Courbet: To Venture Independence

Klaus Herding

COURBET
TO VENTURE
INDEPENDENCE

Translated by John William Gabriel

Yale University Press New Haven and London

Published with assistance from the
Hamburgische Wissenschaftliche Stiftung.

Designed by James J. Johnson and set in Sabon
Roman types by The Composing Room of
Michigan, Inc., Grand Rapids, Michigan.
Printed in the United States of America by
Hamilton Printing Company, Castleton,
New York.

*Library of Congress Cataloging-in-Publication
Data*

Herding, Klaus
  Courbet : to venture independence / Klaus
Herding : translated by John William Gabriel.
    p. cm.
Includes bibliographical references and index.
  ISBN 0–300–03744–9
  1. Courbet, Gustave, 1819–1877—
Psychology. 2. Autonomy (Psychology) I.
Title
ND553.C9H47 1991
759.4—dc20   90–26292

The paper in this book meets the guidelines for
permanence and durability of the Committee
on Production Guidelines for Book Longevity
of the Council on Library Resources.

10 9 8 7 6 5 4 3 2 1

Contents

Preface

Courbet is an artist to whom intensive study has long been devoted in the English-speaking countries. In Germany, thanks to the painter's visit to Frankfurt and an exhibition in Munich during his lifetime, Courbet's work caused great reverberations in German art, influencing Franz Lenbach, Hans Thoma, Wilhelm Leibl, Karl Schuch, Wilhelm Trübner, Otto Scholderer, and many others. Also, Courbet's oeuvre has stimulated research on modern art there since the turn of the century, notably in the cases of Julius Meier-Graefe and Hugo von Tschudi. Nothing, then, could be more appropriate than to contribute to the transcultural exchange on Courbet and to reinforce the compatibility of different approaches to him. The superb Courbet exhibition in Brooklyn (1988–89) revealed that a need for this exchange still exists. If the present collection of essays can help to further an interchange of recent ideas on Courbet's work and milieu, this would be much in keeping with the artist's desire for an art and society that know no national boundaries. His longing for a United States of Europe modeled on the United States of America was an artistic, scientific, and political vision in one. This was closely involved with Courbet's life-long striving for social and personal independence. *Independence* was indeed a key word for Courbet. To him it meant both liberty from academic conventions and a cutting loose from bureaucratic compulsions. Courbet's subjects, style, and personality—all these were intimately connected with his need for independence.

My own concern with Courbet began two decades ago. Still, the present essays amount to no more than preliminary results; they might be compared to exploratory drillings that bring cross-sections of deep strata to light. They are part of a work in progress that corresponds to Courbet's own open-ended thinking and painting. Yet as experience shows, interim results can often be more stimulating than final ones (if such are conceivable at all in Courbet's case). What you have before you, then, is not an exhaustive monograph but an accumulation of thoughts about individual pictures, especially such outstanding ones as *The Wrestlers* or *The Painter's Studio,* supplemented by remarks pertaining to the oeuvre as a whole, for instance on Courbet's palette, the changing aspect of his landscape painting, or the problematic structure of the late work. Finally, I have hoped to shed light on the image of the artist, on his relationship with Proudhon, and on the original and clairvoyant reception of Courbet's work in caricature.

The essays brought together here were written over a period of twelve years, and there is no denying that they bear the marks of their dates of inception, especially as my initial preoccupation with Courbet coincided with the centennial of the Paris Commune. I have thought it best to leave the essays in their original form, and have made few changes apart from citing more recent catalogues for figure references—which was all the more necessary as I have had to do without the numerous color plates that accompanied the original publications. Despite the considerable time range of the articles, they do have a common thread, which consists in an attempt to combine formal analysis with social history. This is an approach that I feel could well prove very fruitful for future Courbet research.

Not everything I have written on Courbet could be included in this volume; specialists are referred to the German publications listed at the back for further studies, for instance on the issue of realism, on Proudhon's influence, on the *Wave* canvases, or on the drawings and sketches (about which the last word remains to be spoken). Still, the selection should suffice to provide what I trust is a meaningful contribution to the discourse on Courbet as a painter on the watershed of modernism.

For references and helpful advice I am greatly indebted to Jean Adhémar, Timothy J. Clark, Pierre Georgel, Robert L. Herbert, Werner Hofmann, Christoph Krämer, Geneviève Lacambre, H. Linda Nochlin, Hélène Toussaint, and Martin Warnke. I am grateful to Yale University Press, especially to John Ryden and Judy Metro, for their interest in undertaking the publication of this volume. My special thanks are due to John Gabriel for his brilliant translation, and to Amy Reid for her help in rendering the French quotations.

1

Redeemer and Charlatan, Subversive and Martyr: Remarks on Courbet's Roles

The Laughing Mask

ANDŔE GILL, in 1872, pictured Courbet's face suffused with laughter (fig. 1). It was the face the artist himself called a mask. "Under the laughing mask," he confided to Bruyas, "I conceal inward distress, bitterness, and a melancholy that lies heavy on my heart and gnaws at me like a vampire."[1] The tendency to veil his true feelings, this gap between self and persona, is often mentioned in the sources and analyses cited below. Yet Gill drew the laughing mask *after* the Commune, at a time when Courbet, excluded from the Salon, subjected to political slurs, facing punishment, displayed anything but a serenely triumphant self-confidence. In these circumstances the artist's laughter, which Gill even brashly described as a reaction to imprisonment and interrogation, could only signify a "nevertheless."[2] A laughing Courbet in 1872—it was bald-faced provocation.[3] His vitality and courage unbroken, the pathological ignoramus,[4] the stonebreaker who had smashed traditional form,[5] the nauseating beggar[6] who had satanically danced the Dance of Death with the Socialist International,[7] suddenly rose like the phoenix from the ashes of the Commune.

Gill's idea of transforming Courbet's "mask" into a symbol of triumph over his adversaries—a prophecy that was not to be fulfilled until years after the artist's death—may serve as a guideline by which to approach the question of Courbet's role. Important as it is to see this role in all its complexity, as part of a masquerade in which Courbet was no less entangled than his opponents,[8] it is equally necessary to draw clear conclusions like that of Gill, to define its essence and influence. What proved lastingly influential about Courbet's stance was the example it set of the independent and at the same time committed artist, the *homme libre*[9] who has found his role in society yet knows how to defend his individualism. This notion of the free artist, of course, was no bolt from the blue. It emerged from what Balzac and Baudelaire, Castille and Thoré described as the crisis of the bourgeois individual who, in the face of mass organizations and the popular press, compulsions from above and new demands from below, drifted into the isolation of a *déclassé* and found himself forced to search for some way out.[10]

Seen in this context, Nadar's *Martyrdom of St. Courbet, Master Painter* (fig. 2) perfectly describes the situation in which the artist had already found himself when he painted his *Portrait of the Artist,* called *The Wounded Man.*[11] Nadar not only demonstrates that Courbet drew more criticism than any other artist before him, but renders his extreme vulnerability as a protagonist of society at large, as if to say that when new ideas must be expressed within old conditions and conventions, the identity of the bourgeois is in mortal danger. As early as 1848, Thoré compared republican society to "a martyr, tormented and pierced by arrows";[12] Daumier harbored similar thoughts.[13] This conflict became even harsher during the Second Empire.

1   André Gill, *Conclusion.*
L'esprit follet, June 8, 1872,
p. 183.

Martyre de saint Courbet, maître peintre.

2   Nadar, *Martyrdom of St. Courbet, Master Painter. Le journal pour rire,* Jan. 5, 1856.

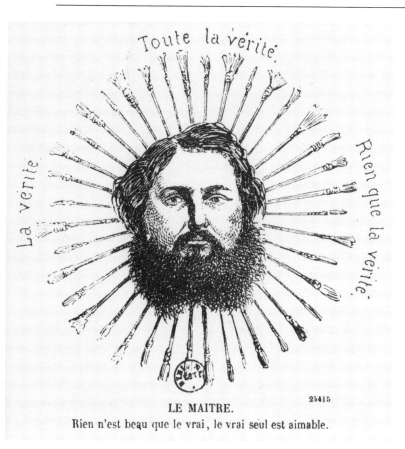

Toute la vérité.

La vérité.

Rien que la vérité.

LE MAITRE.

25415

Rien n'est beau que le vrai, le vrai seul est aimable.

3 Randon, *The Master: Only Truth Is Beautiful, Truth Alone Is Desirable. Le journal amusant,* June 15, 1867.

The topos of the suffering artist—suffering not only from a lack of patronage but from persecution at the hands of the uncomprehending mob[14]—finds its counterpart in the figure of the Artist Triumphant. Nadar, who once caricatured Courbet with his hand raised to bless the world, and again suffering as "peintre et martyr,"[15] in both cases emphasized the master's claim to be in sole possession of truth and morality. Though on the face of it such depictions attacked Courbet's *presumption,* tacitly they acknowledged his *superiority.* In Quillenbois's caricature of *The Meeting* (fig. 71, upper row left), the artist's patron Bruyas kneels before him like an acolyte.[16] Measured against the relationship of court artist to his princely patron, this represents a reversal of historic magnitude—nor, for all its exaggeration, does the caricature falsify the intention of the painting. Even Randon's drawing of Courbet as Redeemer (fig. 3), with his gloriole of brushes and credo "Truth, the whole truth, and nothing but the truth" indicates the universality of the artist's claims.

Courbet as truth incarnate, as Christ—this was an offshoot of a claim to leadership that had its roots in the notion of the poet or artist as high priest of society. Victor Hugo, for instance, celebrated a Last Supper (*cenaculum*) with his apostles, and

Courbet, at the Brasserie Andler, was "the reigning High Priest and Champfleury the reigning Cardinal."[17] This role playing received new fuel when Christ was declared a popular hero, the "great proletarian" of the 1848 uprising.[18] Echoes of the words of Christ are frequent in Courbet's writings. "Yes, *mon cher ami*, I hope to perform a unique miracle in my life," he wrote to Bruyas; "I've always told my friends . . .'Fear not. For should I have to walk the whole earth, I am certain that I shall find people who understand me, were it only five or six; they . . . will save me."[19]

As the last phrase shows, the savior himself needed saving. If the martyr image suggested superiority, that of Christ evokes both a need and a lack. A redeemer requires followers, and if they are not forthcoming, his power collapses. But what if the redeemer-artist declines to establish a school? What if he consciously cuts himself off from his confreres, as Courbet did with his special exhibitions? While an artist like Manet could be depicted Christlike among his pupils,[20] Courbet could not. The only veneration he enjoyed, according to Joudar's caricature of *Return from the Conference*,[21] with St. Gustave riding an ass like Christ into Jerusalem, was that of carousers and drunks. Though his café frequenting might conceivably be considered a popular counterpart of the *cenaculum* idea, Courbet was in the final analysis alone.

This last and perhaps most significant component of his social role surfaced in the oeuvre at a very early date, in the *Self-Portrait with Pipe* (fig. 4), which was also known as *Le Christ à la pipe*.[22] Musingly withdrawn like the "wounded man" of the self-portrait, as if closing his eyes to the world, yet full of self-confidence and latent vitality (collar and shoulder belie the contemplative impression), this "Christ of the people" exudes a calm that was not to reappear, if with a touch of resignation, until Courbet's final *Self-Portrait*—an image that was also compared to Christ, the Man of Sorrows,[23] although the natural light that suffuses the painting, and the Communard's red scarf, bear greater affinities to Gill's "Nevertheless" (Fig. 1).

The artist's missionary zeal and his withdrawal into himself, his both active and contemplative attitude to life, can be explained by a tentative solidarity with the people[24] that included an awareness of the barriers that separated him from them. Courbet's Antwerp speech well illustrates this role conflict. By maintaining an ambivalent balance between an impulse to enlighten the masses and an unwillingness to countenance art education, Courbet refused to be pinned down.[25] It was not until the Commune, that is, through activity *outside* the field of painting, that Courbet was indeed to "bring art to the people."[26]

Yet as soon as his redeemer's role became a reality, another role, that of iconoclast and charlatan,[27] caught up with him and eventually destroyed his life. This role, too, had accompanied the artist from the beginning. As early as 1851, Thierry, a republican, wrote of *A Burial at Ornans* (fig. 29): "Fine. Quite a triumph. Let socialism cheer to its heart's content. . . . Courbet has found the solution. *He has destroyed art at one fell swoop* and replaced it by something else. There is no art, for apparently the *negation of art* can replace art. . . . Fine. My old eyes have been vouchsafed the vision of egalitarian painting."[28] Even the fact that Courbet signed *A Burial* in enormous red letters was considered a demonstrative and destructive *political* act.[29]

4   Gustave Courbet, *Self-Portrait with Pipe*. Oil on canvas, 45 × 37 cm, c. 1846. Montpellier, Musée Fabre.

A Topsy-Turvy World

In 1855, Quillenbois caricatured *The Stonebreakers* (fig. 71, upper row right) as uncouth vandals out to destroy matter, and by inverting the signature also suggested that Courbet's art turned the world upside down—an allusion to the destruction of artistic norms demonstrated on the object itself. But it was not until the razing of the Vendôme column that Courbet came to be most strongly identified with his iconoclastic role. Though he can hardly have been responsible for the desecration, he was branded a stonebreaker of the subversive sort: "This man has perpetrated a wretched, a heinous deed. He has given an example of destruction and has dared to take the lead in tearing down one of the most glorious monuments in Paris. . . . We no longer want these bandits among us."[30] Courbet's "subversive" art brought the wrath and calumny of his opponents down around his head. In a caricature by Schérer[31] he is pictured in front of the toppling column, smashing chunks of rubble like one of his own stonebreakers. His own negative identification with his early work only served to confirm this image: "The man who was predestined to demolish the Vendôme column naturally began as a stonebreaker," reads the caption. That is, if you start as an enemy of art, you will end as an enemy of the state.

But even a full decade earlier, when Courbet's ideas about decentralization and democracy[32] had yet to take clear form, the realists (meaning Courbet) were already being reviled as "iconoclastes de l'art."

> Their rough hands lay waste to every flower,
> Insult every Grace,
> Sully every Virtue,
> Demolish every altar
> On which the sacred flame burns,
> Iconoclasts of Art.
> Their heavy clogs trample
> The mutilated statues of all the virgin goddesses,
> And in rags they dance the Carmagnole
> Around a Venus in the gutter
> Which the hammer of a stonebreaker
> Has chipped into a curbstone.[33]

Part of the charlatan's and iconoclast's role was to supplant the True, Good, and Beautiful (Victor Cousin, 1837) with an ugliness pursued for ugliness' sake.[34] Randon's caption "Only truth is beautiful, truth alone is desirable" was simply a reinversion of Gautier's parody of the classical ideal of beauty: "Nothing is more beautiful than ugliness, only the ugly is desirable"[35]—and *both* were facets of Courbet's image. For he was "Head of the School of Ugliness," as one critic wrote, "and most distressingly, not of the ugly in all its force and grandeur but of the vulgarly ugly, ugliness in its trivial form."[36] To Mérimée's way of thinking, this love of ugliness was associated with a hate of tradition;[37] which indicates that his concern was less to attack a certain personality than to point out a problem faced by the bourgeoisie as a whole. If someone "acted out of character," it was because his role itself had become dubious—the ideal had become flawed. It was not "leftist Courbet research"[38] but Champfleury, Proudhon, and the Goncourts who first saw "le laid *bourgeois*" embodied in *The Bathers* (fig. 8), indeed in Courbet's figure paintings as such;[39] ugliness, even the *mal du siècle,* ennui,[40] had a class-specific role to play in the minds of Courbet's contemporaries, a role of demarcation, accusation, sometimes even of self-destruction. This last aspect was touched on by Clément de Ris, who wrote that "opposites attract one another: all unsuspectingly, Courbet brought forth Gérôme. The one explains the other. Out of an exaggerated need to paint vitally and realistically, to consciously and assiduously seek out physical abnormalities and to find the repellent in reality, they both encourage a search for ugliness even in the domain of the ideal. . . . Courbet has thrown open the gates to the enemy."[41]

So even Courbet's opponents were becoming increasingly aware of the loss of meaning that threatened idealistic art. Nevertheless, they continued to lay the blame for ugliness and triviality exclusively at *his* door, to stamp them as *his* invention. In the popular comedy *Le feuilleton d'Aristophane,* performed in 1852, a character by the name of Réalista declared:

> Ugliness is what we need! By your leave, sir,
> Everything I paint is quite wonderfully ugly,
> Nasty's what my pictures are; and to make them true,
> I root up the beautiful like so many weeds.
> I love sallow skin, noses like papier-mâché,
> Girls whose chins sprout hair,
> The faces of loudmouthed sots and jokers,
> Carbuncles, warts, and corns—
> That, sir, is Truth![42]

Fair was foul and foul was fair; Courbet stood for the revaluation of all values. Proudhon put it in a nutshell: "Our conservative audience . . . wishes to be pictured as *beautiful*"[43]—regardless of their real appearance, and woe be to the artist who did otherwise. This demand led them to condemn anyone who chose everyday life, customs and habits, social conditions as a theme, let alone criticized or attacked them. The fact that Courbet did not *create* an ugly state of affairs but simply tried to *reveal* it through art, was ignored or suppressed. In his caricature of Courbet's audience (fig. 5), Daumier pillories this reversal of cause and effect. While people deplore the ugliness of Courbet's art, they conveniently overlook their own ugliness.

Truth had many faces in this picture-puzzle, but all of them seemed to fit Courbet. "Salute me—I'm the New World! I'm not a school, a church, an idea, a belief—I am Truth! I have interdicted the imaginative power of our eyes, our pencils and brushes.

5   Daumier, *Great Admirers of Gustave Courbet's Pictures. Le charivari,* July 9, 1853.

Grands admirateurs des tableaux de M. Courbet.

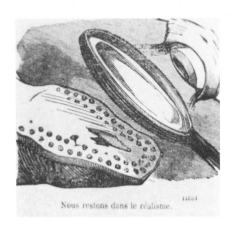

6   Bertall, *We'll Stick with Realism. Le petit journal pour rire* 188, 1859.

Nature—that's me! You have primped and prettified her—I undress her! You have pursued her, I've caught her. . . . I don't paint pictures, I collect them; their design was Creation's own. You were painters—but I am a darkroom!" These words, written as early as 1855, are those of two men who were probably Courbet's most intelligent opponents, the Goncourt brothers.[44] They bring into play another aspect of the destructive role, that of unimaginativeness.

It was an accusation[45] to which Courbet himself later lent credence when, asked about the essence of realistic art, he drew a pipe (attribute of the bohemian; fig. 4) and captioned it "Courbet, without ideal and without religion."[46] Daumier argued similarly.[47] The reproach that realistic art was satisfied, without creative effort, merely to reproduce banal objects—a pipe, a candle, a shoe[48]—became the leaven in the criticism of this style, and in many quarters it still is today. Once this verdict was accepted, realism could be rejected not only as bad art, but as non-art. In 1866, Gill drew a candelabra with portraits in wax of Champfleury and Courbet, a pipe, a hiking boot,[49] and a wooden shoe, titled *Flambeau du réalisme* and flanked by verses like these:

> No creators, thinkers, artists more
> Who forge in their hearts grand plans—
> Mere masons now! Mere copyists!
> Raphael is slain, Daguerre victorious![50]

The road was long from the painted pipe as the quintessence of artistic unimaginativeness to Magritte's use of this motif as a key to the surrealist imagination.[51] Still, the surprise, the element of innovation produced by mere close observation of banal things, was already apparent to Courbet's critics. Bertall's parody of imitative observation of reality turned beneath his hands into a surreal ensemble. In his caricature *We'll Stick with Realism* (fig. 6), an eye, a magnifying glass, and the worn sole of a shoe with protruding nail, form an alienated montage of the everyday world that recalls Grandville's visionary *Crime and Punishment*.[52]

Bertall teaches us, *malgré lui*, nothing less than that realism, in the sense of a blind mimicking of reality, is an impossibility, for "our eye is fortunately no microscope; plain vision already idealizes, otherwise the aphids on a tree, the dust and infusoria in even the purest water, the blemishes on the most delicate of human skin, would rob us of every pleasure we take in them."[53] Nevertheless, Courbet's role as destroyer of "the ideal"—actually of a very few people's notion of it—has outlasted the century since his death. Its meaning for us today lies in the sheer force of resistance it embodies.

7   Gustave Courbet, *The Wrestlers*. Oil on canvas, 252 × 198 cm, 1853. Budapest, Szépmüvészeti Muzeum.

2

"Les Lutteurs Détestables": Critique of Style and Society in Courbet's *Wrestlers*

Aesthetic and Social Conflicts

THE Paris Salon of 1853 included three paintings by Gustave Courbet: *The Wrestlers* (fig. 7), *The Bathers* (fig. 8), and *The Sleeping Spinner*.[1] Very advantageously hung "in the center of the main gallery," the three canvases attracted far more attention than the works of any other artist represented.[2] Yet only *The Sleeping Spinner* received anything like a warm critical reception, probably because it could be taken as a depiction of worthy country folk of the type Champfleury expected of Courbet.[3]

The two other canvases met with vociferous indignation. *The Bathers* was seen as a caricature of the academic ideal of beauty, the critics calling it a mockery of every standard.[4] As for *The Wrestlers*, the critics were unanimous in their rejection of this dirty, revolting picture. Théophile Gautier called it "simply detestable" (Appendix, II); others thought discussing it was a waste of time.[5] More recent publications have tended to confirm rather than revise this verdict, and *The Wrestlers* remains one of the most ill treated canvases in all of Courbet's oeuvre.[6]

Any number of reasons could be found for this rejection and conspiracy of silence. The question is whether the critics' negative reactions were primarily aesthetically prompted, or whether they reveal the presence of a larger conflict on the level of society.

The large canvas (252 × 198 cm) is executed in oil on a reddish-brown ground, patches of which show through the final paint layer. It was painted over another composition done perhaps twelve years earlier, in 1841,[7] a *Classical Walpurgis Night* set on the Aegean Sea and representing an alchemist in pursuit of a young woman.[8]

8   Gustave Courbet, *The Bathers*. Oil on canvas, 227 × 193 cm, 1853. Montpellier, Musée Fabre.

Evidently an attempt to infuse the myth with modern life, it seemed to Champfleury to promise great developments;[9] Gigoux, however, described it as a failed attempt to *reform* mythology.[10]

Seen in this light, Courbet's deletion of the original composition represents a programmatic decision to reject subjects he had neither observed nor could verify with his own eyes. In place of myth, history, and religion, he set everyday life, the here and now. Still, as remains to be shown, this turnabout did not signify a complete rejection of tradition, but merely meant that painters, including history painters, had now come to feel that a complex treatment of commonplace events was more of a challenge to their imagination than an idealization of unusual ones.[11]

Courbet frequently made programmatic decisions of this kind. In 1855, with *The Painter's Studio,* a recapitulation of seven crucial years, he had drawn a conclusion and marked a turning point;[12] just a decade later, in 1864, he was again to cap a phase of his work, and again by painting over an existing composition. This was *The Source of the Hippocrene,* a spoof on poets and painters, which he transformed into *Covert of Roe-Deer by a Stream at Plaisir-Fontaine* (fig. 39), apparently forsaking the level of social criticism and turning to nature.[13]

The Wrestlers had its place in this sequence. Even its form of execution, overpainting, was controversial, because it signified detachment both from Champfleury and from literary themes and classical subjects, as well as being an attack on institutional taste, the direct targets of which were both Delacroix and Ingres. The subsequent history of the painting, its reception and use, merely served to confirm that it infringed on the norms established by art criticism. Painted without a commission, the canvas found no purchaser. Not until Courbet had been dead for years, in 1882, was *The Wrestlers* auctioned in Paris,[14] and not until 1951 did it enter a public collection, the last of Courbet's large figure paintings to do so. Evidently the canvas was expressly intended as a protest, and expressly painted for the Salon. At any rate, there is no statement on record by Courbet or by any of his friends and acquaintances that would indicate that he ever intended or expected to sell *The Wrestlers* to a private collector or to the government. Yet he placed a high value on it, had it photographed even before the opening of the Salon,[15] and exhibited it again at the world fairs of 1855 and 1867, and in the Salon of 1859. We may conclude that *The Wrestlers* represented a kind of confession on Courbet's part. At the same time, it marked a new plateau in his relationship to the public, which he now began to include more directly in his compositional considerations—sometimes even in the role of "victim".[16]

At first sight, the subject of the canvas seems hardly in need of interpretation. Two wrestlers are shown locked in combat on a large grass playing field, watched from a great distance by spectators seated in bleachers at both sides. The natural surroundings play a surprisingly dominant role in the scene; tall trees cut across the field of vision, almost completely obscuring an imposing monument, Chalgrin's Arc de Triomphe. The field appears to have gone to seed; the path running through the foreground is completely overgrown. Lush areas of grass alternate with patches that are worn thin, suggesting the varying frequency with which the different areas of the racecourse are used. The slight discoloring of the foliage and the brilliant blue sky would indicate that the season is late summer.

As the site of his wrestling match Courbet chose the Imperial Hippodrome, also known as Arènes Nationales, which was located between avenue de l'Impératrice and avenue des Portugais. Dedicated in 1845, the stadium (fig. 9) was a splendid place at which horse races and exhibition matches of all kinds were held. Its location on the outskirts of the Champs-Elysées, stomping grounds of the *fashionables* of the Second Empire,[17] made it a favorite gathering place of the middle and upper-middle classes, who at that period comprised the majority of sports audiences everywhere in Europe. Other attractions of this fashionable park were the roofed playing fields of the Cirque d'Eté (rechristened Cirque de l'Impératrice in 1853) and Cirque Napoléon (personally inaugurated by the emperor in late 1852).[18]

The gay atmosphere of the place seems to have left Courbet rather cold. Instead of the oval with its trimmed lawns, banners fluttering on tall poles, barriers, and roofed grandstands decorated with lambrequins, he has depicted what appears to be an improvised arena in which nature has not been domesticated but allowed to proliferate, at the expense of the architecture. The oriental-style portal of the stadium, to the left of the Arc de Triomphe from Courbet's vantage point, is just visible behind a tree. The grandstand roof, which actually continued around the entire arena, has been reduced to an awkward canopy over the royal box;[19] the Imperial Hippodrome has shrunken to the proportions of a fairground booth. In view of the great effort expended during the Second Empire to keep the populace content in the Bonapartist sense,[20] this transformation represents a provocation in itself. That Courbet knew full well how the Hippodrome actually looked, may be gathered from an oil sketch (fig. 10) in which he has taken the bird's-eye view typical of contemporaneous prints, brought the massive Arc de Triomphe into full play, and rendered the stadium facilities with great fidelity.

9 Anonymous, *The Hippo-drome on the Champs-Elysées, Paris.* Edmond Texier, *Tableau de Paris*, 1852, vol. 1, p. 4.

Although this bullfight sketch is mentioned in a letter of 1856, it may have been done several years previously.[21] Whether it served as a preparatory study for *The Wrestlers* or not, it certainly shows Courbet's need to sweep the pompous props off the stage of his final composition. And what motivated him to do so? Courbet disdained the official pageantry and etiquette of the Second Empire, and he truly enjoyed breaking the rules.[22] His desire to retain his personal independence and live as a "savage" among civilized men, though it may have involved play-acting, was certainly a fundamental part of his cult of originality and authenticity.[23] To live up to his credo, "Il faut encanailler l'art" (Art must be dragged into the gutter),[24] he took such steps as to erect his own primitive exhibition tents next to the palaces of the world fairs of 1855 and 1867. It was this stance, in other words, that led Courbet to attack officially sanctioned competitions, sporting and otherwise, which at the time were fast taking on the character of show business. This attack took the form of an alternative staging of events, a more authentic presentation of the current scene.

A Provocative Structure

Its thrust, however, went even deeper. In depictions similar to *The Wrestlers* (figs. 12, 20, 21), audience and athletes are equally prominent. Courbet, in contrast, relegates the spectators to the background; they are nothing, the fight is all.

10 Gustave Courbet, *Bullfight in the Hippodrome.* Oil on canvas, 59 × 48 cm, before 1856. Paris, private collection.

He not only depreciates the gathering place of the *haute volée* but challenges their penchant for self-exhibition. This must have seemed all the more impertinent in that in the Second Empire, such events were frankly used to parade the latest fashions and for a type of socializing quite irrelevant to sports. This was as much the case on the Champs-Elysées as in the elegant new seaside resorts of the period.[25]

However, this shift in emphasis from audience to wrestlers went beyond a provocation to Parisian high society. It led to a disproportionality that affected the means of visual representation themselves. As Delacroix wrote, "The two wrestlers are deficient in *action* and confirm [Courbet's] inability to *invent*. The background overwhelms the figures; the canvas ought to be cropped three feet all round" (Appendix, I). It might seem surprising that Delacroix thought Courbet's wrestlers lacked action, but the import of his words becomes clear when we compare his own mural *Jacob Wrestling with the Angel* (fig. 11) with Courbet's painting. Here the action takes place within a pictorial framework: The protagonists stand firmly on the ground and cast shadows; their movements lead into the picture instead of out of it; and there is an increase and decrease of tension within the figurative composition itself. With Courbet, the pictorial frame of reference has been disrupted. As Delacroix suggests, one could cut the two wrestlers out of the picture, because they really have no ground to stand on. The group has been separated from its context, and the surroundings re-

11   Eugène Delacroix, *Jacob Wrestling with the Angel* (detail). Mural, 1861. Paris, Saint-Sulpice (Photo Giraudon).

duced to mere stage props. This additive procedure was common in the popular imagery of the day, and would experience a revival in early poster art prior to 1900.[26] Courbet, too, achieves a poster-like effect: The proximity of the life-size figures, which are not integrated solidly in the pictorial space, refers beyond the picture in a positively obtrusive way, particularly as the vantage point is especially low—another anticipation of the devices used in early poster design. As a result of its isolation, the group affects the viewer much more strongly than it would if the internal pictorial tensions were taken up by an interaction between wrestlers and audience. Nadar already sensed this attack on the real observer (fig. 14, left) and focused it by adding the shadows that Courbet left out and extending them beyond the frame into real space.

The disproportions of Courbet's figures and the resulting distortion of perspective, as well as the opening of the group outwards, create uncertainty in the viewer and literally challenge him to define his standpoint. This affront differs fundamentally from the methods of visual persuasion employed by other painters (and by early advertising men) in that it infringes on the academic rules for depicting the nude figure, emphasizing the athletes' swollen veins, furrowed foreheads, exaggerated musculature, and protruding knees and elbows. The same holds true by analogy for *The Bathers*.

A parallel to Courbet's image is found in Manet's *Mademoiselle Victorine* of 1862,[27] which evinces a similar negation of the traditional logic of proportions. Here, too, the space of the arena in which the action takes place is disrupted, and the central figure looms up as if bodily disjoined from the pictorial context. But Manet stops short before making his statement so intense as to disturb the spectator; he tries to persuade without offending. Though he establishes a new pictorial rationality, Manet leaves our emotional expectations unquestioned. Courbet's infringement of the rules went farther, and hurting feelings was part of his intention. This provocation was evidently meant to reveal social structures, and in so doing it paved the way for formal, stylistic innovation as well.

A look at *The Wrestlers* provides insight into both of these factors. The composition differs considerably from other, similar depictions of the period. First of all, Courbet has placed his opponents in a stance that suggests anything but a wrestling match according to the rules.[28] Wrestlers usually face one another, standing side by side only in a few holds such as the *coup de hanche*,[29] where one grips the other around the waist and attempts to throw him over his hip. But this is not the hold depicted. The man in the red trunks has applied a headlock with both forearms ("une cravate à la François le Bordelais")[30] and is trying to force his opponent down. To no avail, however, because in this position he cannot shift the weight of his body far enough forward to do so. His opponent's defense seems even less efficacious. Caught in a headlock, he in turn tries to push the other man's head forward, merely expending his energy without being able to free himself. A better tactic would be to go for his opponent's waist, arms, or legs, the only points at which he would be able to apply leverage. It also seems improbable that a man in this position and under this kind of pressure would attempt to keep his balance by throwing out his arms, instead of

12   A. Gilbert after A.
Falguière, *Wrestlers* (Ram-
baud vs. Blas). Wood engrav-
ing, 1875. Paris, Musée des
Arts Décoratifs (Photo Jean-
Loup Charmet).

closing on his opponent and countering his attack. There is a painting by Falguière
(Salon of 1875)[31] that, apparently influenced by Courbet's and reproduced in reverse
in an engraving by A. Gilbert (fig. 12), corrects Courbet's view of wrestling by showing
a fight conducted by the rules and in accordance with the viewer's expectations. This
rendering also sets the dislocated aesthetic norms to rights, having a pictorial field in
coherent perspective, athletes whose ideal forms are unmarred by the strains of their
profession, and spectators who enjoy their accustomed high status.

It is very likely that Courbet had seen wrestling matches; his friend Promayet is
even said to have played in the Hippodrome band for a time. Apparently, however, he
never actually practiced the sport himself. As far as wrestling technique is concerned,
his rendering cannot be called realistic, but then his concerns probably lay elsewhere.
Nor are the inconsistencies in the painting limited to holds and positions. When
Delacroix remarked that the picture had no action, he was certainly not charging
Courbet with having produced an unrealistic depiction of a wrestling match, nor even
with having waived invention or dramaturgy or cut off communication between athletes and audience in favor of a direct appeal to the real spectator. What Delacroix
meant to say was that Courbet had depicted not a process but a state, captured and
fixed like a snapshot. There is indeed no concerted movement, no physical interplay
shared by the two men. Whether they even earn the name group in the artistic sense
remains doubtful.

Formally speaking, the energy of the figure on the right is directed entirely outwards. The figure is based on a prototype that reappeared in art almost unchanged since the Renaissance: Hercules battling Cerberus or Hydra, a pose in which the warrior's strength is concentrated on the legendary beast crouching in front of him. So closely has Courbet reproduced this traditional pose that the only part of the man's body not to conform to it, the lower arm, is entirely obscured. His opponent's pose can be explained similarly, for his upper body and bowed head recall ancient load-carriers or Atlantes, showing an especially close resemblance to Hercules dividing the mountains of Kolpe and Abyla. Both poses are evocations of human labor which Courbet has adopted and demythologized. In fact, the two wrestlers can be traced back to Zurbaran's *Labors of Hercules,* two of which Courbet has combined in reverse;[32] their plasticity and somber colors, too, owe much to Spanish painting, which Courbet held in high esteem.[33]

The circumstance that two separate and differently motivated figures have been forced into an encounter also explains the striking divergencies between them, which extend even to the modulation of the painted surface. Only the body of the man in red has been completely worked through; it evinces most of the "disgusting" details, while the other figure is well shaped and painted with almost academic smoothness of surface. What this implies in terms of content will be discussed below. As far as form is concerned, this divergent structuring creates the impression of a four-legged muscle machine in which the outer pair of legs serves to frame and support the inner pair. For the sake of this effect, Courbet has permitted himself great distortions in foreshortening. Even when viewed as a *whole,* the two figures look as if they had been constructed of random components. The left arm and left leg of the man in black appear grafted on; the other's shoulders seem to have been developed in a separate study, his ribs to bear little relation to the position of the ribcage, and so on. This anatomical puzzle, like the disruptions of perspective, proportions, and plot mentioned above, marks a prevalence of partial structures over the image whole that is new in art—and that represents one of the key prerequisites for the emergence of classical modernity. On the other hand, Courbet persists in sharp-focus objective signification, which prevents him from taking the step from a *representation* of the object to its *presentation* by means of abstract signs or symbols. As we all know, however, innovation arises from trial and error and an acceptance of contradictions.

In *The Wrestlers* Courbet resisted the political and aesthetic norms of the Second Empire in many ways—by reducing the scene of action to a "primitive" state, by relegating the audience to the background, by refusing to allow communication and consecutive action to take place. But his resistance is most apparent in the way he has brought the wrestlers up uncomfortably close to the viewer, lending them a size and drama that vied with the subjects of history painting. Visitors to the 1853 Salon might have added one more infringement to the list, namely, the gray cast Courbet gave to the athletes' bodies (which no photograph can adequately reproduce). This gray nips every thought of heroization in the bud. The way it is used here, grisaille[34] can only signify the mundane grayness of daily life, for as little as Courbet has idealized the wrestlers' bodies, he has idealized their occupation even less. From a wrestler's point of view, the sport is no weekend pastime but a livelihood, and a strenuous one. That this reference was intended would seem to be corroborated by the fact that the gray veil does not extend to the natural environment, which glows in brilliant color. About this time Courbet had indeed begun to discover the theme of primal nature as refuge and as site of reconciliation, connotations which would soon appear unequivocally in *The Painter's Studio*.[35] In *The Wrestlers* an inherent differentiation of color came to fruition that had not yet been evident in such canvases as *Peasants of Flagey Returning from the Fair* of 1850. There the color gray suffused the *entire* image, linking nature (as workplace) with the peasants who worked there. In *The Meeting*, on the other hand, the whole composition is luminous, for Courbet considered it to be a "Sunday picture"[36] and wished it to express a harmony between figures and nature. In terms of the semantics of color, then, *The Wrestlers* occupies an intermediate position between *The Peasants* and *The Painter's Studio*. Its palette augments the social-critical statement of the image, just as it accentuates the formal distortions and divergencies from the norm. This is the gist of Delacroix's other remark, that the (brilliant) background overwhelmed the (somber) foreground—a disharmony into the reasons for which Delacroix sadly declined to inquire.

Political Concerns

The grayish hue of the figures, the contrast in their drawing, the "red" wrestler's contorted face and bulging veins—all these factors point to more than a reaction on Courbet's part to a normative, idealistic aesthetic or, in iconographical terms, a generalized characterization of wrestling as a form of labor. Castagnary, for instance, called *The Wrestlers,* with *The Return of the Peasants,* a "glorification du travail,"[37] implying that Courbet had taken an analytical stance with respect to the actual historical situation in the 1850s. Although this is indeed plausible, it is difficult to prove based on the visual evidence of the painting alone. For assistance, however, we can turn to the contemporary Salon critics and caricaturists. Such witnesses to the reception of his work are especially numerous and revealing in Courbet's case. As Timothy Clark's interpretation of *A Burial* and Hélène Toussaint's of *The Painter's Studio*[38] have shown, it is they who often provide the key to Courbet's content. With regard to *The Wrestlers,* the violent newspaper attacks provide a clue to what it was about the picture that enraged the powers-that-be, and there is a caricature that sheds light on its historical significance, which has tended to be overlooked. As the Salon reviews are still largely unknown, they have been reprinted in the Appendix.

Before I turn to this criticism, it should be noted that *The Bathers,* despite its different format, was considered a companion piece to *The Wrestlers,* explaining why they were so frequently coupled in caricatures and reviews. The caricaturist Bertall even went so far as to call the woman climbing out of the water in *The Bathers* a lady wrestler (fig. 99), giving her a female version of the name of a man then active in the sport, "le terrible Savoyard."[39] The caption runs: "This Terrible Savoyarde offers to anyone who can throw her 500 francs and an honorary tricot; the odds are she'll beat Courbet, alias The Bastion of Ornans." Champfleury anticipated that *The Bathers* would draw the sharpest fire, fearing the effect of a "certain bourgeois nude climbing out of the water and showing her behind to the public. A great scandal, just wait and see."[40] Courbet himself, even before the Salon opened, reported that *The Bathers* had caused reverberations, while *The Wrestlers* had apparently been received with restraint: "As for *The Wrestlers,* no one has said anything thus far, good or bad."[41]

Like his wrestler figures, those of the bathers remained beholden to academic norms while flouting them. The nude seen from the back conformed to a mode of northern European nude painting traditional since the seventeenth century, and her gestures even lent the everyday occurrence something of the pathos of a mythical or religious motif. With this canvas as with *The Wrestlers,* Courbet attempted to square the circle—to mount an opposition and simultaneously to win his opponents' praise; to champion a "liberated" art in the face of official art and simultaneously to beat the traditionalists at their own game.[42]

Despite their similarities in terms of features that appeared objectionable to the contemporary eye, the differences between the two paintings remain obvious. Champfleury may have been able to discern a *bourgeoise* in the woman leaving the water, but he would have been hard put to see *The Wrestlers* as members of this class. The painting confronted visitors to the Salon with the proletariat. This difference also explains why *The Bathers* was perhaps more sharply attacked than *The Wrestlers.* It may have shocked the critics to see the proletariat exalted to a subject for art, but the real issue this raised was something they were still at pains not to face. When Clément de Ris called *The Wrestlers* "less shocking" than *The Bathers* (Appendix, VI), he may have had specific moral, sexual reasons for doing so; but when Gautier introduced his article in the liberal-conservative *Presse* by saying that Courbet's doctrine was developed on different levels in the three paintings (Appendix, II), he was evidently alluding to *social* levels. "The *Bather,*" continued Gautier,

> has had a *succès de scandale.* Imagine a Hottentot Venus leaving the water and presenting to the spectator an enormous backside. . . . As far as the *Wrestlers* are concerned, they are simply detestable. In the Salle Montesquieu[43] we have seen Blas (The Ferocious Spaniard), Arpin (The Invincible Savoyard), Rabasson, "The Ocean," and the whole muscular gang, and they looked just as flesh-colored as normal human beings. M. Courbet's wrestlers, by contrast, rolled in soot and coal dust before the fight, probably for the sake of a better grip. What, in the bright light of day at the racecourse where the painter has placed his group, is one to make of these black shadows, these fuliginous halftones, these leaden lights, this subterranean illumination? . . . For a realist like Courbet these black men . . . are passing strange.

Evidently, these two paintings had a number of dubious, un-French traits in Gautier's view, and he had to ward off the threat to his well-being by using such terms as "Vénus d'hottentote" and "hommes noirs." Even more obviously motivated by racial and class prejudice was Tillot's review in *Le siècle*, where he wrote of *The Bathers* that "if this is a sample of M. Courbet's contribution to the development of the human race, we predict that he will have great success in Turkey, where females are sold by the pound. . . . His *Wrestlers* are as black as two Auvergne colliers; they are not even correctly drawn, and their hold on each other is difficult to fathom. Truly a comedown for M. Courbet" (Appendix, V).

Writing in the *Moniteur universel*, Mérimée succumbed to cannibalistic fantasies: "Surely flesh could hardly be rendered more alive; still, M. Courbet is apparently not going to send his *Bathers* to New Zealand, where the worth of a prisoner is calculated by the amount of meat she provides for her captors' meal."[44] Henry de Pène expressed himself along similar lines in the *Chronique de France* (Appendix, VII). And Lemonnier, finally, apparently with *The Wrestlers* in mind, summed it all up in the phrase "Courbet, he is the virtuoso of bestiality."[45]

These few examples suffice to show how quickly the veil of aesthetics can drop from a critic's opinion to reveal the socially motivated condemnation that underlies it. The critics cited had apparently forgotten the impulse of the Enlightenment to correct the inequities of modern civilization, and that of the French Revolution to establish racial equality. Nor was this a momentary or personal lapse, for Bonapartist propaganda had done its utmost to annul the revolutionary tradition. *La patrie*, for instance, declared in 1853, "The French Revolution . . . is, in essence, satanic. It will never be totally extinguished by its opposite principle, and never will the French take back their proper place until they have recognized this truth."[46] The *Gazette de France*, also in 1853, considered the Salon exhibitions to contain the threat of recrudescent socialism, because revolutionary influences had not been entirely eliminated from the jury.[47]

The Shock of Ugliness

The caricaturists jumped on the bandwagon, too. In the *Journal pour rire* (fig. 13, bottom),[48] Bertall pictured two sooty wrestlers arguing about who was dirtier; Quillenbois, in *L'illustration* (1855), satirized Courbet's painting as two blacks fighting for possession of the "Venus of the lower Rhine" (fig. 71).[49] Even in the shorthand of caricature we find shifts of intention with respect to the painting: Bertall could not understand how anyone could think of concealing the Arc de Triomphe behind trees or reducing the Hippodrome to a bare playing field; Quillenbois would not countenance the ordinary, unattractive physiques of Courbet's wrestlers, drawing *deux beaux musclés* instead. The caricaturists, in other words, did not rise to the critical potential of the painting. Nor were they satisfied with its depiction of wrestling technique, the caption of Bertall's drawing even alluding to the aspect of distortion and alleging that no muscle was in its proper place. Clément de Ris, too, recognized "les difformités physiologiques," though he was not able to understand the historically necessary critique these implied (Appendix, VI).

Gautier, at least, went on to make more profound observations, inquiring into the truth to nature of a painting whose "dirty colors" were so inadequate to the demand for plausibility. He seems to have realized that Courbet's "subterranean illumination"

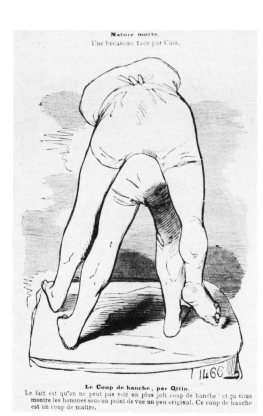

Nature morte.
Une bécassine tuée par Caïn.

Le Coup de hanche, par Ottin.
Le fait est qu'on ne peut pas voir un plus joli coup de hanche ! et ça vous
montre les hommes sous un point de vue un peu original. Ce coup de hanche
est un coup de maître.

13 Bertall, Caricatures of
A. L. M. Ottin's sculpture
(top) and of Courbet's
*Wrestlers. Le journal pour
rire*, July 23, 1853.

Les Lutteurs, par Courbet (tableau prédit par le *Journal pour rire* en 1851).
Ces deux messieurs luttent à qui sera le plus sale : le vainqueur aura droit
à un cachet de bain à quatre sous. — Aucun des muscles de ces lutteurs ne
se trouve à sa place ordinaire : ce désordre s'explique facilement par l'effort
de la lutte. — Souvent un beau désordre est un effet de l'art.

might represent a protest against academicism or resistance to idealization, a device that could be used to convey social content; yet he was not yet able to accept this antinaturalism as artistic truth. For him, Courbet's "brutal" coloration was "merely a new mannerism under a different banner." But unlike such critics as Clément de Ris, who compared Courbet's colors with shoe polish (Appendix, VI), Gautier at least recognized the semantic issue they raised, an issue that distinguished Courbet's approach from naive illustration.[50] Even his polemical final sentence—"A peasant can look just as affected in his homespun smock as a marquis in his violet taffeta swallowtails"—has a progressive core, because it implies that every subject is permitted in art and that a work can be rejected for formal reasons alone. With this review Gautier raised the threshold of tolerance and prepared the ground for a shift of emphasis in the realism debate.[51]

However, the general tenor of the criticism of Courbet's work remained moralistic and political, if only tacitly so. Augustin-Joseph du Pays, for instance, conjectured:

> Probably wishing to compensate for the injustice done to the fair sex by his *Bathers* . . . Courbet has attempted in another painting to depict the ugliness of the common man with increased coarseness and even greater turbidity of handling. Nothing is less pleasant to look upon than his large study of *Wrestlers* in the Hippodrome on the Champs-Elysées. Although the rendering of the figures shows a certain knowledge of anatomy, and despite the unfortunate placement of the four legs, which are aligned like the legs of a chair, and the terribly sloppy drawing, there is true force, modeling, and movement . . . in the left leg of the wrestler on the right. . . . In short, despite all the merits one recognizes and the concessions one makes, one is invincibly dominated by the repugnance caused by this ode to blackness, ugliness, coarseness, and triviality (Appendix, III).

The author makes his conception of ugliness clear from the start, writing that "Courbet remains the master of the School of Ugliness, and, what is worse, not of ugliness in its grandeur and power but of ugliness in its vulgar and common form."[52] That this definition of ugliness represents an ideological defense mechanism becomes quite obvious here.

Attacks on the picture were triggered not only by its repugnant aspects but by the qualities that might be expected to appeal to the masses. Not even ill-wishing critics were able to deny the effectiveness of Courbet's paintings in communicating a message, so they had to make this effectiveness appear ridiculous. "If you've always wondered what a rousing party is like," wrote Loudun, "just step up to Courbet's pictures, where the whole crowd's laughing like crazy. . . . There's no need for introductions, you just know you'd get along" (Appendix, IV). This attempt to make Courbet appear laughable merely conceals the critic's uncertainty, for suddenly the smile disappears from his face: "Wrestlers, and what wrestlers! Enormous black, heavy men with bull necks, blacksmith's arms and boxer's hands that could knock your teeth out with a single blow. They . . . are so real they make you shiver." It is hard to imagine a franker expression of the fear instilled in the middle-class white man by the overwhelming strength of the black races or the proletariat. Nor is this fear much mitigated by the irony with which Loudun continues, "How can they [the wrestlers] stay on their feet with varicose veins like that?"

If such details did not reveal a key source of uncertainty—the depiction of the physical wear and tear caused by manual labor—it would be hard to understand why Nadar focused on this same apparently secondary feature in his caricature of a top-hatted gentleman[53] sniffing contemptuously in front of the wrestlers. This rather cheap joke at Courbet's expense at least indicates the extent to which the picture was felt to be an actual, physical insult, and the immediacy with which this unusual depiction of symptoms of degeneration affected contemporary viewers. The caricature also reveals just how compelling the visual presence of the life-size wrestlers could be when the picture was hung high on the wall, a common practice at the time. Courbet's identification of sheer size with inward greatness proved its truth here—and sheer size can be a threatening thing.[54]

A second Nadar caricature (fig. 90) emphasizes another threatening aspect of *The Wrestlers* by transposing the combatants from Salon to fairgrounds. The caption raises a question that was avoided in the newspaper reviews, that of the use of the picture. It was evidently not a self-sufficient, autonomous work of art like the other paintings in the Salon; it was felt to have a special purpose and a use-value that differed from the traditional one. Nadar, finding this distinctive quality in the picture's poster-like effectiveness, suggests that it be employed as the backdrop of a fairground booth, to advertise "hommes forts" or "Hercules de foire" like the ones Daumier depicted.[55] Nadar's reaction to the unprecedented crowds drawn by Courbet's canvases indicates that, like many others, he feared that Courbet would transform the Salon from a semipublic into a public place, like the railway stations he planned to decorate,[56] thus obtaining for his art the same kind of publicity enjoyed, according to Balzac, by the billboards and hoardings of the big city.[57] Nadar's warning to Courbet, likewise uttered in 1853, that "coarseness is not strength, brutality not the same as frankness, nor scandal the same thing as renown" (Appendix, IX), reflects not only a competitor's envy but a sheer misunderstanding—evidently he feared that Courbet's need for publicity had become an end in itself. Tillot, too, considered Courbet a painter who "fires off pistol shots to draw attention to himself, then lets himself be lulled by the roar of the crowd" (Appendix, V). In these critics' eyes, Courbet's canvases harbored a dual danger, intrinsic and extrinsic—while pointing out the unpretty aspects of an activity that served to entertain the bourgeoisie, their provocative staging exerted an attraction to which "the people" were all too prone (see below) because it shed light on the conditions under which they were compelled to labor.

It was precisely this forensic tendency that made Courbet's paintings seem politically dangerous. There can be no other explanation, for instance, for Loudun's mention of "anarchie intellectuelle" in connection with Courbet,[58] or for Mérimée's approval of a passage from a speech by Nieuwerkerke, the superintendent of fine arts, the target of which was certainly Courbet: "We shall make it our aim to separate all those who abuse the title of artist from the masses of the people"[59]—which can only mean prohibiting them from showing their work. Every artist who, like Courbet, threatened to turn the Salon into a platform for political agitation represented a threat to other state institutions as well. This is why he was branded an iconoclast[60] long before the Commune and caricatured as a "Hercule de foire" (sideshow Hercules) in connection with the razing of the Vendôme column.[61] *The Wrestlers* in fact marked the beginning of Courbet's development of political consciousness, which reached a high point in his activities during the Commune. Persecution set in as early as 1852, and he was able to escape it thanks only to the personal protection of the minister of the interior, comte de Morny.

Both this persecution attempt and the remarks made by Nieuwerkerke are highly revealing. It would appear that Courbet provoked the government in more ways than one, and that, in view of the importance of the Salon, one of them was the tacit political message of some of his paintings, including *The Wrestlers*. If we assume that the critics at least partially understood the allusions they contained, this would help explain why the press was almost unanimous in rejecting them. Considering the strict censorship of the day, it is no wonder that the Salon reviews contain no reference to the political aspects of the painting. In the case of *The Painter's Studio*, too, the only attempt to grasp the historical significance of the composition was a caricature by Quillenbois (fig. 71), and here, too, it by no means did justice to the painting's complexity.

Red and Black

To return to *The Wrestlers*, there is a third, previously overlooked caricature by Nadar (fig. 14, left) that contains interesting allusions. Apart from the fact that the stadium is still shown with its entrance gate (which raises the question whether Courbet deleted this passage after the caricature was done) and, as in other Nadar caricatures,[62] a gingerbread man has been added at the right, the "black" wrestler wears a broad-brimmed hat like those worn by church dignitaries at the time (prelates, Jesuits). If we assume that this characterization of the "black" wrestler as a clergyman was intended, as his black tricot would further suggest, then the "red" one must have a corresponding meaning. Judging by his costume alone, he could well represent an opponent of the church. An additional clue is provided by the fringe on the "black" wrestler's trousers, which adds a slightly noble touch—recalling the festive costume of the "Hercule françois"[63]—while the other's trousers have only the customary white seam. The contrast already noted between the relative health and smoothness of the "black" wrestler's body and the toil-worn limbs of the "red" wrestler might also be explained on this allegorical level.

However, since Stendhal's *Le rouge et le noir* (1830) the color semantics of *black versus red* were no longer open to free interpretation[64] because black stood for the church and red for the army—and also, especially after 1848, for revolutionary movements. The red scarf worn by Courbet in his *Self-Portrait at Ste.-Pélagie*[65] was evidently meant to identify him as a socialist. Still, no juxtaposition of the two colors can be explained in purely abstract terms, but must be seen in terms of the opposition they were intended to signify. During the Second Empire the Catholic church was in principle on the Bonapartist side, and its opponents were increasingly recruited from the socialist ranks. That the Catholic press was loyal to the emperor can be seen even from the Salon reviews, particularly those of 1853.[66] Those socialists who initially wished to ally themselves with the social-revolutionary streams within the church soon became as disillusioned as those who, based on the essay by Napoleon III "L'extinction du paupérisme" (1844), hoped for comprehensive social reform. Among the latter were numerous republicans and Courbet himself; they all turned anticlerical and anti-Bonapartist. As late as 1850 Courbet, in his *Departure of the Fire-Brigade*,[67] could still express a hope that Louis Bonaparte might solve the country's social problems, but in 1851 he declared himself a socialist.[68] Proudhon, who even wrote a pro-Napoleon tract,[69] was sent into exile, as were many other friends of Courbet. Pierre Leroux, who coined the term *socialist*, also wrote an essay on Christianity and democracy, and in 1848 he professed himself a revolutionary Christian;[70] he too now turned against church and state and was compelled to emigrate to London.

In 1853, we may conclude, an anticlerical stance was certainly in keeping with

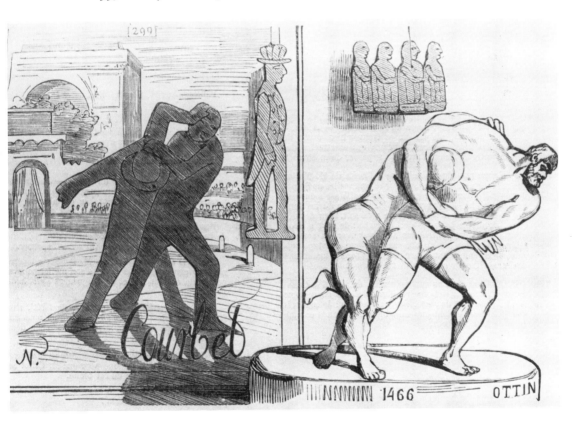

14   Nadar, Caricatures of Courbet's *Wrestlers* (left) and of A. L. M. Ottin's sculpture. *Nadar jury au Salon de 1853*, 1853.

republican and socialist sentiments. This is reason enough to see a tacit reference to the struggle between church and socialism in Courbet's painting, especially as the superiority of the "red" wrestler fits in with his political convictions. If this reading is justified, it would also explain why Courbet's patron Bruyas, though he acclaimed *The Bathers* as a modern, liberated painting, apparently had nothing whatever to say about *The Wrestlers*.

The "black" wrestler cannot be identified because his face is hidden. The "red" one, in turn, clearly bears portrait traits, if not those of any wrestler active at the time, so far as photographs of them exist. Characteristic are the elongated face and its expression of exertion, the beard—not often worn by wrestlers—the slightly incurving nose, and the raised eyebrows. His identity has yet to be determined; Nadar's statement (Appendix, IX) that he knew one of the two wrestlers remains ambiguous. Although Daumier's caricature of Leroux,[71] whose name and personality could well serve as a symbol for "red" in the political sense, does evince a few facial similarities to

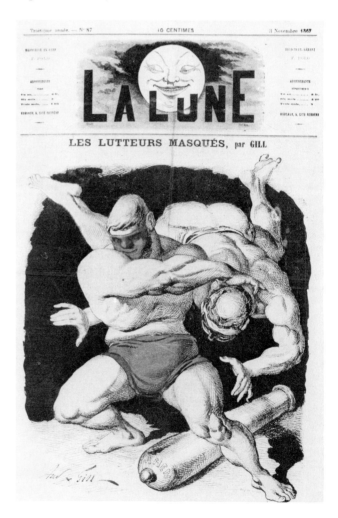

15 André Gill, *The Masked Wrestlers*. Color lithograph. *La lune*, Nov. 3, 1867.

Courbet's "red" athlete, these are not sufficiently close to permit a definite identification. Nevertheless, the man portrayed might be sought among French socialist circles of the day. A link is provided by the contemporary tracts on the poverty question[72] that occupied Courbet ever since he painted his *Departure of the Fire-Brigade;* he was surely aware of the fact that in 1852 the French republicans in London founded the Union Socialiste,[73] a forerunner of the First International, which Courbet himself joined in the 1860s. In his autobiography he expressly states that he had heard "les socialistes de toutes sectes" (socialists of all denominations) and initially leaned to the Fourierists, then to the followers of Cabet and Pierre Leroux.[74]

This iconographical detail, however, does not fully establish the meaning of the picture. Evidently it was still thought to represent the struggle between red and black as late as 1867. Gill, who had undoubtedly seen *The Wrestlers* as it was exhibited for a second time at the 1867 Paris World Fair, employed the subject metaphorically to evoke a political struggle (fig. 15). Here too, the "red" wrestler apparently alludes to a revolutionary, Garibaldi, and the "black" one to the church, personified by Pius IX, and both are masked[75]—a sensationally daring statement in view of the intervention of French troops on behalf of the Vatican. The editors of *La lune* corroborate this reference by asking their readers *not* to take Gill's caricature as a political allegory.[76]

Why Wrestlers?

This caricature will be discussed at greater length in the context of the later metaphoric employment of the wrestler motif. Let us first return to Courbet's painting. The Salon reviews and caricatures of 1853 have shed some light on the pictorial reality it contains, and Courbet's tendency to let contradictions stand instead of eliminating them has made it easier to reconstruct his interest in contemporary concerns. Still, the immediate effect of *The Wrestlers* depends neither on its provocative configuration alone nor solely on the political metaphor it conveys. What remains to be explained is why Courbet chose wrestlers to embody the situation of social conflict that obtained in France in 1853. Such more salient aspects of the Parisian *vie moderne* as factories, department stores, or street scenes might have served better to illustrate the loss of communication between the working and the middle classes, or the everyday lives and working conditions of the proletariat. To explain Courbet's choice, we shall have to look more closely at the contemporary significance of the sport of wrestling, as well as at the then-current conception of the proletariat.

In *The Wrestlers* Courbet took a development into account that was of fairly recent date. The French labor market had undergone a change during the early years of the Second Empire.[77] The private capital accumulated under Louis-Philippe was invested partly in building speculation in Paris, partly in infrastructure, and especially in an expansion of the transportation system; by 1860 the dense French railroad network was almost complete.[78] Trade and tourism accelerated, with a concomitant increase in temporary and seasonal labor. Entire population groups were uprooted from their familiar surroundings, with all the attendant consequences.[79] Among the causes of this development was the pauperization of French rural workers, which more than any other factor contributed to the doubling of the Paris population within the space of a few years. Eugène Sue had good reason to use the term *proletariat* to describe the rural inhabitants of France.[80] Most of them were commuters or day-workers who were unable to find steady jobs on the land, and many of them, like former soldiers, were hired by fairs and sideshows. Only a very few, however, could ever expect to become stars and thus gain regular employment in the entertainment business of the day. In choosing his subjects from among these outsiders, then, Courbet took up a theme that illustrated a very topical and pertinent aspect of the prevailing conditions, if not the only possible one.

His choice of wrestlers also permitted him to depict signs of physical degeneration that were incompatible both with an uncritically heroic image of the working class and with the standardized, classical norms. In this respect, too, Courbet made a direct reference to the current situation; it was during this expansion phase of heavy industry with its officially sanctioned fifteen-hour day that such symptoms were brought to public attention for the first time. His attack had to be mounted in the context of organized leisure, one of the great "improvements" of the Second Empire, because only there could it be effective. Presumably his aim was to show how far the present state of affairs had diverged from the enlightened hope in popular education, defined as the development of physical and mental powers in harmony and on a broad basis. By this time the educational ideals derived from Rousseau's *Emile* and taken up by Villaume, which included wrestling,[81] belonged as much to the past as the Revolution of 1848. Only Proudhon continued to advocate *la lutte* as an adjunct to popular education.[82] The differences between bourgeois and proletarian physical education (the monotony of which anticipated subsequent labor conditions)[83] had already been noted in the eighteenth century; yet instead of being overcome, the barrier grew higher, insofar as the workers had hardly any leisure time at their disposal and the clubs of the day (with their journal, *Le sport,* first published in 1854) accepted only well-off citizens, making sport in France at the onset of the Second Empire a pastime for the prosperous. Laborers entered the picture on a hired basis only, which led to physical and mental stress above and beyond that experienced in the workplace.

The brutality that the Salon critics saw in Courbet's painting and the spread of exploitation into the field of sports had been evoked by no previous artist, for this sort of thing was quite incompatible with the demand for *élévation*.[84] This is why some critics could praise the author of *The Stonebreakers,* which they thought was meant "to elevate the common man despite his shabby clothing, his sunburnt skin, and the furrows graven into his forehead by labor and suffering; to reveal, despite his simplicity, the austere grandeur he possesses in his suffering and labor" (Appendix, V), while deprecating the author of the 1853 canvas, in which they were unanimous in finding none of these ennobling qualities.

The theme and formal treatment of *The Wrestlers* thus work together to illuminate one characteristic aspect of the social situation in 1853. Yet the fact that Courbet elected to depict wrestlers has still further ramifications. Wrestlers came to Paris from

Lutteurs.

16   L'Epine after Valentin,
Breton Wrestlers, 1799.
Jacques Cambry,
Voyage . . . , vol. 3, facing
p. 202.

distant places—from England and Switzerland, but especially from the French
provinces. Natives of Marseille are frequently mentioned in the contemporary articles.
Men from Bordeaux and Franche-Comté, but above all from Brittany, were said to be
the best athletes, and the Salon critics alluded to this when they referred pejoratively to
Courbet's wrestlers as "Savoyards" or "Auvergnats"—the French equivalent of hicks
and hillbillies. By choosing the subject of wrestling, in other words, Courbet tacitly
emphasized the migration of labor that was then so widespread.

The definitely provincial character of wrestling as a sport has still another aspect,
which can best be explained by reference to the province of Brittany. Cambry, who
visited Brittany at the time of the French Revolution and repeatedly called its inhabitants "bons patriotes et bons républicains,"[85] described wrestling as a rough-and-
ready custom perfectly in keeping with the daily activities of the populace, because
"the ways of these folk are those of nature in all its simplicity."[86] Breton wrestling
(which has experienced a revival in our own century)[87] was a popular festival that
included feasting and dancing apart from footracing and other competitive sports with
prizes for the winners, such as bulls, sheep, or colorful costumes. The competitors (fig.
16) swore mutual *franchise* and *loyauté* and agreed not to use prohibited holds.[88] In
Courbet's day fights were held in Rennes, Nantes, and Saint-Brieuc;[89] the participants
were recruited largely from among workers who had once been peasants and who
found in the activity "some of the atmosphere of their native region.[90] Considered a
"renaissance d'un sport celtique" (renaissance of a Celtic sport),[91] Breton wrestling
embodied a claim that was highly important to Courbet and his friends, that of
representing the "true France"[92]—which of course could not prevent the phrase from
subsequently being abused by nationalistic elements. As wrestling was especially
popular in the regions Courbet visited—the southwest, Savoy, and western
Switzerland[93]—it would seem justified to assume that he alluded in *The Wrestlers* to

the upgrading of the provinces which was constituitive for his oeuvre. In his view, these regions represented bulwarks against Bonapartist centralism, which despite occasional flirtations he opposed throughout his career. The theme of Breton wrestling was consciously revived, perhaps with reference to Courbet, in a work shown in the 1864 Salon—Adolphe Leleux's *Lutteurs bretons*.[94]

What may be concluded from the above as regards *The Wrestlers?* By alluding to a popular tradition, the canvas presented a milieu that was familiar and attractive to great numbers of former rural people who now lived and worked in Paris—a group Courbet had already addressed in *A Burial at Ornans*. This assured it of attention of two kinds: negative on the part of the *bourgeoisie*, positive on the part of the *peuple*.[95] Courbet employed the wrestling motif to embody a popular tradition, while lending it new connotations—the antagonism between social forces, and the severity and consequences of manual labor. Although continuing the social impulse of *The Stonebreakers*, *The Wrestlers* surpasses the *commisération* of that painting in being much more aggressive. Even if its tacit reference to current events is left out of account, the picture conveys a powerful moral and political argument.

A Kind of Competition in Depicting Wrestlers

It was opportune for Courbet that in 1852–53 the popularity of wrestling took a tremendous upswing, becoming a veritable fad. Further high points came in 1867, when new wrestling facilities were built, and in 1893, with the founding of a professional association.[96] Before Courbet took it up, the subject had been treated in particular by Decamps and Géricault, whose renderings anticipated his in an exemplary way. In Decamps's picture (fig. 17) the popular, everyday aspect of the sport is emphasized—wrestling as a means to settle a mundane quarrel. (Incidentally, the same point of departure is found in Meissonier's *Rixe* and Thoma's *Roughhousing Boys*.)[97] Like Daumier at a later date,[98] Decamps depicts wrestling in anecdotal terms, showing two thieves fighting over their booty, and adds a moral to the story by letting the stolen donkey escape behind the men's backs. Géricault, by contrast (fig. 18), stages a formal match complete with audience, translating the enlightened, revolutionary idea of equality of the black and white races into a melodramatic if amicable test of strength. There is almost no distinction made between boxing and wrestling here; indeed, both sports were frequently practiced by the same athletes or were combined in one and the same bout. Hence long before Courbet's day, boxing and wrestling had found exemplary expression in French and English art, both as an everyday contest and as a formalized competition.[99] Yet even greater affinities with the "new Géricault," as Courbet was once called,[100] are found in another drawing by his great predecessor in which a characteristic of the 1853 *Wrestlers* is anticipated—the merger of several figures into one, producing a veritable symbol of physical force (fig. 19).

The depictions of wrestling done *after* Courbet's (for instance, Falguière's) either treat it expressly as a formal sporting event or emphasize the current reference to an even greater degree, which of course is especially true of newspaper illustrations and caricatures. Numerous twentieth-century depictions of wrestlers, finally, can be read as conscious metaphors for social conflict, in particular a painting by George Bellows that takes up Géricault's motif and emphasizes its negative aspects.[101]

Courbet himself held the balance between a treatment aimed primarily at rendering the forms of the human figure in motion and an overtly political statement. In concurrent depictions of wrestlers—by Daumier (1852), Doré (1853–56), and Ottin (1853)—as well as in the flood of prints and illustrations that culminated in 1853, we find only isolated facets of this comprehensive approach.

A nonmythological sculpture of wrestlers was exhibited in France for the first and, as far as I know, only time at the Salon of 1853, Ottin's *Coup de hanche*.[102] This sculpture was caricatured by Nadar and Bertall (figs. 13, top; 14, right), in both cases side by side with Courbet's painting, positively demanding a comparison. The

17 A. Masson after A. G. Decamps, *The Thieves' Quarrel*. Lithograph, not dated. Paris, Bibliothèque Nationale.

18   Théodore Géricault,
Boxing Match. Lithograph,
1818. Paris, Bibliothèque
Nationale.

19   Théodore Géricault,
*Wrestling and Boxing
Matches*. Undated pen-and-
ink drawing. Paris, private
collection.

caricaturists seem to have found Ottin's subject no less vulgar and ridiculous than Courbet's, though the former's evidently correct depiction of wrestling technique offered them less of a target. While Nadar had to praise Ottin's "élégance de forme" (Appendix, IX), it fell to Henri Delaborde to detect Courbet's pernicious influence on Ottin's design.[103] As far as we can judge the lost piece from the caricatures and descriptions, we should probably find it naturalistic, technically accomplished, academic in formal approach, and beholden in terms of expression to idealized Hellenistic sculpture.

Also more conventional than Courbet's painting were the numerous graphic depictions of wrestling published in 1852–53. A wood engraving that appeared in 1852 both in Texier (fig. 20) and in *L'illustration*[104] may have partially inspired Courbet. It shows an audience in formal clothes and top hats watching a wrestling match in the Salle Montesquieu, where such events were frequently held at that period. The opponents, two "rois de la lutte" (kings of wrestling) known as "Arpin, le terrible Savoyard" and "Marseille, meunier de la Palud, dit l'Infatigable lutteur" (Marseille, the Miller from Le Palud, alias the Indefatigable),[105] are demonstrating a common

Des lutteurs de la salle Montesquieu, Arpin le Terrible Savoyard, et Marseille.

20 Anonymous, *Wrestling in the Salle Montesquieu* (Arpin versus Marseille). Wood engraving. Edmond Texier, *Tableau de Paris*, 1852, vol. 2, p. 296.

grip, *la cravate*, or headlock. The text gives an idea of the wrestling fever of those years; it also reveals that the government participated directly in establishing the rules, saying that their permission to pit athletes against wild animals was being awaited with baited breath. The text, moreover, confirms that the audience was exclusively upper class ("good-looking young people, all of them members of the Jockey Club").[106]

In the *Journal pour rire* for 1852, Nadar published a caricature of the wrestlers Arpin and Rabasson which also contained a linguistic critique.[107] That same year Randon pictured the Terrible Savoyard appearing on the Champs-Elysées. Randon depicts his wrestler as an extremely uncouth fellow appearing in the midst of a high society public, by which he points up the class conflict described above. Yet he also alludes to the advertising and commercialism that Nadar (fig. 90) had suspected Courbet's painting of exploiting.[108] An 1852 lithograph by Leroux and Rocolin

LES LUTTEURS DE LA SALLE VALENTINO ET LEUR PUBLIC.

21   Gustave Doré, *Wrestling in the Salle Valentino*. Lithograph. *Le journal pour rire*, May 3, 1856.

likewise touches on this forensic connection by illustrating several sports in juxtaposition.[109] Many such prints circulated at the time. All of these renderings show "handsome" wrestlers, avoiding the strenuous nature of the sport and the role of the audience.

In this last respect, Doré surpassed all the other draftsmen of the period. His scene in the Salle Valentino (fig. 21), done in 1856, satirizes both the mock fighting of the wrestlers and the boredom and self-centeredness of the audience. Nevertheless, Doré's lithograph remains affirmative. His concern for physiognomic realism is so strong that although he views the scene with irony, he cannot permit himself to expose it. A detached observer, he does not call the pictorial continuum in question, narrating rather than analyzing. In 1852 Doré submitted to the *Journal pour rire* a number of caricatures (fig. 22) that touch on an aspect of the theme that Courbet left untreated. These are physiognomic studies of aggression, cunning and brutality, deftness and awkwardness, elegance and stupidity—traits superbly characterized in a formal shorthand that recalls that of Daumier.[110]

Two other caricatures, again of 1852, advance a conservative criticism of two British boxers and their "ugly mugs" (fig. 23). On the whole they represent little more than a cheap joke at the expense of the proletariat. The target of two satirical engravings by Dumont (1853)[111] is not so much the athletes themselves as the wrestling fad, and the caption takes ad absurdum the deadly earnest with which victory and defeat are considered a matter of resurrection or oblivion. As the author realizes, the pressure to win robs such matches of all their sporting character.[112] Nadar associates people's attitudes to wrestling with the competition of daily life (fig. 24). However, his allusions

QUELQUES DESSINS DE L'ALMANACH POUR RIRE DE 1853.

Les Gladiateurs pour rire, — par Gustave Doré.

22   Gustave Doré, *Caricatures of Wrestling* (*Les gladiateurs pour rire*). *Le journal pour rire*, Oct. 9, 1852.

23 G. Randon, *Wrestling and Boxing Match on Black Friars Road. Le journal pour rire*, Feb. 13, 1852.

can also be understood as referring to the fistfights and general violence that were never more frequent in France than during and after Louis Napoleon's coup; not incidentally, the scene on the left recalls Daumier's *Ratapoil*.[113] Daumier himself, who like Doré also drew caricatures of horse racing at the Hippodrome,[114] sees the wrestlers from a different perspective. He goes behind the scenes and reveals the events in the ring through the eyes of an observer (fig. 25). Evoking two levels of reality simultaneously, Daumier himself observers the observer, standing aloof from the happenings he depicts. Like Courbet, he refers beyond the pictorial field; the match is shown as a drama staged within the image proper, and the viewer's attention is

24 Nadar, *Hyacinthe and Grassot Testing Their Strength. Le journal pour rire*, Sept. 25, 1852.

— Va te frotter à ce bourgeois-là, Arpin. — Pas si bête ! on dit qu'un homme *averti* en vaut deux : celui-là alors en vaut quatre.

Cependant Hyacinthe et le terrible Savoyard Grassot trouvent moyen de faire oublier la chaleur à tout Paris.

25   Honoré Daumier,
Wrestlers. Oil on panel,
42 × 27.5 cm, c. 1852.
Charlottenlund, Ordrup-
gaardsamlingen.

diverted from an immediate, naive participation in the event to a consideration of the relationship between the two points of view suggested. Unlike Doré, Daumier positively invites us to reflect on the nature of wrestlers' work; his dual viewpoint comes closer to Courbet's than any other artist's.

To sum up our investigation of the contemporaneous illustrations, we can say that in *The Wrestlers* Courbet exploited a fashion that culminated in 1853 and reversed its thrust. Instead of addressing the audience and their elegant ambience, he concentrated foremost on the two wrestlers, but did so without a trace of idealization. His interest focused on depicting the wear and tear of physical labor on the human body, and on expressing the hope that the struggle against reactionary social forces could be won. These aspects are made very obvious to the real viewer, who is confronted with an action that is not completed within the image but continues beyond it, and beyond the Salon as well. In effect, then, Courbet did put in an appearance on the fairgrounds with

The Wrestlers—not in the sense of the emergent culture industry (a phrase first used, to my knowledge, in 1853),[115] but in the sense of a popular custom, although the gravity of his treatment certainly differs from its entertaining character. Seen in this light, the painting takes on a truly historical stature.

A Metaphor for the Struggle of Life

The Wrestlers is far from being the only painting in Courbet's oeuvre to possess this comprehensive significance. If we take its implied subject to be conflict as such, *The Wrestlers* reveals a central trait of the artist's attitude to life. The metaphor of wrestling was highly important to him in many respects, verbal and otherwise. Not only did his contemporaries Silvestre, Ideville, Astruc, and Riat[116] call him a *lutteur,* but he viewed himself as one, writing in his autobiography, "He had to *wrestle* like no other against the infirm institutions that controlled France and paralyzed genius."[117] To Vallès he confessed, "I have *wrestled* against all forms of authoritarian government and of divine right, wishing that man would govern himself in accordance with his needs."[118] After 1871 Courbet decided in retrospect, "Today, I belong . . . to the class of men who died . . . devoted to the Republic, to equality, without self-interest; for it is these men who *wrestled* against the control of Louis-Philippe . . . asking the social question, . . . and who *wrestled* against the war against the Prussians."[119]

Wrestling is a fairly common political metaphor, especially in French, where *la lutte* can connote not only the sport itself but the class struggle or the struggle of life. While the expression "le Breton naît lutteur" (the Breton is a born wrestler)[120] derives directly from the sport, such lines in Breton hymns as "Each man in Scaër will say / I have wrestled well throughout my life / I will be crowned by God / . . . And when we wrestle without fear / We will pin down all the old devils . . . "[121] relate to the purpose of life while retaining clear overtones of the popular custom. In terms of conflict, wrestling can even be equated with living; as Valentine Parisot once wrote, "Wrestling, and then wrestling some more: that's living; if you give up wrestling, you do no more than just exist"; and Mme de Girardin, "In all things, wrestling is life itself: in religion, in politics, in literature, in love." George Sand said, "Be a eunuch and get fat, or be a man and wrestle"; and Balzac, "Work is a never-ending wrestling bout feared by . . . the . . . organizations which often crack under its strain."[123] Victor Hugo wrote, "Those who live are those who wrestle, those whose firm sense of direction fills both soul and mind." And finally, the famous hymn of the First International contains the stanza,

> C'est la lutte finale
> Groupons-nous, et demain
> L'internationale
> Sera le genre humain.[125]

(Now is the final bout / So form ranks, and tomorrow / The International / Will be the human way.)

These few examples will suffice to show how common the image of wrestling was in the language of Courbet's day. It might be traced back to St. Paul, who compared the struggle of life with athletic competition, adopting a popular tradition of late antiquity and transforming it into an instrument of moral and political persuasion. Like the athlete, St. Paul found himself involved in continual struggle.[126] Once it had entered the profane realm, the wrestling metaphor could become a political one, examples of which are found throughout Western philosophy down to the present day.[127] When in 1520 Francis I challenged Henry VIII of England to a public wrestling match,[128] this represented both a demonstration of political rivalry and an expression of self-confidence and power. Similarly, towards the close of the eighteenth century the Third Estate considered boxing and wrestling a symbol of social conflict; during the 1790s Humphrey and Mendoza attributed an emancipatory character to such matches in England.[129] With Géricault the revolutionary demand for racial equality led to the match between black and white discussed above. This egalitarian idea was opposed during the Second Empire, in visual art as in other fields; Julian's etching on Cladel's *Ompdrailles, le tombeau des lutteurs* (1875), in which a colored wrestler is being crushed by his white opponent, has the character of an epilogue (fig. 26). A classical example of the political

Imp. A. Quantin

R. Julian

26   René Julian, *Wrestlers.*
Etching, 19 × 12 cm,
c. 1875. Private collection.

wrestling metaphor is the 1841 bout between Jean Dupuis, the French Hercules, and Bavarian wrestlers: "This time the challenge had a highly political character. Hardly had Thiers publicly proclaimed that he would challenge Germany to fight for the left bank of the Rhine, when Jean Dupuis crossed the Rhine as if to test which nation was the stronger."[130] The widespread popularity of wrestling contributed to the use of the metaphor for mundane political quarrels as well, as may be seen from Nadar's 1856 caricature on the spat between *Le Figaro* and the *Gazette de Paris*.[131]

Political caricature in the Second Empire was hindered by censorship to an extent that can only be called dictatorial. No one dared to associate the wrestling metaphor with high-level politics until toward the end of the period—and then only in veiled form. Gill, for instance, was compelled to give his wrestlers masks in 1867 (fig. 15) and to limit his reference to current events to the colors red and black, the tonsure of the "black" wrestler, and a cannon barrel with the inscription "Amen." Daumier pro-

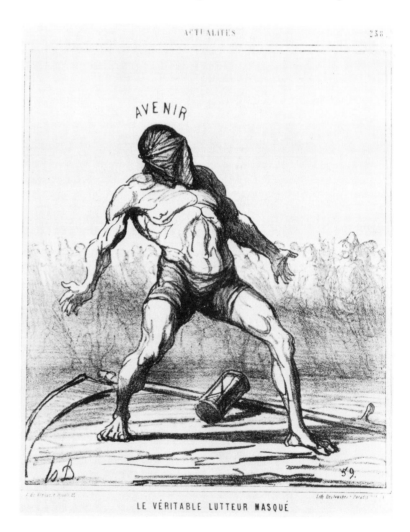

27   Honoré Daumier, *The True Masked Wrestler.* Lithograph. *Le charivari,* Nov. 9, 1867.

LE VÉRITABLE LUTTEUR MASQUÉ

ceeded similarly. In 1867 he depicted Death as a masked challenger symbolizing the future of France (fig. 27).[132] The terrifying message of this lithograph, the fact that no one is strong enough to face state-decreed death, potentiates the demonstrative gravity of Courbet's *Wrestlers* and turns it into an outcry against impending war. Direct reference to political events was avoided until 1873, when Morel-Retz (alias Stop) drew the campaign between republicans and monarchists as a French boxing match from which the exhausted parties are recovering.[133]

Hence Courbet's *Wrestlers* can be viewed in the context of current political metaphor despite its great pictorial complexity as an image, daring as it does to raise the issue of the *glorification du travail* (glorification of labor). The disturbing composition forms a point of reference for the critical analysis of the *société environnante* (surrounding society) by means of which Courbet hoped to bolster democratic ideas.[134] The official sports events organized by the Bonapartist state to pacify the populace and reconcile the class conflict, provided Courbet with an opportunity to view the wrestling ring as something quite different—an arena in which men struggled for power.[135] Although sparing his criticism of none of the groups involved, giving neither wrestlers nor audience a heroic aspect, Courbet projected a vision of the future based on the energy and tenacity of the "red" wrestler. He also embodied the hope that had once been placed in Napoleon, suggested by his great predecessor's Arc de Triomphe.

Courbet carried out his intention of shaking his audience out of their lethargy without resorting to mere propaganda. While bringing the Hercules theme into a normal everyday context, he lent the composition the rank of a history painting, thus equalizing diverse levels of visual statement. But above all Courbet provoked his audience by destroying a historically outmoded pictorial coherency. The atomized nature of the world of work finds a correspondence in the treatment of the image, which is reduced to particles, fitted together as in a montage. Courbet tore the homogeneity of perspective and proportion apart, destroying a notion of beauty associated with figures and objects while nevertheless retaining their sensuous quality. It is precisely the "errors" in the picture that indicate its realistic utopia: to combine formal innovation with revolutionary tradition.

28 Gustave Courbet, *The Painter's Studio*. Oil on canvas, 359 × 598 cm, 1854–55. Paris, Musée d'Orsay.

3

The Painter's Studio: Focus of World Events, Site of Reconciliation

Dramatis Personae

COURBET'S *Painter's Studio* (fig. 28) is still an enigmatic picture.[1] The self-absorbed yet challenging presence of the figures who are gathered in the painter's studio without a hint of shared activity; the indeterminate depth of space out of which only the central group around the landscape emerges into focus; and especially the self-aggrandizing pose of the artist, who has turned his back on his model and is apparently paying no attention to his visitors—all these features have again and again raised the question as to the meaning of the composition.

The question, however, was not always as burning as it has recently become. The nineteenth-century commentaries on this painting were much fewer and farther between than those, say, on *The Stonebreakers* or *A Burial at Ornans, The Bathers* or *The Wrestlers*—the four canvases with which Courbet, according to his friend Vallès, had already "said everything."[2] Indicatively, for a *single* contemporary caricature of *The Painter's Studio* there exist almost two dozen of these four other works. The obvious reason was that the painting was never shown in an official Salon exhibition in Paris; not until 1920 was it acquired from Courbet's sister for the Louvre, and only then was it made continually accessible to the public. These facts, however, raise further questions. Was the painting really without interest for the official institutions, or on the contrary, did it contain information they would rather have hushed up and that stood opposed to its purchase? This question evidently relates to the disturbing aspects of the picture, and it cannot be answered until the facts are sifted, the identity of the figures has been elucidated (so far as this is possible), and the purpose of their common presence has been determined.[3]

Concentrating on the artist's role, Courbet research has addressed itself primarily to the iconography of the painting.[4] First clues were provided by the letters to Champfleury and Bruyas[5] in which the artist described the composition in its early stages, revealing the names of some of the persons depicted and alluding to others. The fact that he gave the names only of those in the right half of the picture—friends, mentors, patrons—would seem to indicate that in these early stages, Courbet was thinking of *The Painter's Studio* in terms of a "friendship painting."[6] He was likely influenced in this by an illustration in the *Magazin pittoresque* for 1849, which not only contained the self-portrait of an artist with a nude model standing behind him but alluded, in image and caption, to the relationship of inspiration to reality[7]—a point of departure for Courbet's attempt to create a topical but not superficial painting, one that was significant without being traditionalistic, "a painting that was both modern and profound."[8] As has been determined, the studio engraving of 1849 shows Théophile Gautier, Henri Valentin, Apollonie Sabatier (as model), and Gérard de Nerval gathered around the artist, in the same places as Champfleury, Bruyas, the nude model, and Baudelaire appear in Courbet's painting.[9]

The iconographic studies have reached their culmination in Hélène Toussaint's hypothesis that not only the figures on the right, but those on the left-hand side of *The Painter's Studio* represent actual historical personalities.[10] The hypothesis is based on Courbet's allusion to a "minister of the interior" represented in the painting, and if it is correct, it would erase the divergence that many observers have noted between the two halves, a history painting with definite individuals on the right, and a genre painting with mere "characters" on the left. But still, then, there would remain some difference in the arrangement of the figures, which emerge in an orderly group on the right, while on the left they recede into the shadows and seem to revolve around a void in their midst. Also, an explanation would still have to be found for the obvious lack of communication among them, because it is certainly strange that nothing links the two groups with each other or with the center of interest—the artist seated center stage, the only person in the picture who is truly "acting," if not really painting.[11]

According to Hélène Toussaint, those represented are (starting in the left foreground): Napoleon III (seated), with two of his ministers; Finance Minister Fould; Courbet's "Jew,"[12] holding the strongbox on the far left; and, seated to the emperor's right, the "purveyor of cheap textiles," Minister of the Interior Persigny. Then come two loyalist newspapermen, next to Fould the ultramontane "priest" Veuillot, and opposite Persigny, a renegade republican, Emile de Girardin, to whom Courbet referred as "the coroner." Behind the emperor would be Lazare Carnot (d. 1823), who voted for the execution of Louis XVI in 1792 and became minister of the interior under Napoleon I; next to him, in the white uniform of the Italian *chasseurs* with the red scarf of the revolutionary armies, Toussaint sees Garibaldi, the first in a series of personifications of foreign countries. Then come Kossuth, with bonnet, representing the Hungarian rebels, and Kościuszko (d. 1817), representing the Polish freedom fighters. The latter, in allusion to these fighters' nickname, *faucheurs* (harvesters), is holding a scythe. Between Persigny and Girardin appear a carnival strongman symbolizing Turkey and a jester in Chinese costume symbolizing European ties with the Far East. Behind Girardin, finally, we see a young woman who may represent an allusion to Greece, and a laborer with the features of Herzen, the Russian socialist. Beneath a life-size lay figure[13] crouches a woman—to whom Courbet himself referred as an Irish-woman—dressed in rags and suckling her baby, an embodiment of abject poverty.

To the right of the central group appear the friends of art: the musician Promayet with a violin under his arm; Courbet's patron, Bruyas; Proudhon, Cuenot, and Buchon; seated, Champfleury, and at his feet, a boy drawing; behind them, a couple representing free love. Then comes another, elegant, couple, the only figures on this side whose identity is still controversial. They probably represent the woman mentioned above, Apollonie Sabatier, and her escort, the Belgian banker Mosselman.[14] Finally, seated in the corner, engrossed in a book, is Baudelaire.

At first glance this decoding of the left-hand section of *The Painter's Studio* would seem highly speculative, particularly as it is predicated on an inconsistent mode of representation—contemporary personalities mingling with symbolic figures and even, in Carnot and Kościuszko, with representatives of a past epoch, ghostly embodiments of republican virtues. However, we have always had to come to terms with the fact that figures like the Irishwoman in the left foreground or the couple interspersed among Courbet's friends on the right exist on a different level of meaning than the identifiable individual portraits. This uncoordinated mixture of inventions of different degrees of reality was characteristic of Courbet's thinking and approach to composition.[15] The painting's subtitle—"a real allegory that closes a seven-year phase of my artistic and intellectual life"—amounts to a program, the intention to create a multidimensional, imaginative world that culminates in the nude figure (which has been erroneously called an allegory of truth, a muse, or a model).[16] Seen in this light, the term *real allegory,* which struck Courbet's friends as merely absurd, would seem perfectly suited to characterize the both intellectual and sensuous, both imagined and experienced history of this phase of his life, a résumé comparable to Goethe's *Dichtung und Wahrheit.* On the face of it, the figures mean no more and no less than what meets the eye; but they also possess an evocative significance that goes far beyond the obvious.

This ambiguity lends the picture a touch of travesty, a device that was familiar to Courbet and his circle. Champfleury wrote an essay on contemporary travesties;[17] Baudelaire's and Flaubert's love of literary "déguisements" was well known.[18] Courbet himself was very fond of puns and wordplays, such as his 1870 allusion, in "une branche d'olivier," to the minister of that name.[19] That *The Painter's Studio* contains a hidden meaning may be inferred, among other things, from his letter of early 1855 to a friend, the painter Français. "You say you'd like to know what the theme of my picture is?" asked Courbet. "It's so complicated to explain that I'd rather *let you guess when you see it.* It's the story of my studio—everything that happens there, intellectually and sensuously. It's all rather mysterious. It's anybody's guess!"[20] That *The Painter's Stu-*

dio was indeed intended to be a visual riddle whose connotations went far deeper than its surface meaning may be gathered particularly from the phrase "je veux te le laisser deviner quand tu verras" (I'd rather let you guess when you see it)—the guessing game won't really get under way until you see the picture.

Guessing games of this kind had a long tradition in France. Back in the seventeenth century, in Jesuit schools, special visual rebuses called *enigmata* were made[21] which besides their obvious meaning had a covert one that the pupils were expected to unravel.[22] Such visual teaching aids were also shown at exhibitions, where the visitors were asked to solve them, and they were published monthly in the form of engravings in the *Mercure galant,* whose readers sent solutions in by mail. Frequently the secret meaning of these mythological or religious picture puzzles referred to current events, and sometimes it was socially critical or blasphemical in intent.[23] This type of image remained popular down to the nineteenth century. In 1834, for instance, Grandville published a lithograph with the caption "Enigme" that criticized, in a veiled representation of Louis-Philippe, the regime of the *juste-milieu.*[24] In contrast to the enigmata of the seventeenth century, however, the puzzle consisted not in finding a hidden key word[25] but in relating the objects depicted to the persons implied. In this sense, Courbet's *Studio* is certainly an *enigma;* nor can we entirely exclude the possibility that, like the seventeenth-century puzzles, it too may have a covert verbal meaning.[26]

His contemporaries cannot have been particularly interested in solving the riddle. If Napoleon was indeed represented in *The Painter's Studio,* this would have made the critics in both camps chary of going into it too deeply. Even if Courbet's intention could be inferred as loyalist, the painting remained politically controversial, for wasn't it an insult to the crown to depict the emperor in a subsidiary role? The omnipotence of the censorship board has been graphically described by Hélène Toussaint;[27] and when one side has a secret police, the other side is compelled to develop a secret language. The contemporary sources abound with references and hints for deciphering it, most of which have been overlooked up to now.

Champfleury, in a letter to George Sand, unmistakably alludes to the disguised nature of *The Painter's Studio,* writing that "the utopians and the mystics are in the habit of twisting language. Courbet doesn't want to be taken for a utopian; yet his *real allegory* does bear a tremendous similarity to the secret letter sent publicly to His Majesty, Prince Louis-Napoléon, by Mr. Wronsky, the god of messianism."[28] Like Wronsky, Champfleury believed, Courbet was making a public appeal in the guise of travesty, that is, covertly; and like Wronsky, we may infer, he was addressing Louis Napoleon (Napoleon III), and with messianic claims much like those of the philosopher. The historical and political connotations of the painting are corroborated by Perrier's statement that the group on the left contained a "personification of our epoch," a term that no mere gathering of representatives of certain professions would have justified.[29] Paul Mantz, one of the best-informed critics of the period, was even clearer on this point, writing about *The Painter's Studio* in 1878 that "Courbet . . . recalls his earlier battles; he has taken up all the memories of his combative youth."[30] This sentence would be hard to understand in reference to a mere depiction of the artist's friends and neutral representatives of "society per se." Its implication that conflicts were worked out and resolved in the painting is predicated on the presence of antagonisms or opposing camps.

In 1881, writing in the catalogue to a sales exhibition of Courbet's work, Philippe Burty declared that "*The Painter's Studio* contains an entire page of contemporary history [tout un côté d'actualité] that eludes us today."[31] Although Burty gives no names for the left-hand group, his reserve might be explained by an intention to convince the decidedly republican government to purchase the painting. An explicit reference to Napoleon would have jeopardized this aim;[32] similar tactics of silence were employed in the next Courbet exhibition (1882), when the portrait of Chaudey was suppressed.[33] However, the most convincing argument for a contemporary political message in *The Painter's Studio* was provided by Thoré, who as early as 1861 lashed out at Courbet's alleged opportunism: "Since he knew . . . that there is nothing more beautiful in painting than *soldiers and kings,* he has avoided jeopardizing his menagerie by including outlaws. . . . He has realized that people have become more interested in *those who have stones broken* than in those who break them." Now, since Courbet never depicted "soldiers and kings" in the 1861 Salon or outside *The Painter's Studio,* Thoré's statement can only refer to this painting.[34] The loyalist stance here attributed to him can likewise only have been inferred from *The Painter's Studio,* assuming, of course, that it actually does contain depictions of Napoleon III and his ministers.

All of this evidence, of course, does not yet prove the correctness of the identifications suggested by Hélène Toussaint. Those for the right-hand half of the picture, in almost every case, are indeed corroborated by clear portrait traits, for these were people whom Courbet had previously portrayed, and he recurred to his earlier work for the depictions of Baudelaire, Champfleury, and even for his own portrait.[35] Other portraits, such as that of Proudhon, are slightly more generalized. This brings up a complicating factor for the identification of the figures on the left side: assuming Courbet indeed wanted to depict politicians, journalists, or even representatives of other countries here—people most of whom he had never seen, let alone sketched—he would have had to rely on photographs, engravings, paintings by other artists, or newspaper illustrations, and their recognizability would have suffered accordingly, particularly as Courbet's portraits generally relied very strongly on the vital impression of the living model.[36]

The identifications suggested for the group on the left, however, are based not only on facial features but on attributes and gestures. The figure identified as Napoleon III, in addition to physiognomic similarities extending even to the waxed moustache and the emperor's way of smiling to himself, evinces such further clues as the dog that accompanied him wherever he went and especially the characteristic boots (since portrait cartoons were considered to constitute *lèse-majesté,* Napoleon III was often caricatured as a boot [*botte*]).[37] Moreover, in Quillenbois's caricature of *The Painter's Studio* (fig. 71), he is shown kicking over the chamber pot, which in Bonapartist lingo represented the vessel of the Republic.[38] Another clue is the "romantic loot" on the floor, objects which—apart from the dagger, about which more later—were attributes of the *carbonaro*, the idealistic republican, which Napoleon III was still considered to be as late as 1848.[39] All of this adds up to a quite plausible identification of the "poacher" as the emperor. (The term *poacher*, by the way, should not be taken as pejorative, for this one identification permits no conclusion to be drawn as yet about the *tendency* of the painting.[40] As with the three following figures, however, the identification is in this case undoubtedly correct.)

Veuillot, whose shifty character was proverbial,[41] is not only a good likeness; his priest's clothing characterizes him as ultramontane, just as Carnot's cap characterizes him as a republican.[42] In Fould's case, his headgear even bears an *F*, and engraved on Garibaldi's rifle butt is a *G*. With respect to Persigny, Girardin, Kossuth, Kościuszko, and Herzen, Toussaint's argument is less convincing because the facial features do not match as well with the known portraits of these men, and because the attributes alone, or additional information whose applicability is predicated on an acceptance of the suggestion (such as Persigny's role as "salesman of Napoleonic ideas"), are not sufficient to permit definitive identification. Yet even if the question of *personal* identity remains open in some cases, as in that of the *faucheur*, there is no reason to doubt the *general*, allegorical significance of the painting, particularly as the military connotation of the word *faucheur* is still more current in French parlance than the civilian one.[43] But whether the "strongman," because he is "fort comme un Turc," or the "fool," because of his Far Eastern pose and costume, or the "laborer," because the position of his arms was typical of Herzen, can be considered to be allegories of Turkey, China, and revolutionary tendencies in Russia would seem doubtful, at least based on this one line of argument. However, when one reviews the newspapers of the period and sees that, as a result of the Crimean War and Anglo-French policy in the Far East, China, Russia, and Turkey were in the headlines every day,[44] one must admit that such considerations do have their justification.

Personal Aims and World Fair Activities

Agreeing, if partly skeptically, with most of Hélène Toussaint's suggestions,[45] I shall attempt in what follows to draw conclusions about the structure and significance of the painting from these iconographic findings. It is secondary whether one or the other of these identifications can be clarified by further research; the important thing about *The Painter's Studio* is that emperor and artist meet here, that part of the Bonapartist entourage is present, and that accompanying this group are representatives of other countries. On the whole—even disregarding the Proudhonist Herzen—an extremely broad range of political opinion is represented, from Proudhon to Veuillot, from the far left to the far right. Also represented are the extremes of social position, from the elegantly dressed Madame Sabatier to the Irishwoman in rags crouching on the floor; the ages of life; and, symbolized by the boy drawing and the boy looking on, the active and contemplative faculties of man. Moreover, in Courbet's own activity, manual and intellectual labor are combined.[46]

This union of all human abilities in that of the artist offsets the often remarked "alienation" of the figures, who have been described as rapt in "collective sleep" as if in a "waiting room."[47] This latter feature, the isolation of the figures around the artist, is indeed what initially strikes one most. Even the formally most consistent group, at the center of the picture, is heterogeneously structured. The key figure here is the nude. The painter has turned his back on his "model," and his visitors pay her no notice, just as they seem to be oblivious of everything going on around them; and dissolved is the mythical triangle of ruler, artist, and the woman as prefigured in the fable of *Alexander and Campaspe in the Workshop of Apelles*.[48] The group is drawn together only by *nature*, which is embodied less in the nude woman than in the virginal landscape.

On what conceptual level does this visually so heterogeneous triptych-like composition coalesce? Why, above all, has the emperor been included in the picture: What was the artist's intention? A tentative answer may be provided by a glance at the real context in which it was painted during the 1850s. Iconographical analysis has led us to forget a fact that is crucial to an interpretation of *The Painter's Studio:* that it was executed for the Paris World Fair, opened on May 1, 1855, by the emperor himself. A great deal of careful and long-term planning went into this exhibition. As early as spring 1853, Napoleon III issued a decree that was forwarded to the prefects and read as follows:

> *Universal Exposition in the Year 1855.* . . . As you know, His Majesty has ordered, by a decree of March 8th, that a world fair of agricultural and industrial products shall take place in Paris in May 1855. . . . It is necessary that you advise your administration, from this date forward, of the significance of this solemn competition, as well as to do everything in your power to further the competition, to which the imperial government has invited enterprises of all countries. . . . You are requested to contact the chambers of agriculture, manufacturing and commerce without delay . . . and to describe to them all the advantages the world fair will have for France, a fair that was prevented in 1849 solely by the economic crisis that came in the wake of the political events of 1848. . . . By setting an opening date of May 1, 1855, the emperor has wisely provided sufficient time for producers here and abroad to prepare for this great competition in an adequate manner. . . .
>
> The Minister of the Interior
> F. de Persigny.[49]

For Napoleon III as well as for Courbet, then, this event represented *a summing-up of seven years of his life*. Elected president of the Second Republic in 1848, he intended, in 1855, to demonstrate the glory of empire and the successes of his reign for all the world to see. After the fact, he declared the Exposition Universelle to have been an aim of Bonapartist policy from the very beginning, implying that it took priority even to the London World Fair of 1851. An attempt to surpass England continued to determine the planning of the event. Two months after the first decree, the emperor announced his decision to combine the commercial fair with an international art competition—something that London could not boast.[50]

This second decree was published in the *Moniteur universel* for June 23, 1853:

NAPOLEON,
Emperor of the French by the grace of God and the will of the nation, extends his salute to all present and future subjects.

Convinced that a world fair, as one of the most effective means of contributing to the progress of the arts, can provide an opportunity for competition to all the world's artists, and that it will create an enormous incentive to achievement and represent a source of fruitful comparisons; considering that advancements in industry are closely bound up with those in visual art and that regardless of this fact no previous industrial exhibition has included works of art to a sufficient extent, and that it is incumbent particularly on France, whose industry owes so much to the Fine Arts, to give them the place they deserve in the coming World Fair; we have resolved and hereby declare that:

1. A World Exhibition of Fine Arts shall take place in Paris concurrently with the World Fair of Industry. The exhibition building will be announced in due course.

2. The Annual Exhibition of Fine Arts for 1854 shall be postponed to 1855 and combined with the World Fair.

3. Our Ministry of State shall be charged with the execution of this decree.

Decreed in Saint-Cloud, on the 22nd of June, 1853,
Napoleon.
For the Emperor: Achille Fould, Minister of State.

This measure was taken with an eye not only to England but to Germany as well. In the first third of the century, Germany had claimed a position of intellectual leadership in Europe to which even the French concurred, and now it had become a major political aim to show that not only could France outpace England in terms of manufacture but that she was indeed the true home of culture and the most highly civilized nation on earth.

As Minda de Gunzburg has shown in detail, the entry requirements for the art exhibition were designed to ensure a French "victory" from the start.[51] These included the composition of the selection and award committees, which were chaired by members of the royal family and had French majorities. Moreover, the government, apparently troubled by doubts as to the superiority of recent French art, hoped to improve the home team's chances by breaking with tradition and permitting artists to hold a great retrospective, in which Ingres and Delacroix, for example, were superbly represented, with forty and thirty-two paintings, respectively.

Considerations of competition and prestige, then, informed both sections of the exhibition, that devoted to the visual arts as much as that devoted to technology. Art and politics, until then kept clearly separated, entered a liaison *ad majorem imperatoris gloriam*. Still, the Paris World Fair was also intended to further the idea of international peace. In his speech on the day of the awards, Prince Napoleon declared that "the bitter rivalries and feelings of hate among nations arise from their division; one need only bring them closer together, and hate will be quenched. In this regard, the

World Fair has had momentous results. Visitors from all corners of the earth have flocked to Paris. The spectacle of real progress . . . has spread feelings of mutual respect among all the foreigners and the French. This is the only way to increase friendship among nations."[52] And the emperor, as he was waging war, emphasized the universal desire for peace and extolled the exhibition as a place of concord and reconciliation.[53]

It is quite unthinkable that Courbet knew nothing of this propaganda. His letters alone, especially those to Bruyas (see note 5), reveal a keen sense of competitiveness with regard to the Salons, and he was obviously involved in a hot debate with the press about the meaning and aims of realistic painting.[54] He continued this debate in *The Painter's Studio* by including a crumpled issue of the *Journal des débats* with a skull resting on it, an attack that likewise had a very concrete reason.[55] In 1853 this periodical had reported that "Courbet's organs of sight are apparently out of order, so distorted and ugly is everything he paints. . . . One even begins to wonder whether . . . he might not be suffering from brain damage. How else can one explain why an artist who must have realized after three exhibitions that the public infinitely detests his ugly paintings, not only declines to shed his crazy aberrations but increases them still further?"[55]

Even more decisive for the genesis of *The Painter's Studio*, however, was apparently a heated conversation Courbet had with M. Nieuwerkerke, superintendent of fine arts, in the presence of the painters Chenavard and Français.[57] In the course of this conversation, which took place in about October 1854[58] on Nieuwerkerke's initiative, the latter told Courbet that the government would be interested in having him participate in the World Fair—a surprisingly liberal attitude in view of the harsh attacks of 1853, yet one that is not unusual in authoritarian regimes planning international events, as we have seen in our own century.[59] When art is seen as a means to international understanding, a certain pluralism is unavoidable, apart from its being desirable in terms of propaganda effect.

Evidently both sides used the situation to sound out each other's intentions. With amazing frankness, Nieuwerkerke simultaneously offered Courbet a government commission and tried to muzzle him. This plunged Courbet into a dilemma which, in his report to Bruyas, he was able only partially to conceal in a flourish of high-sounding words. But he certainly recognized the opportunity presented to him. Before the Commune he was quite receptive to official government recognition, receiving medals in 1849, 1857, and 1861, and being nominated for the Legion of Honor in 1870; and despite all his polemics against "gouvernementation autoritaire,"[60] Courbet felt great respect for the emperor, writing to Castagnary, "Look at Napoleon III— he is progress, France will retain her creative force thanks to him, and he deserves the honor for it." In 1854 the World Fair seemed to present a unique opportunity to show that his claim to being France's greatest painter was justified. His patron Bruyas, a convinced Bonapartist[61] and connoisseur of Courbet's art, could not help but agree.

Proudhon, for his part, was simply elated by the idea of the fair, hoping that it would contribute decisively to the solution of the social question. Between 1853 and 1856 he paid a full dozen visits to Prince Napoleon, the emperor's cousin, who had been named president of the Central Committee for the fair, to explain his plans for a reform of goods circulation, which, once it was tested on a world scale, would soon put an end to the class struggle. Proudhon's "project d'exposition perpétuelle"[62] could not help but impress Courbet, who dreamed of a "musée perpétuel".

On the other hand, Courbet's conversation with Nieuwerkerke gave him the long-craved opportunity to emphasize his need for *independence*—one of the basic ideas behind *The Painter's Studio*. Nieuwerkerke's cautious yet accommodating suggestion that Courbet be commissioned to do a painting for the fair and have it judged by two independent committees, one governmental and the other selected by the artist, raised Courbet's ire "because he assured me that he represented the government, and because I myself by no means feel represented by this government."[63] Courbet continued: "I went on to tell him that I looked upon his government as a normal *private person*"—as which he indeed treated Napoleon III in *The Painter's Studio*—

> and requested only one thing of him, namely, to leave free art in its exhibition and not to support 3000 artists with a budget of 300,000 francs against me. I also told him that I was the only one who could judge my art . . . and of all the contemporary French painters, I was the only one who had the power to represent both my own personality and society in an independent way. To which he replied, "You are very proud, Monsieur Courbet!" I replied, "It's odd you shouldn't have noticed it before. I'm the proudest man in France." . . . He was taken completely aback; apparently he'd promised the gentlemen and ladies of the Court to show them how a man could be bought for 20,000 or 30,000 francs. He asked me again whether I wasn't going to submit anything to the World Fair. I replied that I would never submit to the competition, since I recognized no judge; but that I might conceivably submit my *Burial*, out of cynicism. . . . Anyway, I hope to be able to mount a rival exhibition of my own, which will bring in 40,000 francs. . . . But finally . . . I took his hand and assured him that we were still good friends. Then I turned to Chenavard and Français and asked them to admit that they too had been made fools of;[64] then we went out for a beer. I also remember that Nieuwerkerke said to me: "I don't think, Monsieur Courbet, that you have any reason to complain; the government is really going to great lengths for you, and nobody else can say that of himself. . . ."

In spite of its grotesque exaggerations, this letter is certainly an important document for the art and art policies of the Second Empire, apart from the light it sheds on the ambivalent situation of the "free" artist. But what does it ultimately imply—that Courbet was an opponent of the empire or its propagandist, in continuation of his pro-Napoleonic *Departure of the Fire-Brigade* and portraits of the socialist-haters Wallon and Jean Journet?[65] That Nieuwerkerke was merely a "tamed lion-tamer" (dompteur dompté) who attempted in vain to "buy" a politically ambiguous and artistically highly controversial painter and use him to demonstrate the liberality of the Bonapartist regime? Evidently Courbet was juggling with several balls during this conversation and in his subsequent letter to Bruyas. By self-assertiveness he hoped to gain favorable terms and avoid censorship (limiting himself to good-natured chiding so as not to risk a complete break with Nieuwerkerke), while hinting to Bruyas of the government's offer in order to encourage him to take initiatives of his own. At any rate, Courbet was determined to participate, whether in the official exhibition or outside it, and at the same time to maintain his independence with respect to its organizers. What is more, I believe this letter had an influence on the genesis of *The Painter's Studio*. Conceivably the left-hand side of the picture, with its neither clearly pro- nor anti-Napoleonic sentiment, began to take shape in Courbet's mind at this point, while the other half, inspired by the *Magazin pittoresque,* was already determined.

The government propaganda of the day fairly demanded a reply, a "pictorial manifesto." As Courbet was working on *The Painter's Studio* (from October 1854 to April 1855), all of the French art journals, especially *L'artiste,* were full of inspiring reports that hymned the great event to come. Throughout 1854 *L'artiste* published article after detailed article on "les ateliers de Paris" where work was feverishly progressing for the World Fair, and on "les embellissements de Paris," the great urban planning projects in the vicinity of l'Etoile, the Champs-Elysées, the Place Louis XV, and so on.[66] What becomes especially clear from these reports is the challenge that Ingres and Delacroix represented for the other artists, and how strongly their work was seen from the point of view of political utility. On March 1, 1854, for instance, *L'artiste* described a visit of the emperor and empress to Ingres' atelier, where they inspected his painting for the ceiling of Paris City Hall (*The Apotheosis of Napoleon I*); the following month Théophile Gautier reported on Delacroix's *Salon de la paix,* also located in City Hall, and likewise a political allegory in the service of the empire.[67] That Courbet desired something of the publicity his rivals enjoyed would seem self-evident, and need not be corroborated by the declaration of "moi" (an identification of ego and superego in himself) he made in *The Meeting* and other works.[68] It would seem justified to say that despite his quarrel with Nieuwerkerke, Courbet saw the World Fair as a great opportunity to present himself as an innovator at long last, and alongside Delacroix and Ingres. Courbet as the prime attraction of an exhibition of world art—this expectation may have been objectively exaggerated, but subjectively it was by no means improbable. And the prospect of mounting a rival show *within the exhibition area* would have made his expectation seem all the more realistic.

The Artist and the Emperor

At any rate, the material and ideological conditions represented by the World Fair project were constitutive for the genesis of *The Painter's Studio*, for it is only by reference to this project that the interweaving of autobiographical and universal levels of meaning in the image can be explained. These can be described in terms of four hypotheses (in which issues treated elsewhere, such as the typology of *The Painter's Studio* or the development of artistic self-consciousness,[69] are touched upon only when relevant to the case).

First: Courbet has depicted himself receiving the emperor in his studio, thus according himself an imaginary honor that, unlike Ingres, he had not received in reality. What is more, his invitation to Napoleon has gone out in the midst of an imperial, universal exhibition. As in *The Meeting* (fig. 30), where he relegated his patron to the role of dependent and placed himself firmly in the center of the picture as the true master, in *The Painter's Studio* Courbet made himself the fulcrum around which everything revolves. Although he accorded the emperor a prominent position, it is no better than that of his mentor, Champfleury, who enjoys the same rank in the picture (and an even higher one in the caricatures). And like the gravedigger in *A Burial at Ornans,* with whom Courbet would later identify, in *The Painter's Studio* he figures as judge and ruler in one, a primus inter pares.

Courbet took up the tradition of the studio picture, but turned it on its head. As Huyghe, Bazin, Adhémar, and others have shown,[70] ideas of both a private and public nature were associated with artists' depictions of their own studios. They revealed insights into their craft, justifying themselves to friends, critics, and connoisseurs and thus placing themselves in hierarchical relationship to the outside world. This often involved conflicting claims, particularly in the case of rulers' visits to artists, which were the counterpart of the presentation of artists' plans (drawings, models, and so on) to the court. In the early seventeenth century, descriptions of Michelangelo's relationship to the popes and princes of his era raised the issue of prestige and standing in the eyes of the world.[71] Under absolutism, breaches of protocol indicated that this wrangling for precedence still continued under the surface,[72] and after emerging into the light of day in the cult of genius fostered by the Enlightenment,[73] it issued in postrevolutionary France, as in the Dürer cult in Germany,[74] in a new paraphrase of the *personalities* of the Old Masters. Paintings like *Leonardo Dying in the Arms of Francis I,*[75] *The Pope Paying His Last Respects to the Dead Raphael,*[76] *The Pope's Visit to Raphael's Studio,*[77] or *Emperor Maximilian Visiting Dürer at Work,*[78] emphasize the honorable social position of the artist with respect to men of power—though it is always the latter who pay their respect to the former, the rulers' authority remains unquestioned. That such imagery was not merely intended to glorify a long-past state of affairs but to point out the dependence of *contemporary* artists on patrons, their precarious social position, and their rivalries among one another and with those in power, has been discussed in detail by Haskell (see note 74). How crucial the theme of the ruler's visit to the artist was, is shown by "the fact that even the life of Benvenuto Cellini, which offered such unrivalled opportunities for a 'romantic' interpretation of the artistic temperament, interested nineteenth-century artists almost exclusively because he was visited by François I."[79] Though it was inconsistent with the widespread demand for artistic independence, even Vandyke and other seventeenth-century artists were viewed in light of their dependence on the court.

Courbet reversed this tradition, while maintaining that of meetings between artists and rulers in the studio which were a common subject of nineteenth-century painting. Not even the idea of transposing this *historical* theme into *personal* terms, that is, of claiming equality with the Old Masters, was unusual or unprecedented. Victor Hugo, who styled himself a "lonesome cliff" on Guernsey, was impelled by rivalry with Napoleon: "The important fact was that Napoleon had been a giant. In the 1830s, Hugo decided that he, too, would be such a giant."[80] And Emile Barrault wrote in his famous manifesto "Aux artistes" that only artists were capable of running society.[81] Courbet himself disarmingly stated in 1870, a few weeks before Napoleon's downfall, "I am the foremost man in France."[82] With the comprehensive review of tradition represented by *The Painter's Studio*, however, Courbet disengaged the issue of rank from the personal level and introduced it into a new frame of reference.

This brings us to a second aspect of the painting: Just as the emperor gathered around him "producers from all countries" (First Decree) at the World Fair, Courbet brought the world into his studio for the same occasion. "The world comes to my door to be painted," he wrote to Champfleury[83] after having expressed himself to Bruyas in such universal terms as "Even if I must search the world over, I am sure to find men who will understand me."[84] And while Champfleury spoke of Napoleon III as the "sauveur de la société" (society's savior),[85] Baudelaire, as early as 1855, spoke of Courbet as "sauvant le monde" (saving the world).[86]

Now, although these sources emphasize the idea of universal redemption and the extent of Courbet's claim in this regard, they still do not suffice to explain his universal gathering in *The Painter's Studio*. No meaningful explanation can ignore the context of the exposition itself. Courbet's intention in surrounding himself with Bonapartists and socialists, Frenchmen and foreigners, was not to provide further legitimation for the empire (as Nieuwerkerke wished to do), but to symbolically demonstrate the possibility of the peaceful coexistence of diverse opinions and stances. To fully appreciate the ticklish nature of this idea, we must recall the state of war in which France was involved at the time. On June 2, 1853, the French fleet had been dispatched to the Dardanelles; on March 27, 1854, Napoleon III declared war on Russia and on June 26 Greece was occupied by British and French troops; that fall, the battles of Alma and Inkerman took place and the first public war loans were issued. Seen in this context of foreign policy, Courbet's *Studio* amounted to an appeal for peace. In terms of domestic policy, too, his combination of such heterogeneous figures and stances can hardly be interpreted otherwise than as an appeal to reconciliation (though this idea is not fully developed in the picture). Rather, the image represents an *adhortatio ad principem*, an exhortation to the ruler of a kind common in treatises on statecraft down into the nineteenth century.

Courbet's exhortation, however, far transcends this tradition in terms of concreteness. It includes a lament, a warning, and a symbol of hope. A silent lament is embodied by the mother in rags at the emperor's feet, who poignantly illustrates that his promise to abolish poverty—Louis-Napoléon had published a book titled *L'extinction du paupérisme* in 1844—had by no means been fulfilled.[87] On the floor lies an omen of warning, a dagger pointed toward the emperor, but still in its sheath; if he responds to the appeal for peace, there will be no need to draw it. The same is true of the revolutionaries in the background, the *chasseur* and *faucheur,* who wait passively to see what direction the emperor's policy will take. Hope, finally, is embodied in nature—about which more below.

If this hypothesis is sound, Courbet has inverted the age-old theme of a meeting between ruler and artist in two ways. First, instead of understanding the ruler's visit as an honor and confirmation of his work, the painter uses it to present himself as an intermediary and his art as an instrument to solve and cure[88] temporal problems; second, Courbet has bridged the dichotomy between mind and power by expanding the meeting to a universal gathering whose actors are encouraged not so much to appreciate his art as to serve the more comprehensive end of human understanding and peaceful coexistence. The depiction of fictitious universal assemblies was not unusual around the mid-nineteenth century. Apart from Ingres' *Apotheosis of Homer,* which Hourticq already compared to *The Painter's Studio,*[89] Chenavard's conception for murals in the Pantheon may well have had a seminal influence on Courbet. He had met with Chenavard several times during these years, and in 1855 Chenavard had developed, in his cartoon for *The Philosophy of History,* a universal scheme of redemption whose connection with the World Fair has been pointed out by Werner Hofmann.[90] What is new about Courbet's conception, however, is a concise reference to daily life, to the domestic and foreign policy of the government, which was designed to appeal as much to the people as to their rulers. The early insight of 1851, "with M. Courbet, art has become one with the people,"[91] found new confirmation in *The Painter's Studio.*

In this regard, Courbet's conception has much in common with Victor Hugo's poem "L'art et le peuple," a call for international reconciliation through art which was published despite a censors' ban in 1851:

> L'art, c'est la gloire et la joie . . .
> L'art, splendeur universelle,
> Au front du peuple étincelle. . . .
>
> L'art est un champ magnifique
> Qui plaît au coeur pacifique. . . .
>
> L'art, c'est la pensée humaine
> Qui va brisant toute chaîne!
> L'art c'est le doux conquérant! . . .
>
> Bon peuple, chante à l'aurore! . . .
>
> Chante la sainte Italie,
> La Pologne ensevelie,
> Naples qu'un sang pur rougit,
> La Hongrie agonisante . . .
> O tyrans! le peuple chante
> Comme le lion rugit![92]
>
> (Art is glory and joy . . .
> Art, universal splendor,
> Sparkles on the brows of the people. . . .
>
> Art is a magnificent field
> Pleasing to the peaceful heart. . . .

Art is the thought of mankind
Which can break any chain!
Art is the sweet conqueror! . . .

Good people, sing at dawn! . . .

Sing of sainted Italy
Of shrouded Poland,
Of Naples reddened with pure blood,
Of Hungary in agony. . . .
Oh tyrants! the people sing
Even as the lion roars!)

Here too we find the combination of a peace appeal and enumeration of suffering nations—like Courbet, Hugo refers to Italy, Poland, and Hungary—with an invocation to tyrants; here too, *art* as an element of resistance and a factor in international understanding is clearly contrasted to the *politics* which have failed to bring about peace.

Third: Courbet directed his two-edged petition to the emperor at the very moment when industrial mechanization had triumphed in France and the Bonapartist regime was preparing to celebrate itself as a modern, progressive system. Precisely at that point in time and on that occasion when the industrial capacity of the country was to be demonstrated, Courbet held up to the public—to the audience of the official exposition (for which the picture originally was done)—a vision of *nature*, a landscape representing a view of the Loue Valley in Franche-Comté, the painter's native region. Its river, cliffs, trees with autumn foliage, its thatched-roof mill and a ruin silhouetted against a bright sky present the aspect of an unsullied and seemingly almost inaccessible stretch of wild countryside. That Courbet intended the landscape as a reference to nature in its virginal or primordial state, and that this, in connection with the peasant boy, a symbol of unsophisticated naturalness, was an allusion to the fruitful soil of social regeneration, has long been recognized and corroborated by many sources.[93] Within the closed interior space of Courbet's Paris studio, the landscape inset into the composition like a composite icon takes on fundamental significance. Its meaning is augmented by other traits recalling religious painting—the artist receiving inspiration, like the Evangelist from an angel, from his "Muse" (who is really only looking admiringly over his shoulder)[94], or, surrounded like Christ by the ailing, setting out to heal the ills of his time (perhaps influenced by Rembrandt's *Hundred Guilder* etching, which was reprinted by Dumesnil in 1850 with a new, social-critical interpretation).[95] But Courbet's "cure" involves neither the proclamation of eternal religious truths—as a French critic demanded in 1853, with an eye to the work of Overbeck[96]—nor an acceptance of the urban *vie moderne* in Baudelaire's sense, but rests solely on a direct reference to unsullied, primordial nature. This Rousseauian thought, both retrogressive and progressive, had remained vital in Franche-Comté and informed Courbet's view of nature throughout his life.

His origin in the Jura Mountains of this region bordering on Switzerland was the emotional point of departure for Courbet's critique of modern civilization. Claiming the liberty of the *montagnard,* with the mountains like fortresses[97] behind him, he turned as a regionalist against centralist government, as a man from the country against hyper-sophisticated city mores, and as a follower of Proudhon against the urbanization of modern industrial society. In this stance we find an explanation for the central group and the landscape painting in *The Painter's Studio,* which represent the counterproposal that Courbet dared to make to the emperor: that instead of encouraging the dubious progress of industry he should recall the forces of renewal inherent in nature. This idea could serve all the better as a ferment for a utopia of reconciliation in that it combined so many otherwise antagonistic positions. Veuillot, for instance, was no less violently opposed to the "horrors of industry" from a conservative, Catholic point of view than Proudhon was from a socialistic one.[98]

My fourth point is that the content of *The Painter's Studio* is rounded off by a statement on the social role of art. Courbet's entire philosophy revolved around a liberated painting based on the truth inherent in nature.[99] In his eyes, this kind of art alone was capable of reuniting an atomized society—yet in *the future,* for he believed that in his times realist art was accessible only to the "day side" of society, the open-minded, liberal bourgeoisie and his socialist friends, while its significance remained hidden to the "night side," the only representative of which to have a view of the landscape is Napoleon.[100] In terms of the intensity with which he addressed the outside world, Courbet held a position midway between the solipsism of a Flaubert, who believed art could emerge only from an individual's heroic struggle with him-self,[101] and Castagnary's hope that for the coming generation art would play the role of a "social agent"[102] and thus lead to a renewal of society.

The principal force behind this renewal, Proudhon declared in 1853, would be *work,* by which he meant, based on the Fourieristic concept of "travail attrayant," a type of work that would permit human beings to become "more beautiful and free" than they could be under present conditions.[103] This utopia took on precise form in *The Painter's Studio,* for while the visitors on the right are still watching and waiting, and those on the left plot and haggle, the artist himself works, an active, liberated man.

The artist as the center of the world, art as an instrument to save society—this high claim for the *métier* is really only the logical continuation of the romantic notion of the artist as godlike in his genius, and it is tempered only by the "realism" with which Courbet alludes to the isolation of the freelance artist, which is the price he pays for his high moral standing.

The idea of a *reconciliation of society through art* is also one that can be traced back to the early nineteenth century.[104] The two leitmotifs that Courbet redefines by raising them to a universal, historical level and alluding to the truth of nature—the meeting of artist with ruler and the notion of reconciliation through art—are found particularly in the work of artists whose aims were quite opposed to those of realism. A few examples may make the difference clear. In Ingres' *Apotheosis of Homer* the poet, despite his exaltation above the present and posterity, still remains the focus of a *world of art and artists* which, exempt from the present, pays its reverence to genius. In this type of gathering, which Delaroche took up in his decoration of the Ecole des Beaux-Arts (1841), it is true that the "artist himself"—as in Courbet's painting—"takes the place of the allegorical figure of art"[105] But Courbet has relinquished the temporal and spatial aura of the "devotional image" as well as its inherent hierarchy by depicting a number of authorities all of whom have equal compositional rank. By so doing he overcame the "authoritarian" formal harmony of which Ingres' picture is a typical example. Where emperor and entourage, painter and model, critics and friends all possess equal dignity and importance, the only type of formal harmony possible is an "equalization of interests," that is, a nonhierarchical visual harmony. Courbet achieved this by tying the figures into the huge zones of shadow and the expanses of wall in the background, which occupy a space almost equal to that occupied by the human protagonists, and by distributing light and shadow equally across all three sections of the image.

This attempt to create a "balance of forces" differs from related attempts to represent the idea of human equality in art as a compensation for inequality in the real world[106]—a pessimistic approach that, at least in Germany, often led to the idea of a pacification from above.[107] In Courbet's *Studio*, by contrast, art is seen as a means to reconciliation that relies not on official authority but on the naturally given common interests shared by all human beings, undeveloped as these may be.[108]

Courbet's reference to natural equality, which represented the end of a development and a new beginning, also revealed the outlines of a new aesthetic. When an artist like Courbet, up to then a bohemian and outsider, suddenly and programmatically made himself the center of attention of a painting intended for a universal exhibition, it was like the return of the prodigal son. With this gesture, an art dedicated to freedom and based on a natural primitivism raised the historical claim of taking effect *within* the given social order, of playing as central a role as philosophy and religion, politics and poetry. In this regard artistic truth indeed claimed not merely equality but superiority, for while the truths of philosophy might mean something only to their adherents, the natural truths conveyed by an art that mirrored nature could figure as universal and universally intelligible. An art that was open, no longer dependent on previous knowledge, and accessible to all was therefore the prerequisite for the claim that art could occupy the *center* of society and its processes.

Admittedly, Courbet's "déguisement" was predicated on the existence of *cognoscenti*, and, assuming that the interpretation of *The Painter's Studio* as a Freemason's lodge should prove correct,[109] it would present a visual language no less hermetic than that of the Renaissance. But with this decisive difference: Courbet's "sens caché" (hidden meaning) can be cognitively separated from the immediately intelligible, visual message of the picture. Its cross-section of society and its slice of the natural scene are understandable even to those who have no insight into the deeper semantic levels of the picture.[110]

With regard to this sloughing off of traditional devices, too, Courbet's *Studio* represents an end and a new beginning in one. In this it resembled the World Fair itself. "In retrospect," wrote the critic Loudun in 1855, "this great exhibition of mid-century marks, as it were, a historical caesura between two societies—one that is coming to an end and one that is beginning."[111] The new beginning, we now realize, has been delayed; the caesura continues.

4

Equality and Authority in Courbet's Landscape Painting

Landscape—A Neutral Genre?

COURBET'S landscapes have received little attention in the literature, and most commentators consider them secondary to his work in other genres.[1] Even Clark, in his pioneering study, declares Courbet to have been a failure as a landscape painter,[2] a judgment diametrically opposed to that of the nineteenth-century critics of the Salons.[3] Granted that their praise was often a defensive ploy, intended to divert the force of Courbet's explicitly social-critical figure paintings, it is not enough simply to turn the tables, no matter how good one's political reasons; for this would merely be to confirm, and perhaps even sharpen, the distinction made at the time between the political intentions of France's bourgeois opposition and the forms these took in art. Courbet can no longer be considered a "mere eye" and political ignoramus,[4] nor can he figure exclusively as an anticapitalist worker-artist whose life work was ostensibly crowned by the Paris Commune.[5]

These two accepted, conflicting views might be assimilated to each other by adopting an approach broad enough to overcome the superficial division between the "political" and "unpolitical" aspects of his oeuvre. The hypothesis that no "themes of social relevance" are treated in Courbet's landscapes is particularly untenable.[6] A strong case can be made for the proposition that it is precisely here, in these supposedly unpolitical landscapes, that the social changes and conflicts of the day are manifested.[7] This interpretation would facilitate a new evaluation of Courbet's oeuvre and also permit an adequate definition of programmatic realism—as a historical phenomenon that can be defined in aesthetic terms only if and when the historical substratum of these terms is considered as well.[8] As Edmond Duranty realized as early as 1856, "Giving an *aesthetic* definition of realism would be a waste of time; opening a lock to a flood of discussion on its wording."[9] Thus any reconstruction of historical processes between 1848 and 1871 that is meant to shed light on Courbet's oeuvre must pay greater attention than hitherto to the fundamental problems that emerged during this period, and trace the way they were reflected and refracted in Courbet's art. One such problem during the third quarter of the nineteenth century, France's first period of economic expansion and speculation, was certainly the confrontation between capital and labor.[10] This was reflected, in the visual arts, not only on the level of *motifs* (such as depictions of industrial plants and workers) but on the level of *intentions*—the commitment of artists to social progress or their need to escape social compulsion; and their awareness of being involved in a struggle for dominance marked by a growing competition among the social classes and a growing antagonism between city and country.[11]

The more anarchic production came into conflict with hierarchic industrial organization,[12] the more the gap between equality and authority was felt. It was not by chance that after 1848 the promise of the French Revolution that stood most in need of fulfillment was that of equality. While fraternity was prevented from resulting in general social solidarity[13] by the continued "morcellement de la société française,"[14] liberty, since the 1830 revolution, had been corrupted by Guizot's propagation of freedom as the opportunity for unlimited personal enrichment, and was generally recognized to be an insufficient basis for an equitable social order.[15] In art, the original idea of liberty remained effective only as an undercurrent up to the Commune.[16] Not so equality—defined as equal rights for all citizens, fair consideration for every intellectually serious position in scholarship and science, and a balance of economic interests.[17] Equality was the quintessence of republican demands before and after the coup d'état of Napoleon III,[18] not only in Paris but in the provinces: "Here too [that is, in the Vendée and Bretagne] as throughout France, the people are imbued with the *principle of equality*," declared the author of a report to the emperor.[19]

In art, the Le Nain brothers and the Dutch seventeenth-century painters were thought not only to possess stylistic quality but to stand for equality and democracy.[20] The socialist critic Thoré's hope that Delacroix would paint *Equality on the Barricades of February*[21] as a companion piece to his *Liberty* of 1830 was symptomatic; four years later, in 1852, Thoré stated that the prime goal of insurrectionary movements in the nineteenth century, after they had abolished proletarian misery, was to establish equality.[22]

The failure of this ideal cannot be blamed solely on high finance and Bonapartist rule, for it was abetted by the schematic nature of the equality theories themselves. Wholesale and abstract leveling, as Maxime Du Camp remarked *post festum*, might well create "un besoin farouche d'autorité" (a fierce need for authority) in politics and art, and above all make people long for the great man, the absolute ruler, the divine artist.[23] This nostalgia indeed affected not only the lower classes but the intellectual opponents of the bourgeoisie, who, by pitting authority against authority and claiming to be a "shadow government" of nonaligned individuals,[24] partook of the behavioral antinomies of their opponents. Auguste Comte, who expressly understood his work as the completion of the French Revolution,[25] spoke out against all "futile equalizers" and yearned for "powerful leaders."[26] Proudhon, as if to compensate for the unrealizability of his political demands, developed a patriarchal conception of authority,[27] and Champfleury, the theorist of programmatic realism, after 1852 propounded an ambiguously hierarchical theory of art that ideologically reinforced the Napoleonic appeasement policy toward the rural populace.[28] Artists and writers like Meryon and Dupont, originally republicans, humbled themselves before the usurper;[29] Daumier and Millet faced the tension between equality and authority in their art, but under the Second Empire, they resolved it only at the cost of a weakening in critical thrust.[30]

In my view, two major periods must be distinguished in Courbet's work.[31] The first, from about 1845 to 1857, which has almost always been investigated in context until now, is characterized by the predominance of figure paintings. In these Courbet identified with the demands, current since 1848, for equality for the less privileged classes, from whom the bourgeois intelligentsia hoped for a regeneration of society at large.[32] Courbet's work was both understood and fought as furthering democracy in art and, more generally, as being a concrete realization of the abstract ideal of equality.[33] It was thought to contribute substantially to republican agitation, although its effectiveness in this regard was overestimated.

During the second period I discern, from about 1857 to 1871, Courbet increasingly construed equality to mean equal rights for the individual and social regeneration through an involvement with nature that had nothing of control or mastery about it (that is, that was anarchistic in the original sense of the term). This second period is marked above all by landscape paintings, in which nature came to stand in for the artist's earlier demands for equality, a shift that increasingly determined the technique and the form of his work. In this less spectacular field, Courbet's criticism of society proved even more profound and lasting than in his figure paintings; this is why, as remains to be shown, his contemporaries judged both by the same criteria. This shift in the problem called for a choice of different means—this, and not solely historical factors, is the reason for my two periods. But now let us turn to a number of paintings from the first period by way of comparison.

Toward an Egalitarian Art

At the end of his career, Courbet decidedly rejected one of his major early works. On February 9, 1873, he wrote to his friend, the republican art critic Castagnary: "L'enterrement ne vaut rien" (The burial's not worth a thing).[34] He was referring to *A Burial at Ornans* (fig. 29), the picture that had provoked his first scandal and that he described, a short time later, as "mon début et mon exposé de principes (my debut and the exposition of my principles).[35] It was an attempt to express everything at one fell swoop: his identification with his social origins and detachment from

29 Gustave Courbet, *A Burial at Ornans*. Oil on canvas, 315 × 668 cm, 1849–50. Paris, Musée d'Orsay.

them, his high regard for the provinces and for the rural middle-class populace, whose equality with the Parisian bourgeoisie he symbolized by the two Jacobins of 1793. But at the same time, the painting was intended as a moral critique of the valorized classes, combined with an attack on the clerics and on traditional funeral ritual.[36]

The critics censured the ugliness of the figures and the "wooden" and artless way in which they were lined up—the very feature in which Courbet's supporters discovered the principle of equality, and a plea for the abolition of barriers between classes. If the figures were ugly, they said, that was the fault of the bourgeoisie and not of the artist. Yet it is obvious that the figures of the Jacobins work only in terms of content, for they are not formally integrated in the group, while the gravedigger, with whom Courbet later identified,[37] occupies its central position. "He alone throws his chest out with pride; he alone commands," observed Buchon.[38]

This betrays a problem that makes the representation of equality through human figures difficult, if not ultimately impossible: whenever one figure is raised to the status of main protagonist, the notion of equality is automatically forfeited. Nor is this inherent contradiction between equality and authority in the picture resolved by the merging of the largest part of the mourners into a "black mass."[39] That this represents "compositional egalitarianism" is an opinion that I cannot entirely share.[40] The gap between intention and evidence is too great—equality may have been advanced in this passage, but it has not been established. By picturing the conflict in this manner, Courbet took into account the actual circumstance that in the opinion of the day, the rural populace, despite its internal divisions, not only equaled the Parisian bourgeoisie but was superior to it. This being the case, a painting like A Burial seemed not so much egalitarian as threateningly insurrectionist.[41]

The letter of 1873 cited above was written not at an arbitrary juncture but on the occasion of the Vienna World Fair, to which Courbet planned to send works; all the more reason to ask why he should have rejected the painting that caused fear and trembling among conservative critics and enthusiasm among republicans. Accommodation or resignation can hardly have been the reason, for, as the sources indicate, Courbet's work at this period had received new impetus,[42] and his artistic outlook and approach had changed. That his rejection cannot have been brought on by a few critics is sufficiently indicated by the works and documents themselves.

In The Stonebreakers of 1849,[43] as in The Bathers and The Wrestlers of 1853 (figs. 8 and 7), for all the egalitarian distribution of emphasis among everything in the picture, the main figures have the character of anti-academic monuments—formally substantial and isolated from their surroundings.[44] It is this feature, together with their claim to be treated as history paintings, that gives these canvases a traditional aspect despite their transgressions of the academic canon of beauty, and despite the fact that they have no plot and communicate no message in the traditional sense.[45] In the case of The Bathers and The Wrestlers, two characteristic features may be noted: first, a sharp opposition between human figure and natural surroundings that extends even to the paint handling; and second, an unresolved tension in the central figures between activity and suspended animation. Even though Courbet's emphatic accentuation of the main figure may have stimulated, even provoked, observers like Delacroix, it was achieved at the cost of isolating the figure and depicting it in a perspective that is incongruent with the perspective rules governing the whole. Classical perspective is used here as a code of recognition, and thus acknowledged; yet at the same time Courbet continually infringes upon the code, without being able to offer a substitute perspective.[46]

Nadar understood the crux of this anti-authoritarian approach, warning Courbet in 1853 that "coarseness is not strength . . . nor scandal the same thing as renown."[47] Since to his way of thinking the "maître d'Ornans" behaved a bit too much like a sideshow barker, Nadar caricatured The Wrestlers as a sideshow poster.[48] Perhaps he realized that this was precisely Courbet's intention—to use the Salon to exercise influence beyond it, in the public domain. Nadar's words, however, imply that a committed, anti-authoritarian art which, by raising the status of "low" subjects, aimed at democratizing art and advancing Republican sentiment, might well bypass the very strata that counted around 1850, the middle- and upper-class opposition. The first works of Courbet that were inspired by the events of 1848 and the egalitarianism of 1789 were in fact highly idealist, in that they were based on the view that art could and should accomplish what history had been unable to: the reconciliation of the classes and the realization of democracy.[49] Yet could these paintings satisfy their own express aim—to reveal reality in a new light and overcome bourgeois strictures, institutions, behavioral norms—while in effect offering social positions no less rigid? This contradiction still informed the earlier paintings of the second period. It was not until Courbet turned to new subject matter—a turn often too glibly described as a retreat—that a pictorial form emerged in which he could express his longing for equality in universal terms.

The unresolved problem of dominance versus subordination came to light clearly at the end of the first period, in The Meeting, or "Bonjour Monsieur Courbet" of 1854 (fig. 30).[50] The carefully balanced composition can hardly hide the fact that here, the traditional patron-artist relationship has been not merely equalized but reversed. Yet since Courbet thought of himself as the protagonist and the itinerant prophet of modern painting, even as its redeemer,[51] he does not simply demand subordination (though one is tempted to take his "I disdain patrons"[52] to be the painting's tacit message). He also advocates support for "peinture libre," which both he and the Bonapartist Bruyas considered a cure for social ills.[53] What struck the contemporary public as insolent self-aggrandizement actually resulted from the sharp competition among the artists supported by Bruyas, indeed among Parisian artists in general, only a fraction of whose paintings submitted to the coming World Fair would be accepted. Courbet, like other migrant workers of all classes who flocked to Paris, was an alien in the city, but depended on it to sell his wares, which in turn alienated him from the country.[54] Due to unsureness about his social position, which after his break with Bruyas contributed to his political calamity, Courbet was continually over- or under-estimating his relationship to other individuals and groups.[55] Nor could his repeated insistence on the social role of the artist apparently suffice to give him an identity,

30 Gustave Courbet, *The Meeting* or *"Bonjour Monsieur Courbet."* Oil on canvas, 129 × 149 cm, 1854. Montpellier, Musée Fabre (Photo Giraudon).

though his emphasis on insecurity was a significant step in overcoming the romantic aporia of an artist's position in society ("his giant's wings prevent him from walking")[56] and placing it in a more realistic light. What Courbet evidently says in *The Meeting* is that the path to equality, in a competitive society, must begin with individuals who make exaggerated claims to personal authority. Shroder has made a similar point with regard to Hugo and Flaubert; the topos of the "titan" deserves to be investigated in this context.[57]

Between City and Country

The question of the artist's position in society immediately raises that of the hierarchy among the various strata of the Parisian and provincial bourgeoisie, as well as that of the relationship between city and country as a key problem of mid-nineteenth century art. This is particularly visible in *The Painter's Studio* (fig. 28), which in many respects introduced the transition from Courbet's first to second period. It is a group portrait, but without group cohesion; the figures occupy a common stage, but, as Delacroix remarked,[58] it is split open by the naturalistic sky in the center. It is an interior, but also a landscape. *The Painter's Studio* advances in the direction of equality by arranging the various social orders paratactically, a choice of people and arrangement which strengthens both the artist's identification with his environment and his separation from it. Often caricatured as a savior,[59] Courbet communes with nature while turning his back on society, isolating himself. Nor is there much communication among the others in the picture.[60] This reflects the new phenomenon of an atomization of society, which Thoré noted when he said that "in France today there are but isolated individuals and an all-powerful government."[61] And Courbet's authoritative attitude in *The Painter's Studio* would merely seem to be the other side of his complaint that he stood alone against society.

Those gathered around the artist share in his activity only to the extent that they share his absorption in nature, which they see before them, rendered "true to life". Nature, instead of the "gens qui me servent" (people who serve me),[62] has now become Courbet's true subject. This lends an entirely new aspect to the conflict between equality and authority, as well as to the artist's relationship to the outside world. *The Painter's Studio* may represent a conclusion, but it certainly also marks a new beginning. Yet none of the five monographs on the painting treat its central motif, the landscape, in any detail.[63] This despite the fact that the unity of nature and society, depicted in a *single* image, is the key to Courbet's conception.

The landscape represented is in Franche-Comté, the Loue Valley near Ornans.[64] We see an almost totally inaccessible wooded area, with a high cliff looming up on the right. A footbridge leads over the rapids in the foreground; this, a small cabin, and a ruin in the valley are the only signs of civilization, and nature has begun to reclaim even these. All the man-made objects, moreover, are assimilated in color to the environment (the bluish greens and browns of water, forest, and earth). Courbet had originally depicted the story of the miller, the miller's son, and the ass, but he deleted the figures later, divesting the landscape of all genre and anecdotal traits and making it appear grave, even gloomy—nature in its primeval state. One symbol of nature's reclaiming force is the ruin on which the tip of Courbet's brush rests as if demonstratively. That this message was intended may be inferred from the fact that the gesture cannot be explained by the process of painting.[65]

The meaning of the primitiveness of Courbet's image of nature and its function in *The Painter's Studio* becomes clearer when we consider what unspoiled nature signified during the Second Empire. Dissatisfaction with the big city was growing, and many artists turned with abhorrence from the "decadence" of Paris to the unsullied natural countryside.[66] This attitude was typical of the political opposition in particular, because *their* Paris was the old, revolutionary city which was threatened by demolition to make way for pompous Bonapartist edifices. Nor was the Loue Valley just any natural locale, for the Franche-Comté region as a whole was considered the antipode to Paris, an alternative realm of freedom.[67] Courbet's friend Buchon extolled the Loue in his poems as a genuine, untamed, and above all *free* river, whose banks, unlike those of the Seine, were unwalled.[68] Buchon and others even went so far as to speculate that the last refuge of the ancient Gauls lay in Franche-Comté.[69] If the Loue Valley embodied the true, unsullied Gallia, then ruined castles signified the former independence of the French provinces.[70] Courbet frequently drew castle ruins in his sketchbooks, and also included them in his paintings in such a way that they evoked the integrity and self-sufficiency of precentralistic France.[71] Even Courbet's *Château d'Ornans,* done some years before *The Painter's Studio,* has with good reason been interpreted as a plea for independence.

Now, if *The Painter's Studio* can be supposed to suggest liberty—through primal nature and man-made objects with which this meaning was associated by social consensus—then obviously it cannot have been merely an expression of the artist's own personal independence and love of nature.[72] He sits, as is so often remarked, not so much in front of as *in* the landscape, as if to approach as close as possible to his evocation of nature, for it is to nature that he owes his prominent and dominant position. But nature, though represented as the highest authority here, cannot mediate between the urban and rural people who have come together in *The Painter's Studio.* We as spectators might consider the image of primal nature to be the only medium that can unify and regenerate the isolated visitors, who are trapped in their individual thoughts and actions; but this "mirror of truth" held up to them apparently goes unperceived. Courbet broaches the subject of how society should confront nature, but, like Proudhon,[73] only to give it the form of a contradiction left unresolved. Not until the pure landscape of the second period would he supply an answer.

Transition to Nature—The Crisis of 1857

Yet before doing so Courbet had to pass through a crisis that deeply affected the compositional structure of his figure paintings between 1857 and 1863. A comparable upheaval occurred in the work of other artists and writers at this time, and it corresponded with turning points in economics and politics. A brief review of the historical background may help us to understand Courbet's position.

The world economic crisis emanating from England in 1857 caused great social unrest in France.[74] For the first time, members of the opposition were elected into Parliament that year, and the clergy began to lose ground. "In many ways, therefore, the year 1857 ought to be regarded as a prominent landmark in the history of the Second Empire."[75] The words of Napoleon III upon the opening of the National Assembly, "that all over Europe signs of insecurity and dissolution have appeared, and the old state edifice is disintegrating piece by piece,"[76] show the degree of ideological insecurity that had already been reached. The government agreed to modest, conciliatory reforms, which were really attempts to take the wind out of the opposition's sails.[77] This objective was made easier by French successes in foreign policy and trade. A trade agreement was concluded with England in 1860 which, after initial setbacks, facilitated the development of heavy industry. The conquest of Savoy and Nice strengthened the conservative forces' sense of national self-confidence, and despite internal convulsions in France, Napoleon III outwardly reached "the zenith of his success." By 1861 he was beloved by the masses as never before, although he had brought no real liberalization about.[78] He figured as the great conciliator who had even managed to drive the "irréconciliables" from the National Assembly and establish a grand coalition, while claiming egalitarianism for his own principle.[79] Actually, he had no choice but to compromise and form a coalition. His ostensible policy of liberalization both strengthened and fragmented the Republican opposition;[80] as the contradictions increased, so did the attempts at reconciliation.

In literature and art the productive unrest of 1857 (the year in which Baudelaire's *Fleurs du mal* and Flaubert's *Madame Bovary* appeared, and Courbet's *Young Ladies at the Banks of the Seine* and Millet's *Gleaners* hung in the Salon) was followed in 1859 by perceptible insecurity on the part of the state, as evidenced by a sudden falling-off of its art purchases.[81] In 1861, attempts at integration and appeasement took hold, and by 1863 Maxime Du Camp could diagnose a "repos absolu" or pervading dullness in the Salon,[82] which, along with artists' vehement protests against the limitation of the number of exhibitors, apparently induced Napoleon to concede a Salon des Refusés.[83] Here, too, the opposition grew, but here, too, it was to some extent lulled by prospects of social integration.

This period also saw the theory of realism enter a new phase. In 1857 Champfleury (who had to revise his judgment later) thought he could cap things by editing an anthology of realism, hoping by this gesture to distance himself from Courbet's art, which seemed to him to grow continually more contradictory.[84] Even more importantly, Champfleury saw his career as a writer jeopardized, and envied Courbet the publicity he had received.[85] Castagnary, the young Republican critic who was influenced by Champfleury and would later become the principal defender of programmatic realism, thought in 1857 that he could review Courbet's entire oeuvre, and declared, "The dust and the scandal that he had raised . . . are today well settled. Since our ideas have tended to become more liberal, . . . one hardly concerns oneself with realism,"[86] and even Courbet "may previously have believed that painting needed to have a social intent; but at the present time, he no longer believes a word of it."[87]

Subsequent commentators have accepted this judgment all too readily. Bouvier has dated the end of the "Battle of Realism" in 1857; Sloane has rehearsed the widespread view that after that date, Courbet seldom depicted controversial subjects. Nochlin and Bowness have called *The Painter's Studio* the termination of Courbet's career, even the "swan song" of realism.[88] Still, the drift of Champfleury's opinions, which not much later would earn him a decoration from Napoleon, together with the subsequent controversies over Courbet, indicate that though he had reached a turning point, he by no means had finished his work or resolved his artistic problems. Champfleury's retreat is more indicative of the explosive force of increasing demands for *égalité, indépendance,* and *vérité.*[89] If a termination point is needed, there is more justification in placing it with Théophile Gautier's *Histoire du romantisme* of 1857.[90] Programmatic realism, by contrast, was neither fully developed nor publicly accepted by 1857;[91] Courbet's own "program" had merely been intimated in *The Painter's Studio,* and it would take him the next twenty years to gradually fill it with substance. If the exhibition of 1855 was the highpoint of Courbet's first period, the second culminated with that of 1867. The young editors of the journal *Réalisme* rightly understood their title as a *challenge* in 1856–57, a promise whose fulfillment lay far in the future.[92]

Castagnary had to amend his original judgment only six years later, declaring Courbet to be "le premier des peintres socialistes" (the foremost socialist painter) and his approach to embody "les seules forces subsistantes" (the only strength remaining) in French painting.[93] The artist himself had withdrawn from the fray in 1857 and 1861, not least in order to go hunting in Germany. He apparently needed time to come to terms with social developments and integrate them in his art. This period was a transition phase for him as well.

By comparison to *The Painter's Studio,* two great changes now occurred: first, what might be termed a crisis of space, marked by an indeterminacy in the location of figures and objects within the composition; and second, the potential this crisis offered for an assimilation of defined, individualized objects to a larger continuum. At least two works can be compared and contrasted to *The Painter's Studio* in this regard. In *Dressing the Dead Girl* (1858, Northampton, Mass., Smith College), five groups are arranged in an indeterminate pictorial space such that no communication can take place among them, despite the extreme proximity of the figures.[94] In *The Hunt Breakfast* (fig. 31), painted around 1858–59, the figures' positions and gazes, gestures and attitudes, work against each other. Each figure inhabits a world of his own; the group dissolves into isolated individuals, which again seems irritating due to their forced proximity. The game and dogs to the right are self-sufficient, like a still life. The variety of colors enhances the impression of a heterogeneous medley.

Although earlier paintings also had isolated figures, they filled and firmly occupied the pictorial space. *The Hunt Breakfast* differs from such earlier works as *A Burial,* with which it shares a critique of traditional ceremony, in terms of two key

31   Gustave Courbet, *The Hunt Breakfast*. Oil on canvas, 207 × 325 cm, c. 1858–59. Cologne, Wallraf-Richartz-Museum/Museum Ludwig.

factors: first, the figures no longer appear tethered down or wooden, nor is there a competitive relationship among them as in *The Meeting*, and even in *The Painter's Studio*. Second, they are affected to a much greater extent by the environment; unlike *The Bathers* or *The Wrestlers*, nature enters between and surrounds the figures, rather than simply functioning as a backdrop. While the farmers in *The Peasants of Flagey Returning from the Fair*[95] show the same authority as do historical heroes, even against their surroundings, the hunting party is strongly individualized in both features and clothing, and relinquishes itself to nature. The composition is held together neither by a unified mass nor by a selected main figure, but is only loosely framed by the woods to the left and the rocky bluff to the right. The seated figure, earlier believed to be a self-portrait, may rather be seen as the huntmaster, possibly the landlord;[96] yet he is much less dominant than the figure of Courbet in *The Painter's Studio*. This might appear to solve the authority conflict; indeed *The Hunt Breakfast* is said to have influenced early impressionism, which was attacked as egalitarian.[97] But at the same time, Courbet's egalitarian notion of human community reached its crisis in this painting. Equality can come about only through solidarity—yet in *The Hunt Breakfast*, the disparate groups are hardly united in shared activity as in *Dressing the Dead Girl;* the prevailing mood, as commentators have recognized, is melancholy and loneliness.[98] Courbet has abandoned the earlier principle, still used in *The Painter's Studio*, of constructing a picture of figures that reinforce each other by opposition, but he has not yet replaced it by a new type of composition that would transcend objects and to which the bright local colors would also have had to be sacrificed.

Both the precarious poses of Courbet's figures and the stability they obtain from the natural environment were carried to an extreme in an 1863 satire on *The Return of the Priests*.[99] Thereafter, the large figures, incompatible with nature, began to disappear from the landscapes, or were reduced to insignificant accessories.[100] The authority they lost was projected into nature itself—only as a landscape painter could Courbet "become, for the younger artists of the sixties, the modern example of a pure painter,"[101] and only as such could he develop a form of social criticism appropriate to the Second Empire. Now, what may have prompted him to concentrate on depicting nature?

Resignation certainly played some part in this. Equality could no longer be adequately represented through explicit commitment, nor even by the detour of a genre-like celebration of rural life. Nor did a target group, an audience, for such works exist, since Napoleon had silenced the great majority of the bourgeoisie, expanded the police department into Europe's first modern bureaucracy, and quashed the revolutionary hope that had been placed in the peasantry. Thoré, who accused Courbet of slackened critical interest, said that while he himself had once spoken in Jacobin clubs on the connection between art and politics, now, in 1864, he was afraid to.[102] Thus for Courbet pure nature represented, in the first place, a "terrain neutre" where he could expect less trouble from the censors.[103] In the second place, nature offered experiences which could help him develop his art unhindered by contemporary problems, and also to find solutions which would be valid beyond the immediate present and its pressures.

This suggests the ambivalence of nature as a place of "retreat"; an imaginative flight into the great outdoors does not necessarily mean an escape from history and political change, but can actually prepare the way for it, as was the case in German romanticism. Of course, this view is predicated on a conception of nature not as being "eternally the same" but, like history, as being a complex of perennial and innovative factors.[104] A philosophy of this kind was prevalent in Courbet's circle. Victor Hugo, who wanted to sit for Courbet in 1864, conceived primal nature to be part of the historical process;[105] in his watercolor *The Wave* (1857), Hugo described the sea as "ma destinée."[106] He viewed the cliffs of Guernsey as a symbol of freedom: to him, as to the intellectual opposition in general, the archaic represented a prime guarantor of the future.[107]

On the other hand, societal exploitation and transformation of nature proceeded apace after 1860. The systematic cultivation of the woodlands began;[108] the sea came to be understood as "an immense factory of provisions, a laboratory of sustenance more productive than the Earth itself," and national sea exploitation rights were demanded.[109] All of this lent increased significance to nature during this period, both as a repository of emotional appeal and as an economic factor. As early as 1859, Champfleury ironically discussed both of these aspects in his novel *Les amis de la nature,* in which a wildlife club is simultaneously concerned to improve the forests, to use them as a political stage, and to further their true-to-life representation in art.[110] Such representation obviously figured, to Champfleury as to Buchon and Thoré, as an expression of society, and it did so in a much more precise and pointed way than, for instance, in the romanticist nature movement, where communing with the great outdoors was primarily a surrogate or compensation for artists' loss of social security.[111]

When in 1861 Thoré saw the sole salvation of painting in a "sincere return, naive and even a bit primitive . . . to *nature* of the wilder sort,"[112] it was not by chance that he justified his statement by reference to Rousseau. Like Rousseau in his early writings, Thoré and Du Camp felt that inequality had resulted from the corruption of civilization, which was now compounded by the effects of industrialization on city and country. Proudhon was perhaps the most ardent follower of Rousseau in this respect.[113] However, for Rousseau and on through the French Revolution, the return to nature had been primarily moral and symbolic. Thoré understood it in a more comprehensive way—as a real goal, not a moral fiction—while on the other hand limiting it by stating that only artists could grasp the primitive force of nature, its "pure et sauvage beauté" (pure and savage beauty).[114] In the course of this renaturalization of history, arts relating to nature were held—for the last time in the nineteenth century— to have a responsibility to society at large, "in order to protest against mannerism and civilized dissolution."[115] Growing Rousseauianism around mid-century also brought a revival of the Swiss Enlightenment tradition, particularly in Franche-Comté, which borders on Switzerland.[116] For Courbet, the intellectual concerns of the opposition movement in Paris were a continuation of those of his home region. His country squire friends—Buchon, Dupont, Trapadoux, and to some extent Hugo and Sabatier-Ungher—read early nineteenth-century southern German literature (Schiller, Uhland,

Hebel, Körner) and classic German philosophy (Hegel) from the point of view of the French Enlightenment tradition, translated these works, and cited them in defense of programmatic realism.[117]

Landscape as a Symbol of Resistance and Freedom

Meanwhile, Courbet had made practical progress toward this end. While still struggling to establish balance in his figure compositions, he succeeded in the landscape and hunt pictures in making forceful historical statements. In 1856, on a trip through Belgium, he did *The Meuse near Freyr* (fig. 32). The river begins right at

32   Gustave Courbet, *The Meuse near Freyr*. Oil on canvas, 1856. 58 × 82 cm. Lille, Musée Wicar (Photo Giraudon).

the canvas edge in the foreground, with no embankment to act as *repoussoir,* and runs diagonally through the picture, its mirror-smooth surface contrasted to almost vertical limestone cliffs behind. Both elements, the gray-brown illuminated cliffs and the blue-green shimmering water, may have reminded Courbet of his home region; such memories were indeed a constitutive factor in his landscape paintings.[118] Similarly to *The Meeting,* a low vantage point has been chosen; and the cliffs, like the figures in that painting, have the effect of towering height and invulnerability. The river course, by contrast, seems inviting and accessible, an effect partly deriving from its broad curve, which to a modern eye resembles a superhighway. The viewer is pulled right into the picture, only to be repulsed. The landscape is represented as unspoiled, free, and accessible, yet at the same time as inaccessible, repelling, rough, and harsh. This reflects Courbet's ambivalent view of nature in pure form: primitiveness as a symbol of both liberation and threat.[119] The image evokes both nature's equalizing effect (the promise of reentering a natural state) and its authoritative power (its indifference to man's existence).[120]

Also ambivalent is the aim of Courbet's approach to nature. On the one hand, as in *The Painter's Studio,* unspoiled nature was meant to represent freedom from Napoleonic oppression (this was also a motivation of the Barbizon group, whose influence on *The Meuse near Freyr* is particularly evident).[121] On the other hand, Courbet's awareness of the landscape's vulnerability[122] prompted him to record it before it was changed by progress (whether a railway was already planned for this stretch of the Meuse would be worth investigating). So, combined with a flight from industrialization marked by Courbet's frequent choice of such remote areas as motifs,[123] we are put in mind here of the increased travel made possible by the rapid expansion of transportation networks in the late 1850s.[124] In this regard Courbet, unlike the Barbizon painters or Hugo, indirectly *accepted* the technological achievements of the Second Empire.

Courbet, indeed, produced "travel landscapes," pictures of tourist spots.[125] By the same token, he was fascinated by the idea of painting murals in Paris train stations, depicting the destinations of excursion trips.[126] This idea was part of the plan for general art education which was propagated during the meetings of the "démocratie pacifique" (pacifist democracy) during the 1848 revolution.[127] Courbet picked up the idea and passed it on to Hittorf and Sainte-Beuve, who publicized it.[128] While Champfleury saw the decoration of train terminals affirmatively, "à mettre l'art au service de l'industrie" (putting art at the service of industry),[129] Thoré developed the notion further with anti-Bonapartist intent, proposing that instead of being strongholds of church or state, the terminals should be meeting places for the people, decorated with appropriate sculptures.[130] Baudry had similar thoughts. In *Le camp des bourgeois,* which Courbet illustrated, he conceived the project as an expansion of the didactic possibilities of art education.[131] Baudry's lucid, popular style, designed to win a broad readership, should not delude us into thinking him shallow, for he had such fundamental insights as that art, and especially landscape painting, could be a historical force toward liberating and educating the entire populace. It is indicative that he used the phrase "*l'histoire* de nos départements" when discussing the depiction of contemporary *landscapes*. He declared landscape painting to belong as much to history painting as previous depictions of the rural populace (fig. 29), and believed in its efficacy as a tool of agitation.

Courbet's project was never realized. Only its completion could have shown whether it was possible "to inaugurate a monumental style of painting that would be in keeping with the new society,"[132]—a demand that I think should be seen as a reply to the decoration of the Paris Pantheon with old-fashioned, idealized murals. Courbet's position can only be inferred from the paintings he did at the time. In their bleakness, these indeed represent a *terrain neutre*, insofar as the scenes depicted were still open to utilization, still awaiting penetration by society and hence still removed "anarchically" from power or control.[133] Recalling Kleist's criticism of Friedrich, the reproach leveled at Courbet, "You have stripped your painting,"[134] applies in a deeper sense to the evident bleakness of his landscapes, their lack of the charming qualities which are a prime requisite of advertising. Another aspect of these landscapes that made them resistant to official appropriation is the seemingly arbitrary cropping, which entails negation of a priori, generally accepted notions of scenic beauty or *points de vue*. Courbet once recalled a conversation with Baudelaire at the seaside: "'There, this is what I wanted to show you,' Baudelaire said to me, 'this is the viewpoint.' Pretty bourgeois, isn't it?! Just what are viewpoints? Do viewpoints even exist?"[135] In other words, Courbet did not recognize any generally binding perspective, nor any hierarchy of visual values, which was precisely what the later train station decorations and their views of established "sights" demanded (see note 126). Any fixation on a single viewpoint (literally and figuratively) he considered bourgeois, a contradiction of the equality principle. Another time, he remarked to Corot, "Wherever I sit myself down . . . it's all the same to me; it's always fine, provided that there is nature before one's eyes."[136] This was *one* factor of a "relative art," as Du Camp was later to dub this leveling of values.[137]

However, Courbet's neutrality, under closer scrutiny, turns out to be a combination of opposing attitudes. While the landscape in the center of *The Painter's Studio* (fig. 28) was perceived as primal nature, juxtaposed to society as a symbol of freedom, now nature itself appears contradictory (fig. 32), both available and inaccessible, both inviting and hostile. This rendered the image unusable to arouse interest in travel; Courbet's train terminal project succumbed to its own inherent contradictions. The formal dichotomy of these landscapes, moreover, points to a dichotomy of content that requires explanation.

Accessibility and forbiddingness—with these two qualities, depictions of nature were granted a dual role. First, they offered, to urbanites and country-dwellers alike, an opportunity to appropriate reality, a realm of experience that had become aesthetically or actually foreign to them. Second, these landscapes alluded to the provinces' right to self-determination and federative independence. In this respect, the Meuse landscape may very well allude to Belgium as a country of freedom.[138]

The structure of this composition continued to be used in the many views Courbet painted of Franche-Comté. Common to all of them[139] is a direct, flat introduction in the foreground (sometimes a road running into the distance) and the blocking off of the background (usually by a line of high cliffs); these two elements are often connected in the middle ground by some form of animal life, integrated in the natural environment.[140] Some pictures of this type have craggy mountains that resemble castles, such as *Valley with Deer* or *Wire Stringers' Mills on the Loue* (figs. 33, 34), where the dramatically lighted rock formation evokes a fortress under whose protection the mills seem to stand. Since in Courbet's circle nature was frequently substituted for history, it is not only permissible but necessary to state that here, nature at once embodies and negates social authority. Although no widely accepted social symbol existed for Courbet's notion of a decentralized France with self-sufficient provinces, the primitiveness and authenticity of nature served him as such a symbol by which to defy Bonapartist centralism. The comparison of the Jura Cliffs with castles must have been familiar to Courbet: Buchon and Champfleury expressly celebrated the cliffs at Ornans as "citadels,"[141] and during the Second Empire castles were frequently depicted and described to recall earlier provincial resistance to the monarch's encroach-

33 Gustave Courbet, *Valley with Deer*. Oil on canvas, 80 × 100 cm, 1866. Formerly Dresden, Coll. Schmeil.

ments.[142] We may conclude that in his landscapes, Courbet continued to proclaim, in a metaphorical way, the counterauthority he had evoked in the earlier figure paintings.

If in 1852 he could still confront the Bonapartists, the "nouveaux maîtres de l'opinion," with his farmwomen as if with the model for a healthy society,[143] now, after the rural populace had turned to Napoleon, he confronted them with nature itself. The self-sufficiency Courbet envisioned, despite his quotation of the comte de Chambord and *The Wire Stringers' Mills,* was not to be feudally organized, but it was almost certainly to embrace the memory of the independence maintained up to the reign of Louis XI (as "good simplicity"),[144] which is why a natural formation, or something returning to a natural state (cliffs or ruins) could take the place of a castle, or a castle that of rock formations.[145] But nature does not subjugate; this metaphor therefore includes the negation of all domination. The wire stringers' mills could assert the same thing as the decayed Château de Saint-Denis overlooking the Loue at Scey-en-Varais.[146] This would

34   Gustave Courbet, *Wire Stringers' Mills on the Loue.* Oil on canvas, 55 × 66 cm, c. 1860. Charlottenlund, Ordrupgaardsamlingen.

support the supposition that Courbet had social intentions with his *Mill by Ornans* (1869; Providence, Rhode Island School of Design).[147] In this late work, the egalitarian structure of the humble house with its uniform windows as an "arbitrary major subject," stripped of genre or anecdotal dressing, superseded earlier views of manors or protecting cliffs—and, by the way, blazed the trail for Cézanne.

Opposing the propagandistic use of nature, aimed at a new audience, and, despite the amalgamation of provinces caused by industrialization and the railroads,[148] insisting on the importance of simplicity and naturalness as expressions of individual and regional self-assertion, this series of paintings was emphatically terminated and transcended by *Cliffs by the Sea in Winter* (fig. 35). It shows a cliff descending in three steps to the middle of the picture, where it forms a barrier to the winter landscape in the middle ground. A path leads directly from the viewer to the cliffs. On the right is a hill with snowy bushes; behind them spreads the open sea. This background considerably qualifies the barrier function of the cliffs. Very often in Courbet's landscapes and seascapes, a relatively near, isolated object is combined with a comprehensive overview,[149] but while in the seascapes the *relationship* between the two elements prevails over the substantiality of the main object, the two are held in equilibrium in the winter landscape. The leveling effect of the blanket of snow also plays its part here. The earlier principle of individuation, the attempt to define and establish separate things, to distinguish one substance from another, tends to be reversed by this equalization of matter. And the cliffs, despite the voluminous and solid appearance of each single object, form a coherent flat surface. Unlike the paratactically composed early landscapes, the later ones have a planarity that anticipates Cézanne, while in content retaining a clear connection to the visible world.[150] This development, as will be shown below, roused the critics to attack.

But what disturbed them even more was the insignificance to which the human figure had sunk. "Man, the great model, disappears almost completely. . . . He seems to have become some sort of boring accessory; landscape painting is invading genre painting, which itself invaded historical painting," feared Du Camp,[151] who thus unwillingly conceded to landscape painting the rank of history painting. Thoré, who saw this valorizing positively, was even clearer: "The revolution in landscape painting . . . has certainly brought back true nature, but nature for itself; a forthright theater, but almost without actors. . . . In this brilliant school of landscape artists the human figure is but an accessory."[152] With these words, which apply as much to the Barbizon school as to the last-mentioned paintings of Courbet, Thoré implied the increasing isolation of the individual in the Second Empire. But "solitude," which was much described at the time, was also perceived as a healthy alternative to life in the city. Michelet called "solitude," as well as "sociabilité," prerequisites for creativity.[153] When Henriet, in 1857, valued the peace, freedom, and loneliness in the imagery of Barbizon, it was not in the ubiquitous romantic sense, but rather as an actual antipode to the modern city.[154] Being alone in nature caused Thoré not only "mélancolie" but also "sérénité";[155] Castagnary found in Courbet's wood and stream paintings the freshness and health of the outdoors for the sake of which he often holidayed in the Jura.[156] The painter

Gigoux commended Courbet in the face of the widespread criticism of his Proudhon portrait, saying, "Let him profit from the solitude in which he finds himself and, when he shall be face to face with nature, perhaps his good instincts will return to him."[157] Nature as medicine, the painter as doctor: "These doctors . . . of forests and mountains," Thoré said of these subjects in the hands both of Courbet and Millet.[158]

The natural scene and paintings of it could have this salutary effect only if they appeared "rude," "simple," and "sincère" in the sense of the French Revolution,[159] and if the painter was expected to heighten this effect, it was because he was obliged "to reproduce nature by bringing it to its *maximum strength and intensity*."[160] With this

35   Gustave Courbet, *Cliffs by the Sea in Winter*. Oil on canvas, 54 × 65.5 cm, 1870. Pasadena, Norton Simon Museum of Art.

dual requirement and the disposition in the Second Empire toward a literary and political reception of visual art, any representation of unsullied, primitive nature at that period could not help but suggest indestructible force and hope for the future. This was especially true of natural features whose symbolic significance was generally agreed—besides certain cliffs and streams, above all trees. If a random pine forest could become a historical metaphor,[161] how much more easily could a "significant" solitary tree, as earlier in the work of Caspar David Friedrich.

Courbet's *Oak at Flagey* (fig. 36) relied on just such public agreement in this regard. An isolated object, as it were a generic term for nature, the oak figured as an

36   Gustave Courbet, *The Oak at Flagey*. Oil on canvas, 89 × 110 cm, 1864. Tokyo, Murauchi Museum of Art.

embodiment of regional rights and traditions, and thus as a tree of liberty by implication of the people. This, then, is a symbol of the kind generated in the French Revolution, and at the same time an actual, physical site associated with personal memories.[162] This double connection is decisive for an understanding of Courbet, who
knew that a diffuse adherence to the French Revolution no longer sufficed, and that a
new one with emotional roots in the individual was needed. As late as the Commune he
still opposed a merely schematic adoption of the idea of 1789.[163] This double allow-
ance determined the form of the painting. Basically, it can be read in the same way as
Courbet's "tourist" pictures, where nature was given a sort of authority with demands
to make on society. It also reveals a similar opposition between horizontal expanse and
towering vertical; it is an image of great concentration achieved by bringing the tree
palpably near and cropping it, which veritably explodes the pictorial field.[164]

For Courbet the tree of liberty was not only a sign that history is based on nature, a
symbol of national strength or of a "grand history," as it was for Théodore Rousseau;[165] in accord with the anti-Bonapartist thrust of Second Empire opposition, it
was a physical embodiment of individual and regional resistance to Napoleon III.[166]
Like the activities of regional associations in Paris, manifestations of one's love of home
at the appropriate rural sites were part of French republican tradition. A concern with
natural things (or artifacts with the authenticity of nature) thus had an ethical significance, for it was to redeem society from corruption and the individual from isolation.[167] The Bonapartists initially supported this cult of the archaic, but when they
realized that this might spur republican sentiments, they prohibited all such manifestations, including even the publishing of folk songs.[168] Napoleon was not able to
incorporate the cult of nature into a legitimation of power.[169] Though landscape
painting was generally encoded enough to be tolerated, even it occasionally fell to
censorship. *The Oak at Flagey* reveals this ambivalence. Not until 1867 in Philadelphia was it shown under its full title: *The Vercingetorix Oak at Flagey on the
Battlefield of Caesar near Alesia in Franche-Comté,*[170] with which Courbet protested
against official attempts to establish Napoleon III as a national hero in the tradition of
Vercingetorix.[171]

The Hunter Hunted

Although Courbet's animal and hunting scenes deserve a separate exam-
ination,[172] in what follows I shall consider them insofar as they support or modify the
hypotheses advanced above. Courbet's identification with and dissociation from his
environment, which began with *A Burial at Ornans,* continue in these paintings, if in a
sublimated form suited to the altered historical situation. The painter himself called
the 1861 *Battle of the Stags* (fig. 37) and 1867 *Kill: Episode during the Deer Hunt in a
Snowy Terrain* (fig. 38) companion pieces to *A Burial.* The two later canvases, in turn,
can be seen as counterpoints in terms of content.[173] Instead of depicting animals in
their "Sunday best,"[174] Courbet invariably showed them either under normal conditions, or in suffering—this still in the old metaphorical sense in which Grandville,

37 Gustave Courbet, *The Battle of the Stags*. Oil on canvas, 355 × 507 cm, 1861. Paris, Musée d'Orsay (Photo Giraudon).

38 Gustave Courbet, *The Kill: Episode during the Deer Hunt in a Snowy Terrain*. Oil on canvas, 355 × 505 cm, 1867. Besançon, Musée des Beaux-Arts (Photo Lauros-Giraudon).

Cham, and others used the theme of the hunt.[175] Politically persecuted people were compared to suffering animals; as Courbet wrote of Buchon, "He was hunted, like a wild beast. . . . While trying to escape, he had fallen into the wolf's jaws."[176] Likewise, "la chasse à l'homme" (the manhunt) and "le gibier à guillotine" (prey for the guillotine) were current descriptions, in a novel written in defense of Courbet by Jean Bruno,[177] who compared the persecutors, representatives of the bureaucracy, to reptiles and bulls.[178] In 1870 Courbet likened the German soldiers advancing on Paris to wild beasts that had been lying in wait for their prey for forty years.[179] The painter also identified with the hunter, however, for with Champfleury he sounded the horn to "hunt the bourgeois"[180] and saw himself as a "wild animal tamer."[181]

The actual hunt also had different levels of meaning for Courbet. His self-confidence profited from this activity outside the realm of professional competition and beyond the censors' incursions, and it gave him a feeling of independence that was hard to come by as an artist.[182] Here, at least, he was occasionally able to "face nature on more equal terms," as Kane has remarked.[183] But his anarchic craving for equality also prompted him to criticize the hunt, particularly the 1844 regulations, which, although they permitted the rural populace to hunt, also brought more strict regimentation. Courbet defied this by hunting out of season[184] and by elevating the poacher, that "romantic, anti-authoritarian figure," to a subject of painting.[185]

The link between this anarchic stance and Courbet's formal approach is important to note. In *The Battle of the Stags* (Fig. 37), various procedures are combined. The stasis and plasticity of the light-flooded wood,[185] contrasts with the agitated linearity of the animals' bodies, which were painted from stuffed models. Indicatively, the firmly contoured animals found the approval of the Frankfurt Academy director, who in turn condemned the loose, comparatively "inexact" foliage.[187] With the awkward, unnoble attitudes and positions of the stags' bodies, Courbet again declined to establish that stylized center of interest (and climax of plot) found in trivial game paintings, where the need for authority and idealization prevail. The movement of *The Battle of the Stags,* moreover, would suggest that Courbet's notion of equality also holds valid for temporal relations, for each instant in time depicted, and every form arising from it, possesses equal importance.

When one considers that *The Battle of the Stags* was originally to form a trilogy with *Stag Taking to the Water* (Marseille) and *Runaway Horse* (Munich), one sees that Courbet's main intent was to evoke the restlessness and suffering of animals and nature in general[188], not to mention the allusion to the emperor inherent in the latter picture. This was lost on the Salon critics. In the landscapes of this year Thoré found the peace he missed in the other Salon entries, writing, "In this period . . . uncertain of its ideas and feelings, of philosophy and morality, of literature and the arts, of the meaning of history as well as of that of the trends of the present day—nature and landscapes have great attraction."[189] Also Thoré noticed Courbet's protest against academic tradition in *The Battle of the Stags:* "I prefer Courbet's stag to Alcibiades' dog."[190] The ambivalent agitation and expressiveness of the painting are certainly significant, since they reveal that even nature depictions could be caught up in the general feeling of unrest, if in a different way than the "pure" landscapes, with their primarily static oppositions. Just a few years later Thoré himself recognized this, when he wrote that "nature and society are equally troubled. In France, above all, there is a permanent state of alarm."[191]

This unrest is heightened in *The Kill* (fig. 38), becoming an inherent opposition within the painting on both a semantic and a technical level and marking the close of the anti-authoritarian phase of Courbet's second period. In 1873, Courbet planned to show *The Kill* together with *The Battle of the Stags,* in place of *A Burial* (see note 173), which was no longer pertinent to the social reality. These two paintings were to be his new history paintings, depicting his view of "truth." Courbet emphasized his social responsibility in this regard by borrowing, for *The Kill,* the figure of the rider from Delacroix's *Massacre of Chios,* a history painting meant as an appeal for independence.[192]

Since 1866 hopes for independence and an end to Bonapartism had grown, paralleled by an increase in government surveillance.[193] The bourgeoisie was able to make gains only in the increasingly important area of leisure—for those whose alienation from nature had not ruled out this source of recreation.[194] The ersatz function of the natural environment ensured that depictions of it could be used to convey social protest. While in 1856–57 the programmatic demand for artistic truth, directed polemically against the hypocrisy of the prevailing order of the Second Empire, had inhered principally in figure paintings, by 1861 it had shifted to depictions of the outdoors.[195] In that year Delaborde already took issue with the "vérité brute des paysagistes" (raw truth of the landscape artists),[196] and when in 1867 Thiers commented during his secret viewing of Courbet's special exhibition, "M. Courbet cares too much for truth, one must not love truth,"[197] he meant the landscapes and hunts. Only against this background is it understandable why Courbet attached such great importance to his canvases of 1866–67, *Mounted Hunter* and *The Kill,* and to others he wanted to paint in autumn 1868 in Ornans, which he called "socialistic"[198]— a term that he, like his critics, used synonymously with anarchistic and anti-Bonapartist.

The "Paysage Autoritaire" Dissolved

The triumph of the individual in an open nature, however, was made a theme of painting at a time when the individual object was already losing meaning.[199] The greater the gap became between opposing interests and relations toward the end of the Second Empire, the less nature could be used to symbolize a tangible opposition. The individuals in *The Kill,* who no longer even pretend to act, are frozen like heraldic symbols. Although the previous categories of "diversified units" and "individual colors . . . confined to separate areas" still apply to them,[200] other passages in the painting, especially the landscape, show the borders of objects being called in question. The model of individuation inherited from David[201] and largely valid for Courbet's oeuvre as a whole, is here synthesized into a color continuum and a patterned pictorial surface that deserves closer description. Indeed, the partial overlap of these two approaches in *The Kill* is the chief reason for the picture's appeal. Under the surface of formal definition and self-sufficiency appears a new unity that reflects the late Courbet's humanitarian ideas, which transcended both individuals and classes. However, this dissolution of the object, often glibly associated with impressionism, should not be understood solely as a technical phenomenon; changes in approach imply changes in conception or philosophy. To Courbet's contemporaries, this process bore a highly charged social message. Let me attempt to describe its symptoms step by step, though admittedly the development was not linear or even always consecutive.

If the visual transformation of primal nature into a symbol of social authenticity and promise required clearly contoured objects as vehicles of meaning, the attempt to convey this message by means of egalitarian structure also required a removal of borders between objects, a search for unifying characteristics, links, analogies. This new approach was promoted through scientific observation and an intuitional feel for natural phenomena.[202] Over the long term, this entailed suspending the metaphorical use of nature for explicitly agitational ends. Terms like "le paysage prolétaire" or "le paysage autoritaire" (the disappearance of which from the visual arts Du Camp bemoaned in 1867)[203] no longer applied. They were superseded by Castagnary's truly symbolic phrase about humanity being a landscape painter, which even then was associated with world economic ties and the developing internationalism of politics.[204] Only now, in the high capitalism of the 1860s, did Hegel's conception of a world marketplace approach fulfillment.[205] Insofar as landscape painting was able to assimilate this development, it became for one last time, figuratively speaking, "universal landscape."

Courbet's version of this was a type of landscape in which the old iconology, fixated on objects, was discarded in favor of a new, if equally socially oriented, semantics of color and light conveyed largely by a new paint application and treatment of the ground. In the landscape detail from *The Kill*, the rust-red ground, visible as particles, emerges as a structure in its own right.[206] The result is a new transparency of surface that stands in contrast not only to academic painting, but also to Courbet's own opaque paint handling. The support now functions as a unifying element that emerges almost unnoticeably between the objects and within them, dissolving them into particles and allowing them to merge with the surrounding parts of the picture. By working up from the ground and letting it show through, Courbet mitigated the distinction between the paint layers and laid the painting process bare. As Schug has shown, this includes the canvas in the artistic confrontation with reality.[207] It is this dissolution that first gives the impression of all things being "of equal visual value" in a painting.[208] However, it would be just as superficial to attribute this phenomenon to political events alone as to reduce it to stylistic terms. Rather, it evinces a new mode of perception that takes fuller account of the mutability of nature and its susceptibility to human intervention.

This new approach to the object is enriched, in *Covert of Roe-Deer by a Stream at Plaisir-Fontaine* (fig. 39), by a further factor. The light-flooded background appears to

39 Gustave Courbet, *Covert of Roe-Deer by a Stream at Plaisir-Fontaine*. Oil on canvas, 174 × 209 cm, 1866. Paris, Musée d'Orsay (Photo Giraudon).

leach the substance out of things, making it difficult to associate the patches of reflected light with particular objects. This procedure, which Courbet had studied in Rembrandt and which was considered a revolution in perception,[209] had already been assayed in the *The Battle of the Stags* (fig. 37) and intensified in the later *Terrasse of Bon-Port*.[201] Yet while the stags' bodies in the former still, as it were, resisted assimilation, and those in *The Kill* were starkly silhouetted against the landscape, those in *Covert of Roe-Deer by a Stream* are integrated in the surrounding vegetation by color and shading. The painter's faith in harmony with nature here takes the form of a social harmony expressed by proxy through "nature naturante."[211] This would appear to bring Courbet's vision of harmony very close to the Bonapartist one, as if he had made concessions to the prevailing taste with this pleasing subject;[212] in fact, the painting was being considered for a medal.[213] This in itself indicates the force which this as yet unhackneyed theme still possessed during the Second Empire. Courbet's desire for harmony and reconciliation, however, by no means contradicted his basic oppositional stance. This idea, always latently present among the anarchists, was already expressed in *The Painter's Studio*. But only now, with the granting of right to assembly and other civil rights, had a general disposition for this sentiment arisen.[214] There was certainly also an element of opportunism in this desire for harmony, which all the progressives in the Second Empire shared. Proudhon, as early as 1848, wanted to "concilier dans un même principe toutes les questions" (reconcile all the questions in just one principle);[215] Hugo too, and above all Michelet, tried despite persecution to achieve national renewal through a reconciliation of class antagonisms.[216] With Hugo, Courbet, and Castagnary, the idea of reconciliation was directly associated with a rejection of Bonapartist nationalism. To them, the demand for regional independence and for cosmopolitan cooperation based on a United States of Europe seemed to be two sides of the same coin,[217] permitting them to consider such regionally motivated painting as Courbet's a medium of a general renewal of culture. Finally, Thoré and Du Camp saw in landscape painting toward the close of the Second Empire the possibility of reconciling the diverse streams in art.[218]

This context explains the widespread acclaim which Courbet received for *Covert of Roe-Deer by a Stream*: its pictorial harmony evidently answered a general need for reconciliation and neutralization of conflicting interests. This mutual "embrace" certainly involved a danger of watering down the painter's demand for emancipation; but beyond the surface of harmony, Courbet was already thought to have undermined the limits of pictorial and political tolerance. For as soon as Courbet advanced from an assimilation of oppositions to a dissolution of pictorial surface, this was taken to be a sign of impending catastrophe. Courbet was caricatured as a Christ dispensing truths—on account of his landscapes, as he had been earlier for his figure paintings. And just as his *Wrestlers* had once been condemned for being "dirty," now his seascapes were.[219] To a modern eye, this is hardly visible; the charges remain incomprehensible without knowledge of the historical connotations. Yet one can find certain grounds in the paintings for the controversies they touched off at the time.

Courbet's *Stream of the Black Well* (fig. 40) anticipates Cézanne's "interference of nonobjective formal values with object-derived abbreviations"[220] in more than a strictly formal sense. The site near Ornans, which Buchon had characterized as a haven, a simile for unspoiled nature, is depicted in a manner far removed from earlier positivistic description. Here the subject has become arbitrary. The picture is based on relations instead of an exact nomenclature of objects, and above all on the effect of light penetrating the foliage, which transforms objects without rendering them completely unrecognizable. The experimental character of the painting is obvious; apparently, Courbet found it easier to integrate *planes* of impinging light into his previous approach than, for instance, the *rays* of light falling obliquely from the left, which leave objects unaffected.[221] On the whole, there is greater interest here in the communica-

40   Gustave Courbet, *The Stream of the Black Well*. Oil on canvas, 65 × 89 cm, 1865. London, private collection.

tion among things than in individuation. This is corroborated by the way we tend to perceive the picture: only on second glance can such details as the deer or the trees on the cliff be identified. If previously Courbet had replaced Balzac's "great man" with the authority of "the great outdoors," now he lessened the burden of significance placed on nature[222] by taking the same familiar natural objects merely as points of departure for more general probings of natural physical processes (reflection and refraction of light).

Courbet's use of color developed in a similar way. In the *Source of the Lison* (c. 1864, Berlin)[223] such local colors as the yellow of the autumn leaves or the green of the grass also appear in small particles on cliffs and water. Beyond this, a nonlocal color, a red, is introduced and flecks of it distributed over everything in the picture. The color correspondences thus produced on the surface are quite different from that object-related polychromy which dominated the figure paintings of the first period and occasionally thereafter.

Castagnary, the first to comment on these correspondences in the late paintings, referred to Courbet's increasing use of a new tool, the palette knife.[224] This was indeed decisive in producing the material quality of his *peinture* and in equalizing compositional emphases. The quality of the late seascapes, which Champfleury called "l'immatériel"[225]—a term really more applicable to Turner's watercolors—consists precisely in an exact materialization of the atmosphere, and in a transition from one object to another produced by broad paint application. In this respect, *Seaside* of 1866 (fig. 41) is one of Courbet's most highly developed paintings, for here the differences between sky, sea, and beach are overcome (unlike the later painting in Caen; see note 206) by renouncing objective definition of the foreground, polychromy, and decided gradations of color, combined with a flocculent paint application that avoids all clear definition.[226] The chiaroscuro contrasts used in *Stream of the Black Well* have also disappeared. It might be objected that while this establishes pictorial equalization, it also divests the picture of any critical relationship to reality, but I think this misses the point. The picture's statement about reality consists in a representation of the equalizing effect of nature and its suppression of individual objects, which is precisely why paintings like this one were opposed as anarchistic.

Before concluding with a discussion of the contemporary controversy over "relative art," let us turn to Courbet's relationship to external nature as exemplified by one of the wave pictures, which can be viewed as complementary to the beach paintings. The wave pictures are particularly important because they represent the culmination and summing-up of the artist's complex relationship to nature, especially as regards the factors of equality and authority. In motif and technique, *The Wave* in Lyon (fig. 42) holds an intermediate place between the more official, smoothly finished versions (Paris, Musée d'Orsay; Berlin, Nationalgalerie) and the freer, more strongly dissolved ones (Bremen; Frankfurt, Städel),[227] the first of which are dominated by the frontally approaching wave, and the second by a dissolution of the surf in spray, observed from the side. The lack of distance common to all of Courbet's wave paintings again confronts the viewer with nature as a threat; unlike the beach scenes, which are emptied of motifs, their masses of water and clouds affect the viewer like a surprise attack. Yet behind the initially perceived, very low vantage point which elevates nature above humankind, there is a second and separate one located at the height of the horizon which gives an overview of nature and suggests human superiority. What does this dual perspective signify?

Apparently, Courbet was no longer willing at this point to clearly define man's relationship to nature, and left it ambivalent. In the wave paintings he qualifies both the notion of human subjugation to a natural order that brings everything to its own level, and the ideology of human domination and omnipotence. His attack is directed equally at the belief in nature as a quasi-mythological redeeming force and at its total utilization—both of which were publicly propagated under Napoleon III.[228] Neither of these concerns, however, was wholly negative in the sense of being an attempt to liberate the individual from industrialization and dominance.[229] They also reflect an

41   Gustave Courbet, *Sea-side*. Oil on canvas, 54 × 64 cm, 1866. Cologne, Wallraf-Richartz-Museum/Museum Ludwig (Photo Giraudon).

attempt, through exact observation of nature, to collect experience which could be fed back as imagery into society, in conformance with Courbet's desire to work through art for individual freedom and finally for democracy.[230]

In what sense has Courbet observed nature in these paintings? In the first place, he has recognized its coherence. Instead of perceiving the surf and the water masses behind it as separate phenomena, he evokes their interdependence and continual amalgamation. Second, he has observed that there is a successive movement which, at its climax, makes a wave appear to stand still; that is why Courbet's contemporaries found his waves "frozen" or "like walls."[231] Yet they can just as well be perceived as being in motion, simultaneously swelling and breaking. Finally, and concomitantly, Courbet's recognition of the mutability of all matter has led him to dissolve the wave into countless interconnected particles. This also produces a texture which is indepen-

42   Gustave Courbet, *The Wave*. Oil on canvas, 65.6 × 90 cm, 1869–70. Lyon, Musée des Beaux-Arts (Photo Giraudon).

dent, autonomous, as seen for example in the nonobjective white crown of foam spreading across the foreground to the left edge of the canvas. It was probably innovations like this that prompted Du Camp to lament the disappearance of landscapes with "authoritarian" principal subjects[232]—a change in *shape* quite apart from the loss of authoritarian *meaning:* the sea stood now as a metaphor for the people.[233] The method of applying perceptions from the natural sciences to social relations is already to be found in Comte, Taine, and Zola;[234] contemporary art criticism had posited links between painting and the larger social reality. This permits us to conclude that in Courbet's late work, the romantic utopia of a unity between *solitude* and *sociabilité* was fulfilled, and to apply the term *equality* to his late landscapes. It also explains why Champfleury could place the wave pictures on the very same level as *A Burial at Ornans.*[235]

One aspect of Courbet's landscapes on which the critics focused was the equality of subject matter they evinced. This was merely to associate Courbet with the secular side of the pantheistic tradition which Caspar David Friedrich had expressed thus: "Holiness is everywhere . . . once I depicted it in reeds."[236] The radical force of such statements was proved in the events of the German Vormärz and in French realist theory, for their literary pantheism was viewed as covert materialism, indeed as a threat to the state.[237] Among the "tendances panthéistes en France" which caused concern in Germany, Champfleury counted the return to nature in reality and in art.[238] Courbet himself may have become associated with pantheistic streams around 1854.[239] In 1873, Dubosc de Pesquidoux, a critic who despite his irony deserves to be taken seriously, attacked realism as a form of pantheism: "Everything in nature is of interest; everything, if presented by a painter of talent, can please," he conceded, though he felt that the quality of a work of art depended on the dignity of its subject matter. The realists' insistence on the equality of all things was by no means a simple "réhabilitation picturale et agreste" (rustic pictorial rehabilitation). Their claim "could be surprising, if one is unaware of the affinity of the realist painters for innovations of another kind," by which de Pesquidoux meant their connection to the Commune. "'Let's turn tradition upside down,' say the realists, . . . 'let's exalt the humble and the small: let's cut a wide path for the new social strata of the forests': . . . This is a new form of democracy which is going to suffocate us."[240] This fear of leveling in art, difficult to understand today, culminated in a condemnation of Courbet, whose landscapes threatened society in the same way as his political misdeeds: "Here is this *work of subversion on which all of the realist landscape artists collaborated,* these accomplices, willing or not, of our most dangerous visionaries, these too docile henchmen of the infamous sacker of the Column, the painter Courbet *who has but transferred to politics his ideas on leveling* and on an artistic tabula rasa."[241]

The contemporary German critics similarly rejected vulgar subject matter. But by 1855 in France, even the conservative faction had acknowledged that all *subjects* were of basically equal value, Perrier, for one, being disturbed only by the *form* of such equivalencies.[242] During the 1860s, the criticism of realist form grew increasingly harsh (up to 1857, this approach had been only lukewarmly criticized).[243] The reproaches can be

summed up in the terms *pandemonium, pantography,* and *anarchy.* They were formu-
lated most clearly by Du Camp, who noted a general decline in art which had become
particularly apparent in the "folie lucide" of the 1863 Salon des Refusés. Wherever he
looked he saw "negligence du dessin" and "tendances ultra-matérialistes," by which Du
Camp, like Delaborde before him, meant the thematic prominence of the sheer materials
of painting. Painting had regressed to the state of mere sketching; these "peintres
rudimentaires" worked in a "manière de pochade" (quick, sketchy style)[245] and were
content with mere strokes (*touches*) or flecks (*taches*) of color.[246] Landscape painting
was most susceptible to this type of "dissolution"[247] because it required less psychological precision than figure painting; not by chance had "the landscape been invading
painting" for years now.[248] The seeds of this development, said Du Camp, had probably
already been planted in the "dissolution"[249] of prerevolutionary society, which, tired of
civilization, had turned to nature. His words bear unmistakable parallels to the present
day: "We want to escape at any cost, to conquer the freedom of our individuality . . . and we are going to inquire into nature . . . asking from her a peace which we
find neither in nor around ourselves."[250] Art followed these tendencies, leading to a
spate of landscape painters, said Du Camp, implying that social *and* stylistic causes both
contributed to a predominance of landscape painting, which in turn led to the dissolution of painting itself. At this point, Du Camp took up the critique of a leveling of subject
matter and combined it with a critique of formal dissolution and its social causes, asking
"Hasn't the sort of vague and consoling pantheism promulgated by modern socialist
schools taught artists that God is everywhere, in trees as in man, in animals as in plants?"
As with Pesquidoux, this differs from romanticism only in its more directly political
motivation. But then he adds, "The ease and rapidity of [modern] communications
encouraged painters. . . . Seeing that . . . they would never be able to fully portray man,
they turned to landscapes, which are always easier to treat, more obscure, less defined; in
a word, feeling themselves incapable of rendering an expression, they were content to
convey an impression."[251] To produce a mere impression, summary means sufficed,
concluded Du Camp, thus closing the circle of his equally polemical and clairvoyant
argument. It is important to note that Du Camp's terms are linked throughout with
moral judgments.[252] He felt that the liberation of the painting process—"French art is in
a state of utter licentiousness"—would lead to a general disregard of moral standards, of
the kind found typically in republican societies.[253]

All of these reproaches were leveled in concentrated form at Courbet, whose
ostensible lack of imagination and discrimination made his painting a prime example
of the relativizing of truth. "To take at random what one sees, is to reduce oneself to
being a mere pantograph . . . it reduces observation, comparison and choice to noth-
ingness."[254] Du Camp stood trembling before the consequences of this development:
"Only the future will be able to say whether this change was for the better; our only
mission is, trembling, to make note of it, *for we believe it to be disastrous.*"[255]

Writing the same year, 1868, Castagnary described the quality of dissolution in
the landscape painting of Courbet and the younger generation as "a revolution . . . and a revolution in content as well as in form."[256] Pissarro and Cézanne

consciously followed Courbet in their "anarchistic" approach to landscape, and were opposed as anarchists for their painting alone.[257] In a sham session of the National Assembly, the landscapist Monet, friend of Courbet, was even called "le Marat de la peinture" (the Marat of painting).[258] But to the same degree as landscape painting was believed capable of suggesting reconciliation, combating nationalistic narrowmindedness, and presenting nature as a model of social equality, it lost its semantically unequivocal, agitationally effective, and generally understandable mode of representation. What affected Du Camp as a shocking disintegration of all accepted standards, appears in hindsight to have been a broader understanding of individual experience and of the ways painting can influence society. But what it in fact led to was a separation, at least temporarily, of moral and political commitment from artistic expression. Seen in this light, Courbet's participation in the Commune would appear to be a consequence of his realization that too much had been expected of painting as a means toward social transformation, an insight that can be called realistic if one takes into account the overtones of resignation this term bears in ordinary speech.

Courbet's artistic protest against hierarchical structures, fixed systems of perspective, the ostensibly unalterable nature of things and the values associated with them, nevertheless contained implications that were not to be fully explored until the twentieth century. His protest formed the negative, anti-authoritarian background against which the utopia of a community of self-determined individuals could appear in high relief—though initially in terms merely of a liberation of subject matter from formal limitations and an emphasis on the appearance of objects in color and light. When these elements of equality were rendered autonomous, divested of their oppositional content, and torn out of historical context, of course, they could just as well be used to confirm existing authority, a circumstance to which Courbet's landscapes owed their art-historical rehabilitation in the later nineteenth century.

The question that Courbet's painting still poses is that of the conditions of artistic analysis of reality in a period of both social disintegration and ossification like that of the 1860s in France. One might ask whether under conditions such as these, artists should not exploit even the least promising but appropriate means in order to assert the demand for a humanitarian transformation of the status quo. This is what Courbet did.

5

Proudhon's *Carnets intimes* and Courbet's *Portrait of Proudhon*

Art as a Means of Regeneration

ON August 20, 1861, Proudhon noted in his diary: "Success. Four friends. Chaudey, Madier-Montjau, Courbet, Hagelmann, are thwarting the intrigues of literary propriety. These same, minus Hagelmann, pledge themselves to my antidogmatic name."[1] These unnoticed lines in the unpublished portion of the *Carnets*, jotted down during the Antwerp Artists Congress of 1861, reveal the sort of relationships the philosopher maintained—self-centered, and for the most part professionally motivated. Proudhon *expected* friendship, but apparently rarely took the initiative himself. This reserve is reflected in the dearth of private comments in the *Carnets;* even where the rare *ami* occurs,[2] it seems to be little more than a word, and Proudhon's relations with women were limited to his wife.

Anyone who expects revelations about the Paris and Brussels Salons or about the diarist's personal feelings about his contemporaries on the literary and artistic scene is bound to be disappointed, the most recent instance being Alan Bowness with respect to Proudhon's relationship to Courbet.[3] Based on the low number of mentions, Bowness felt compelled to conclude that the painter can hardly have been closely acquainted with the philosopher, and that Proudhon's influence on Courbet was much less important than Courbet himself maintained.[4] This view leaves many questions unanswered—for instance, why Courbet was one of the few of Proudhon's friends who remained faithful to him and visited him in prison in 1852 (something Proudhon did not even permit his wife to do on occasion),[5] or why, as indicated by the above quotation, he publicly sided with Proudhon during his exile. It should be taken into account that Proudhon tended to discuss personal matters at length only when they presented considerable difficulties for him, an example of which will be given below. Moreover, with seven mentions in the *Carnets,* Courbet stands quite close to the top of the list. Bowness's statistics, one cannot help but feel, were intended to prove something entirely different—that Proudhon was indeed the dry, artistically insensitive moralist that Zola[6] and many others made him out to be, a man who may have indoctrinated Courbet but who gave him no support, and that Courbet for his part neither understood Proudhon's philosophy nor required it for his work in painting.

When one looks beyond mere statistical frequencies, the *Carnets* prove to be a rich source of information that shed light both on Proudhon's art theory—and concomitantly on his relationship to Courbet—and on the philosopher's personal situation. In giving the diaries another reading, my intention is not so much to rehabilitate Proudhon's sensibility or Courbet's intelligence as simply to trace their mutual *interest in art* as a subject of personal identification and social involvement. The effort is especially worthwhile since it reveals new aspects of Proudhon's essay *Du principe de l'art et de sa destination sociale*[7] and of Courbet's *Portrait of Proudhon with His Family.*

The widespread view to the contrary, Proudhon became interested in art long before the last years of his life. As early as 1843, ten years before the publication of *La philosophie du progrès* and fifteen years before *De la justice*—the two works published during the author's lifetime that contained discussions on art theory— Proudhon included "the principles of aesthetics" in his list of projects. At the very beginning of the first diary, we read: "*Style:* Look for the expressions, figures of speech, and turns of phrase proper to each industrial speciality which would lend themselves to common speech and to the new art."[8]

Before Baudelaire[9] and before Semper,[10] both of whom were self-professed followers of his theories for a time, Proudhon advocated an art that would conform to the industrial era in terms of style, technique, and approach. Demands of this type were indeed later violently opposed by advocates of realism such as Desnoyers, who wrote: "There are as well some new romantics . . . [who] have invented industrial literature, Crampton-poetry. They argue that the best way to regenerate literature is to sing the praises of gas, of the sewing machine, etc. This would preclude the need for advertising on the part of inventors and notable businessmen."[11] Still, in the 1840s the avant-garde itself demanded an art with contemporary content.[12] Proudhon's note on style aptly summed up the demythologization strategy of progressive artists, though in his limitation to an art in *conformance* with industry he admittedly remained far behind Marx, whose famous statement "Who is Vulcan by comparison to Roberts & Co., Jupiter by comparison to the lightning rod, or Hermes by comparison to the *Crédit mobilier . . . ?*"[13] went to the heart of the *problem,* namely, the incompatibility of a naive orientation to classical mythology with a society that had been shaped by capitalist technologies.

With the onset of the Second Empire, the demand for an art in conformance with the era took on a different shade of meaning. Although in 1857 Proudhon could still associate with the "industrialized romantic" Gustave Doré, whose project for a *Battle of Inkerman* apparently fascinated him,[14] he had already evidently begun to feel the doubts that would lead him to write, on July 8, 1858: "The Empire has inherited corruption from the reign of Louis-Philippe, from romantic literature, and from industrialism";[15] and even more pointedly on July 20: "Literature follows the example of industry."[16] By this Proudhon was criticizing many things: the romantic "libertinage" of a George Sand, the "sophism" of an Ingres that ignored the needs of the people, the lack of perspective on the part of such mere "faiseurs" as Jean Gigoux, or the Bonapartist conformism of writers like Alexandre Dumas *fils*.[17] Not until late in life was Proudhon to find a solution, and then only in the field of visual art—personified by Courbet.

Another of Proudhon's interests was the *effect* of visual art and its institutions. Long before Champfleury,[18] he conceived the notion that modern art should be involved in everyday life, that it should be a part of the public domain, not merely filling the museums but adorning city squares, reading rooms, schools, cafes, government offices, markets, courtrooms, even army barracks. The museum, in turn, should be a *place of learning* and a repository: "A museum is not a place where works of art should last forever; it is no more than a place of study and a temporary place for antiquities, things which, under certain circumstances, have nowhere else to go."[19] This larger view admittedly sometimes led Proudhon to overlook the works of art themselves, as in the case of the Städel Museum: "We visited the Frankfurt museum, where there are some beautiful things, which, however, interest me little."[20]

Proudhon's thinking about the relationship between art and daily life also infused his approach to the *history* of art, especially to that of the medieval period, which he felt was better integrated in people's everyday affairs than the art of his own time—a basically Hegelian idea discussed extensively in *Du principe de l'art*. On his way to exile in Belgium, Proudhon interrupted his journey only once, in Tournai, to inspect the cathedral.[21] He had previously noted literature on medieval art history: Alexis-François Rio, *De l'art chrétien* (Paris, 1855) and Arthur Murcier, *La sépulture chrétienne en France du XIe au XVIe siècle d'après les monuments* (Paris, 1855).[22] In the same passage he commented on Savonarola's relationship to the Medicis, no doubt tending to identify with the martyr and his troubles with the powers that be.[23] A desire to serve the people also motivated his study of seventeenth-century Dutch art, to which Proudhon was inspired particularly by Bürger-Thoré's essay on the Dutch museums, a publication which he reviewed.[24] In his diaries for September 16, 1858, he wrote of Dutch art that "The true movement in painting is found in the Dutch school. . . . People are surprised that this cold, phlegmatic, positivist nation has succeeded so well in art. But it is quite simple. These optimistic folk have painted themselves: and this painting is of greater worth than those of peoples who create allegories."[25]

Proudhon's occupation with art history has been given as little attention as his involvement with contemporary art, which was broader than is generally thought. By no means concerned with Courbet alone, he maintained contacts with other republican artists of the period, including David d'Angers.[26] Proudhon visited the Salons of 1846, 1855, and 1857, worked out a detailed plan for the beautification of Besançon which included demolishing the fortifications,[27] observed art tourism in Brussels, went hiking with Bürger-Thoré, and visited the Museum of Industry and the Musée Wiertz. About Wiertz he commented, "This gentleman has much talent, but no judgment; he has set off down the wrong path: the path of the fantastic, the mystical, the monstrous, the horrible. A few gracious pieces, quite different, show that he is gifted by nature, but that he disdains his gift."[28] As far as I can see, Proudhon's involvement with both historical and contemporary art served the same purpose—to answer the question how visual art could be made more permeable to everyday concerns and more accessible to plain people.

In spite of this social impulse, however, Proudhon's art theory remained largely beholding to German idealism, at least initially. In the *Carnets* the "socialiste caricaturé"[29] expressly reveals his debt to Kant, Lessing, Fichte, and Schelling.[30] He lists Hegel's *Phenomenology* and *Aesthetics* among the first works that influenced him.[31] On the other hand, Hegel's conception of God and truth became an open question for Proudhon at an early date ("Truth = reality, or the appearance of the spirit?"),[32] and in the critique of religion he followed Feuerbach and Auguste Comte.[33] This process was accelerated by his contacts with Bakunin and Karl Grün, who was agitating in Paris for the goals of Junges Deutschland.[34] Proudhon's art theory initially remained unaffected by these concerns, tending until the onset of the Second Empire to culminate in an idealization of reality. His prime witness was Raphael: "Raphael used to say that a painter had to represent things not as nature has made them but as she ought to have done. Everything contrary to the pure form of each object is evil. Evil, at its lowest level, is imperfection, then ugliness, disorder, chaos, deformity, illness, suffering, crime, and destruction."[35] As later, in 1851 with regard to Courbet,[36] Proudhon's moral rigor apparently prevented him from recognizing the truth in ugliness. Not until late in life, in *Du principe de l'art,* would he manage to overcome his doubts.

An even clearer statement is found in the *Carnets* for August 2, 1843:

> I read *Lucretia:* a beautiful tragedy that misses being one. As in painting, according to Raphael's precept, the representation in tragedy must be idealized, not realistic. Consequently, the style, the language, cannot be vulgar language: on the contrary, it must be raised a bit above the human. . . . Local color, local anecdotes, local style, oral allusions and manners . . . must not be allowed to suffocate the essential side of tragedy, which is humanity.[37]

In this passage Proudhon may seem to cleave to the very academic tradition he otherwise opposed. Yet he employs the concept of the humane in a sense different from that of the classical, idealistic generalization invoked, for instance, by Théophile Gautier.[38] Like Castagnary, a follower of Proudhon and outspoken advocate of Courbet, he was concerned foremost with a humanization of content, a moral renewal—with art as an expression of the "perfectibilité" of the human race.[39] There can be no other explanation for Proudhon's statement, in face of Courbet's *realistic* oeuvre, that it was an "*idealistic* representation of nature and ourselves, aiming at the physical and moral perfection of our species."[40] It also explains his hate of the "depraved" art of the Second Empire, which to him was directly related to the moral and political decline of the period.[41] One may conclude that Proudhon's concern with everyday life, his preoccupation with the "mundane" painting of Holland, and even his call for a "humane" and "unsullied" art, were in the end all prompted by one and the same motive—to contribute to the independence and self-reliance of the ordinary citizen.

Perhaps even more important than the statements pertaining directly to visual art are the links Proudhon established between art and his theory of human community, for it is these which shed light on the function he attributed to artistic production. As early as 1846 he based his theory of productive labor on the special case of artisanry and craftsmanship. To his way of thinking, the workshop represented the "school of the nation": "The true school is the workshop."[42] With this reference to the small crafts shop, Proudhon propagated a society based not only on nonalienated labor but on individual achievement. This, however, involved him in a continual conflict with his own postulate of an art adapted to the needs of industry. For instance, he defended the special organizational form of the "atelier domestique" with the dictum: "Maximum strength, the individual. Minimum strength, the state or the strength of the nation."[43] This exaggerated emphasis on individualism seemed problematical even to Proudhon's likeminded friends, as may be seen from Courbet's portrait of Proudhon as an "écrivain sans lecteur" (readerless writer),[44] the meaning of which becomes clear in this context.

For Proudhon himself, in turn, the work process in society was to take place as an interaction and cooperation of autonomous individuals like the "artistes-ouvriers."[45] To illustrate the idea of channeling surplus back into production, Proudhon likewise chose an example from the field of art, declaring, "What a start! A million commissions for works of art, on the first try, for all public places."[46] In the same context he goes on to state, "Germans [are] metaphysical entrepreneurs, like English industrial ones = misery, misery. It is neither with metaphysics nor with capital that we will be cured."[47] In a work ethic based on craftsmanship, we may conclude, Proudhon believed he had found an antidote to greed and to an abstract longing for redemption, because it would satisfy *both* the human need for achievement and for emotional wholeness and render the surrogate that Proudhon so feared, the *cafés-concerts*, superfluous.[48]

Equality versus Ideal

As we have shown, Proudhon's interest in art tied in with a manual skill, a craft activity, which was the definition later favored by the realist artists in particular. When we come to the question of how this model was to be put into practice and expanded, however, we face a problem of Proudhon's philosophy that is just as fundamental as it is insoluble: his doctrine of equality.

Although he does not employ the concept of *égalité* in the political sense derived from the French Revolution, but as a category of social compensation which he also terms *équité*,[49] Proudhon obviously has difficulties in applying this principle in the cultural sphere: "Disciplining this race of artists is a difficult thing: nothing but equality will do it."[50] The word *discipline* strikes a discordant note, which to Zola sounded a bit too much like regimentation. [51] Proudhon, however, believed that if artists could be integrated in the workforce, the result would be an expansion and wider dissemination of art. Everybody would be an artist: "The people need historians, scholars, writers and artists: but . . . one must bear in mind that what is accorded to them is accorded at the expense of the individual's well-being, and that this supposed category of workers must be progressively reduced, *for everyone ought to be an artist;* everyone ought to make art for himself; and consequently, everyone ought to contribute, without pay, to public pastimes."[52]

This view bears close similarities to Marx's observation about the "exclusive concentration of artistic talent in the individual and his concomitant suppression in the great mass," and to Marx's famous prognosis that "in a communist society there will be no painters but at most people who paint among other things."[53] For Proudhon, however, this expansion of artistic activity was not the result of a leisurely process of finding oneself; it was a program of democratic education. The arts were to prepare the ground for social equality, which they could do only insofar as they *both* embodied an "infinite" ideal *and* sprung from social reality: "A third revolutionary agent is indispensable: the ideal. The infinite in thought. . . . This ideal is something we create within ourselves, with our own hands. Art is the representation of this ideal."[54]

Yet this concept of the ideal has now become a front, behind which a tacit reversal of idealistic positions would take place. This is why Proudhon, as early as 1843, classified his traditional statement "The arts, sciences and trades are, in man, the special formulations of the absolute"[55] under the rubric of "égalité." Proudhon wanted to bring "the ideal" down to earth, but was unable to take the step of waiving this hackneyed concept completely. It would be up to Courbet, unconcerned with an intellectual disengagement from German idealism, to state in 1861: "The ultimate aim of realism is the negation of the ideal."[56] For both, however, art was an expression of the egalitarian principle, which Proudhon advanced just as much in opposition to the "principe autoritaire" (authoritarian principle) of Napoleon III as to "les socialistes hiérarchiques" (hierarchical socialists).[57]

Taken together, the factors just discussed add up to a contradictory picture. Proudhon was unable to resolve the tensions between the popular art he demanded and the idealistic art that existed, just as he was scarcely able to resolve the contradictions in his life. Yet it is precisely these difficulties that shed light on the conflicts of the Second Empire and on the nature of Proudhon's personal and intellectual problems.

A Proudhonist or an Anti-Proudhonist Painting?

A great deal can be learned about the philosopher's thinking and his personal situation from Courbet's *Portrait of Proudhon with His Family.* The *Carnets,* in turn, contain much previously overlooked material that can contribute to a better understanding of the picture.

Courbet depicted the philosopher, who died in 1865, in the situation that obtained in 1853, the significant year in which *La philosophie du progrès* was published.[58] The first state (fig. 43) showed Proudhon seated on the second of three steps in front of his house, meditating chin in hand, separated from his wife and children by a shrub placed adjacent to the steps—a monument set off from nature and from the living, as if time present and time future coexisted in the same moment. The situation is domestic, almost anecdotally treated, and its calm is enhanced by the pervading roundness of form. Yet the image is fractured to the core. Proudhon's immobility (to which the use of a photograph certainly contributed), the bland features of his pregnant wife, who was unable to model for Courbet—all of this lends the painting the character of a montage, an artificially fixed state that gives the impression of a glimpse into a *hortus conclusus*.

In view of the diverging directions of husband's and wife's gaze and pose, their total isolation from one another, it was only logical that in the second state, reacting to the Salon reviews and to Madame Proudhon's criticism, Courbet should have deleted her figure (fig. 44). Characteristically enough, he finally called the picture *Portrait of*

43 Gustave Courbet, *Portrait of P.-J. Proudhon in 1853*. Oil on canvas, 1865 (first state, before revision).

44   Gustave Courbet, *Portrait of P.-J Proudhon in 1853*. Oil on canvas, 147 × 198 cm, 1866–67 (second state). Paris, Musée du Petit-Palais.

P.-J. Proudhon in 1853, a title which completely omits the rest of the family. He also made the thinker's forehead higher[59] and lengthened the worker's smock which, in the first state, hung from Proudhon's shoulders like Anacreon's cape. This change, with a darkened hue in the trousers, increased the gravity and solidity of the figure. Moreover, the steps were reduced to two in number and Proudhon placed on the top step as if seated on the base of his own monument, while the motifs that recalled a sepulcher— slightly open door and gray wall—were toned down, decreasing the mood of reverence for the dead while increasing that of a vision of the future. By the same token, Proudhon's daughters, embodiments of his educational ideal, have been emphasized to the point of being independent figures. This processual dimension of the image is underlined by the diagonal of the steps, a device intended to mitigate the impression of stasis (both that of security and that of resignation). Although the philosopher's melancholy remains the dominant trait,[60] a process has nonetheless been set in motion, as may be seen from the combination of old bound books (historical knowledge) with new uncut ones (contemporary literature) and a manuscript (emergent ideas that point to the future). Even the hiker's hat symbolizes movement; Proudhon was continually on the road, walking from Paris to Besançon and even to Toulon,[61] recalling the itinerant preacher Jean Journet. Of Proudhon's two daughters, the elder one (with the slate) embodies the rational basis of education, and the younger one (with watering can) its emotional component. Both, incidentally, are very much *comme il faut,* obedient and studious, as Courbet rather denigratingly remarked.

It would seem that the artist felt a certain ambivalence toward his subject.[62] Wanting to honor Proudhon's memory with a *tombeau,* as such paintings of the deceased are called in France,[63] Courbet wanted at the same time to depict him in his everyday surroundings, at work, in the intimacy of his home—showing his reverence not only for the personality but for the philosophy of Proudhon by translating his ideas about the function of visual art into an actual painting, turning theory into practice. Hence the philosopher in this history painting[64] is both an exalted hero with a "front du génie"[65] and a common laborer in his smock; and the laborer is a *pater familias* as well.[66] Never before had the private life of an intellectual been so compellingly rendered, nor, for that matter, the intellectual's neglect of his family been made so painfully obvious—that very family which, in his own view, represented the model for society. In short, the painting contains both a description and a critique of Proudhon's doctrines.

An exhaustive analysis of the painting would go beyond the bounds of this brief discussion of sources. In what follows I shall neither review the tradition of the family portrait and the emergence of the small-family motif in art nor go into the history of philosopher portraits; neither the intellectual opposition between thinking and acting[67] nor the structural opposition between harmoniously rounded and disharmoniously faceted forms will be given the consideration they would otherwise deserve. What I am concerned with here is Courbet's exposure of Proudhon's patriarchal individualism, which is reflected particularly in his cool relationship to women.

Although the painting takes up Proudhon's idea of the small family as a core of the self-organizing society, at the same time it rejects this idea. For Courbet certainly could have retained the figure of Madame Proudhon in the second state, perhaps with alterations; yet he decided to completely expunge the portrait of the pregnant woman, which was thought scandalous. The change thus has a programmatic significance. Not only did Courbet raise a situation-oriented genre picture to the rank of a history painting with a claim to permanence, like a monument, but he showed a sensitive knowledge of Proudhon's relationship to his family and, what is more, addressed the existential issue of individual self-reliance—a central issue of the nineteenth century. It was not without good reason that Hippolyte Castille wrote in 1853, "Individualism is the idea of the century," and "Individualism, born of the great French Revolution, was received into the democratic family like a deformed child,"[68] leaving only two alternatives to the increasing "fragmentation of French society,"[69] both of them risky: either a "moi érigé en doctrine" (egotism raised to a doctrine) or "les tendances communistes" (communist tendencies).[70] Whether Castille, Engels, or Baudelaire—thinkers of the most varied persuasion agreed in considering the increasing isolation of the individual, in spite of continual advances in communication, to be the true paradox of the century. Courbet struck to the nucleus of this problem—not as might be expected by suggesting Proudhon's isolation from the masses, the feared "rouges,"[71] but by exposing the contradictions and ruptures in that very sphere where Proudhon still felt the identity of the individual was secure—in the family.

Isolation and Togetherness

There is a related, long passage in the *Carnets* that reads like a cry of despair. It is so personal in nature that one hesitates to publish it. Be this as it may, Proudhon's notes share a feature in common with many diaries of the nineteenth century—an almost schizophrenic vacillation between top-secret dossier and public announcement. Occasionally Proudhon even addresses posterity with a "cher lecteur";[72] the passage in question has a similar tone. Hence it would seem justified to quote this entry for January 1, 1855, in full, particularly as it seems to be based on a conversation with Courbet:

> One of my friends asked me the other day whether I regretted getting married. I tried to make him see that the question was badly put; that it could have no meaning except in personal terms, relating not to marriage, but to one's wife.
>
> As for this, a husband never confides his secret feelings; but perhaps I may be allowed to confide them to paper.
>
> I regret marrying so late. . . . I regret not marrying for love . . . something which had, moreover, become impossible for me more than twenty years ago; but something that I believe to be good in and of itself and, therefore, something that one can regret. My only love, never avowed, was but a dream. . . .
>
> I regret that my wife is not rich: no need to explain that. . . .
>
> Perhaps I would regret not having chosen a wife of spirit and of a more distinguished education: for spirit, education, talents, and knowledge are in and

of themselves, like wealth, good things. But today, as at the time when I met my wife, I remain firmly convinced of two things. One, no longer in love—and given that *my individuality would remain mercilessly true to itself*—that a better rounded education, talents, etc. . . . would in my wife be incompatible with the sort of life that I intended to live and that, in fact, I do live in a married state. Two, that these same qualities, incompatible with my objective, would be even more so given the qualities that I require in my wife: an absolute abnegation, limitless devotion, a zeal for housework, an unblenchingness in the face of any repugnant task, a complete abstention from any meddling whatsoever in my business, my work, my ideas, my contacts, etc.

My wife reads nothing; has never read a page of my publications, is wholly uninformed about my studies, doesn't poke her nose into my manuscripts; my heart being what it is, you have no idea what precious advantages I find in this behavior, in these marital relations.

And with all of this, this wife of mine possesses a fund of severe virtue, an abnegation, a natural generosity which I value highly, and for which superior talents and other advantages would be of no compensation to me.

I hereby close this chapter on the regrets, more or less persistent, of all of those who marry and which prove absolutely nothing against marriage itself. . . .

For me, marriage is one of the essential periodic forms of existence. . . .

First, there is paternity, which is for me a like a doubling of existence, a sort of *immortality*. In our times, paternity is feared. . . . This egoism, to my way of seeing, is death itself. A circle of children is a crown for the father of the family, from society's point of view as from that of nature. . . . I am so profoundly a family man and *patriarch* that for several years, after the fading of my first and only love, I had the idea of becoming a father, in return for certain monetary compensation, with the help of some poor young girl I might have seduced. . . .

After paternity, there is the household, the domicile, one of the most substantial things in civil and natural life. A bachelor really has no home. . . . The domicile, paternity, in a word marriage . . . has produced for me other priceless advantages. First, a greater amount of *work accomplished* . . . .

Second, an almost complete protection against the needs of the flesh . . . in short, a way of life, a discipline, an inner strength, a consistency, such as I had never found in bachelorhood. In a word, *with work, marriage has increased my liberty*.

For me, work and age, and for my wife, the fatigue of maternity and the wearing down which results from it, have brought about an almost total suspension of marital relations: we each have our own separate bed. I have the satisfaction of thinking that, if I have no more children, at least it is not a question of my cheating nature, neither my own nor my wife's; it is nature itself which shows itself to be impotent and which says to us: "Enough."[73]

This incredibly frank and basically despairing description shows, first, how strongly the need for rationalization and compensation influenced Proudhon's misogynist theories,[74] which appear in a different light when seen as a result of personal unhappiness. Second, it illustrates the degree to which the family had to serve as a refuge in circumstances of political helplessness and professional discrimination, where organized resistance was impossible.[75] This is why Proudhon was able to tell his opponents, "What is authority's function? Where is its seat? I place it in the family; you place it in the state, which fact I deny."[76] This patriarchal attitude took on an almost missionary quality with Proudhon, who saw himself in the role of Christ: "If I find twelve weavers, I am sure of conquering the world: what obsession I have to pursue men of property!"[77]

In conclusion, let us return to the painting. Courbet raised the monument of a patriarch to Proudhon; he also revealed his isolation. But at the same time he rejected the family ideology that, in the first state of the painting, was already shown to be untenable. He depicted Proudhon as a *counter-authority*, a personification of an authoritarian resistance to the "principe autoritaire" of the Bonapartist state, including a transition, made manifest in the image, from the past and the memory of his friend's death to the future, which will live on in Proudhon's children.

This brings us back to Proudhon's theory. His theory of society rested principally on the notion of equality, to the realization of which belonged an approach to art oriented to social needs. However, the plausibility of the equality principle was considerably shaken by Proudhon's authoritarian attitudes, in private life as well as in the field of economics (wage theory). Courbet, in turn, showed his awareness of this problem, not in theory, but in his portrait. Basically he depicted the philosopher in the guise of a republican, romantic artist, a "solidaire, solitaire."[78] Proudhon, like Flaubert, believed that he had to make a decision between his wife and his work, feelings and intellect.[79] In the painting, this decision has been made in favor of scholarship—at the price of loneliness.

6

Color and Worldview

Color as an Argument

TWO things are commonly associated with Courbet: a redefini-
tion of the artist's role in society,
and an upgrading of mundane
subject matter, depicted on large formats. But these alone explain neither the change he
precipitated nor the indignation his work touched off. His declaration "That's right,
art has to be dragged into the gutter"[1] implied not only a new appreciation of lowlife
and low subjects but above all a new approach to color, in which his philosophy found
concrete expression.[2]

Courbet argued his case with color. For him it embodied both utopia and
protest; his impulse to criticize society manifested itself in paint. Apart from his choice
of subjects, it was the way he handled the medium that prompted his contemporaries to
call him a dirty anarchist. His most lasting influence on posterity, too, proved to be his
palette. This was Courbet's true contribution toward the nineteenth-century transformation in the structure of painting, for once again he shifted imagination and artistic
innovation into the domain of color. If Delacroix called Courbet revolutionary, it was
not because of his political convictions but because of his palette;[3] and his friends
predicted a great future not for the self-styled "premier homme de France"[4] but for the
"roi de la couleur."[5]

From the vantage point of the present, neither appellation seems quite credible. To
us, most of his paintings look tranquil, homogeneous in tone, low in contrasts. In none
of them does the palette seem in the least scandalous, as it did to Courbet's contemporaries. To find out why this was so, I shall attempt to reconstruct the relationship

45 Gustave Courbet, *Château d'Ornans* (detail). Oil on canvas, 81.6 × 116.8 cm, c. 1850. Minneapolis Institute of Arts, John R. van Derlip Fund and William Hood Dunwoody Fund.

between color and content in Courbet's work, and to determine the place his palette holds in the force-field of emerging modernism, between Delacroix and Cézanne.[6]

Inner versus Outer World: Ego against Society

One of the basic features of Courbet's painting, and one that his contemporaries found particularly obtrusive, is a lack of distancing. His first attempts to draw attention to himself in this way date from the mid-1840s.[7] After the *Portrait of the Artist with Black Dog*,[8] he dramatized his features in irritating close-up in the two versions of *The Desperate Man*.[9] Here, the confrontation with the viewer, thanks to an unusual palette, becomes almost an assault. The intense bluish-green background propels the figure into the foremost plane, where backlighting leaves it in semi-obscurity. At the same time, this light-dark contrast draws a sharp line between individual and exterior world: one could cut the figure out of the canvas, as Delacroix later remarked about *The Bathers*.[10] It is by color that the artist expresses his need both to identify with and to detach himself from society. In unreal illumination, head and arm project from an immaterial, concave torso. A sparingly used red in the cape throws the upper part of this hollow shell into relief against a complimentarily hued natural backdrop. As in the *Self-Portrait as Sculptor*[11] done shortly before, yellow and red are evidently employed as historical references, *civilized* colors derived from a study of earlier painting. Courbet has begun to swim the river of tradition,[12] entered the battle between bright Salon colors and dull earth colors, that was soon to be decided in favor of the latter.[13] In this respect, too, the artist was engaged in defining his individuality. The conflict between inner and outer world, between civilization and nature, has led him not only to the verge of a theatrically staged catastrophe, but to the limits of material substance. Courbet can find no solution for the extreme foreground; no intervening ledge is present as a natural correspondence to his iconic fixation on self.

The unfinished character of this passage gives us a first insight into Courbet's painting process. Over the black, he has applied two patches of impasto white; these are the two noncolors that he was later to use as the basic constituents of an increasing abstraction. Over these (and over ocher) he then applied, with a wide, dry brush, that dull gray with which he was subsequently to protest against Ingres' distinguished Salon gray,[14] indeed against brilliant colors of any sort. Finally, we see a dull green, a color symbolic of the elemental power of nature in the raw. Color thus may be used with threefold significance in Courbet's early work: to separate disparate objects from one another; to concentrate the action in a single pictorial plane; and to express protest against the Academy.

Château d'Ornans of about 1850 (detail, fig. 45)[15] reveals a surprisingly different aspect of the artist's struggle with reality. As the detail of the small valley town shows, the surface of this painting is dry and gritty. Courbet apparently mixed his paints with a cheap, insoluble sand additive, as in *The Peasants of Flagey Returning from the Fair*,[16] which gives these pictures a rough, unacademic feel. The material nature of the compound itself precluded a smooth, flowing application, necessitating meticulous brushwork which is occasionally mitigated by textures loosely brushed over it—trees stretched over the slope like dark nets, houses set like mere points of light against black. Two painting procedures collide here: careful, consistent description of objects versus agitated forms that have lost almost all objective reference. Although the former approach, aiming to create a conventional objective context, still predominates, the tendency to produce an overall, abstract pattern is already strong. This dual manner communicates itself to the matter of the image as well. The village lies in shadow, like an isolated island; but it is not transfigured into an idyll. For all the charm of scene and rendering, the discontinuity of technique creates an atmospheric ambiguity much like that already described as a problem of individuation, in *The Desperate Man*,[17] and that invoked as a situation of social conflict in *A Burial at Ornans* (fig. 29).

In *A Burial*, Courbet relinquishes the fussy, timid articulation of *Château d'Ornans* in favor of blocky, dense passages in which objects have an equal intensity, and within which a free play of light across the surface occasionally develops.[18] The revolutionary paint handling in this picture is often commented on.[19] Yet what is decisive about it is Courbet's rejection of self-sufficient, "arty" colors, which brings the image into dangerous proximity to the real, unaesthetic, everyday world. The colors also tie visible things into an impenetrable obscurity, such that "the ground and the things depicted clash—each is given an equal but opposite pictorial weight. In *A Burial . . .* there is no neutral substance. . . . This is probably why the handkerchief with which Courbet's sister Zoë covers her face is so disturbing; instead of the face we expect beneath it, we find only blackness, which is just as matter-of-fact as it is terrifying. . . . The conflict between matter and human individuality . . . [remains] basically . . . unresolved."[20]

Courbet himself explained his method of working up a painting from a black ground in these instructions to young artists:

> Look for the darkest tone in the picture you want to paint; when you've found it, mark the place and apply this tone there with a palette knife or bristle brush; probably, no detail will be visible within this dark area. Then gradually go into the less dense, intermediate tones, trying to put them where they belong, then likewise with the half-tones. Finally, all you have to do is bring out the highlights, of which there should be much fewer than the Romantics are wont to use. Your work will light up at one stroke, once you've got the knack of it; the chance lights will just fall into place.[21]

At another opportunity he said, "You wonder that my canvas is black. But nature, too, when the sun isn't out, is dark and black; I do what light does, I just brighten the projecting points, and the painting gels."[22] With this, Courbet gives the organization of the canvas surface priority over a faithful depiction of separate objects. His aim was to lift objects from the coherence of nature, in order to plunge them back into that primordial black mass from which all things once emerged. In the case of *A Burial*, this frightening black mass, to a part of the Parisian bourgeoisie, seemed to materialize into masses in the political sense—the impending invasion of Paris by the rural populace.[23]

Neutral Light and Positivist Color Handling

Clearly, Courbet used colors in highly contradictory senses. They served to separate objects by complementary contrasts, and at the same time to unify them through a common coloring. Both approaches may appear in a single painting; both arose from Courbet's renunciation of the illusionistic handling of light. When Clark talks about "neutral tonality" in connection with *The Young Ladies of the Village*,[24] what he means is an even illumination of the picture surface, no accenting of significant elements to create a traditional center of interest. The colorful costumes only apparently belie this. Their hues cannot hold their own against the rest of the canvas; they find no echo. This is quite in keeping with the painting's intention. It was not for nothing that Gautier scoffed at these women as "graces after Courbet's particular manner"[25]—spruced-up country girls, without urban chic, but not rural enough to seem at home in their surroundings. This is why they appear so posed, so immobilized, a quality that did not go unnoticed by the caricaturists of the day. Reduced to puppet size, they stand more in front of than in the landscape, an opaquely self-sufficient mass of paint whose dull green fields and dense blue sky anticipate the impenetrability of Courbet's later landscapes. As Clark observes:

> It is not a dark painting, not a light one, it has a peculiar, neutral tonality. And it manages to suggest a certain kind of lighting—a certain kind of sunshine—without presenting light to us in the usual way with a register of shadows and highlights. There *are* shadows in *The Young Ladies of the Village*, but they hardly register as such—what establishes the light is the evenness of the pigment . . . just flat enough to make us perceive them as one substance, just worked and marked enough to carry the traces of sunlight. It is a painting which . . . allows us no convenient way to look at it except as one thing, one whole surface demanding an equality of attention.[26]

Courbet's positivistic handling, his egalitarian method of organizing a picture, achieved at the price of immobilizing figures and objects by color—precisely the method the critics derided as "wooden"—culminated in this canvas, and in *The Bathers* and *The Wrestlers* of the following year. But the peculiarity of Courbet's color is not restricted to a homogeneous pigmentation. Notably, the background is rendered more precisely than the foreground—flying in the face of every law of aerial and color perspective. By heightening the verisimilitude of the background, Courbet compensates the blurring of distant objects to the eye. Everything is of equal value; that is his point, a kind of positivistic corrective. His contemporaries, Champfleury and particularly Hippolyte Castille, the "socialist Job" of the Second Empire,[27] already recognized the affinity between realistic painting and positivistic philosophy.

Hasty Painting, Dirty Colors: Courbet as "Muckraker"

Almost every statement about Courbet's palette is qualified by evidence to the contrary. This is due to his anarchic love of experiment, augmented by the complex upheaval in art and society that took place about mid-century. Courbet continually changed his technique; he never adopted the systematic procedure of priming, under-painting in grisaille, using cool and warm colors in alternation, painting thick over thin—or any other standard method. Nor did his paint handling develop in any logical way; such accepted notions as a firm touch in youth and fluency in old age do not apply in his case. Finally, Courbet often used extremely diverse procedures simul-taneously. Nevertheless, his work contains enough clues to establish a sequence into which undated paintings can be fit;[28] in some cases, an analysis of color even permits a redating, or uncovers a misattribution.[29]

At about the same time as *The Young Ladies of the Village,* Courbet painted the *Portrait of Adolphe Marlet,* one of his most astounding works in this genre.[30] The dissolution of object-consistency just attained is decisively advanced here, with the aid of paint patches that continue beyond the borders of things, mitigated only by the traditional dark portrait background. The artist is now in full control of his means; bristle brush and spatula permit the paint to be laid on in broad swaths of heavy impasto, wet-in-wet, without the upper paint layers flowing into the lower ones. This "impatient" procedure allowed Courbet to exploit fleeting portrait opportunities or to finish a picture quickly when forced to, without needing to abandon differentiated color, though the resulting carelessness often later collided with the "master painter's" claim to craftsmanlike solidity. In the portrait of Marlet there is no unified facial tone. Over yellow and ocher Courbet has applied short strokes of gray-green, brown, pink, light yellow, and white; the beard is wiped over the mouth; the flesh colors are even run over the black of the hat. This type of multilayered application, particularly in render-ing flesh, is of course met with in seventeenth-century Flemish painting, whose influ-ence Courbet's portraits betray; but his blurring of contours goes far beyond anything ever attempted there. This procedure requires a perceptual shift on the part of the spectator, for the picture does not pull together into a consistent whole until seen from a certain distance. The issue of separation versus merger of ego and environment is decided here by an opening out of color to the outer world. In so doing, Courbet offers an alternative solution to that given in *The Desperate Man.* The color is about to open a dialogue between self and world.

In *The Bathers* of 1853 (fig. 8) and *The Meeting* of 1854 (fig. 30), Courbet again takes up the palette knife he began using in 1844, to apply large patches of impasto, an employment to which he also puts the broad spatula generally used as a scraper. This permitted a rapidity of execution comparable to that of the Marlet portrait and hitherto unknown in the nineteenth century. This skill proved advantageous particu-larly for the mass production demanded of the artist after the Commune. Swaths of paint pulled along and across the contours of objects (light green in *The Bathers,* dark green in *The Quarry*)[31] seem at first a mere supplement to local color, before more comprehensive color planes gain the upper hand. Yet the objects are already becoming assimilated to one another. This fact gives Courbet a key position in the development from Delacroix to Cézanne, from the romantic palette of the imagination to positivistic, object-linked color, and from there to abstract color fields. The direction Courbet would take was decided in 1853.

The palette of *The Sleeping Spinner*[32] may appear more subdued, but this is for good reason. The "stationary" rhythm of the color corresponds to the static composition the theme requires. The color scheme is "homey," dominated by a medley of gray, brown, and green, and a muted red, which are broadcast across the entire surface, without regard even for anatomic plausibility (as in the dress, which dissolves into the larger field). More important than anatomy to Courbet was the unfolding of a story calmly, expansively, over the whole picture plane. The tranquility of this image results even more from the paint handling than from the motif itself. Unlike *The Young Ladies of the Village,* the spinner is at home in her environment; the red of her dress accordingly recurs on the chair and in the bouquet, and the same is true of the nuances of white. In all, this lends the picture an open, planar, field-like structure all points of which are perceived simultaneously, a structure that to sympathetic critics like Champfleury communicated a feeling of rural calm and epic breadth. Most spectators, however, were dumbfounded by the pervading obscurity of *The Spinner,* which gave rise to the cliché that Courbet's paint was dirty, that it even "stank." That same year, in the wake of the 1853 Salon, appeared the caricature by Cham (fig. 98), in which a careless viewer is poisoned by the smell of Courbet's palette. "Dirty" now became the generic term to characterize the artist's renunciation of clearly defined objects, luminous colors, and idealization. For contemporary critics, this adjective implied not only an aesthetic but a political judgment. To use dirty colors (*couleurs boueuses*)[33] was to render not the dramatical aspect of ugliness but its dulling and leveling effect.[34] In fact Courbet did level; showing mundane life in a transfiguring light would have meant doing history paintings. And that was exactly what he did not want. Already in *A Burial,* and in *The Peasants of Flagey Returning from the Fair,* he used a gray monotone to give the proceedings the character of the everyday, familiar, mundane.

In turning to the people, by whom he said he was "nourished,"[35] Courbet sought precisely the "ugliness" of daily life, in order to revalue the base and insignificant not only in thematic terms, but also through form and color. The insults leveled at this painting as vulgar and ugly indeed contained a kernel of truth, residing in Courbet's programmatic "négation de l'idéal."[36] His attack from "the gutters of society" was also what provoked the caricaturists to whitewashing: purified color in art was tantamount to a preservation of public decency. The uncouth bodies of *The Bathers* and *The Wrestlers* (figs. 8 and 7) were objectionable enough, but it was their coloring that aroused racist sentiments; the swarthy wrestlers were decried as "niggers" and the bathers defamed as "Hottentot women."[37] Neither was a fundamental distinction made between light and dark paintings, provided that their colors were not unmixed and clear but grayed or oxidized, and thus dull even in substance. The lighter *Grain Sifters,*[38] for instance, was attacked on just these grounds. The later seascapes met as well with opposition because of their gloominess. On the other hand, if there is any luminosity in Courbet, it occurs in landscape paintings. The park background in *The Wrestlers* shines with relatively unbroken hues, as does most of *The Meeting* (fig. 30). Like the "dirty" colors, the "luminous" ones can be interpreted semantically. Nature had just been discovered for the purposes of personal recreation and social regeneration; Courbet's landscapes had brought him the title of "doctor" for society,[39] and like a doctor, or even a messiah, he confronts his patron in *The Meeting,* and the emperor in *The Painter's Studio,* at the center of which he places a landscape. Yet some figure paintings evince brilliant passages as well. That Courbet complied with the wishes of patrons like Khalil-Bey seems certain. But he also resorted to brilliance and over-naturalistic handling in reaction both to the competition of photography (against which he was later to set abstract structures) and to the academic competition of the Salon. *Sleep* of 1866[40] alludes to Ingres' coloration, but in renouncing that artist's suave, hothouse gray, it also represents Courbet's most concerted attempt to challenge his opponents' methods by taking them to the point of absurdity.

Dirty and pure colors, hasty paint application and old-master craftsmanship, were polarities which Courbet necessarily had to work through in reaction to the competitive situation just described, in which his self-assertion as a painter brought him both ever-increasing opposition and a spur to continuing innovation.

Object and Planar Color

The year 1855, in which *The Painter's Studio* was achieved, appears to have been a watershed not only in terms of content but in terms of technique as well. While in this secular painting Courbet squared off against tradition, dismissing "studio tone,"[41] in *Bunch of Flowers* (fig. 46) he recapitulated all of his attempts to turn his back on tradition. It should be said to begin with that this still life did not, as is often claimed, "pave the way for impressionism." Rather, this light picture provides a perfect demonstration of the theory that black is the primal source of all other colors. The extraordinary thing here is not the dark priming, but that instead of effacing this substructure by overlaying it, Courbet lets it participate in the final color effect. This wrenches the object open, leaves it unfinished in the traditional sense of the word. Out of protest against the meticulous finish of the Academy developed a new, open painting, liberated from the cage of norms, a painting that Bruyas called "free" as early as 1853, thus making it acceptable to the liberal bourgeoisie. The art critics, however, had no better term at hand to describe it than "sketch"; not unjustifiably, they felt this dissolution in painting anticipated a dissolution of social structures (the same word is used for both in the contemporary sources).[42] This is why later paintings, in which the whole surface is ripped open and "infiltrated" with black, could be termed "anarchistic."[43] For Courbet, this approach permitted a laying bare of the painting process from first to last, leaving preliminary stages to coexist with the final layer. The spectator is invited to reconstruct the process, whereby his distance from the picture is just as crucial as before: while the close view reveals the process of making, the subject matter does not cohere until seen from a distance.

In *Bunch of Flowers,* another technical idiosyncrasy appeared that would recur with increasing frequency from then on. The color of the ground that shows through in places is reapplied over it, in the same tone but thicker, so that the upper, raised paint layer interlocks with that beneath. Yet despite this optical leveling, the haptic difference between the paint applications remains. This lends the objects a vibration that

46   Gustave Courbet, *Bunch of Flowers*. Oil on canvas, 84 × 109 cm, 1855. Hamburg, Hamburger Kunsthalle.

they have neither in smooth-surfaced academic works nor in later impressionist paint-ings: there, this effect is mitigated by closer matching of colors and, at least initially, by an equal thickness of strokes. In this context, the Hamburg *Bunch of Flowers,* as an experiment in color, takes on a key significance for emergent modernism: it reduces objects to abstract color planes that lack indicators of depth; the pictorial space, instead of being defined, is left open to the spectator's imagination. Instead of a defined table top, we are given a mere rectangle; instead of a wall in the room, a green field that merges into black without a logical, objective reference to explain it; instead of a back wall or window, we see a light blue field, whose flocculent lighter passages lead us to read it as sky.

In this painting, Courbet stands at a crossroads. Though he may still depict the flowerpot conventionally, with shadows growing gradually lighter through gradations of brown and beige, apparently determined by light falling from the above right, at the same time, on the opposite side beneath the flowering branches, he places nonobjective black flecks as shadows on the table that seem independent of his ostensible light source. Description of the object and autonomy of color are held in equilibrium. A transition between the two is suggested by a few tones (reddish-brown, green, and white) that spread over the entire picture yet remain linked with objects, making them both objective and planar colors. Moreover, there are no major colors to which the others are keyed. Equality governs palette as well as theme. In this regard, Courbet uses color differently from his contemporaries and followers, not reveling in contrasts, as does Manet, for instance, in his *Lilac Branch,*[44] in which the full effect of the whites is brought out by a dark background. Courbet sets light hues against a light ground, and lets the blossoms in shadow recede into darkness. His flowers hold a position halfway between Delacroix's brilliant artificial arrangements and Cézanne's simple meadow flowers; their color lends them a quality intermediate between nature and artifice. The *Rocky Landscape near Ornans*[45] of about 1855 reveals a similar structure. The white on the trees in the foreground (fig. 47) can be read as blossoms or as pure paint, in a tone which, distributed over the pictorial field, suggests hope in personal and social regeneration. In what Théophile Thoré called "nature naturante"—vital, creative nature, as opposed to static, created nature—landscape and still life connect, in terms not only of subject matter but of coloration. This affinity is not accidental, as will be shown below.

The independence of approach and palette that Courbet strived for was more easily achieved in studies than in finished salon paintings. Yet the study for *The Young Ladies on the Banks of the Seine (Summer)* (fig. 48) is an important stage in the development of his color. Two color fields dominate the canvas, the English red of the dress, rendered with almost no interior structure, and the summarily articulated blue-green of the surrounding landscape. But simplification does not end here. The two colors interpenetrate, the reddish-brown ground surfacing in the middle of the riverbed and the dress being interspersed not only with the green of the leaves and ferns but also with that of the meadow beneath. To the right, the impasto surface is torn open with the spatula, revealing the underpaint here as well. The latent conflict between figure

47   Gustave Courbet, *Rocky Landscape near Ornans* (detail). Oil on canvas, 85 × 160 cm, c. 1855. Paris, Musée d'Orsay.

48 Gustave Courbet, Study
for *The Young Ladies on the
Banks of the Seine (Summer)*.
Oil on canvas, 78 × 100 cm,
1856. Private collection.

and nature, first sensed in the unfinished version of *The Desperate Man*, is reconciled
in this sketch. The uniformly applied red makes the figure tip forward, immaterial,
flat. The increasing lightness of the blue and green surfaces toward the river enhances
this effect. The eye, instead of being led gradually into the depths, stumbles over a series
of light and darker tones employed in disregard of aerial perspective—foreground and
background are no longer applicable terms here. Although the color scheme rests on
complementary contrasts, these merely reinforce the calmness of the motif, since the
contrasts are mitigated and made to seem natural by the dull (and also, by the way,
inexpensive) iron-oxide red. Seen thus, Courbet's red is still a protest against
Delacroix's Salon red—a fixation he was not to shake off until the 1860s.[46]
    His stay in Saintonge (1862–63) seems to have helped Courbet escape the pres-

sure of Parisian competition. *Portrait of Gabrielle Borreau* (fig. 49) is one we now tend to view, in terms of color, through the medium of Manet; that is, through Courbet's historical influence. Here the "irreconcilable opposition of black and white" that Elie Fauré[47] considered a romantic relic in his work, becomes the point of departure for a new integration of the subject in its surroundings. A network of light-blue and black and white touched with yellow spreads across the picture plane, regardless of the fact that the lace and broad black bands considerably diminish the figure's three-dimensionality. Another transition from objective delineation to color field is created by the

49   Gustave Courbet,
Portrait of Gabrielle Borreau,
or *Dreaming*. Oil on canvas,
63.5 × 77 cm, 1862. Art
Institute of Chicago, Winter-
botham Collection.

red flanking the subject, a stripe whose objective reference—to a sunset—remains ambiguous. The figure is, moreover, outlined with a brown band of thin, liquid paint, which propels it bodily into the foreground without transition. From above and below, the red is gripped, as in a vice, between passages of gray; the relationship this gray might have entered with the reflection of sun on water is avoided. Even where Courbet treats a theme like a sunset, he destroys the mood associated with it by introducing a black band to trip up the spectator. In *Portrait of Gabrielle Borreau,* the environment indeed takes on an aspect of threat, as the painting technique itself suggests—while the face is painted meticulously with a hair brush, the landscape is hastily, even brutally, thrown on with bristle brush and palette knife. So the opposition between civilization and nature remains, but the procedure used to express this relationship enters a state of flux.

Girl with Flowers[49] was also done at Saintonge. A nonobjective red, applied over a dark ground, accentuates the figure; the white of the dress, a flat expanse of color, unites with the white of the flowers. Never before had Courbet dared to so question the physicality of a figure, the closedness of contours, and the continuous surface of a garment, and all this on a relatively large format. Full vermilion, too, is used to create free color fields which, here and there defined as blossoms, designate no objects at all on the sides of the basin. Although Courbet's claim to autonomy is still expressed in such flecks of color, these no longer represent a protest, as in 1853, but a counterproposal. Basically, painting here belatedly demands a right long granted to business and commerce: free disposal over the object. Flower subjects could take the lead in this development because their polychromy was particularly conducive to an expansive, flat treatment without prejudice to the plausibility of the motif. Now, however, even narrative sequence and pictorial logic are "disturbed": the girl's dipping and bending, the movement of her hands, and the line of the garland hardly agree; or can be understood only as the result of different points of view. The color correspondences alone hold the picture together.

"Drama" and "Atmosphere"

Courbet's color is often said to lack atmosphere. *View of Frankfurt*[50] from the Deutschordenshaus over the Main River, which, unlike Quaglio's view, shrinks the city down to the size of Ornans, reveals a totally different side of the painter. Clearly, he has tried to capture the atmospheric quality of the local red sandstone, a color he lets pervade and link river, trees, buildings, and sky. Complementary contrast is reduced almost to monochromy in an effort to produce a unified, overall effect. The reddish-brown is applied partly impasto, partly as thin glaze, a distinction apparently intended to evoke both the lasting, substantial quality of the stone and its resonances, and also the evanescent atmosphere of late afternoon. The latter is also true of the sketchy *Lady of Frankfurt.*[51] It is amazing that this picture was accepted at all, since its summary handling and lack of brilliancy were like a provocatory gesture—in Frankfurt as in Paris. Maybe the painting served only as a "travel note" and was later to have been finished. Its mood, unlike that of *View of Frankfurt,* is ambiguous. There is a contradiction between the personal intimacy conveyed by the color and the stagelike presentation created by three equivalent horizontal bands—also an effect reliant on color. This effect is further enhanced by the dark green curtain in the middle, while the empty, sand-colored plane in the foreground reveals the loneliness and isolation of those acting "on a stage." In the first state, when the canvas still depicted a couple, this isolation was even more marked, a lack of communication between the figures that is detectable even under the final paint layer. At the same time, this self-dramatization is questioned by the dual perspective of the image, which combines an extremely low and an extremely high point of view.

The symbolism of *The Desperate Man* is raised to metaphor in *Stag Taking to the Water.*[52] Again the artist's concern is existential threat: the hunted animal, symbol of suffering and persecution, is a recurrent image in Courbet's work and one with which he identified.[53] The mood is set by a gloomy color-scale related to the monochromy of the late seascapes. Almost more threatening in effect are the bands of color at and above the horizon, brilliant yet icy cold; together with the masses of smoky black clouds, they lend the painting the mood of apocalypse. The tines of the animal's horns, raised into the light like hands in supplication, also belong to this iconology of death. The creature's isolation, its Passion, its vain struggle against fate, are all conveyed through color. The semantic significance of the subject as a traditional nature metaphor still holds during this pantheistic, neo-romantic phase of the 1860s. Such deep levels of meaning distinguish Courbet's hunting and history paintings from the mass-produced bellowing stags that came in their wake.

In a letter about the color of the Marseille painting, Courbet himself remarks on a further aspect, that of movement. "The way the light falls on the stag increases his speed. . . . The light beam striking him is sufficient to outline his form; he flashes by like a shot, like a dream."[54] What Courbet alludes to here is the theory of flecks of light as a means to depict fleeting movement, a theory frequently mentioned in the art criticism of the 1860s, if usually only to denigrate the careless paint handling it led to.[55] But this is only part of the story; the unnatural spotlighting of the stag's chest, though evoking its sudden emergence from the dark woods, isolates this area and freezes the movement, much as in the poised waves in the late seascapes.

Not because of its subject, but simply because it was "badly painted," the *Portrait of P.-J. Proudhon in 1853* (fig. 44) touched off a scandal in 1865, even though by then Courbet had long achieved recognition.[56] In hindsight, the reason is clear enough— Madame Proudhon was not pleased. More importantly, the picture seemed to provide incontrovertible evidence of Courbet's vices—dirty colors and careless painting. Even in its second state this work has the look of a study; today the deleted portrait of Madame Proudhon (like the man in *The Lady of Frankfurt*) is bleeding through again. As far as dirtiness is concerned, the preponderant gray and dim illumination (of everything except Proudhon's brow) are closely related to the provocative pictures of 1849–53. It cannot be ruled out that, to support his recourse to 1853, the date given in the inscription, Courbet might have employed these "dirty" colors to tone down the "memorial" character of the portrait. Proudhon as a man of intellect, and Proudhon as a man of the people, is the quintessence of the picture, mediated by color. The light-gray worker's smock, pigeon-gray trousers, sand-colored ground, the related hue of the children's clothing, and the gray-blue drapery into which Madame Proudhon's dress is transformed—all these point to the normal, everyday life of which even the great philosopher partook.

The circumstance that the picture was done in memory of Proudhon immediately after his death may explain the total lack of warm colors (with the exception of the red edge of a book, possibly a reference to the philosopher's undying influence). This cool palette further increases the detachment created by Proudhon's melancholy gaze and the void around him—factors that isolate the philosopher from his surroundings and strengthen the character of an obituary. This is color in mourning.

Abstraction and Concrete Reference

For Courbet's thoroughgoing transformation of painting technique, 1864 was a crucial year. It brought a nonobjective deployment across the canvas surface of mostly unmixed, light colors. In paintings like *The Oak at Flagey* (detail, fig. 50) and *The Bridge,*[57] a pure lemon yellow occurs seemingly at random in various passages regardless of the thing and the distance depicted. The same is true of the red sprinklings in the 1864 canvases *The Source of the Lison* and *Forest Glen.*[58] Strongly reducing the importance of the central motif, this technique neutralizes dominating elements such as trees, cliffs, and waves. Without entirely negating their existence, Courbet develops an almost homogeneous, egalitarian pictorial surface. This effect is enhanced by an undiminishing light and color intensity from foreground to background, collecting all the energy into a single plane. This is the source of the obtrusiveness remarked upon by the critics, the things and figures threatening to crush the spectator by "falling out" of the picture (see Nadar, figs. 14, left; 88).

Now, for the first time, a detail from one of Courbet's paintings can be read as totally nonobjective (*The Source of the Loue,* 1864; figs. 51 and 52). This depiction of primordial matter in an amorphous state can be seen as an abstract symbol of the primeval, and not merely as the material substratum of some philosophical formula. Admittedly, the suggestive nature of such a detail can lead one to falsify the intention of the whole painting. But this reading does fit in with the general character of Courbet's paintings around the mid-1860s.

As against the situation of 1855, Courbet is now evidently much less concerned with local, object-related color, a property he now distributes evenly across the canvas. This puts the academic principle of verisimilitude to flight, since here no body can be distinguished from any other by its color. We recall that the individualistic color of 1849—based on the "principle of diversified units"[59]—worked only because the separated elements or units were held together by a mass of black. Now, after having dissolved object contours, Courbet ceases to work towards separation and concentrates on unification, on a bridging of oppositions.[60] Yet still he proceeds cautiously when it comes to figures. He consistently pursues the principle of dissolution, so crucial to modernity, only where a certain plausibility can be retained despite it. That is why Courbet dares most where water, rocks, or foliage are concerned, that is, when he is depicting objects over which light freely plays. In *The Source of the Loue,* the color range extends from light yellow through ocher, green, and brown to a deep black, yet their juxtaposition or coexistence never seems particularly harsh or obtrusive; and the same holds for the even bolder color in *The Source of the Lison.* However, for all its abstract play of color, the threshold of comprehensibility in this image is never transgressed.

In figure painting, there is more uncertainty involved. To permit figures to merge in the natural scene would have contradicted the demands of exact representation too sharply for Courbet to have pursued this path to the end. In this regard, the study for

50   Gustave Courbet, *The Oak at Flagey* (detail). Oil on canvas, 89 × 110 cm, 1864. Tokyo, Murauchi Museum of Art.

51 Gustave Courbet, *The Source of the Loue*. Oil on canvas, 98 × 130.5 cm, 1864. Hamburg, Hamburger Kunsthalle.

52 Detail of fig. 51.

The Young Ladies on the Banks of the Seine and the sketchy Saintonge pictures remain exceptions. In pure impressions of nature, by contrast, a hasty technique appropriate to changing atmospheric conditions seemed admissible, because exactness in this field was harder to define, and imaginative experiment had greater leeway. Significantly, *Dressing the Dead Girl*,[61] the only large-format, scenic picture in which Courbet attempted to negate the separation between figures and space by assimilating their colors and dissolving the contours, remained unfinished.

Courbet proceeded, then, on two tracks. While forcing the process of dissolution ever further in the realm of nature, in figure painting he held fast to a separation of figure from environment. Figure and nature remained two different things for him. Unlike Cézanne, for instance, in whose *Large Bathers*[62] the ambient colors transmit themselves to the bodies and their contours dissolve continuously into the background, Courbet often frames his figures with wide bands of color, demarcating them from an exterior world in incessant motion. In *Woman at the Well* or *The Woman in the Waves*,[63] both of 1868, this principle becomes especially clear. Again, more movement and change is suggested in vegetal nature than in animal nature. This is also the source, in *Deer Hunting in Franche-Comté: The Ruse*,[64] of the discrepancy between immobilized deer, which as motif should be movement itself, and a natural setting rendered in almost violent motion. Courbet's quarrel with the director of the Frankfurt Academy, Herr Becker,[65] involved this very conflict. While the beautifully contoured stag, done "true to life" from stuffed models, found Becker's approval, the loosely painted foliage did not, because the leaves had not been drawn with botanical exactitude.

This dichotomy in paint handling can even occasionally be found in Courbet's figures. It sometimes led him to distribute different procedures among the different people in his paintings, thus as it were dividing a complex mental structure into its several components, making the image a montage of various approaches. In this way, *Three Bathers* of 1869[66] becomes a metaphor for a complex attitude toward reality. The picture is an incarnation of Champfleury's "art nouveau," an art at once poetic and brutal.[67] Most clearly separated from the surroundings, inserted into them in the most artificial way, is the nude in the middle, and the paint consistency is correspondingly strong, while the instability of her pose implies that she cannot exist as an autonomous being. Her companions are adapted to nature in color, the surrounding green running over one's skin and over the other's garments. Belonging to nature, dream state and the state of waking observation interpenetrate; but none of these states is fully integrated or expressed in any *single* figure.

On the Way to Synthesis

Courbet was not to bring together the strands of his analysis of reality into tentative synthesis until the late sea pictures, which have been called the culmination of his oeuvre.[68] They indeed reveal a new view of the world, and at the same time a new quality in painting. This development proceeded in two phases, in rapid succession. At

Trouville in 1865, Courbet still worked very much in the traditional vein of seascape. The *Sunset*[69] he did that year recalls the dramatic maritime scenes of earlier Dutch painting. In the following years he then began to use the same motif to show the primordial power of the open sea, as an antidote to mythological or "touristy" beach scenes. He confronts the usual tasteful arrangements in this genre with an arbitrary choice of viewpoint,[70] which in turn renders the choice of motif arbitrary—image and individual motif in effect coincide. The sea is the wave, the wave the sea. The issue of the equality of objects, indeed their definition and with it the question of liberating color from discrete objects, is raised to a new level. Even the reference to a specific time of day or year loses pertinence. As Castagnary writes, "It is no longer a matter of partial and local description . . . [but of] the eternal drama that is played out on all coasts in all countries."[71] This negation of time and place has consequences for color. Especially in the small canvases, it becomes *overall* color, identical with the image both as means of production and as product. *Seacoast with Sailing Ship*[72] is striking for its cloud masses laid on thickly with the spatula and shot through with blacks, reds, and blues, clouds of that extreme atmospheric density which Cézanne would develop further in such paintings as *Quai de Bercy*.[73] These clouds are the true subject of the picture. Beneath them stretches a sea that might be composed of sand, with no *repoussoir* of any kind, separated from the deserted beach by a thin black bar. A few light yellow stripes evoke sunlight on the water, and (as a concession) we are given a golden yellow sail against blue—one of the few places where Courbet allows himself the pleasure of a complementary contrast.

The tendency to telescope depth and melt the planes into one, the lack of any definite vantage point for the spectator, the way everything in the picture is pulled together into a single entity without sacrificing legibility—this is the surprising synthesis achieved by an artist who began by firmly establishing discrete objects. Yet what one might have expected to develop—an impressionistic technique—does not materialize. What is astonishing about the big late pictures is that they gain in solidity *despite* the increasing tendency to dissolution. The Paris version of *The Cliff at Etretat* (detail, fig. 53) and the two large wave canvases in Paris (detail, fig. 54) and Berlin have a static, cold effect. Their resemblance to marble, even to solid walls, has indeed been justly emphasized, even though they as yet reveal no trace of the iciness of color that entered Courbet's work after the Commune.

This consolidation indicates that Courbet's path toward abstraction was by no means straight and narrow.[74] Rather, he adopted abstract structures *only as a means to depict movement in a static medium*. He resolved waves or the play of light on cliffs into abstract structures in order to translate the motion of the motif into an activity on the picture plane.

Color has a totally different function, for example, in Monet's *Beach at Trouville* (1870, London).[75] The bold, unmediated white on the dress of the woman in the left half of the picture serves to relate unconnected objects, a use of color to create pictorial unity. But Courbet, even where he scatters a color across the entire surface, works with clear oppositions. The uniting and separating powers of color are equally strong; the

53   Gustave Courbet, *The Cliff at Etretat* (detail). Oil on canvas, 133 × 162 cm, 1869. Paris, Musée d'Orsay.

54 Gustave Courbet, *The Wave* (detail). Oil on canvas, 117 × 160 cm, 1869. Paris, Musée d'Orsay.

picture is held together by this very equilibrium, which lends it the appearance of monumental timelessness despite the activity, even agitation, of the surface. This is why Courbet can afford so much "disorder" in detail, without a loss of solidity. In *The Cliff at Etretat,* the whitest white occurs in the middle of the picture, where the base of the cliff meets the sea; then come alternating bands of dark and light (and also of warm and cool) laid out parallel to the edge of the picture, zones continued by the yellow sand in the foreground, the sand-colored clouds, and the cool blue sky. This organization of motif and colors from the center outwards not only lends formal stability to the whole but corroborates Courbet's conception of the power of elemental nature to resist the exploitation of civilization. Courbet's Etretat is worlds apart from the Etretat of the Bonapartist *haute bourgeoisie*.[76] No tourist has strayed onto *this* beach, and even the seldom remarked figures in the foreground are associated with and subordinated in meaning to the sea. This elevation of nature is accomplished through color.

The pictorial organization just described culminates in the wave pictures. Seldom has the concrete appearance of paintings been so determined by their materials, and seldom before has paint been so thickly, densely applied, as if to evoke the invincibility of nature by sheer coarseness of surface. The evanescent phenomena of the elements water and air—foam and clouds (and, in other pictures, snowflakes)—are used symbolically to express the tension between permanence and change. These opposites are held together by color, which now, in the shape of discrete, abstract patches, does what object-related color did in the beginning—place concrete substance in a relationship to the world.

This new use of color refers beyond the work of art. Seemingly autonomous, this liberated color yet made the reproduction of reality appear problematical at exactly the time when the function of painting was being displaced by new media, and familiar conditions of life and perception were being dissolved. In this context, Courbet's method of painting might be described as a dual reaction to modern society and technology. The artist was concerned to find structural correspondences to a reality increasingly shaped by bureaucracies and industrialization (which disturb the individual's rapport with nature) while at the same time retaining his naiveté of vision in the face of this abstraction. He showed that even a mechanized society still has resources at its disposal by which it can approach freely, without obstacles or the greedy stare of domination, a reality still in the making. With this both revolutionary and retrospective approach, which stood for progress not only in the history of style, Courbet ventured into problems of modernity that remain particularly acute today.

7

A Note on the Late Work

Demystification

COURBET's late work has a slightly dubious reputation. Not that the final phase of his career is lacking in outstanding canvases—it is enough to recall *Lake Geneva at Sunset* in St. Gallen, *Château de Chillon* in Essen, or the *Portrait of Régis Courbet, the Painter's Father* in Paris.[1] What is really lacking is a consistent view of this final period. Meier-Graefe's opinion about the gradual "decline" of Courbet's painting after the mid-1860s still stands opposed to Champfleury's praise of the "immaterial" quality of the late seascapes he so admired,[2] and subsequent research has yet to provide an explanation for such conflicting views.

The phenomenon of an artist's late work is frequently defined in terms that transcend the individual and his epoch, being treated as something of an anthropological constant in art. Such determinations are in turn generally influenced by the commentator's tendency to identify and empathize with his subject, to project his own self-image into the artist under discussion. Psychologically speaking, artists' mature periods are just as often said to reflect a withdrawal from society as an adaptation to its demands; objectively speaking, they are just as often called a heterogeneous skein of divergent approaches as they are believed to be a distillation of a lifetime's experience. Formal elision or simplification are read as an attempt to achieve harmony or to bring about a reconciliation, whereas complication in this regard is thought to indicate a dealing with setbacks, or an attempt to justify divergent expectations. Judgments of this type are invariably based on that *equation of life with work* the inadequacy of which, one would have thought, has been amply demonstrated.[3]

Created in the shadow of death, an artist's late works fall easy prey to categorizations of this type. Where they succeed in eluding them, criteria for comparison are in turn often lacking. For instance, it would be hard to draw conclusions about Courbet from the observations on specific forms in Beethoven's late works made by Theodor W. Adorno.[4] The problem is not that none of the above hypotheses holds true for Courbet's oeuvre, but that, even excluding the obviously irrelevant aspects, several of them apply *simultaneously* to the final period. The only way to arrive at a more precise definition, it seems, would be to take the sum of a large number of separate, detailed analyses. This would appear all the more desirable for the fact that the contributions of assistants, particularly in the late period and most obviously in the slightly less than five years of Courbet's Swiss exile (mid-1873 to his death in late 1877), throw open the door to attributions and disclaimers.

Any attempt to distinguish certain characteristic traits of the final period is bound to be complicated by the fact that Courbet lived to be only fifty-eight, which makes it difficult to speak of a mature style in the usual sense of the word. Then, too, breaks in the development of his oeuvre are barely discernible. From beginning to end—from his initial attempts to capture the spirit of the Franche-Comté region to his last visions of the château de Chillon on Lake Geneva—we find old-masterly verisimilitude combined with a great capacity for abstraction; we see both solid masses of paint and rapid, slashing strokes; in one and the same picture, often abruptly juxtaposed, we find cold and warm colors, impasto and thinned or glazed paint application. Also, Courbet favored earth colors throughout his career. The same holds for the uppermost paint layers: from the early 1850s to the end of his life, Courbet applied the paint with a combination of brush and spatula and scraped off excess paint with the aid of his famous palette knife.[5]

Steps of Evolution

Nevertheless, there are turning points in the oeuvre which can be evaluated as such even when subsequent works occasionally show symptoms found in earlier ones or vice versa. In a previously unknown oil sketch from the early period, depicting the Brême brook where it emerges from a wooded cleft (fig. 55), Courbet has remained mimetic despite the verve of his paint handling; that is, he reveals a continuing interest in objective fidelity (as in the rendering of the crows).[6] With *After Dinner at Ornans* of 1848–49,[7] his involvement with seventeenth-century Netherlandish painting—which at that period was seen primarily in terms of chiaroscuro—reached its culmination. The *Portrait of Adolphe Marlet* of 1851[8] represents probably the first finished canvas in which the colors extend beyond the contours of the things they designate, as in the flesh color brushed over the black hat. In *The Meeting* of 1854, the surprising feature is the light-hued palette with which Courbet took leave of his previous subdued tonal range reminiscent of the Old Masters. As the detail illustrated shows (fig. 56), lights and darks are interwoven in a wild tangle even in the areas of shadow; from this point on, light and shade were to become "autonomous" in the sense that, no longer depen-

55   Gustave Courbet, *The Brême (Winter Landscape with Birds)*. Oil on canvas, 21.5 × 40 cm, dated 1836. Schweinfurt, Coll. Georg Schäfer.

dent on the direction of impinging sunlight or the quantity of displaced light, they could advance to the status of independent pictorial values. Nevertheless, the traditional, subdued tonal range continued to be used as a secondary device, as evinced by a major work begun that same year, *The Painter's Studio* (fig. 28), in which both approaches are juxtaposed.

It is true that the crisis of 1857 brought changes in conception and induced Courbet to depict the cliffs of his native Franche-Comté as impregnable fortresses—the word was Champfleury's[9]—as well as to consider unsullied nature a repository of "indépendance."[10] Yet actual changes in *form* really did not occur until his collaboration with Corot in Saintonge: in the stemlike tree trunks in the canvases of 1862–63, an erosion of objective substance seems to take place, and in *Undergrowth at Port-Berteau: Children Dancing*,[11] these attenuated growths have become mere *ciphers* for trees. This graphic abbreviation is paradoxically interwoven with the corporeality characteristic of earlier phases in *The Charente at Port-Berteau* of 1862 (fig. 57), where individual trees, hardly recognizable as such, stand interposed like stakes between bushy willows and seem to have no more than a provisional existence. The foliage of the willows, too, appears to have been thrown on in extreme haste.

A decisive step in the direction of a desubstantialization of the object was taken in

56   Gustave Courbet, *The
Meeting* (detail). Oil on can-
vas, 129 × 149 cm, 1854.
Montpellier, Musée Fabre.

the source paintings of 1863–64.[12] Every subsequent development toward "facile"
rapid paint handling—an attempt to find pictorial equivalents for flux in nature—was
based on the flecks of light playing over a dark ground seen here. When extended over
the entire picture plane regardless of observed nature, this fleck structure, initially it
seems without design on Courbet's part, resulted in compositions whose character
approached the abstract. The artist's penchant for handling large areas with the palette
knife augmented this effect, which to his contemporaries must have seemed grossly
negligent. Examples are the 1866–67 state of his *Portrait of Proudhon* (fig. 44) and
The Rest during the Harvest Season (Mountains of the Doubs) of 1867,[13] images that
coalesce only when viewed from a certain distance—or on the reduced scale of
reproduction.

    To complicate matters, Courbet's color now began increasingly to lose its char-
acter of objective designation. The first state of his Proudhon portrait drew criticism

57   Gustave Courbet, *The Charente at Port-Berteau*. Oil on canvas, 43 × 61 cm, 1862. Philadelphia, Philadelphia Museum of Art, John G. Johnson Collection.

from his friend Thoré because the philosopher had been rendered in the same gray as the wall behind him.[14] Although this had the semantic effect of emphasizing the mood of mourning, such color handling no longer fulfilled the expectations of Salon audiences. At the same time, Thoré noted a decline in content, a diminishment in the protest character of Courbet's work.[15] The remark was perspicacious, for the artist's interest in addressing societal issues indeed seems to have flagged, even before the Paris Commune.[16] His tendency to focus provocatively on certain figures or objects evidently decreased as well. Although the figure remained present as an objectively designated *opposite number* into the 1860s, it was attacked from the edges, and, apparently under the influence of a "freer" landscape approach, subjected to the new, sketchy, abstracting manner. The best example of this is Courbet's extremely free 1869 copy of *Malle Babbe* by Frans Hals. A detail of the ruffles (fig. 58) makes it abundantly

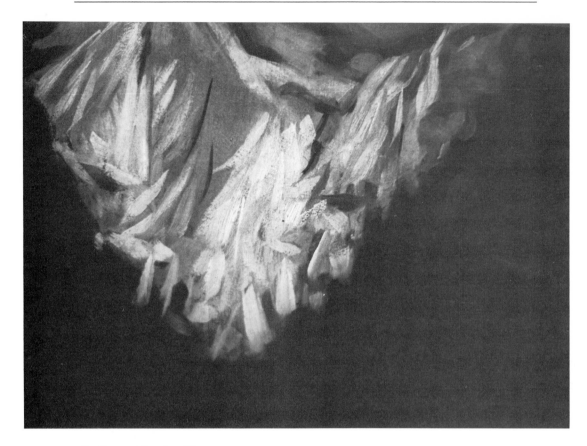

58 Gustave Courbet, *The Witch* (*Malle Babbe*), after Frans Hals (detail). Oil on canvas, 85 × 71 cm, 1869. Hamburg, Hamburger Kunsthalle.

clear how the paint, applied in various directions with a stiff-bristle brush, fans out into pure pattern.

The salient quality of the final creative period, the years between imprisonment and death (1871–77), lies in the fact that without explicitly addressing contemporary problems and current events—unless by negating them through a turn to unspoiled nature—Courbet renewed his concern with the objective opposite number, yet in such a way that the entire picture surface now assumed this function. In *The Trout* of about 1873–74 (fig. 59), principal motif and pictorial plane coincide. There is no escaping this creature; in terms of pictorial effect, it is victim and culprit in one.[17] The artist's opposite number in nature—whether fish or tree, cliff or ocean wave—was now given so much visual weight that, at least theoretically, it could once again be read as a reference to social conflict—as barrier, wall, barricade, or as a symbol of primitive authenticity or profound injury. At the same time, *The Trout* reveals a growing insubstantiality of the objective realm, producing uncertainty as to whether soil, stones, and clouds were really intended to designate these things or to remain pure paint. By implication, this means that terms like *solidity* and *dissolution* begin to lose relevance to Courbet's art at this point.

As this brief review indicates, Courbet's form was caught up in a continual tension between integration and disintegration. This makes it difficult to detect evolutionary criteria in his art. The attempt is complicated by another circumstance: instead of logically developing a conception once arrived at, he repeatedly rejected one aspect of it or another. For instance, the pervasive brightness of *The Meeting* or of *Bunch of Flowers* (figs. 30, 46) was a passing phenomenon and did not lead to impressionism. By the same token, quiet, almost static compositions are found in the 1870s alongside agitated, well-nigh nervous imagery, and smooth, transparent paint application alongside heavy impasto. The agitated seascape *The Wave* in Winterthur (1869) and the tranquil winter landscape *Les Dents du Midi* in Hamburg (1876)[18] cannot be reduced to any meaningful common denominator. And even paintings with shared motifs like the numerous variations of *The Cliff at Etretat* or *Château de Chillon*, done during the last ten and five

59   Gustave Courbet, *The Trout*. Oil on canvas, 55 × 89 cm, c. 1873–74. Zurich, Kunsthaus.

years of his career, respectively, are as different as they could possibly be with regard to paint handling and evocation of movement and change.[19]

Collaboration Problems

In sum, great contrasts and abrupt divergencies in quality must be taken into account when dealing with Courbet's late work in particular. Added to this is the increased cooperation of assistants, with the result that the final period appears largely determined by what might be called "hybrid imagery." Courbet's first mention of assistants occurred in the year 1872, when he wrote, "The painters are arriving in our area. Rapin, Jean-Jean Cornu, a few Swiss and Pata are already here."[20] Whether these artists were already working for him at the time is a moot point. During his Swiss exile, which began on July 23, 1873, Courbet evidently relied on the assistance of Ernest-Paul Brigot (1836–1910), Auguste Morel (dates unknown), Marcel Ordinaire (1848–96), and André Slomczynski (1844–1909), but especially on that of his earlier collaborator, Chérubino Pata (1827–99).[21] His entourage also included such painters as François Bocion (1828–90) and Auguste Baud-Bovy (1848–99).[22]

In the discussion that follows, I shall focus only on those artists from the list who created original works, permitting a distinction to be drawn between their style and Courbet's: Pata and Ordinaire. Original paintings by Brigot and Morel have not come to light; Baud-Bovy and Bocion, like Cornu, who was of the same age as Courbet (Cornu's dates are 1818–76), appear not to have been involved in any coproduction. Nor has evidence turned up that the pupils who from time to time gathered around Courbet in Paris (such as H. Hanoteau)[23] actually collaborated with him.

Still another complicating circumstance is that Courbet occasionally "lent" his signature to his assistants, thus conniving in the counterfeiting of his works: "No one has succeeded as well as he at false Courbets."[24] An actual forger's studio was raided in Marlotte in 1890; it had supplied Courbet imitations to Brussels, where they were signed and, to produce the craquelé effect, even heated. One of the motifs frequently "reproduced" in this way was the *The Stream of the Black Well* (*Puits noir*), which Courbet had depicted several times during the 1860s. The forger employed assistants who specialized in light-green foliage, undergrowth and rocks, and deer à la Courbet. Brussels also provided the market for imitations by an anonymous pupil who had previously worked with him in Switzerland and who concentrated on cliffs and the Lake Geneva motif.[25] On the whole, the fakes and imitations blur the picture of Courbet's last twelve years more than any previous phase. After 1866, when *Covert of Roe-Deer by a Stream at Plaisir-Fontaine* earned him a medal and international recognition, his canvases were all too easily marketable.[26]

As necessary as it is to follow up the traces of the forgeries,[27] this would go far beyond the scope of the present essay. However, no serious discussion of the late work can dispense with a glance at Pata and Ordinaire. As long as Courbet research continues to ignore the distinction between these two artists' hands, every remark on the final period is bound to remain speculative.

Pata's paintings evince a limited repertoire of motifs and stylistic traits; his preference for rugged cliffs and tree groupings with foliage dabbed with highlights is obvious. Apart from these scattered lights, his palette is somber. As regards his treatment of objects, a development can be discerned. Pata's *Mountain Landscape* has not unjustifiably been called "hyper-realistic,"[28] on account of the precise, well-nigh academic rendering and contouring of the things represented. This painting was likely executed prior to 1870. In his *Winter Landscape* of 1873 (fig. 60), clearly bounded "color fields" begin to appear, as in the sharply delineated patches of bare ground under the pines. In the foreground, a looser technique has been employed to suggest bushes, which are composed of paint particles applied with a stabbing brush. Some of these particles have even been spread with the palette knife à la Courbet.

Yet despite this dexterous technique, there is little sense of movement in Pata's work. This is especially true of *The Cliff at Etretat*, a canvas of 1878.[29] Here the paint application is rougher, heavier; the cliffs and the rocks on the beach are built up of flecks of impasto. The intermediate areas are filled in with thinned color, giving rise to

60   Chérubino Pata, *Winter Landscape*. Oil on canvas, 50 × 78 cm, 1873. Ornans, Musée Maison Natale Gustave Courbet.

numerous small, separate zones which have a pattern-like effect. Pata's generally have a rougher appearance than Courbet's, but they also seem more uniform and therefore less surprising—nature in suspended animation. A further reason for this static effect is found in the *Black Well*.[30] Evidently Pata was in the habit of first establishing a focus around which to arrange the composition. As this focus usually lies in the lower third of the central vertical axis, the beholder has an unhindered view and free access to the middle ground of the picture. But basically this center remains empty—in contrast to the tension-filled core so characteristic of paintings from Courbet's own hand.

The distinction is less easily drawn in the case of later canvases by Pata. In his *Seaside* of 1877 (fig. 61), composition and paint application evince a looser and more energetic approach that seemingly comes very close to that of Courbet. Still, there is an obvious tendency in works of this period to a scattering or isolation of impasto passages, accompanied by a waiver of coherent color masses.[31]

Based on these criteria, a whole series of canvases can be ascribed to Pata which are either dominated by a flocculent technique with particulated fields, as in several

61   Chérubino Pata,
Seaside. Oil on canvas, 64.5
× 81 cm, 1877. Private
collection.

wave paintings, or which have the character of a silent, empty scene loomed over by a precipitous cliff.[32]

Marcel Ordinaire is a different case entirely. His paintings have a lighter feel, and his objects, apart perhaps from his initial attempts, are much more smoothly rendered than Pata's. Courbet's tendency to abstraction, to a dissolution of the object in his later work, is something Ordinaire seems almost oblivious to; his versions of the Puits-Noir motif indulge in a literal enumeration of branches and leaves, and as loosely as the lighter areas of foliage, highlights, and foaming water are brushed over the darker ground, a coherent interweave never quite comes about. Ordinaire's paintings are composed additively rather than "d'un seul jet." His fall landscape *Ravine of the Brême at the Black Well* (fig. 62) completely lacks that gnarled, tangled effect that Courbet, and even Pata, were able to lend such remote stretches of countryside. *The Source of the Lison*, dated 1880,[33] is another clear example of Ordinaire's tendency to narrative enumeration—mill plus cliff plus waterfall. And the colors seem to form superimposed layers that look as though they could be peeled off; the foaming water-fall is spread over the rocks like a loose veil.

Based on such observations, a number of paintings hitherto considered authentic Courbets could be attributed to Ordinaire, as for instance the landscape *The Loue at Scey-en-Varais,* executed around 1873, on which doubt was indeed cast years ago. The same holds for *The Pool* and *Swiss Landscape at Sunset,* canvases that are dated to the exile period.[34]

Several of the criteria mentioned are found in the compositions we have termed hybrid. One example may suffice: *View of Franche-Comté,*[35] a painting of 1873 that evinces the full professionalism of Courbet's spatula and palette-knife technique, but whose repeatedly altered date and signature might provide reason to doubt its authenticity. Still, the image was obviously created "d'un seul jet," and its alternation of light and dark, tranquil and agitated passages is very much in the vehement manner characteristic of many securely identified Courbets. Except for the aquatic plants in the foreground (perhaps by Ordinaire, who may also have added the final touches to the shrubs on the left), this canvas would seem to be largely from Courbet's own hand.

A great deal more fieldwork of the kind just attempted will have to be done before the debate on Courbet's late period can really get underway. If we were to employ the rigorous yardstick of such critical catalogues raisonnés as that now being compiled on Rembrandt, the category A (undoubtedly by his own hand) could seldom be applied to the work of Courbet's exile years, or even to most of the post-1866 oeuvre; almost everything would fall into category B (uncertain attribution) or C (authenticity doubtful; workshop contribution probable). It is well known that most of the paintings Courbet supposedly executed in Ste.-Pélagie Prison in 1871 were actually done at a later date, or were not done by him at all; even the unsigned *Self-Portrait at Ste.-Pélagie* was likely begun after his release, and possibly finished by Marcel Ordinaire.[36] We can only speculate on the extent to which Courbet and his friends exploited the pathos of authentic "prison work" to boost sales; the defamation campaign that came in the wake of the Commune would have been ample justification. Successful exhibitions with Durand-Ruel provided further fuel for extensive "coopération." Soon Courbet was able to report to his parents from Switzerland: "We are earning 20,000 francs a month,"[37] which implies that he and his assistants were able to sell a good dozen medium-format paintings a month. As I have argued in another place, about a fifth of the canvases by Courbet's own hand are virtually muffed,[38] and a good proportion of these unfortunately date to the exile period.

Creating a Swiss Identity

Despite the considerable problems involved, I shall discuss several works of Courbet's late period that not only deserve the mark of authenticity but reveal the

62   Marcel Ordinaire,
*Ravine of the Brême at the
Black Well.* Oil on canvas, 73
× 92 cm, 1874. Besançon,
Musée des Beaux-Arts.

63 Gustave Courbet, *Grand Panorama of the Alps with the Dents du Midi.* Oil on canvas, 151 × 210 cm, 1877. Cleveland, Cleveland Museum of Art, John R. Severance Fund.

outlines of a final and mature worldview. On the face of it, this outlook on life was largely determined by the artist's second home in Switzerland. Apart from a few portraits, he used his exile to depict Lake Geneva and the Alps exclusively. Yet for all their "local color," the results frequently reached a level comparable to true history painting. In *Grand Panorama of the Alps with the Dents du Midi* (fig. 63), this holds even for the format; measuring 151 by 210 centimeters, the painting fulfills Courbet's self-imposed demand for *grandeur* in terms both of subject matter and sheer size. According to Castagnary, Courbet intended to submit the canvas to the Paris World Fair of 1878, and he worked on it until May 16, 1877, the day on which the fall of Minister Jules Simon quashed all hopes of a pardon.[39]

A hundred years later, at the Paris Centennial Exhibition of 1977, *Grand Pan-*

orama of the Alps was justly spotlighted as representing Courbet's legacy. Viewed as a summing-up, it also contains his reply to impressionism, which might be paraphrased thus: Modern painting does not consist entirely in an aesthetic valorization of the boulevards and cafés-concerts of Paris, nor in painters' appropriation of the industrial landscape and recreation areas on the city's outskirts; at least equally important is its recourse to nondomesticated nature, as the truly progressive "pièce de résistance" of the individual. In other words, with his late landscape painting Courbet mounted objective resistance to Haussmann's modernism, but without taking up the subject matter of the "nouvelle peinture."[40] Still, if in earlier pictures he had declared the Franche-Comté region a refuge from Bonapartist centralism, he now depicted the high Alpine region as a landscape which the beholder could view but scarcely enter. The broad "approach" in the foreground of earlier compositions[41] was now replaced by an "island" cut off from its surroundings on all sides, which became as inaccessible as the distant mountains.

A reply to the impressionists might also be seen in the technique employed in *Grand Panorama*. While in the foreground the paint handling produces an effect of dissolution, in the background peaks it evokes one of denseness and solidity. This confirms, on the one hand, Courbet's method of describing material properties in terms of paint application—the high meadow ground is differently composed from the mountains, more subject to weathering and decomposition, and therefore rendered with a higher degree of dissolution. On the other hand, the paint handling constitutes an objection to axiomatic impressionism—Courbet too is fully aware of the fact that things are in continual flux, but he considers this merely *one* aspect among many others. To him, impressionist technique is a means of painting, not its end. This may explain why both dissolution and resolution of paint structure are found side by side in *Grand Panorama*.

Whether the broken, serried earth in the foreground was intended as finished or was due to an abrupt interruption of work (Castagnary noted that, "discouraged and broken, he stopped painting")[42] must remain an open question in this particular case, though similarly disintegrated zones exist in other paintings of the exile period.

In sum, as a culmination *Grand Panorama of the Alps* provides a good basis from which to review Courbet's late work as a whole. This late work includes two previously unknown canvases which I should like to discuss in some detail. One of these is titled *Grand Landscape with Goats* (fig. 64).[43] It represents a high mountain valley irrigated by a branching stream. Beyond scattered rocks, brush and sparse ground cover, a cleft opens to reveal distant meadows. Above them hang heavy gray clouds, shot through with red and tinged with yellow from below by the setting sun; the view to the horizon is cut off at the left by rocks and trees. The stream forms a deep pool, then falls in rapids toward the foreground, where its course is divided by a huge boulder; to the right it disappears behind a grassy outcrop to reappear, tinged dark, swampy brown, in the lower right corner, where it forms a background for the signature. This zone is enlivened by yarrow, water lilies, and a variety of long-stemmed red flower. In the middle ground, a shepherdess rests on her staff as three goats browse around her.

64 Gustave Courbet,
*Grand Landscape with
Goats.* Oil on canvas, 70 ×
120.5 cm, c. 1873–74.
Private collection.

The topographical situation—a high mountain meadow with goat pasture—
suggests Switzerland, which places the picture in Courbet's exile period. This is not
necessarily to say that it represents an actual landscape. Courbet frequently combined
memory with observation and composed his landscapes of heterogeneous elements,
employed like set-pieces. Even the coloring of the vegetation suggests such a procedure: while the tree behind the boulder has dark brown autumn foliage, the under-
brush to the left is rendered in the vivid light and dark greens characteristic of early
summer. This combination of different seasons occurs in a number of the artist's Jura
landscapes, but also and especially in his flower pieces, where spring and fall flowers
often bloom simultaneously.[44]

On the whole the composition is related to Courbet's earlier treatments, though it
does evince certain late traits. A familiar feature is the way objects are interposed and
superimposed on one another, including occasional caesuras like the foreground boulder or the overgrown cliff that cuts across the view at the left. This screening effect has
grown stronger than in earlier works. While there a visual barrier tended to occur only
in the middle ground,[45] here the boulder in the foreground serves to create distance
between shepherdess and viewer. The paint application also differs from earlier examples. Both human figure and animals are rendered so thinly as to resemble shadow-
plays, almost devoid of corporeality. This tendency to dematerialization, already noted

by Champfleury, is also found in the vegetation, though here "incorporeal" zones alternate with others suggesting tangible, even plastic substance, such as the foreground boulder. On the slope at the right (much as in a fragmentary picture in Kassel),[46] we find not an evocation of physical substance but mere swaths of rapidly applied paint in gradations of green and brown, which serve to suggest depth.

An extreme diversity of technique can be seen throughout the picture; light and dark, cold and warm passages alternate in close juxtaposition. Water and soil are rendered partly in wash, partly in impasto. The grass, depicted with a stiff-bristle brush, seems to grow wildly in all directions. Toward the cliff the paint layers are partially applied with a palette knife, as abruptly terminated paint swatches indicate. The goats were added at a relatively late point in the painting process, over green that had not yet completely dried, causing splits in the upper paint layer through which the green shimmers. While in the right half of the composition the light-colored ground shows through in places, on the left, impasto passages predominate; the tree behind the rock, for instance, is covered with a gray layer meant to represent lichen. Characteristically for Courbet's work after 1864, certain dabs of color are scattered over the entire pictorial field regardless of objective designation—in this case, blue and red.[47] Other color combinations are familiar from Courbet's seascapes—for instance, a red cut with white placed in close proximity to a dove-blue (at the left edge just above center).

The picture is remarkable, first, for its fresh and furious attack and variety of paint handling; and second, for its combination of fields of equal weight that support one another without forcing the eye to stumble over pedantic detail. The homogeneous density of this structure is such as almost entirely to blur the distinction between foreground, middle ground, and background. Ever since *The Young Ladies on the Banks of the Seine (Summer)* of 1857,[48] this frequently remarked equality of emphasis on all objects in the scene constituted the modernity of many of Courbet's canvases. Nevertheless (and this is also characteristic), there is a central motif, namely, the boulder in the front middle ground, which is so strikingly angular as to suggest a prehistoric altar stone. This rock is *repoussoir* and main figure in one; by comparison to it, the shepherdess seems not merely offhandedly rendered—as so often in Courbet[49]—but veritably engulfed by the natural scene.

Two key features distinguish this new work from the workshop products of the exile period: variety of paint handling and an entire lack of prettiness. The painting has nothing in common with the pleasing sentimentality associated with pastoral motifs of this kind.

On the other hand, it reveals certain similarities with other Courbet canvases that permit it to be dated with some certainty. The heavy sky (including the color combination of grayish-blue, red, and yellow) and the loose structuring of the foreground recall *Stag Taking to the Water* of 1859–61, which is the earliest parallel.[50] Yet in this canvas, and as late as *Covert of Roe-Deer by a Stream at Plaisir-Fontaine* of 1866, the animals' bodies are clearly delineated and possess corporeality. The rapidly rendered goats and fissured earth[51] of *Grand Landscape*, on the other hand, are more closely related to the treatment of *Grand Panorama of the Alps* of 1877 (fig. 63). This leads me to think that, although a date of around 1860 or later is not entirely improbable, the picture was more likely painted around 1873–74. This would put it among the few works by Courbet's own hand from the final phase of his career, and it would confirm the agitated yet fragile vitality of this last phase. In terms of a "dissolution" of the object, Courbet goes far beyond impressionism in *Grand Landscape with Goats*, as he had in *Grand Panorama of the Alps*. This, together with his waiver of hierarchical composition, justifies speaking of "anarchical" painting—not so much in the political sense of the word as in the sense of the explosive effect that such canvases had on the art of the period.[52]

Other qualities of Courbet's late work appear in another previously unknown

65   Gustave Courbet, *Fisherman at Lake Geneva*. Oil on canvas, 22.3 × 27 cm, 1877. Private collection.

canvas, *Fisherman at Lake Geneva* (fig. 65). This painting is dated " '77" and signed by the artist's own hand (as easily forged as signatures are, in every case known to me the forged signatures appear more facile, less awkward and unwieldy).[53]

The subject is a stretch of rocky shoreline along Lake Geneva, with the gentle breakers characteristic of fine weather. Two sailboats and billowing, agitated clouds suggest a cool breeze. In the foreground, a fisherman stands in the shallows, and discernible among the rocks is the summarily sketched figure of a woman with sunshade. Above the low-lying horizon, a point of land rises to the edge of the canvas at the left.

There is a second, somewhat larger version of the painting which, while not including figures and with different cloud formations, shows exactly the same spot on Lake Geneva, near La Tour de Peilz, the town of Courbet's exile; Fernier gives the same inscription, "77 G. Courbet," though neither date nor signature are visible in his reproduction.[54] At any rate, the site is one that Courbet evidently visited repeatedly, probably to go fishing as well as to paint. The date is reliable; an alteration of the type Courbet frequently undertook would have brought no commercial advantage in the last year of his life. Also, the fact that the canvas was purchased in Geneva agrees with the information we have about Courbet's habits.[55]

This having been said, we can turn our attention to the composition and palette. An idiosyncracy frequently found in his work turns up here as well: unsureness as to where to place the horizon line. In the present case the horizon apparently initially lay higher and was lowered in the process of painting; similar shifts were observable particularly in those paintings from private collections that were first exhibited at the Paris and London Centennial Exhibitions.[56] Yet while in those canvases the definitive horizon line was marked by a renewed application of paint, here the paint has been scraped off. Courbet was apparently unwilling to completely expunge the traces of this change and others (for instance, in the water at the right). Might *Fisherman at Lake Geneva* possibly be Courbet's last painting? I do not wish to state this definitively; yet Castagnary's report that the artist broke off painting in May 1877 can hardly be construed to mean complete abstinence, and very probably he continued to execute such small oil sketches as the one under discussion.

Another striking feature is the loose treatment of the figures and rocks in the foreground. As regards the figures, parallels are found in the early, Paris version of *The Cliff at Etretat*, whose eleven tiny washerwomen are visible only on close scrutiny (detail, fig. 53), or in the oil sketch *Bon Port* of 1874, or in the red-clothed traveler in *Les Dents du Midi*.[57] Pata's figures, by comparison, are characterized by clearly contoured, closed form. The foreground rocks, loosely rendered in sheer black and ocher, recall those in several versions of *Château de Chillon* (fig. 66), the famous gathering place of émigrés, and parallel the treatment in *View of Lake Geneva by Cloudy Sky*[58] and, especially, in the rugged *Grand Panorama of the Alps* (fig. 63), where similar cumulus clouds occur.

Courbet's cloud formations deserve a separate study. It would be difficult to name an artist who lent them more variety and contrast, from dark and threatening to light and airy. It is enough to recall the so different beach scenes in Warsaw, Caen, or

London; clouds with a delicate purple tint like those in *Fisherman at Lake Geneva* are met with in numerous Courbet canvases.[59] A great variety of clouds can even appear in one and the same painting. In *Fisherman at Lake Geneva*, the lower band of distant cumulus clouds is rendered in thin, silky paint that approaches the character of a glaze, while the clouds gathering above are thicker, more dense, and partially painted in impasto. Such twin layering of clouds is typical of Courbet; in this respect, as well as in the ragged, torn effect of certain passages in the water and ground, *Fisherman at Lake Geneva* is related to the 1865–66 *Seaside* in Cologne (fig. 41). The looser and lighter

66   Gustave Courbet, *Château de Chillon*. Oil on canvas, 54 × 64.5 cm, 1873. Ecublens, Coll. André Held (Photo André Held).

character of the later canvas, however, should not tempt us to posit the workings of a law of biographical evolution; rather, it would seem that Courbet, much as any romantic artist, had attempted to express in the clouds something of his own strongly oscillating state of mind.

There can be no doubt that the contrasts in cloud formations grew increasingly strong during the exile period. But whether this can be attributed to the artist's inner conflicts, or whether his increasing emphasis on variation expressed his hope for change in the interpersonal realm, are questions that in the absence of additional sources must remain speculative. All we can say is that the phenomenon is detectable particularly in the paintings of Lake Geneva, one of the most striking examples of which is *Lake Geneva at Sunset* of 1874 (fig. 67), where the lake is bathed in the red of the twilight. In terms of paint application, this canvas anticipates *Fisherman at Lake Geneva,* for in both the subtle treatment of the clouds contrasts with the rough, heavy

67   Gustave Courbet, *Lake Geneva at Sunset.* Oil on canvas, 55 × 65 cm, 1874. Vevey, Musée Jenisch (Photo Eric Ed. Guignard).

strokes used to characterize the foreground rocks. Although in both cases the impression of delicacy and lightness must be slightly qualified due to the fact that color photography tends to absorb the gray that made Courbet's palette seem dirty and somber to his contemporaries, his *Fisherman at Lake Geneva* nonetheless remains a vibrantly sketched leisure picture that eloquently contradicts any categorization of Courbet's late work as unrelievedly melancholy. On the other hand, the painting shows some of the self-reflection inherent in *The Seaside at Palavas* of 1854.[60] Indeed, like this earlier work, the late one may be interpreted as a kind of self-portrait.

The few paintings discussed here may suffice to take the notion of a unified, consistent late style ad absurdum. Perhaps this will be seen as a chance to abandon, at long last, the fiction of anthropologically valid developmental constants in art. It may even lead to the insight that the accepted, largely normatively justified assumptions about the consistency of artist's hands, especially in the late nineteenth century, are in need of revision. The fact that Courbet set no *point final* and achieved no synthesis already offers the advantage of keeping his oeuvre free of arbitrary determinations.

If despite this open-endedness we were to draw a conclusion, it would be that Courbet's late style tends, in traditional terms, toward the antirealistic and is for that very reason adequate to his era. Figures and objects are merely *placed* on the canvas as the needs of composition demanded, instead of being firmly located in the context of a scene. This permitted Courbet to achieve a virtual congruence of paint material and subject matter. In other words, abstraction advanced to become the most realistic method of appropriating reality. Courbet's surprising statement of 1873 "L'enterrement *ne vaut rien*" (A Burial is *worth nothing*),[61] with which he rejected one of his own major early works—this statement is not a sign of debility but reveals insight into the continual shifts in reality that make the effectiveness of provocations only short-lived. That he was able to face these changes unflinchingly proves that he indeed possessed the quality so important to him—that of *indépendance*.

8

Courbet's Modernity as Reflected in Caricature

Salons, Media, and Audiences

CARICATURES of paintings have become rare. Hardly any work of art nowadays is thought worthy of satirical treatment and published in the mass media in this form. Art has apparently lost much of its provocative character, nor do art audiences react to it with the same defiant humor they once displayed.[1]

The situation was different in mid-nineteenth-century Paris, where periodical exhibitions of contemporary art in the Louvre—the famous Salons—provided a forum at which the acceptance or refusal of submitted works amounted to a verdict on the professional careers of entire generations of artists.[2] With growing official interest in art there emerged a sale and exploitation of cultural goods of the kind familiar to us today. During the Second Empire the Salons were opened in the presence of the emperor, who in 1863 even established a Salon for rejected artists, the Salon des Refusés.[3] In the course of a new public involvement in art, caricature took on a significance equal to that of written criticism. Of course, this shift in critical focus to the field of visual art had much to do with the fact that criticism in other areas was largely prohibited.

In this function of a safety valve and surrogate for political criticism, the caricature of works of art developed into a historically determined, independent genre that reached its absolute apex in France between 1848 and 1871. In 1843 Bertall published caricatures of this type in a special brochure,[4] followed in 1846 by the renowned *Salon caricatural* with texts by Baudelaire, Banville, and Vitu,[5] and, after mid-century, a spate of new journals devoted to art caricature such as *Le journal pour rire* (also titled *Le journal amusant*), *La lune, Le grelot, Le nain jaune, Le monde pour rire, La vessie, La charge, La silhouette, Polichinelle*, and others. Older magazines like *Le charivari* also opened their columns to this special genre, and artists like Cham and Nadar regularly issued their own brochures on the Salons, the former beginning in 1851 and the latter in 1852.

This burgeoning of art criticism through caricature coincided with the emergence of Courbet's first sensational canvases, which drew attacks of unprecedented harshness, the caricaturists leaping into the fray long before the critics. Their target was what became known as the trilogy of realism—*A Burial at Ornans, The Stone-breakers*, and *The Peasants of Flagey Returning from the Fair*, depictions of those classes and strata of society in which the urban bourgeoisie suspected a source of continued revolutionary ferment. Accustomed to the noble and sublime, the Salon visitor was bound to feel affronted by an emphasis on plain people and everyday subject matter in art, and to feel positively shocked by Courbet's provocative stagings of such themes.

Admittedly however, there was no such thing as *the* Salon visitor. The *Salon*

68   Bertall, Caricature of *The Beggar's Alms. Le journal amusant*, May 30, 1868.

caricatural for 1846 already distinguished Saturday from Sunday audiences; the price of admission was higher on Saturday, with the result that the upper strata could foregather pretty much among themselves. On Sunday, however, admission to the Salon was free and the audience made up accordingly—going to the Salon on Sunday became a regular popular entertainment.[6] Courbet reacted to this new situation at an astonishingly early date, by attempting to make his paintings accessible to the average viewer in terms both of content and form. The unseemliness of this attempt (and the clash between two different social spheres at the Salon) is strikingly illustrated by two caricatures of 1868. In the one (fig. 68) Courbet's beggar is shown approaching a lovely model in the midst of the "fine" Salon audience; in the other, Courbet himself appears dressed as a street sweeper with the beggar's mangy dog, surrounded by his artist colleagues.[7]

While Courbet attempted to reach both working people and the middle strata of the bourgeoisie, the caricaturists aimed primarily at the social elite. To them, Courbet's work seemed the embodiment of irregularity, the pinnacle of bad taste; his paintings were even decried as caricatures in themselves.[8] This is why the "Courbet case"—in allusion to the "Böcklin case"[9]—permits us to draw general conclusions about the predominant norms of the period and the expectations of a broad audience with regard to visual art. No other painter was more frequently caricatured than Courbet; ridicule was heaped not only on the content of his work but on its color and form as well. The caricaturists were both biased and clairvoyant, because while correcting Courbet's innovations from the point of view of convention they also augmented the provocative and unprecedented character of these features by emphasizing them out of all proportion. The caricatures, in short, were unconsciously innovative, in the end helping to pave the way for a development they were intended to prevent.

Gingerbread Men, Children's Toys, Jumping Jacks

The criteria developed by the caricaturists in reaction to Courbet's oeuvre became standard equipment in the field of art lampooning for thirty years. Still, their work evinces specific traits that cannot be explained solely in terms of the simplification inherent to caricature. Bertall's spoof of *The Peasants of Flagey Returning from the Fair* illustrates both points (fig. 69). Here the structure of the painting has undergone a decisive change.[10] Shadows have been expunged, figures and trees placed farther apart, and the animals and humans have been given big round eyes open in a happy, stupid stare. The oxen seem made of tin, the arms and legs of the figures look bolted on, and their hands as if cut out of paper. Wherever Courbet was concerned to integrate forms, Bertall has dismembered them, isolating and increasing the size of such details as umbrella, wooden shoes, and the figures' legs. Although Puvis de Chavannes was once accused of creating a similar montage of jumping-jack figures,[11] in Courbet's case the lifeless frieze with faces in strict profile or frontal aspect and oversized motifs enters a new unity that to contemporary eyes expressed the key issue raised by the painting—its foreground massing of peasants, the rural populace so

Le retour du marché, par Courbet, maître peintre.

Rien n'égale l'enthousiasme produit sur le public par les tableaux de Courbet. — Voilà de la *vérité vraie*, sans chic ni ficelles. — On ne sent point là le poncif de l'école, et les absurdes traditions de l'antique Tout y est naïf, heureux et gai. Courbet avait dix-huit mois quand il a peint ce tableau.

69 Bertall, Caricature of *The Peasants of Flagey Returning from the Fair. Le journal pour rire*, March 7, 1851.

despised and yet so feared by the urban bourgeoisie.[12] This anxiety, which was acute around 1850, also comes out in the caption, which makes fun of Courbet's lack of technical finesse and ignorance of classical tradition.[13] At this point in time Bertall was still able to attack Courbet's "naiveté" and to compare his painting to children's scribbling without qualms. Yet a few years later, people would realize that children's drawings possessed a unique autonomy and that naiveté contained a potential for social change and renewal—big-city life would be permeated by a vision of the contented savage.[14] It was a development the caricaturists continued to ignore for a long time.

A year later Bertall rendered Courbet's *Young Ladies of the Village* as carnival dolls and reproved him for distorting the proportions (fig. 70).[15] Actually, in his attempt to overcome academic traditions, Courbet quite consciously negated atmospheric perspective and size relationships.[16] By transforming the figures into "dolls," he was at liberty to dispose them at will—the key prerequisite for a visual synthesis of freely composed set pieces. Bertall unwittingly prepared the audience for this experiment.

A third prong of this attack on Courbet's ostensibly naive and mechanistic view of natural phenomena was mounted by Quillenbois, who in 1855 trained his guns on a whole series of paintings, including those of rocks and meadows (fig. 71). The stiff toy cows on wheels and rocks devoid of all vegetation[17] attest to the surprise that Courbet's radical waiver of decorative appurtenances could not help but evoke in contemporary viewers. By using rudimentary forms that translated the French Revolutionary pathos of the primitive into mundane terms, Courbet achieved a high degree of abstraction that ran counter to the imitative narrative structures which were then the

70   Bertall, Caricature of *The Young Ladies of the Village. Le journal pour rire,* April 16, 1852.

Les demoiselles de Village.

M. Courbet, en profond observateur, a voulu prouver que les demoiselles de village sont *fichues comme quatre sous,* il leš a représentées en poupées de la foire et comme, dans ce monde à part, les animaux sont plus petits que les personnages, il a maintenu les proportions... . de la foire. On dit que ce tableau a été acheté 5,000 fr. par M. de Morny, nous en faisons compliment à M. Courbet.

norm. This new, nonperspective, disproportional, and simplified order of things was a program with Courbet. During the 1850s his principal concern was to focus as sharply as he could on separate objects without regard for an overall, ideal frame of reference. A silent collection of isolated objects or figures, however, can certainly develop intrinsic and dynamic force. This is why the "wooden" figures in *A Burial at Ornans* could take on the appearance of a threatening mob[18] and even Courbet's "wooden sea" could affect viewers as a menace (fig. 72). They even felt insulted by his broad paint application, considering his use of the palette knife to create swaths of color a mere device to smear the canvas full. In an 1870 caricature of *The Wave* (fig. 73), for instance, the surf is treated as a solid mass of pigment, Courbet's pigment—a notion predicated on an experience of the painted object as "pure" painting (*peinture*), if only in order to denigrate it as heavy-handed and insensitive.

The most disturbing factor of all, however, was the equal emphasis Courbet placed on everything in the picture, his replacement of pictorial hierarchy with objective neutrality. "I look at a human being," he wrote to Bruyas, "with the same interest as at a horse, a tree, or any other object in nature."[19] To this positivistic view of reality the caricaturist could only reply with a leveling sequence of lifeless objects. In his eyes, Courbet's paintings neglected to fulfill key expectations with regard to visual art, for instead of evoking activity and life and reverberating with associations, they apparently cut off all lines of communication with the viewer. In the caricatures this was symbolized by toys, tin or wooden figures and plants, or by gingerbread men lined up in ranks (figs. 70, 74, 77, 78, 91).

La peinture réaliste de M. Courbet, par Quillenbois.

AU SALON. INTRA MUROS.

L'adoration de M. Courbet, imitation réaliste de l'adoration des Mages.

et atelier de l'art.

Une Espagnole en cuir de Russie.

Une fleur qui ne s'est jamais débarbouillée.

HORS DU SALON, EXTRA MUROS. — (PRIX : 4 FRANC, SI ON ENTRAIT.)

Réapparition de la Vénus du Bas-Rhin.

M. Courbet dans toute la gloire de sa propre individualité, allégorie réelle déterminant une phase de sa vie artistique. (Voir le programme, où il prouve victorieusement qu'il n'a jamais eu de maître… de perspective.

Lutte entre les adorateurs de la Vénus.

M. Courbet chantant sa gloire.

M. Courbet de face.

M. Courbet blessé.

M. Courbet enrhumé.

Les terres à M. Courbet.

Les vaches à M. Courbet.

L'enterrement de M. Courbet.

71   Quillenbois, *The Realist Painting of Monsieur Gustave Courbet.* L'illustration, July 21, 1855.

72   Cham, *Gustave Courbet Proves That the Sea Is Made of the Same Stuff as Boats.* *Le monde illustré,* 1870, p. 365.

671. — LA VAGUE, PAR COURBET.
Permettez-moi de vous offrir une tranche de cette peinture légère.....

73   Stock, Caricature of *The Wave. Stock-Album,* 1870.

The apparent contradiction in Courbet's work between motifs in motion and rigidity of form—basically no different than the photographic principle of capturing a fleeting movement with the precision and focus of a stationary object[20]—comes out in the caricatures of *Hunter on Horseback* of 1861 (figs. 75, 76). Nadar, on account of its dark colors, transposes the scene into a cellar and suggests that Courbet might as well put it in a bottle, the epitome of the inanimate toy. Oulevay is even more direct, for

Oh ! maman, vois donc ces beaux courbet! Achète m'en !
Quatre pour un sou !

74 Nadar, *Oh, Mom, Look
at the Pretty Gingerbread
Men! Le journal pour rire,*
July 2, 1861.

though his horseman is depicted in full gallop, he is fixed to the spot, because his toy horse is mounted on a spring—that is, he can be set in motion only by external agency. The appearance of verisimilitude is paradoxically negated by the introduction of this second level of reality. Courbet's alleged unconcern with truth to nature is pilloried even more sharply in the caption, which reads: "Mounted on his high horse, Pegasus, and equipped with his famous trumpet . . . [Courbet] sounds his fame throughout the wide world and the suburbs. If they still call him a realist after this horse, they're in for a big surprise." To Oulevay, in other words, the picture seemed unrealistic—it fell apart because horse and rider were of a different quality than the surrounding landscape.

The caricaturist indeed put his finger on a sore spot in Courbet's work. His landscapes are in fact quite differently handled than his figures; nature frequently functions much more as a vehicle of movement than do the figures, which ought intrinsically to express movement. By addressing this paradox, the caricatures draw attention to a conflict arising from Courbet's practice. While he frequently painted landscapes on the spot, he usually painted figures and animals in the studio, and we can assume that he felt less beholden to tradition in the former case than in the latter.

This conflict is at the bottom of Nadar's spoof on *The Young Ladies on the Banks of the Seine (Summer)* (fig. 77) and an 1869 caricature of *The Rest during the Harvest*

75 Nadar, Caricature of *Hunter on Horseback. Le journal amusant*, July 13, 1861.

76 Henry Oulevay, Caricature of *Hunter on Horseback. L'art pour rire*, June 15, 1861.

Season (*Mountains of the Doubs*) (fig. 78), where the landscape appears largely abstract and the figures awkwardly solid.[21] As the caption to Oulevay's drawing explains, "It is our duty to warn the Master of Ornans. If he keeps on this way, even the most docile of ruminants will refuse to enter his landscapes. Have the poor animals on

77   Nadar, Caricature of *The Young Ladies on the Banks of the Seine (Summer)*. *Nadar au Salon de 1857*, unpaginated.

78   Henry Oulevay, Caricature of *The Rest during the Harvest Season (Mountains of the Doubs)*. *La parodie*, June 4, 1869.

the right caught a cold, perhaps? There's a draft, *mon cher maître*, there's a draft!" This "trop d'air"—the airy, free, modern aspect of the painting—is what bothers the commentator most. Yet by pointing out the internal contradiction between figures and nature, the caricature suggests its solution, tacitly demanding that the toy figures, which have become mere set pieces, be treated as freely as the landscape; that is, that they be distributed at random in the pictorial space without regard for traditional perspective. In this regard, too, the "reactionary" caricature anticipates future developments.

The Void, the Moon, and the Oculist

Caricatures of a work of art are like magnifying glasses, emphasizing some aspect or detail of the whole and lending it symbolic value. Certain disturbing features of a painting are brought to light in which its very message lies. As we have seen, by attacking these features the caricaturists serve *both* as defenders of established standards *and* as promoters of the very advances they criticize. Particularly those drawings in which a single object is isolated and blown all out of proportion achieve a degree of abstraction far in advance of developments in fine art. A similar result can be achieved the other way around, by dissolving the objects of a painting and dividing the pictorial continuum into separate zones. The painter as iconoclast, as a destroyer of form—this view of the situation, in Cham's caricature *Gustave Courbet Quarreling with His Models* (fig. 79), gives rise to a new picture in which the artist is characterized as the victim of his own intentions. It shows Courbet standing in front of his canvas, attempting to protect it from an angry farmer who is bombarding it with various objects as a stubborn pig beside him expresses its disapproval in its own swinish way. A spade and

79 Cham, *Gustave Courbet Quarreling with His Models. Le charivari,* March 7, 1852.

M. Courbet ayant, juste au moment de l'exposition, un démêlé avec ses modèles, ce qui compromet furieusement sa toile.

Courbet.

Mer orageuse — on vient d'y jeter l'*ancre*.

80   Somm, *Le Salon de ct'*
année, The Wave. La charge,
1870.

a wooden shoe are already lodged in the canvas and a goat is leaping through it at the lower left. Painting and reality form a conglomerate of heterogeneous motifs that, by allusion to *The Peasants of Flagey Returning from the Fair,* symbolize Courbet's repertoire and imagery as a whole.

In a caricature of *Rocky Landscape near Ornans,* the pictorial context, basically unaltered, is divided into separate components and abstract signs.[22] This dissolution of the object, which went further in the landscapes than in the figure paintings, was later to be considered an "emptying" of the canvas. Referring to the high degree of abstraction involved, a commentary on *The Wave* of 1870,[23] in a play on the like-sounding words *ancre* and *encre* (Fig. 80), says that in stormy seas one drops the ink— meaning that as far as the caricaturist is concerned, the picture consists of dark paint splotches and nothing more. Or, in another caption, "Just as God created Heaven and Earth out of the void, Courbet creates his seascapes out of nothing, or almost nothing: three hues on the palette, three brushstrokes," which allegedly suffice Courbet for the rendering of a coastline.[24] The protest against the emptiness of *The Waterspout* takes a similar form (fig. 81).[25] Although "empty" paintings were occasionally executed as curiosities and uniformly dark pictures were caricatured as black planes from 1843 onwards,[26] this sort of reception is surprising in connection with a painter who was as interested in precise renderings of objects as Courbet. Caricatures of this type seem strange at first glance, and yet they conform to the increasing prevalence of planar structure and flat color over the designation of separate objects and their definition in terms of local color (see essay on Courbet's color).

In his caricature of *The Bathers* (fig. 82), Nadar was content merely with drawing a full moon, alluding to the nude figure's backside. This reduction of Courbet's paint-ings to round forms required a capacity for visual abstraction that was new at the time. Manet once called Courbet a painter of billiard balls;[27] even compositions that actu-

81   Randon, Caricature of
*The Waterspout. Le journal
amusant*, 1867.

Mais maintenant que M. Courbet vous a fait voir sa
lune, que diable pourra-t-il nous montrer l'année
prochaine!

82   Nadar, Caricature of
*The Bathers. Le journal pour
rire*, July 2, 1853.

ally contained few rounded objects, such as *Portrait of P.-J. Proudhon in 1853* (fig. 44),
were caricatured as a pile of sacks filled to the bursting point (fig. 83)—a persiflage one
would have thought more appropriate to the swelling forms in *The Grain Sifters*.
However, the aim of such caricatures would seem to be a quite general expression of the
force and density of Courbet's paint handling and approach to form, as for example in
the gypsy woman in Bertall's spoof on *The Beggar's Alms* (fig. 84).

The formally oriented caricatures reveal Courbet's modernity with particular

Le jour du blanchisseur; par M. Courbet.
Hommage au talent convaincu de M. Courbet. Au moins
celui-là, on ne l'accusera pas de travailler pour la vente. —
Pas plus que M. Manet.

83   Bertall, *Laundry Day*
(Caricature of *Portrait of P.-J. Proudhon in the Year 1853*
[first state]). *L'illustration*,
June 3, 1865.

608   A MENDIANT MENDIANT ET DEMI, par COURBET.
    M. Courbet a voulu prouver ici qu'un grand artiste peut facilement se passer de
forme, de couleur et de style quand il est soutenu par une grande et généreuse pensée. Ce vieux mendiant privé de tout, même du plus nécessaire dessin; offrant son
obole à l'enfant qui se plonge résolûment le doigt dans le nez, sans souci de l'avenir,
nous attendrit profondément. Le ton merveilleusement approprié se compose des
boues d'Ornans combinées savamment avec les balayures Mouffetard, le tout relevé par
un petit glacis de macadam. Un trait de génie! La femme dans un paquet de linge
sale est un chef d'œuvre.

84   Bertall, Caricature of
*The Beggar's Alms. Le jour-
nal amusant*, May, 16, 1868.

85   Cham, *The Dying Fox . . . . Cham au Salon de 1863*, 1863.

Renard mourant inconsolable de s'être laissé forcer par un cheval qui avait des jambes en manches de veste.
Nota. Ce tableau a été exécuté par le jeune Toto Courbet, âgé de trois ans, fils de M. Gustave Courbet, le fameux peintre.

86   Cham, *Riding the Quickest Way to the Oculist's. Cham au Salon de 1863*, 1863.

TABLEAU DE M. COURBET.
Cavalier conduisant au plus vite son cheval chez un oculiste pour qu'il lui remette son œil en place.

clarity. This quality was also remarked by an art critic, Castagnary, and by a sculptor, Perraud; when they said of *The Beggar's Alms* that the true significance of the painting lay in its abundance of light,[28] they were expressing an insight anticipated by the caricaturists, namely, that Courbet's perceptual interests had shifted and that as a

Ce que M. Courbet sait faire d'une jolie femme   car nous
parierions que la dame qui a posé pour ce portrait est très-
jolie.

87   Cham, Caricature of
The Lady in the Black Hat.
Cham au Salon de 1863,
1863.

result his concern with form had begun to take precedence over, indeed actually to reshape, his subject matter. This is why the cubists and surrealists could claim Courbet for one of their own.

Courbet's distortion of form was a prerequisite for his break with tradition, and it is in those very features which the caricaturists branded as errors that we find him anticipating the painting of the twentieth century. One of these features was a disregard for anatomy, which was remarked even in such early canvases as *The Peasants of Flagey Returning from the Fair* and *The Stonebreakers.* The caption to Cham's caricature of the latter reads, "Until now painters used to put legs in trousers; Courbet has deemed it necessary to abandon this custom"—in other words, he has decided not to bother about anatomical correctness any longer.[29] Bertall's caricature of *The Wrestlers* (fig. 13, bottom) is captioned: "Not a single muscle of these wrestlers is in its accustomed place, a disorder probably explained by the effort of the fight. A beautiful disorder is often the result of art." Misdrawn in key passages, the painting indeed has the effect of a montage of heterogeneous parts. The caricaturists and critics noted only the drawing errors and considered them signs of a degeneration of painting, which was no longer capable of fulfilling its mission of idealization. *The Bathers* and *The Wrestlers* were even attacked as racially inferior,[30] and in the caption to Cham's version of *The Foxhunt* we read, "Unlike the Jockey Club, Courbet is working on a deterioration of the horse species."[31] In another caricature of the same painting (fig. 85), the fox is "disconsolate at having been chased by a horse that has legs like coat sleeves." And when Sainte-Beuve gives Courbet "a horse of the type he likes," it can only be an anatomically impossible one.[32] The possibility of taking artistic license with anatomy is even more clearly addressed in the caricature of *Hunter on Horseback* (fig. 86), who is getting his steed to the oculist as fast as he can in order to have its eye put back in the "right" place. Cham's drawing after *The Lady in the Black Hat,* captioned "What Courbet can make of a lovely woman . . . " (fig. 87), has a particularly avant-garde look, anticipating the cubist device of superimposing frontal and profile views.

From Pictorial Space to Public Spaces

Courbet's paintings are frequently characterized by close-up views that seem to force themselves on the spectator to the point of obtrusiveness. Caricaturists accentuated this feature by letting the figures actually protrude into real space, thus emphasizing the offensive, reality-oriented nature of Courbet's approach. Nadar, for instance, extended the shadows of *The Wrestlers* (omitted in the painting) across the frame and into the exhibition space (fig. 14, left) or, vice versa, showed a spectator's dog trying to chase the painted deer in a landscape (fig. 88).[33] In the latter case we find—for the only time in Courbet—that type of realism described by Pliny in his story about Zeuxis, who imitated nature with such skill that one could mistake his painted creatures for real.[34] In general, however, as indicated above, Courbet's style was described as being quite the opposite, namely, lifeless and unrealistic.

The extension of a painted image into real space took on various forms in caricature. In 1859 Courbet depicted Marc Trapadoux leafing through an album; waiving the traditional *repoussoir,* he showed the philosopher's legs stretching out toward the viewer. Nadar interpreted this pose as a badly arranged snapshot in which the feet loom disproportionately large (fig. 89).[35] In the caricaturist's view, Courbet's painting bore similarities to photography, and this fueled the accusation that his approach was

88   Nadar, *A Dog Trying to Chase the Painted Deer. Gazette de Paris,* 1868.

Perspective nouvelle ouverte par le talent
de M. Courbet.

89 Nadar, *A New Perspective . . .* (Caricature of *Portrait of Marc Trapadoux*). *Petit journal pour rire,* 1861.

mechanistic. More than this, Nadar implied that Courbet had adopted merely the distortions and errors of the new medium, in order to depict an unseemly pose. Nadar's emphasis on certain effects of photography served to illustrate Courbet's aggressive appropriation of real space.

This sort of appropriation confronted his contemporaries with problems of more than a formal nature, and it went beyond the walls of the exhibition space. The aggressiveness of Courbet's imagery resulted from an intent to provoke, and to extend its influence beyond the Salon. Extremely skilled at publicity, Courbet was continuously propagating his work.[36] To him the Salon exhibitions were an instrument of opposition to the Academy, for they gave him an opportunity to mobilize a different audience, by creating a scandal if need be. Nadar realized this as early as 1853, warning Courbet that "coarseness is not strength, brutality not the same as frankness nor scandal the same as renown."[37] In one of his caricatures, Nadar suggested that *The Wrestlers* be treated as a sideshow poster, quite correctly recognizing the painting's intent to influence and persuade (fig. 90). Another caricaturist lined up the hunters from Courbet's *Kill: Episode during the Deer Hunt in a Snowy Terrain* (fig. 38), together with motifs from Manet, Isabey, and other artists, as targets in a shooting gallery (fig. 91). Courbet actually did intend to show his works in a fairground booth at one point;[38] he also planned to do murals in railroad stations in order to appeal to the people directly.[39] In this regard, too, caricature assumed a pioneering role, for it

Qui est-ce qui demandait donc à quoi pouvait servir la
peinture de M. Courbet ! U. 1362

90 Nadar, Caricature of
*The Wrestlers. Le journal
pour rire*, July 2, 1853.

LE TIR AU PISTOLET ET A LA CARABINE.

Pif, paf, pan. Quels enragés! En fait on du bruit autour de ces poupées. — Voici d'abord le balcon de Manet, les pipes de Ribot, la
Veuve Lambron, puis le chasseur de Courbet, le lapin de Taylor et le St-Antoine, d'Isabey.

91 Anonymous, *With
Pistol and Rifle* (Caricature
of *The Kill*). *L'éclipse*, 1869.

was in this medium that the tendency to break down the barriers between fine and trivial art and to gain new audiences for art was reflected for the first time.

Dirt, the Barn Smell, and the Hayseed

"Even his bitterest opponents had to admit that . . . this peasant who smelled of the barn had a certain worth," wrote d'Ideville about Courbet in 1878.[40] For a long time, however, his worth was definitely disputed. "Why do they call this painting socialistic, Dad?" asks a boy in Cham's caricature of *The Stonebreakers* (fig. 92). "Well, because it's not rich but poor painting," replies the father. The quality of poverty is still associated here with the vulgar nature of the *subject matter*, that is, with a disappointment of visual expectations schooled on sublime and ideal motifs. The same reaction is evident in a caricature of *The Stonebreakers* that, by taking offense at their shoddy clothing, labels the working man as offensive (fig. 93). In other words, the coarse and vulgar subject itself was felt to be threatening; the fact that a tangibly close and unprettified presentation of the subject implied a new form and technique which enabled a more intensive involvement with everyday life was not yet taken into account around mid-century. Indirectly, however, this insight gained headway. In Cham's *Preview of the 1852 Exhibition* (fig. 94), a single subject, a pair of wooden shoes, could fill the entire pictorial field, a novelty in terms of form as well as content. Still, Cham was primarily concerned with the latter, fearing that if Courbet's example caught on, the next Salon would consist of nothing but pictures of hayseeds.

The lowest, most boorish and disgusting, and the most dangerous painting in Courbet's oeuvre, as far as his contemporaries were concerned, was *The Stone-*

— Pourquoi donc, papa, qu'on appelle ça de la peinture socialiste?
— Parbleu ! parce qu'au lieu d'être de la peinture riche, c'est de la pauvre peinture !...

92   Cham, *Why Do They Call This Painting Socialistic, Dad?* (Caricature of *The Stonebreakers*). *Revue comique du Salon de 1851*,

93   Cham, *The Stone-breakers, a Remarkable Canvas . . . of Trousers. Revue comique du Salon de 1851,* p. 4.

Les *Casseurs de pierres,* remarquable toile... de pantalons.

94   Cham, *Preview of the 1852 Exhibition. Revue comique du Salon de 1851,* p. 16.

EXPOSITION DE PEINTURE EN 1852.

M. Courbet ayant fait école, on ne trouvera en 1852, en fait de peintures, rien que des tableaux représentant des paysans.

breakers. "Democratization of art," reads the laconic caption to a caricature of the painting (fig. 71, top right) in which the two laborers, clad in huge clogs like dwarfs in seven-league boots and as red-nosed as the sextons in *A Burial at Ornans,* seem just as threatening as they do ridiculous.[41] That the target was the artist himself is indicated by a caricature called *Courbet's Burial* (*L'enterrement de M. Courbet;* fig. 71, bottom right), where Quillenbois turns the subject of the canvas against its author. This double-edged drawing also reveals that *A Burial,* as T. J. Clark was the first to remark,[42] was understood to represent a class that threatened the urban bourgeoisie, a confrontation which the caricaturist brings to a point by contrasting the rough footwear of a crowd of peasants with the fine clothes of Salon visitors.

The Bathers and *The Wrestlers* provided even more fuel for controversy. Quillenbois (fig. 71, second row left) called one of the bathers "Venus of the lower Rhine" (that is, of the gutters) and let her two black admirers, the wrestlers, fight for her charms (fig. 71, second row right), while critics like Gautier reviled *The Wrestlers* as dirty, soot-smeared workingmen.[43] "Venus" is shown wearing wooden shoes, a paradox that in itself points up the extent to which Courbet had violated *the* ideal figure of Western art. His intention, in *The Bathers,* of changing ideal figures into less delectable realities was brought to a focus in the caricatures, which transformed the two women into fat farmer's wives—representatives of the rural populace—which turned the point of Courbet's attack away from the urban bourgeoisie. While this interpretation probably conformed with the artist's own, it shifted the moral emphasis of his critique, bringing the two figures suggestively close to each other. Perhaps this also represented an attempt to resolve the crisis of communication remarked by Delacroix, who noted the meaninglessness of the figures' gestures.[44]

Poking fun at farmers, a perennial form of self-righteousness on the part of city dwellers, was increasingly used as a weapon to combat Courbet's ideas from 1853 onwards. As many as four caricatures—two of *The Sleeping Spinner* (figs. 95 and 71, second row right), one of *The Bathers,* and another of *The Grain Sifters* (fig. 96)—recommended that the main figures take a good hot bath; two others even referred to "stinking" pictures (figs. 97, 98), implying that it wasn't enough for the good citizen to sniff at them—he had to hold his nose. A caricature by Bertall (fig. 99) turns the bathers into ugly female wrestlers, thus relegating them, like the wrestlers themselves, to the lowest rung on the social ladder.[45] At least these drawings had the effect of popularizing what was probably Courbet's most provocative innovation, for while the other "realists" protected the image of woman against the coarsening of the mundane—Jules Breton's *End of the Day* (1859) is a prime example[46]—Courbet put women at the center of his "depictions of common reality,"[47] that is, he stripped them of idealization. It is no wonder that his image of woman drew the caricaturists' special scorn.

They also took careful note of the contrast between rustic coarseness and city elegance, thus revealing the artist's precarious position between city and country.[48] In Quillenbois's caricature of *The Meeting* (fig. 71, upper row left), the wooden shoes (not worn by the artist in the painting) stand for the former quality and the Assyrian beard

La Fileuse de Courbet.   D. 1362

— Pendant que Courbet la peignait, on voit bien qu'elle ne se peignait guè
— Quand elle se réveillera, ça ne lui ferait pas de mal de filer au bain a

95 Bertall, Caricature of *The Spinner. Le journal pour rire*, 1853.

Une jeune fille travaillant avec tant de zèle dans une grange qu'elle n'a pas encore pu trouver une seule minute pour se livrer à quelques soins de propreté.

96 Cham, Caricature of *The Grain Sifters. Le charivari*, June 26, 1855.

LA FILEUSE, PAR M. COURBET.

La fraicheur de cette villageoise tend à nous prouver que la
malpropreté n'est pas aussi nuisible à la santé qu'on le croit
généralement en société.

97   Cham, Caricature of
The Spinner. Le charivari,
May 29, 1853.

Un monsieur ayant eu l'imprudence d'entrer sans précaution
dans l'atelier de M. Courbet est asphyxié par sa palette.

98   Cham, *A Gentleman
Asphyxiated by Gustave
Courbet's Palette. Le char-
ivari*, June 19, 1853.

for the latter. This is a lucid characterization of Courbet's role of hayseed turned city
slicker, of country boy come to town in search of success. The paradoxical mixture of
Jeannot[49] and dandy is even more extreme in Hadol's caricature of 1857 (fig. 100),
which shows heavy, nailed shoes with dung and straw still clinging to them, dangling
from the maestro's easel in front of his nose, and includes a barn-lantern and back-
basket as further symbols of the artist's peasant origin.[50] Although Courbet has
exchanged his rough work clothes for an elegant suit, the vulgarities of his realistic art
still come to the fore: while at the bottom of the picture he arrives in miniature, in a toy
coach, swelled with pride (an allusion to *The Meeting*), there looms up in the corner the
"Venus of realism" (an allusion to the model in *The Painter's Studio*), ugly, crosseyed,
and resting her foot on a wooden shoe. The main point of the attack, however, is

99 Bertall, *The Terrible Savoyarde. Le journal pour rire,* June 25, 1853.

100 Hadol, *Gustave Courbet (at His Easel).* 1857.

directed against *The Young Ladies on the Banks of the Seine* (caricatured on the easel). As far as the caricaturist is concerned, Courbet has abused his new career in the city to render vulgar subjects that, in true city people, can only raise repugnance. To convey this, Hadol transforms the picture into a bedroom scene in which the female figure becomes a coarse country girl. In the mass, this type of ridicule merely represents an attempt to exorcise the city dweller's fear of noncity and low strata of the populace.

The outsider figures in the later paintings seemed both wooden and boorish to the caricaturists (figs. 101, 102). While the gypsy woman in Bertall's *Beggar's Alms* is depicted as an overblown bag and the boy as a little brat, the beggar himself becomes a scarecrow (alluding to the two "left" feet he has in the painting) on which the dog relieves itself as on an inanimate object. In Ancourt's caricature, the picture is cited as a prime example of Courbet's primitive "sign painting" (a term that would now be applied to other artists as well).[51] The caricature thus combines a critique of Courbet's formal primitivism with an attack on his vulgar content. In the eyes of his opponents, his programmatic statement "That's right, art should be dragged into the gutter"[52] implied a reversal of more than aesthetic values, casting doubt on the cultural policy of the government and indeed on the entire bourgeois system of values. This is why their laughter soon gave way to frank hate. In the wake of his activities in the Commune, the wish expressed in the caricature *Courbet's Burial* would be fulfilled.

101   Attributed to Bertall, Caricature of *The Beggar's Alms. Gazette de Paris,* 1868.

102   Ancourt, Caricature of
*The Beggar's Alms. Le
bouffon,* 1868.

Revolution, Empire, and Commune

That political allusions were widespread in nineteenth-century French art
is now a matter of accepted fact, and the caricaturists were instrumental in revealing
and popularizing these references. They also employed earlier works of art to convey a
political message.[53] The political aspect of Courbet's work was frequently revealed,
even augmented, by caricatures, especially those which depict peasants or day-laborers
(figs. 69, 71, 92–94) or those of the red-nosed sextons in *A Burial at Ornans* (fig. 103)
who are having a good laugh over the reconciliation between Church and Revolution
that was widely propagated after 1848.[54]

Another caricature sheds light on the implicit meaning of *The Painter's Studio* (fig.
28). The maestro's claim to stand at the center of society and at the same time above its
concerns is made to look ridiculous, in a way similar to Joudar's drawing after *The
Return from the Conference,* where Courbet appears as a drunken Messiah complete
with halo.[55] He was a Messiah in *The Painter's Studio* as well; but who was he out to
convert? According to the caricaturist, the world of art and the world of politics,
including Napoleon III, who is shown knocking over the chamber pot that, to loyalists,
symbolized the "stinking outhouse" of the Republic. By changing the painting in this
way, the caricature reveals its political message—an attempt on Courbet's part, against
the background of the 1855 Paris World Fair, to confront the empire with his anarchistic approach to art and to reconcile social conflicts by referring to the propitiatory
forces inherent in nature.

L'enterrement d'Ornans, par Courbet, maître peintre.   D. 1362

Cette toile est celle que l'on remarque le plus au Salon, et à juste titre. Un enterrement est généralement chose assez triste. M. Courbet qui n'accep[...] ne marche pas dans les sentiers battus, a combiné son enterrement de telle sorte qu'on est pris d'une gaieté folle en

103   Bertall, Caricature of *A Burial at Ornans. Le journal pour rire*, March 7, 1851.

M. Proudhon travaillant désormais aux tableaux anti-religieux de M. Courbet.

104   Cham, *Proudhon Collaborating on Courbet's Antireligious Pictures. Le charivari*, April 24, 1863.

In another caricature Proudhon, who also puts in an appearance in *The Painter's Studio*, is shown collaborating on Courbet's "antireligious" pictures (fig. 104)—an allusion to *The Return from the Conference*, but also to *The Wrestlers* of 1853. The latter symbolizes a battle between red and black in Proudhon's meaning of these terms; he thought it necessary to "subordinate the church to the Revolution."[56] Since in view of Bonapartist censorship such opinions could not be printed except in exile, or could be propagated in France only by word of mouth, the form they take in the paintings is extremely veiled, and even in the caricatures this veil is only occasionally lifted. An example is one by Nadar (fig. 14, left), in which the significance of the fight between black and red is elucidated by the broad-brimmed Jesuit hat worn by the weaker man, which characterizes him as a member of the clergy.

In a caricature of a landscape,[57] the color red is employed in a quite different sense (only the ribbon is printed in red). The caption reads: "A masterpiece, these deer! But they are obviously baffled by it. Do we perceive a red band on the horizon of this landscape—or are we mistaken?" The powerfully advancing red, rather than the socialist threat, in this case signifies an imperial honor: in 1866 Courbet was being considered for the red ribbon of the Legion of Honor, which, when it was offered to him in 1870, he indignantly refused. The hope expressed in *The Painter's Studio* of a reconciliation with the powers that be was shattered; with the Commune, Courbet went over to the other camp for good. Now the caricaturists opposed him outright, even turning his still lifes against him politically (fig. 105). "The fruits of reflection— fallen unripe from the tree after six months in the dark. 17,000 francs a pile!" was the

105   Faustin, *The Fruits of Reflection*. *La chronique illustrée,* May 6, 1872.

— Le jury ayant eu le mauvais goût de refuser les deux tableaux d'un honorable citoyen peintre que la pudeur me défend de nommer, nous sommes heureux de pouvoir donner aux lecteurs du *Journal amusant* un léger aperçu de ces œuvres ingénieuses et patriotiques; l'une représentait — *les Pommes de discorde;* — l'autre avait pour sujet — *la Colonne-des-reins d'une jeune citoyenne.*

106   L.-P. Morel-Retz, alias Stop, *The Apples of Discord* (*Female Nude with Vendôme Column*). *Le journal amusant,* May 18, 1872.

caption of a caricature of a still life of fruit painted in prison after the defeat of the Commune (the six months refer to the length of his sentence). Although Courbet was excluded from the Salon in 1872, his "poor" paintings were caricatured along with those actually exhibited (fig. 106). Embarrassment has obscured his signature with a fig leaf; his nude has a Vendôme column as a backbone: both still life and nude are treated as political statements.

Courbet—a peasant, an iconoclast, a subversive element. After the fall of the Commune he was branded all of these and more. It was easy to identify him personally with his "dirty" oeuvre, especially with *The Stonebreakers,* now seen as the quintessence of his life's work (fig. 107). This painting was apparently so well known that a mere depiction of someone breaking stones, no matter how formally unrelated to the picture, was enough to call it to mind. In the caricaturists' view, Courbet had degraded himself to a stonebreaker, and one who had proceeded from smashing aesthetic standards to smashing the state. His choice of a vulgar subject, his involvement in the razing of the column, and the "imbecilic" cheering of the populace over these heroic deeds, were all inextricably mixed in the caricatures. Courbet's painting and his political activity were considered equally villainous; the same political and moral verdict was passed on his image and his imagery—revealing the significance of the

107 Léonce Schérer, *The Man Who One Day Would Demolish the Column, Began His Career as a Stonebreaker. Souvenirs de la Commune*, Aug. 4, 1871.

108 Attributed to André Gill, *Two Portraits of Courbet, by Alexandre Dumas. Le grelot*, February 1882.

motif of the dirty peasant in the class struggle. As late as 1882, during the phase of Courbet's rehabilitation, the impropriety of realistic painting was still considered such a challenge that a drawing of a pig was thought sufficient to characterize Courbet and his work (fig. 108). However, this sort of thing was merely a parting shot, for after the fall of the Commune the critique of content was deprived of targets and gradually lost its point.

In the long run, it was largely due to the caricaturists that a sensibility for Courbet's innovations emerged at such an early date and became so widespread. Behind their back, and with their inadvertent aid, the art they so detested experienced its breakthrough. Facing backwards like Don Quixote, the caricaturists unwittingly broke a lance for modernity.

Appendix:
Contemporary
Statements on the
Courbet Paintings
Exhibited in the
1853 Salon

I. Eugène Delacroix, *Journal,* ed. André Joubin, vol. 2, Paris, 1932, pp. 18–19 (April 15, 1853):

J'avais été . . . voir les peintures de Courbet. J'ai été étonné de la vigueur et de la saillie de son principal tableau; mais quel tableau! quel sujet! La vulgarité des formes ne ferait rien; c'est la vulgarité et l'inutilité de la pensée qui sont abominables; et même, au milieu de tout cela, si cette idée, telle quelle, était claire! Que veulent ces deux figures? Une grosse bourgeoise, vue par le dos et toute nue sauf un lambeau de torchon négligemment peint qui couvre le bas des fesses, sort d'une petite nappe d'eau. . . . Elle fait un geste qui n'exprime rien, et une autre femme, que l'on suppose sa servante, est assise par terre. . . . Il y a entre ces deux figures un échange de pensées qu'on ne peut comprendre. Le paysage est d'une vigueur extraordinaire, mais Courbet n'a fait autre chose que mettre en grand une étude que l'on voit là près de sa toile; il en résulte que les figures y ont été mises ensuite et sans lien avec ce qui les entoure. . . . Les *Deux Lutteurs* montrent le défaut d'action et confirment l'impuissance dans l'invention. Le fond tue les figures, et il faudrait en ôter plus de trois pieds tout autour.

II. Théophile Gautier, "Salon de 1853," *La presse,* July 21, 1853 (eleventh article):

Il se fait, depuis trois ans, beaucoup de bruit autour du nom de M. Courbet; il a des fanatiques et des dénigreurs outrés. Selon les premiers, tout est admirable chez M. Courbet; selon les seconds, tout est détestable, en sorte que le public ne sait trop à quoi s'en tenir sur le jeune peintre d'Ornans qui est entré dans le domaine de l'art comme un paysan du Danube, vêtu d'un sayon de peau de bique, de sabots pleins de paille aux pieds, un bonnet de coton sur la tête, une pipe culottée au coin de la bouche, un bâton de houx retenu au poignet par une ganse de cuir.

Que cette rusticité soit sincère ou non, elle a produit un effet de surprise, et M. Courbet a obtenu tout de suite une réputation qui n'est ordinairement le fruit que de longues années de travail. . . . Quel élément nouveau apportait M. Courbet pour soulever tant de discussions tumultueuses et passionnées?

De tout temps la peinture est divisée en deux camps: les idéalistes et les réalistes; pour les uns, l'art n'est que le moyen; pour les autres, il en est le but. Les idéalistes empruntent à la nature des formes pour revêtir le type qu'ils portent en eux ou vers lequel ils aspirent; les réalistes se contentent de la reproduction brute et sans choix de la nature elle-même: Michel-Ange, Léonard de Vinci, Raphaël, Corrège, Lesueur, Poussin sont de la première école; le Caravage, le Guerchin, l'Espagnolet, le Calabrèse, le Valentin, Ostade et presque tous les Flamands sont de la seconde. . . . Examinons les trois tableaux envoyés par M. Courbet, qui exposent la doctrine à des degrés différens.

Le meilleur de tous est assurément la *Fileuse*. . . . La *Baigneuse* a obtenu un succès de scandale. Figurez-vous une sorte de Vénus hottentote sortant de l'eau, et tournant vers le spectateur une croupe monstrueuse. . . .

Quant aux *Lutteurs*, il sont franchement détestables. Nous avons vu à la salle Montesquieu Blas (le féroce Espagnol), Arpin (l'invincible Savoyard), Rabasson, l'Océan et toute la bande athlétique, et ils nous ont paru couleur de chair comme les autres hommes. Les lutteurs de M. Courbet se sont roulés préalablement dans la suie et le charbon, sans doute pour avoir plus de prise.

Comment admettre au plein jour de l'Hippodrome où le peintre a placé son groupe, ces ombres noires, ces demi-teintes fuligieuses, ces lumières plombées, ce jour de cave? Hercule et Cacus se colletant au fond de la caverne ne seraient pas plus bistrés et plus bitumineux. Pour un réaliste comme M. Courbet, ces hommes noirs s'étreignant en plein soleil sont passablement fantasques.

Quoique nous préférions la recherche de la beauté, nous concevons cependant que l'on copie la nature comme elle se présente, mais il faut être d'une sincérité scrupuleuse, et d'une conscience extrême, et d'une naïveté parfaite, et ne pas se faire comme Courbet le Watteau du laid; c'est une erreur de croire qu'on n'est maniéré qu'avec des lignes coquettes, des tons roses et une touche papillonnante, on l'est également avec des tournures épaisses, des couleurs boueuses et une facture brutale; c'est le maniérisme inverse, voilà tout. Mais un paysan peut être aussi affecté dans un sarrau de toile qu'un marquis dans son frac de taffetas zinzolin; il y a la fausse rusticité comme il y a la fausse élégance, et il est regrettable que M. Courbet continue à dépenser, dans des toiles qui semblent des gageures tenues contre l'art et la critique, des qualités de premier ordre. Il nous donne la caricature et non le portrait de la vérité.

Adolphe Leleux, bien avant M. Courbet, a fait du réalisme, mais sans exagération, sans charlatanisme, sans pose.

III. Augustin-Joseph du Pays, "Salon de 1853," *L'illustration*, June 18, 1853 (fourth article):

C'est sans doute pour se faire pardonner l'injure de sa baigneuse au beau sexe, comme on disait autrefois, que M. Courbet a essayé de produire avec plus de rudesse et d'une façon

plus triste encore les laideurs du vilain. Rien de plus déplaisant à voir que sa grande étude de
lutteurs au prises, dans le cirque de l'hippodrome des Champs-Elysées. Qu'il y ait un
certain savoir anatomique dans le rendu de ces deux figures: que, malgré l'agencement
malheureux de leur quatre jambes, alignées comme les supports d'un meuble, que, malgré
des exagérations incorrectes de dessin, on remarque l'énergie vraie, le relief de dessin et de
mouvement de la cuisse et de la jambe gauche du lutteur à la droite du spectateur; qu'on
consente à oublier un instant ces tons noirs abominables qui enveloppent, qui ensevelissent
une des deux têtes, qui salissent les deux corps et forment à leur ligne de rencontre une sorte
de cavité obscure placée dans l'axe du tableau. . . . Quels que soient les mérites reconnus et
les concessions faites, on sera dominé invinciblement par la répugnance que cause cet
ensemble voué au noir, voué au laid, au grossier, au trivial.

IV. Eugène Loudun, "Salon de 1853," *L'union,* June 5, 1853 (second article):

M. Courbet jouit d'un grand avantage: il attire tout d'abord les regards; nul n'est plus
connu à l'Exposition; on voit les provinciaux naïfs, qui ont entendu parler de ses ex-
centrités, s'arrêter devant toutes les toiles burlesques ou bizarres, s'imaginant qu'elles ne
peuvent être que de lui. Non, monsieur; non, madame, ce n'est pas encore cela. Mais quand
ils arrivent au milieu de la principale galerie, et qu'ils aperçoivent certaines formes que l'on
n'est pas accoutumé de voir, il n'y a plus d'incertitude: Voilà bien les Courbet! on ne s'y peut
tromper. Heureux peintre! il fait épanouir tous les visages; il déride les plus sérieux. Si l'on
veut avoir une idée d'un parterre égayé, il faut se placer devant les toiles M. Courbet; chacun
se laisse aller à un fou rire; on se communique ses impressions; on n'a pas besoin de se
connaître, on est sûr de s'entendre. Avez-vous vu les Courbet? me disait un critique le jour
de l'ouverture de l'Exposition. Ce qu'il y a de mieux à faire, c'est de n'en pas parler. Je ne
suis pas de cet avis: Il en faut parler, au contraire; d'abord parce que le public en parle
beaucoup, ensuite parce que l'on n'a pas tous les jours la bonne fortune de rencontrer une
peinture aussi amusante.

M. Courbet a donc exposé trois toiles: une *Fileuse dormant:* c'est le morceau sage. . . .
Puis des *Lutteurs,* et quels lutteurs! des hommes énormes, noirs, épais, des têtes de tau-
reaux, des bras de forgerons, des mains de boxeurs qui vous démonteraient la mâchoire
d'un seul coup. Ils *s'empoignent,*—pardon du mot, c'est le seul juste,—et s'étreignent, et se
poussent. C'est d'une vérité à faire trembler. Je ne suis inquiet que sur un point: comment
peuvent-ils se tenir si fermement sur leurs pieds avec les varices qu'ils ont aux jambes? Mais
la pièce capitale, et sur le succès de laquelle M. Courbet a évidemment compté, c'est son
tableau des *Baigneuses.* Comment donner une idée de ces baigneuses? . . . L'une, sorti de
l'eau la première, est assise sur un banc de gazon, et se sèche au soleil; elle est à peu près
habillée. Mais la seconde! Ma foi, la seconde est habillée jusqu'à la mi-jambe. . . . Et il faut
voir ce cou, ce dos, ces reins etc. Quelles gaillardes! quelles chairs! quels muscles! quel
épanouissement de formes! Et quelles couleurs! le rouge et le noir se mêlent et s'unissent
pour faire rebondir une peau épaisse, rude et bistrée. On aperçoit, suspendus aux branches
d'un arbre, une robe de soie, un mantelet et un chapeau! Il paraît que ce sont des *dames!* les
dames des *lutteurs* peut-être. . . . Il n'y a point à désespérer d'un pays où les *dames* peuvent
présenter des formes qu'envieraient les plus robustes vachères!

Pour parler plus sérieusement, il me semble que la plaisanterie que M. Courbet se permet vis à vis du public est assez prolongée. . . . Le public se demande quel est le but de toutes ces mascarades; si M. Courbet a voulu, à force de bizarrerie, acquérir rapidement une réputation, il a réussi; on s'occupe de ses tableaux plus que des oeuvres les plus éminentes et les plus consciencieuses. Il serait temps, maintenant, qu'il nous montrât ce qu'il sait réellement faire.

V. Charles Tillot, "Exposition de 1853, Revue de Salon," *Le siècle,* June 25, 1853 (fifth article):

Nous avons remarqué que M. Millet est . . . sincère et naïf comme M. Hamon. C'est que l'amour de la nature les a conduits au même but. M. Courbet, qui accuse la même intention, y est-il arrivé? C'est ce qu'il est bien permis de lui contester. Aussi avant d'entrer dans un examen détaillé de son œuvre, voyons si M. Courbet a justifié le titre de réaliste qu'il prend si souvent. . . . Qu'entend-on par réalisme? Il est bien utile de s'entendre là-dessus, car de quoi n'a-t-on pas accusé le réalisme! C'est, a-t-on dit, la mort de l'art. C'est l'imitation et non la chose; le réalisme, c'est la célébration du laid; enfin, le réalisme, c'est la peinture de M. Courbet. Fort heureusement, le réalisme n'est rien de tout cela, et nous avons même la conviction que c'est la seule voie que puisse prendre l'art pour s'élever à la hauteur qu'il est destinée à atteindre. . . . C'est là pour nous le réalisme, c'est-a-dire la reproduction des objets avec l'impression qu'ils ont laissé dans le cerveau du peintre. Aussi, plus que la pensée de l'artiste est élevée, plus il éprouve d'impressions; plus il est poète, plus il approche du réalisme pur. Si au contraire l'artiste ne perçoit que des formes et des couleurs, il cesse d'être l'homme de la pensée, il n'est plus que l'homme de la matière. C'est en cela qu'on fait, selon nous, un trop grand honneur à certains artistes en les traitant de réalistes. M. Courbet est de ce nombre. . . . M. Courbet est un artiste qui, avec des facultés merveilleuses de peintre, ou s'est laissé étourdir par le bruit qu'il a fait, ou a manqué de la force nécessaire pour continuer son œuvre. . . .

Entreprendre de relever l'homme malgré son costume, malgré les rides et le hâle que la fatigue et les passions tracent sur son front; malgré son ignorance, le montrer grand et austère parce qu'il souffre et qu'il travaille, telle était, nous en avons la croyance, l'idée première de M. Courbet. . . . Mais M. Courbet n'a pas su s'en tenir là. Est-ce par suite d'un système? Est-ce défaut d'élévation dans les idées? On ne saurait le dire. Toujours est-il qu'il est presque impossible actuellement de trouver dans ses œuvres aucune des qualités qui nous avaient si vivement frappé dans ses premiers tableaux. On a accusé l'artiste de charlatanisme, d'avoir voulu amener la foule par ses excentricités, en attirant l'attention par des coups de pistolet. . . . M. Courbet se trompe évidemment s'il croit que la peinture doive reproduire les objets tels que les offre la nature. Il y a un choix à faire. . . . M. Courbet a eu pendant quelque temps la gloire d'avoir renversé le fameux axiome de Platon: »l'art c'est la célébration du beau«. Pour notre artiste, l'art c'est la célébration du laid. . . .

Si M. Courbet pousse par cet exemple au développement de la race humaine, nous lui prédisons grand succès en Turquie, où les femmes se vendent au poids, ou en Angleterre, s'il veut exposer ses productions en concurrence de ces énormes bœufs que les Anglais défigurent sous prétexte de les améliorer. . . . Ses *Lutteurs* sont noirs comme deux Auvergnats adonnés au commerce du charbon; ils ne sont même pas dessinés, et on ne sait comment ils se tiennent embrassés. C'est pour M. Courbet une véritable chute.

VI. Clément de Ris, "Salon de 1853: Lettres à un ami, à Bruxelles," *L'artiste*, June 1, 1853, pp. 129–131 (first article):

Les extrêmes se touchent, et, sans s'en douter, M. Courbet a formé M. Gérôme. L'un explique l'autre. En voulant exagérer le sentiment de la vie et de la réalité, en étudiant avec soins et conscience les difformités physiologiques, en recherchant le hideux dans la réalité, on autorise la recherche du laid dans l'idéal. . . . C'est M. Courbet qui aura introduit l'ennemi . . . M. Courbet est parvenu à révolter le sens général. Sa femme est ignoble, grotesque, monstrueuse: c'est la réunion de toutes les laideurs imaginables. Pourquoi a-t-il fait un pareil choix? car c'est un choix; c'est là où est le tort. . . .

Les *Lutteurs* sont moins choquants. Malgré des imperfections (la cuisse droite du lutteur de gauche), ils sont bien dessinés; mais il est impossible que M. Courbet n'ait pas fait exprès de donner aux ombres cette noirceur qui doit réjouir les marchands de cirage, mais qui surprend sur les poitrines humaines. La peinture de M. Courbet ne m'exaspère pas comme certaines personnes, elle me rend triste pour lui d'abord, dont je regrette de voir les remarquables moyens employés à un si triste usage, et ensuite pour l'école moderne, contre laquelle ses déplorables exagérations deviendront de cruels arguments un jour.

VII. Henry de Pène, "Salon de 1853," *Chronique de France,* June 1, 1853, pp. 470–474 (first article):

Si M. Courbet est sincère, ce dont je me permets de douter, l'horreur qu'il a pu éprouver pour la peinture de M. Winterhalter . . . a peut-être contribué à le jeter dans les extrémités opposées. Mais M. Courbet porte un masque, et joue un rôle. Il manie avec adresse deux instruments dont il se moque également: son propre pinceau, et la naïveté publique, et il fait chanter son nom sur tous les tons. . . . Mais, observez comme il procède: En même temps qu'il produit l'Enterrement villageois, les Casseurs de pierres, avec mission de faire la parade et de rassembler la masse autour de son nom, il n'oublie pas d'exposer une tête d'homme où les connaisseurs saluent de rares qualités. Cette année, à côté des *Lutteurs*, à côté de ce quartier de viande décroché à l'étalage d'un boucher qu'il lui plaît d'intituler *Baigneuse*, il nous montre une paysanne, endormie sur sa quenouille, où certaines parties sont traitées en main de maître. . . .

M. Courbet a du talent, c'est incontestable; mais, qu'il y prenne garde: maintenant qu'il s'est de vive force emparé de l'attention, elle sera sévère pour lui.

VIII. Henri Delaborde, "Salon de 1853," *Revue des deux mondes,* 1853, pp. 1143–44:

Quant à certaines toiles, où la méthode réaliste est appliquée à des scènes d'un autre ordre, nous ne croyons pas, malgré le bruit qui se fait autour d'elles, que ce soit pour nous un devoir de nous y arrêter et de les décrire. Bien qu'il soit possible peut-être, et en y regardant de fort près, d'y reconnaître quelque indice d'habileté matérielle, quelque promesse de talent énergique, elles sont à tous autres égards si peu conformes aux lois essentielles de l'art, que nous ne voulons pas contribuer, même par la juste sévérité de nos critiques, à leur donner une importance qu'en somme elles ne sauraient avoir.

IX. Félix Tournachon (Nadar), "Nadar jury au Salon de 1853," *Album comique . . . texte et dessins par Nadar,* Paris, 1853, unpaginated:

J'ai dit que je haïssais surtout les torts de ceux que j'aime le plus. A ce compte, j'en veux terriblement à M. Courbet. Pendant deux ans, l'apparition de ces grandes figures d'Ornans m'émut d'une façon tout à fait enthousiaste et fraternelle. *L'Enterrement* reste surtout, pour moi, une admirable toile, pleine d'impression et de sentiment. Courbet se montrait là bon peintre et psychologue, ce qui ne gâte jamais rien, et ne se fût-il montré ni l'un ni l'autre, il lui restait encore une très-sérieuse raison d'être: si par ces essais il n'ouvrait pas précisément une voie nouvelle, car Goya et autres avait passé déjà bien près de là, au moins indiquait-il qu'il y avait à chercher des inspirations, une manière et des types à côté et au delà des habitudes actuelles.

L'année dernière, M. Courbet s'était comme reposé. Le paysage des *Demoiselles de village* était sans grande signification. . . . Cette fois voici trois toiles, dont deux d'importante dimension, qui semblent vouloir poser la question. La couleur, dans toutes les trois, est terne, triste, boueuse. Je ne reproche pas à sa *Baigneuse* l'exagération des formes, qui choque tant de gens. J'accepte volontiers, dans leurs amplifications et leurs débordements, ces natures de femmes-là. C'est comme une espèce percheronne, et je n'y vois rien à dire. Si, maintenant, ceux que la Baigneuse de Courbet irrite à ce point de vue, acceptent, sans y faire même attention, les natures de Rubens en leurs chairs bourreletées, Courbet doit comprendre que toute la question est dans la peinture proprement dite. Ce n'est pas une hymne à la laideur qu'il nous donne, c'est un état de malpropreté. . . . On dirait que Courbet peint dans une boutique de charbonnier, au milieu de la poussière et des scories.

Les *Lutteurs* sont au-dessous encore. Je croyais que Courbet nous rappellerait le public ordinaire de ces luttes, et je comprenais alors le tableau. Il y a, dans cette salle Montesquieu, une galerie ordinaire de personnages étranges, généralement pervers et brutaux, types accentués des profondeurs parisiennes, race bien distincte et tranchée en dehors des habitudes générales, et qui n'en tiennent pas moins leur place, comme une espèce d'Etat dans l'Etat.

Il y avait peut-être une raison pour un homme qui s'appelle Courbet en si grosses lettres de constater sur la toile cet échantillon assez terrible d'un des côtés de notre société moderne. Au lieu de cela, deux bons hommes d'un dessin douteux, et qui me touchent tout juste autant que l'œuvre d'un jeune élève de Suisse ou Dupuis. La couleur est fausse en tous points et abominable. Je connais l'un des deux modèles, et cette carnation verdâtre à peine dorée par le ciel marseillais, je ne la retrouve guère dans cette débauche de bitume. Les articulations ne sont pas lourdes ni écrasées comme cela. Voyez donc ce même coup de hanche que le hasard indiquait en même temps à M. Ottin—un sculpteur, à la bonne heure! Ses lutteurs ont une élégance de formes dont il n'y avait pas à se passer ici; ceux de M. Courbet sont patauds et issus des flancs de sa baigneuse. Je ne puis voir dans cette toile autre chose que deux bons hommes en pain d'épices variqueux,—et la peste soit de la varice!

La Fileuse, dont j'avais vu une très-belle préparation, est obscure encore et terne. . . . M. Courbet s'est posé en peintre du Danube, à la bonne heure, mais il ne faut pas qu'il s'y trompe: la grossièreté n'est pas la force, non plus que la brutalité n'est la franchise, ni le scandale la réputation. Il ne faut pas non plus se frotter les mains et dire: Vous voyez bien que je suis le plus grand peintre, puisque c'est moi qu'on attaque le plus. . . . Jamais les attaques, surtout générales et sincères, n'ont servi l'homme attaqué: ce n'est pas pour avoir été nié que M. Delacroix a prévalu, c'est parce qu'il était Delacroix.

X. Théophile Silvestre, "Courbet d'après nature" (1861), Courthion, vol. 1, p. 45:

Les *Lutteurs* et les *Baigneuses* soulevèrent une tempête au Salon de 1853. Le ton des lutteurs est noir, sans transparence, tout à fait en désaccord avec le fond du tableau qui représente l'Hippodrome des Champs-Elysées au plein soleil de l'été, et le dessin visant à la justesse manque d'ampleur. L'une des deux baigneuses, la plus célèbre, celle qui tourne le dos au spectateur avec cynisme, est un monceau de matière puissamment rendu. Le tableau qui devait faire passer les *Baigneuses*, c'est la *Fileuse endormie*, figure simple, solide, noire et lourde.

XI. Jules-François-Félix Husson (Champfleury), "Salon de 1853," *Souvenirs et portraits de jeunesse*, Paris, 1872, p. 227:

Je ne sais plus que penser des tableaux de Courbet au Salon de cette année. Les sottes admirations, les détracteurs acharnés finissent par enlever le libre examen. Il est difficile de se dégager de ces influences, et le sentiment personnel en est troublé. En lisant une vive critique à propos des *Lutteurs*, j'ai d'abord cru que le feuilletonniste avait raison; mais les maladroits éloges qu'il donne à un peintre médiocre qui a les défauts de Courbet sans aucune de ses fortes qualités, m'ont rendu la netteté nécessaire aux appréciations. Courbet est violemment attaqué à cause de ses prêches, de sa personnalité bruyante; il serait cependant équitable de ne pas lui opposer de honteuses médiocrités.

XII. Zacharie Astruc, "Les 14 stations du Salon (1859) suivies d'une histoire douloureuse," *Le quart d'heure* 11, July 20, 1859, p. 203:

Vous parlez d'études académiques. Quel plus émouvant drame de muscles que ces deux fiers *lutteurs*, enlacés, tordus, haletants, au milieu de cet élégant paysage, contre ces verts massifs derrière lesquels jaillissent les tours carrées d'un château, sous ce beau ciel pur d'une lumière si heureuse. Comme la chair est bien exprimée! comme ils vivent violemment ces deux hommes. Quelle couleur! quelle large exécution! Il y a des bras admirables, des torses de toute beauté; la tête penchée du lutteur lymphatique, vue du côté des cheveux qui s'épandent sur sa poitrine, est superbe. Ribéra s'effraierait d'une telle vigueur. Et quel beau dessin!

Notes

The following abbreviations are used in the notes. See the References for other works cited by author's name or short title.

BM   *The Burlington Magazine*
BN   Bibliothèque Nationale
GBA   *Gazette des beaux-arts*
JHK   *Jahrbuch der Hamburger Kunstsammlungen*
RDM   *Revue des deux mondes*

CHAPTER 1. Redeemer and Charlatan, Subversive and Martyr

1. Borel, p. 47. On page 46 Borel quotes from Gill's *Souvenirs:* "The truly wonderful thing about this *mask* of an Assyrian idol leavened with village rusticity was the gaze."

2. This "nevertheless" also had its financial aspect. Courbet's exclusion from the Salon and rejection on the part of official institutions created a kind of counter-audience. His pictures found many buyers, and the renowned dealer Durand-Ruel showed them with great success.

3. The reaction to this provocation was correspondingly harsh. Gill's partisanship with the Commune cost him dearly, for his commissions decreased and in 1881 he was interned in Charenton.

4. See Emile Bergerat, *Sauvons Courbet,* Paris, 1871, p. 8:

> Il appartient à la pathologie interne,
> Et ce fait est depuis longtemps accrédité
> Que, pour la profondeur de la stupidité,
> Si le puits est Hugo, Courbet est la citerne!

5. Concerning the identification of Courbet with *The Stonebreakers,* see the essay by Michael Nungesser in *Cat. Hamburg,* 1978–79, pp. 560, 571 (with reference to Courbet as a "Raphael des tas de cailloux").

6. See chap. 8 in this volume.

7. Bertall's caricature of Courbet's *Beggar's Alms* (with a lovely lady taken from Lefèvre; ibid.) found its sequel in another caricature by the same artist, of the Socialist International as a product of the devil; see Hofmann, "Gespräch, Gegensatz und Entfremdung—Deutsche und Franzosen suchen ihre Identität," in *Cat. Hamburg,* 1978–79, p. 150.

8. See Karl Marx, "The Eighteenth Brumaire of Louis Bonaparte" (1852), English ed. Moscow, 1967, p. 63, with regard to Napoleon III: "An old crafty *roué,* he conceives the historical life of the nations as a masquerade where the grand costumes, words and postures merely serve to mask the pettiest knavery."

9. Letter to Bruyas of May 1854, in Borel, p. 20: "There is one other [portrait] I still have to do—that of a man who is sure of his principles, that of a free man." These words, mistakenly associated by Toussaint with the *Self-Portrait in Striped Collar* (*Cat. Paris,* 1977–78, no. 37), can only have referred to the artist's depiction of himself in *The Painter's Studio.*

10. See Shroder, p. 40; Werner Hofmann, in *Ossian und die Kunst um 1800,* exh. cat., Hamburger Kunsthalle, 1974, pp. 49ff.; and my own essay "Meryons 'Eaux-Fortes sur Paris'," *Kritische Berichte,* n.s. 4, 1976, nos. 2–3, pp. 47ff.

11. Repro. in *Cat. Brooklyn,* 1988–89, p. 100.

12. Théophile Thoré, in *La vraie république,* April 13, 1848. See also Viollet-le-Duc's comparison of poets to martyrs, quoted in Shroder, p. 51.

13. Compare Daumier's caricature of Sébastien Véron as a "new St. Sebastian" (1849); reproduced in Loys Delteil, *Le peintre-graveur illustré* 25, Paris, 1926, no. 1917. See also Daumier's drawing for a St. Sebastian (1849) and the commentary on it by Clark, *Bourgeois,* p. 113.

14. See Shroder, p. 31 (with reference to "l'homme fatal" and the isolation of the artist); also Wolfgang Kemp, "Das Bild der Menge," *Städel-Jahrbuch,* n.s. 4, 1973, pp. 249–270, esp. pp. 251f.

15. See Léger, *Caricatures,* p. 38; *Cat. Hamburg,* 1978–79, p. 496.

16. Léger, *Caricatures,* p. 29; *Cat. Hamburg,* 1978–79, p. 19.

17. Delvau, *Histoire anecdotique des cafés et cabarets de Paris,* Paris, 1862, p. 4; also Peter-Klaus Schuster, in *Cat. Hamburg,* 1978–79, p. 214.

18. See Clark, *Bourgeois,* p. 112, and the present author's review of Clark in *Kritische Berichte,* n.s. 6, 1978, no. 3, p. 48; also Frank Paul Bowman, *Le Christ romantique,* Geneva, 1973.

19. See Borel, p. 21; on this and the following discussion, see also Peter-Klaus Schuster, "Der karikierte Courbet," *Cat. Hamburg,* 1978–79, pp. 494–500. Courbet's words include allusions to the topic of the Wandering Jew; see Nochlin, *Meeting,* pp. 209–222.

20. See Bertall's caricature *Jésus peignant au milieu de ses disciples ou la divine école de Manet, tableau religieux par Fantin-Latour, Le journal amusant,* May 21, 1870.

21. See Léger, *Caricatures,* p. 51; *Cat. Hamburg,* 1978–79, p. 273.

22. See Charles Léger, *Courbet et son temps,* Paris, 1948, p. 54.

23. Werner Hofmann, in *Kunst—was ist das?* exh. cat., Hamburger Kunsthalle, 1977, p. 97.

24. In Michelet's sense of the term; see Jules Michelet, *Le peuple,* Leipzig and Brussels, 1846.

25. In an unpublished passage of his speech, he says: "Thanks to realism, which expects everything from the *individual* and his achievement, we have realized that the *people* must be instructed in order to bring forth everything themselves; while with idealism . . . that is, with authority and aristocracy, [the people] received everything from above . . . and therefore succumbed to ignorance and resignation."

26. Although Courbet did reach this goal for a short time in 1851 when Louis Peisse, the director of the Ecole des Beaux-Arts, wrote: "Thanks to M. Courbet, art has become one with the people" ("Par M. Courbet l'art s'est fait peuple"). See Clark, *People,* p. 186, n. 39 (without further reference).

27. Champfleury, in "Courbet en 1860," quoted in Lacambre, p. 186; Gautier expressed himself similarly; see chap. 2 in this volume.

28. Clark, *People*, p. 186, n. 41. Thierry is alluding to Luke 2, verses 29–32.

29. Courbet's oversize red signature was indeed considered to play its part in the painter's diabolic behavior.

30. Arnold Mortier; quoted in Courthion, vol. 2, p. 303.

31. Reproduced in *Cat. Hamburg*, 1978–79, p. 155, 520, 571.

32. See Courthion, vol. 2, pp. 47–52.

33. Quoted in Champfleury, "Courbet en 1860"; see Lacambre, p. 179.

34. On the concept of the ugly, see Ursula Franke, in *Historisches Wörterbuch der Philosophie*, vol. 3, Basel, 1974, cols. 1003–1007.

35. Théophile Gautier, "Salon de 1850–51," fourth article: "M. Courbet," *La presse*, Feb. 15, 1851.

36. Augustin-Joseph du Pays, "Salon de 1853," *L'illustration*, June 18, 1853, p. 392.

37. Prosper Mérimée, "Salon de 1853," *Le moniteur universel*, May 17, 1853, p. 1: "En haine de la noblesse de convention, on s'est jeté dans le trivial; en dégoût du beau idéal, on a recherché le laid de parti pris."

38. Hofmann, "Wirklichkeiten," p. 607.

39. For Proudhon's opinion, see his essay *Du principe de l'art et de sa destination sociale*, Paris, 1865, reprint Farnborough, 1971, pp. 215f. Champfleury expected that the main figure of *The Bathers*, whom he called "une bourgeoise," would provoke a scandal; Edmond and Jules de Goncourt noted in their journal for Sept. 18, 1867: "Le laid, toujours le laid, et le *laid bourgeois*, le laid sans son grand charactère, sans la beauté du laid" (quoted in Courthion, vol. 2, p. 301).

40. See Pierre Barbéris, *Balzac et le mal du siècle: Contribution à une philosophie du monde moderne*, 2 vols., Paris, 1970; vol. 1, p. 55 ("mal du siècle aristocratique"), p. 75 ("mal du siècle bourgeois").

41. Clément de Ris, "Salon de 1853: Lettres à un ami à Bruxelles," *L'artiste*, June 1, 1853, p. 129.

42. Quoted in Lacambre, p. 157. The allusions refer, among other paintings, to *The Stonebreakers* (papier-mâché noses) and to *A Burial at Ornans* (drunkards' faces).

43. Pierre-Joseph Proudhon, *Philosophie du progrès* (1853), in *Oeuvres complètes*, vol. 12, Paris, 1946, reprint Geneva, 1982, pp. 88–96.

44. Edmond and Jules de Goncourt, *Etudes d'art; Le salon de 1852; La peinture à l'exposition de 1855*, Paris, n.d., p. 170.

45. An attempt to refute this accusation has been made by the present author, in "Realismus—eine Frage des Ziels," *Als guter Realist muß ich alles erfinden*, exh. cat., Hamburger Kunstverein, Hamburg, 1978–79, pp. 12–23.

46. According to the report of Champfleury, in *Souvenirs et portraits de jeunesse*, Paris, 1872; reprint Geneva, 1972, p. 179. As early as 1855, Eugène Loudun wrote: "Enfin la matière, la matière sans idéal, l'objet tel qu'il existe, le réel en un mot . . . , MM. Courbet, Bonvin etc., le représentent dans son impudente nudité" (*Le salon de 1855*, Paris, 1855, p. 13).

47. See his caricature *The Battle of Schools: Idealism and Realism*, repro. in Delteil (see n. 13 above), vol. 26, no. 2629.

48. See Nadar, *A Realistic Painter, Le journal pour rire*, Jan. 17, 1857; repro. in my essay "Realismus—eine Frage des Ziels," (n. 45), p. 16. Also Daumier's *They Rejected It—the Philistines!* *Le charivari*, April 6, 1859; repro. in Delteil (n. 13), vol. 8, no 3135; and especially Daumier's *A Realist Can Always Find a Still Greater Realist to Admire Him* (woodcut, 1868, with pipe and candle), repro. in Eduard Fuchs, ed., *Honoré Daumier, Holzschnitte: 1833–1870*, Munich, n.d., p. 205.

49. The term *wanderer* meant both the Fourierist missionaries, who, like Jean Journet, walked through France, and, on a metaphorical level, the artists and writers who "envisioned

themselves as . . . restless voyagers at home nowhere" (Nochlin, *Meeting*, p. 216), hence the identification with the "Wandering Jew." In 1870, the same term was used to designate the traveling exhibitions organized by contemporary painters in St. Petersburg and elsewhere.

50. In *La lune*, Aug. 12, 1866; reprinted in Léger, *Caricatures*, p. 63.

51. See *Realismus und Realität*, exh. cat., Darmstadt, Kunsthalle, 1975, p. xxi; also Michel Foucault, *Ceci n'est pas une pipe: Deux lettres et quatre dessins de René Magritte*, Scholies, 1973.

52. See Grandville, *Das gesamte Werk*, introduction by Gottfried Sello, 2 vols., Munich, 3d ed., 1972; vol. 1, p. 312.

53. Friedrich Theodor Vischer, *Ästhetik oder Wissenschaft des Schönen*, 6 vols. (1846–57), ed. R. Vischer, 2d ed., Munich, 1922–23; part 2, p. 363. For a discussion, see George L. Mosse, *The Nationalization of the Masses: Political Symbolism and Mass Movements in Germany . . .*, New York, 1975.

CHAPTER 2. "Les Lutteurs Détestables"

1. Repro. in *Cat. Brooklyn*, 1988–89, p. 111.

2. See Eugène Loudun, Appendix, IV, to this volume; also Jules Vallès, "Courbet," in Courthion, vol. 2, p. 224: "La foule s'arrêtait devant ces toiles, mais avec plus de stupeur que d'émotion. . . . Courbet fut traité de vaniteux féroce et de charlatan comique. Quand il eut ajouté aux *Casseurs de Pierre* et à l'*Enterrement d'Ornans* les *Lutteurs* et la *Baigneuse*, tout fut dit. Il devait pendant douze ans être appelé un excentrique, et passer aux yeux de la foule pour un fanfaron de vulgarité." A more exhaustive discussion of the crowd's reaction is found in Clark, *Buchon*, pp. 209, 289; see also Bertall's caricature of *The Peasants Returning from the Fair* (fig. 69), whose caption runs: "Rien n'égale l'enthousiasme produit sur le public par les tableaux de Courbet." One can hardly agree with Vallès's last remark, however, as the "vulgarity" of Courbet's pictures very likely shocked the critics more than the hoi polloi.

3. On Champfleury's attitude, see Clark, *People*, pp. 53ff., 66ff. See also Charles Tillot (Appendix, V) and Nadar (Appendix, IX), both of whom preferred the "naive" Courbet of 1850–51 to the "critical" Courbet of 1853.

4. See Riat, pp. 102, 104; also Appendix, I–IX.

5. Eloquent silence was the best reaction, said Henri Delaborde in the *Revue des deux mondes* (Appendix, VIII); the Salon reviews in the *Gazette de France*, the *Magazin pittoresque*, and *La patrie* did not mention Courbet; Léon Aubineau, writing in the Catholic paper *L'univers* for July 3, 1853, was contented with a reference to Courbet's "toiles impossibles," and Louis Peisse in *Le constitutionnel* for May 20, 1853 with the statement, "Dans la peinture de genre, M. Courbet continue, dans trois tableaux, ses cruelles expériences sur le goût publique." Similar sentiments were expressed by André Jubinal in *L'abeille impériale* for May 31, 1853, p. 10. "Pourquoi chercher l'ignoble?" asked Louis Boyeldieu d'Auvigny (*Guide aux Menus-Plaisirs, Salon de 1853*, Paris, 1853); Horsin Déon called *The Wrestlers* a "tableau repoussant dont nous ne pouvons expliquer la présence au Salon" (*Rapport sur le Salon de 1853*, Paris, 1853, p. 18). Gustave Le Brisoys (Gustave Desnoiresterres) limited his comments to *The Bathers* in his review in *La mode* for July 25, 1853, pp. 149–150, as did Prosper Mérimée in his *Moniteur universel* contribution of June 5, 1853.

6. The painting is mentioned only in passing and seldom reproduced in the monographs, except in Marie Kálmán, "Le Centenaire des 'Lutteurs'," *Bull. du Musée National Hongrois des Beaux-Arts* 4, 1954, pp. 43–47; Nochlin, *Style and Society*, pp. 185–188; *Courbet à Montpellier*, exh. cat., Montpellier, Musée Fabre, 1985, pp. 49–51 (with color plate, p. 17). The first publication of the present article (*JHK* 22, 1977) contained an excellent color plate, p. 139. István Genthon (Museum der bildenden Künste Budapest, *Die grosse Zeit der neuen fran-*

zösischen Malerei, German and French eds., Budapest, 1972, pp. 12–13) suggests that an X ray study of the painting be made, but this has as yet proven infeasible. For a more recent negative opinion, see Joseph C. Sloane, *French Painting between the Past and the Present,* Princeton, N.J., 2d ed., 1973, p. 156.

7. Riat, p. 31. The original composition was not exhibited until the Salon of 1848, where it was praised by Champfleury; for a more recent discussion, see Marie-Thérèse de Forges, in *Cat. Paris,* 1977–78, p. 26. The astonished tone of Champfleury's and Gigoux's remarks of 1848 would seem to speak against the early execution date. Above all, the artist's meeting with Gigoux ("Mônsieur, me dit-il, je viens vous demander si vous pouvez venir voir mon tâbleau!") suggests that Courbet did not finish the canvas until spring 1848 (see Jean Gigoux, "Courbet," *Revue Franc-Comtoise,* 1884, p. 455).

8. Riat, p. 31: "Un alchimiste poursuivant une jeune femme, qui personnifie la nature." If the depiction was in fact "provoquée par l'idée générale du Faust" (Jules F.-F. Husson, alias Champfleury, "Revue des Beaux-Arts," *Le pamphlet,* Sept. 28–30, 1848; quoted in Lacambre, p. 153) or even represented a satire on Goethe's drama (Riat, p. 31), the figures were probably Faust and Helena. At any rate, this is more plausible than Gigoux's version (see n. 10).

9. Lacambre, p. 153: "Je le dis ici, qu'on s'en souvienne! Celui-là, l'inconnu, qui a peint cette *Nuit,* sera un grand peintre."

10. Gigoux, "Courbet", pp. 455–456: "Je vis sur la toile énorme une Nymphe poursuivie par un Apollon quelconque, les bras étendus, courant au pas gymnastique, et pour comble, portant une queue de morue—un frac—dont les pans flottants accompagnaient le mouvement de la jambe, et un large feutre sur l'oreille à la mode du temps." Courbet's attempt to modernize the myth with satirical intent finds a parallel in *Faust,* part 2, act 2, verses 7087–7089:

> Yet I think antiquity's much too alive;
> You could tackle it the modern way
> And plaster it over with the latest fashions.

Courbet was acquainted with *Faust* in the translation made by his friend Sabatier-Ungher.

11. On Courbet's notion of imagination in art, see his letter of Dec. 25, 1861, which was inspired by Castagnary: "L'imagination dans l'art consiste à savoir trouver l'expression la plus complète d'une chose existante, mais jamais à supposer ou à créer cette chose même" (quoted in Courthion, vol. 2, p. 206).

12. For a recent discussion, see Hélène Toussaint, in *Cat. Paris,* 1977–78, pp. 241–272.

13. In this case, too, the rejected composition is unknown; an X ray investigation is not feasible (see *Cat. Paris,* 1977–78, no. 97). As I have attempted to show, social problems (the idea of reconciliation, redemption through communing with nature) are indeed involved in Courbet's *Covert of Roe-Deer.* See chap. 4 in this volume.

14. See *Catalogue de tableaux . . . par G. Courbet dépendant de sa succession . . . ,* 2ᵉ vente, Hôtel Drouot, June 28, 1882, no. 1. Although the price was set at 10,000 francs, the painting brought only 5,800 (as compared to *The Wounded Man,* 11,000 fr.; *Return from the Conference,* 15,000 fr.; *The Studio,* 21,000 fr.; *The Kill: Episode during the Deer Hunt,* 33,900 fr.; *Fighting Stags,* 41,900 fr.). *The Wrestlers* entered the Léon Hirsch Collection, Chenonceaux, then was sold to Cassirer, Berlin, where it was purchased by F. Hatvany.

15. According to Courbet in a letter to his parents, May 13, 1853; see also Riat, p. 102.

16. See Shroder, 1961, pp. 30f., 54, 73, 151.

17. The best contemporary description of the Champs-Elysées as a "promenade du beau monde" is given by E. Texier, *Tableau de Paris,* vol. 1, Paris, 1852, pp. 5–23. See also Jacques Hillairet, *Dictionnaire historique des rues de Paris,* Paris, 1963, pp. 297–302; and *La mode,* July 5, 1853, p. 18: "Le Paris de théâtres et du plaisir n'est plus dans Paris, il est aux Champs-Elysées, au Cirque d'Eté, à l'Hippodrome, au Ranelagh, à Mabille, partout où il se trouve vingt

pieds carrés pour tricoter des jambes; aussi ces entreprises dansantes et masourkantes sont-elles assiégées et par le public qui paie, et par un public tant soit peu équivoque qui voudrait bien ne pas payer." This suggests the friction that existed among the different classes at leisure places.

18. The Cirque Napoléon, designed by Hittorf, was inaugurated on November 12, 1852. It was described by Pitre-Chevalier as "un ensemble à la fois riche et grandiose, orné de sculptures magistrales, par MM. Pradier, Duret, Bosio, Husson et Dantan. On y voit . . . les luttes et les scènes antiques, au milieu des cavaliers, des amazones, des Dieux païens" (*Le musée des familles* 20, 1852–53, pp. 158f.). Courbet's attack was directed against this pompous official architecture.

19. Seated in the front row of the royal box are men in uniform and well-dressed civilians with their ladies, evidently representatives of the *beau monde*, which Courbet relegates to the background.

20. See Alfred Messel, "Ausstellungsbauten," *Handbuch der Architektur*, Darmstadt, 1893, p. 483; E. Schmitt, *Zirkus- und Hippodromgebäude*, Stuttgart, 1904, pp. 15ff. For a general discussion of sports events as bolstering the established order and its norms, see Franz Joachim Verspohl, *Stadionbauten von der Antike bis zur Gegenwart. Regie und Selbsterfahrung der Massen*, Giessen, 1976, passim.

21. See *Bull. de la Société des Amis de Courbet* 31, 1964, p. 12f. As indicated by the letter to Gautier published here, Courbet sold the sketch to a Brazilian collector.

22. An example is his meeting with the superintendent of fine arts, Nieuwerkerke; see Courthion, vol. 2, pp. 79–84.

23. See the letter by Courbet to Wey (1850): "Dans notre société si bien civilisée, il faut que je mène une vie de sauvage" (Courthion, vol. 2, p. 78); also Urbain Cuénot to Juliette Courbet (Feb. 13, 1851): "Cet homme est un sauvage" (ibid., vol. 1, p. 98).

24. Courbet to Wey, Nov. 26, 1849 (Courthion, vol. 2, p. 76).

25. See, for example, "Dieppe or the Champs-Elysées by the Sea" (*L'illustration*, Nov. 1, 1862, p. 300), which also contains six further depictions of this kind by Bertall and Dumont.

26. See A. Bénard, *Wrestling*, advertising poster, c. 1895, Paris, BN; repro. in *JHK* 22, 1977, p. 142.

27. See *Manet*, exh. cat., Paris and New York, 1983, no. 33, p. 111.

28. See Hugh F. Leonard, *A Handbook of Wrestling*, New York, 1897, which is still one of the best-documented handbooks. None of the 220 positions it illustrates comes anywhere near that rendered by Courbet. On the development of the sport in France, see particularly Léon Ville, *La lutte et les lutteurs (avec 39 vignettes et 25 planches photographiées par Nadar)*, Paris, 1891; and Edmond Desbonnet, *Les rois de la lutte*, Paris, 1910.

29. As in a lithograph by Nadar, ill. in Ville, *La lutte*, p. iv; repro. in *JHK* 22, 1977, p. 142.

30. Claude Augé ed., *Le Nouveau Larousse illustré*, Paris, 1898–1903, vol. 5, s.v. "lutte," fig. 27.

31. Falguière, who was active primarily as a sculptor and may well have appreciated the plasticity of Courbet's treatment, probably owned one of the photographs that Courbet had taken in 1853 (see also n. 15).

32. See Martín Sebastián Soria, *The Paintings of Zurbaran*, London, 1953, cat. nos. 99, 101, figs. 68, 70 (*Hercules Dividing the Cliffs of Kolpe and Abyla; Hercules Struggling with Cerberus*). A depiction of Hercules fighting the Hydra of Lerna may also have inspired Courbet; presumably he knew these paintings through engravings. With regard to this classicizing tradition, which underlies even Courbet's picture, I should add that shortly after the first publication of this article, appeared the study of Marcia Pointon, "Painters and Pugilism in Early Nineteenth-Century England", *GBA* 92, 1978, pp. 131–140. As the author shows very convincingly, English artists at the turn of the nineteenth century followed and even practiced this sport in order to corroborate academic principles by life studies. Younger artists were also interested in the social

and psychological experiences offered by these contacts; in this respect they may be considered to be forerunners of Courbet.

33. See Appendix, XII. On the influence on Courbet of Spanish painting (especially that in the Musée Espagnol, Paris) see Clark, *People*, pp. 41f. Both the typological and the color idiosyncracies of the painting speak against the influence of Italian art (Pollaiuolo, Guido Reni), which various authors, including Nochlin (*Style and Society*, p. 187) have detected.

34. Riat, p. 99: "des grisailles sur cartons."

35. See chap. 3 in this volume.

36. See Toussaint, in *Cat. Paris*, 1977–78, pp. 124f.

37. See Courthion, vol. 1, p. 146.

38. See Clark, *Buchon*, pp. 208ff.; and Toussaint, in *Cat. Paris*, 1977–78, p. 251.

39. Nickname of the wrestler Arpin, who was active in 1852–53; see Desbonnet (n. 28), p. 3.

40. " . . . une certaine bourgeoise nue, qui sort de l'eau et qui montre les fesses au public. Grand scandale, attendez-vous-y." Champfleury to Buchon; see Riat, p. 102.

41. "Pour les Lutteurs, on rien dit ni bien ni mal jusqu'ici." Courbet to his parents, May 13, 1853; Riat, p. 102.

42. According to Castagnary, when Bruyas saw *The Bathers*, he exclaimed, "Voici l'art libre, cette toile m'appartient"; see Courthion, vol. 1, p. 113.

43. A multipurpose auditorium for sports and musical events; see Texier, *Tableau de Paris*, vol. 2, p. 295. Ville writes, "Les Parisiens ne se passionnèrent pour la lutte qu'à partir de 1848, époque où l'on ouvrit les arènes de la rue Montesquieu; alors, les athlètes accoururent de tous les points de la France. Les arènes Montesquieu durèrent trois ans" (*La lutte et les lutteurs*, p. 31). Hence, in selecting the Hippodrome, Courbet was quite up to date.

44. *Le moniteur universel*, June 5, 1853: "J'avoue qu'il est impossible à faire des chairs plus vivantes; mais aparement M. Courbet n'envoie point ses *Baigneuses* à la Nouvelle-Zélande, où l'on juge du mérite d'une captive par ce qu'elle peut fournir de viande au dîner de ses maîtres."

45. "Courbet, lui, est le virtuose de la bestialité." Camille Lemonnier, *Courbet et son oeuvre*, Paris, 1888, p. 44.

46. "La Révolution française . . . est satanique dans son essence. Jamais elle ne sera totalement éteinte que par le principe contraire, et jamais les Français ne reprendront leur place jusqu'à ce qu'ils aient reconnu cette vérité." *La patrie*, May 21, 1853. The paper approvingly quotes Joseph de Maistre, *Considérations sur la France*, London 1797 (expanded ed. Paris, 1852, chap. 10, § 3), a decidedly counterrevolutionary book that was widely read during the Second Empire.

47. Thénot, "Salon de 1853," fourth article, *Gazette de France*, June 7, 1853: "Lorsque le socialisme dans l'art se crut tout à fait organisé . . . il fit apposer, le 15 avril 1848, sur la porte du musée du Louvre . . . une grande affiche . . . qui convoquait en assemblée générale, . . . les peintres français qui avaient atteint l'âge de 21 ans. . . . *Eh bien! les hommes choisis parmi ceux qu'on venait de nommer par ce vote . . . ont encore aujourd'hui la plus grande influence sur nos Salons*" (my italics).

48. In Léger (*Caricatures*, p. 52), the artist's name and the date are erroneous.

49. *L'illustration* for July 21, 1853, printed another caricature by Quillenbois that is related to the first in this respect: *Réapparition de la Vénus du Bas-Rhin* (Léger, *Caricatures*, p. 30).

50. Many critics, including Gautier, considered Millet's paintings to represent the sort of "naive" description of nature that they increasingly missed in Courbet's work. Yet Millet also employed color to help define the social position of his subjects. In contrast to Courbet, however, Millet's color tends to affirm rather than to disillusion; even in *the Man with the Hoe* (1863), it expresses not so much the effort of labor as a hope of redemption.

51. Gautier's review formed the prerequisite, for example, for Castagnary's treatment of the concept of truth in Courbet's work on the level of form regardless of the subject, even in the case of such socially critical canvases as *The Return from the Conference* and *The Beggar's Alms;* see Castagnary, vol. 1, pp. 150, 289.

52. Augustin-Joseph du Pays, "Salon de 1853," *L'illustration,* June 18, 1853, p. 392: "M. Courbet reste définitivement le chef de l'école du laid, et ce qui est plus triste, du laid, non dans sa grandeur et dans sa force, mais du laid vulgaire, du laid ignoble."

53. Nadar, *Des lutteurs avec des varices comme ça!,* Le journal pour rire, July 2, 1853; repro. in Léger, *Caricatures,* p. 20, and *JHK* 22, 1977, p. 149. The chronology makes clear that Nadar was indebted to Loudun, whose review had appeared just one month before (on June 2). Nadar in turn corroborates the social impact: the top hat that his visitor wears was a class-specific attribute of the bourgeois at this period.

54. Courbet to his family (1845): "Les petits tableaux ne font pas la réputation. Il faut que j'exécute pour l'an qui vient un grand tableau qui me fasse décidément connaître sous mon vrai jour. Car je veux tout ou rien" (Courthion, vol. 2, p. 71).

55. For instance, Daumier's *Hercule de foire (Un lutteur),* c. 1865, Washington, Philipps Coll. (K. E. Maison, *Honoré Daumier: Catalogue Raisonné,* New York, 1968, vol. 1, no. 189, pl. 139). Even greater similarities are found with Daumier's allegorical drawing *L'Hercule des Champs-Elysées,* 1851 (D. 2102).

56. See chap. 4 in this volume.

57. Honoré de Balzac, *Histoire de la grandeur et de la décadence de César Birotteau* (1838) Paris (ed. Garnier), 1964, pp. 16f., 45f., 256f., 290.

58. In *L'union,* June 19, 1853.

59. "Nous avons pour but de séparer de la foule ceux qui usurpent le nom d'artistes" (*Le moniteur universel,* May 17, 1853).

60. "Leurs mains sauvages saccagent toutes les fleurs," / Insultent toutes les graces, / Flétrissent toutes les vertus, / Renversent tous les autels, / Où brûle le feu sacré, / Iconoclastes de l'art" (G. Merlet, 1860; quoted in Lacambre, p. 179).

61. Caricature by Marcia; see Léger, *Caricatures,* p. 98.

62. See the caricature *Oh! maman, vois donc ses beaux courbet!* (Léger, *Caricatures,* p. 20, top). Nadar's gingerbread men are a spoof on the woodenness of Courbet's figures (see also Appendix, IX).

63. This was the name assumed, among others, by Jean Dupuis (see n. 132), turning Hercules, who was traditionally associated with French kings, into a popular hero. A "Hercule français" in fringed costume is depicted in a color lithograph by G. Engelmann, in Paris, BN, Cab. des Estampes, Carton Mat. Kg. I.

64. Naturally, Stendhal cannot be considered the sole source, particularly as the greatest effect of his novel came at a later date. However, new editions of *Le Rouge et le noir* were published in 1846 and 1854, and were thus presumably known to Courbet.

65. See my *Realismus als Widerspruch,* color plate 12.

66. E.g., Léon Aubineau, "Salon de 1853," *L'univers,* July 3 and 16, 1853.

67. Color plate and interpretation in *Cat. Paris,* 1977–78, pp. 56 and 111.

68. "M. Garcin me nomme le peintre socialiste; j'accepte bien volontiers cette dénomination; je suis non seulement socialiste, mais bien encore démocrate et républicain, en un mot partisan de toute la révolution et par-dessus tout réaliste" (letter by Courbet to the editor of the *Journal des faits,* Nov. 19, 1851; *Bull. de la Société des Amis de Courbet* 52, 1974, p. 12).

69. *La révolution sociale démontrée par le coup d'état du deux-décembre,* Paris, 1852.

70. See Pierre Leroux, *Du christianisme et de son origine démocratique,* new ed. Paris, 1848. On Leroux's revolutionary and religious stance in the year 1848, see Jacques Droz, *Histoire générale du socialisme,* 2 vols., Paris, 1972; vol. 1, p. 376; and *Cat. Paris,* 1977–78, p. 102.

71. D. 1806 (*Le charivari*, Dec. 30, 1848). The caption reads, "Ce grand philosophe se dirigeant vers la tribune de l'assemblée nationale avec sa collection d'aphorismes sociaux."

72. See, among others, Pierre Leroux, *Malthus et les économistes, ou: Y aura-t-il toujours des pauvres?* (1846), new ed. Paris, 1849.

73. See *Union Socialiste. Acte de société. Manifeste signé Louis Blanc, Cabet, Pierre Leroux*, London, May 10, 1852. A great deal of hope seems to have been placed in this "party in exile." On Courbet's link with the First International Workers' Association, see Clark, *Buchon*, p. 208.

74. Courthion, vol. 2, p. 27.

75. Likely based on an actual event: in 1867 an anonymous wrestler appeared in Paris as the *lutteur masqué* and drew great crowds.

76. The caption reads, "Il est expressément défendu aux 500.000 lecteurs de la Lune de voir dans cette lutte de l'Homme rouge et de l'Homme noir aucune insidieuse allégorie. Qu'ils n'oublient pas que certaines actualités nous sont interdites." Gill's caricature was published in the issue for Nov. 3, 1867. The next day French troops intervened in Magenta on behalf of the pope to expel the followers of Garibaldi. Revealing insights are found on page 2 of the same issue: "L'arène est ouverte. On vient d'y répandre du son frais. Puisse-t-il ne pas s'imbiber du sang des lutteurs. Que cette arène ait la forme d'un chapeau ou la forme d'une botte, peu nous importe." Whether the battle lines were drawn by the pope (*chapeau*) or Napoleon III (*botte*) is of no consequence, since they are allies. "Hourrah pour le lutteur au masque rouge! Il tient victorieusement la tête de son adversaire sous son aisselle velue, et cherche à l'enlever de terre. Le vent qui passe, c'est singulier, rappelle vaguement la brise dans les voiles gonflées d'une flotte en marche." That is, Garibaldi is underway, but the French troops are approaching. "Courage, athlète au masque rouge. Tiens ferme. Pas de fausse générosité. Tu es fort, mais ton antagoniste est plein de ruse; ses yeux étincellent sous son loup noir, qui rappelle vaguement, c'est étrange, la cagoule." The "black" wrestler is now clearly characterized as a representative of the church by his cunning and his monk's habit. The following description corroborates the identification and, moreover, typologically recalls Courbet's painting (see n. 29): "Le lutteur au masque noir, aux larges épaules faites pour porter un monde comme Atlas et comme Saint Christophe, a perdu pied. . . . Serre-le bien fort, encore plus fort, héros au masque rouge; prends garde! Celui que tu combats est plus glissant qu'une aiguille." For clues to interpreting this text, I am indebted to Michel Melot, Paris.

77. On the economic and political development of France at this period, see, for example, Joan Margarete and Brian Chapman, *The Life and Times of Baron Haussmann: Paris in the Second Empire*, London, 1957; Theodore Zeldin, *The Political System of Napoleon III*, London, 1958; Patrick Kessel, *Le prolétariat français avant Marx*, Paris, 1968.

78. More information in *Les débuts du chemin de fer*, exh. cat., Paris, Archives Nationales, 1977.

79. See Clark, *Buchon*, pp. 287–289.

80. See Eugene Sue et al., *Le républicain des campagnes*, Paris, 1851, p. 61.

81. See Verspohl, *Stadionbauten* (n. 20), p. 119.

82. Pierre-Joseph Proudhon, *Philosophie du progrès* (1853), in *Oeuvres complètes*, vol. 12, Paris, 1946, reprint Geneva, 1982, p. 93.

83. Verspohl, *Stadionbauten* (n. 20), pp. 119–120 and further sources given.

84. Aubineau writes, "Si elle [painting] a le pouvoir et la mission d'entrer en communication avec les âmes, de les élever . . . , ces maîtres chrétiens . . . ont été dans la condition véritable où doivent se tenir les efforts humains" (*L'univers*, July 3, 1853). See also Tillot (Appendix,

85. Jacques Cambry, *Voyage dans le Finistère ou état de ce département en 1794 et 1795*, 3 vols., Paris, n.d. [1799], vol. 1, pp. 69, 106.

86. "Les moeurs de cette peuplade sont celles de la nature dans toute sa simplicité." Ibid., vol. 1, p. 179.

87. See Fédération des Amis des Luttes et des Sports Athlétiques Bretons, *La lutte bretonne: Organisation et règlement,* new ed., Quimperlé, 1970.

88. See Cambry, *Voyage dans le Finistère* (n. 85), vol. 3, pp. 202–203. J. Anthony quotes the following oath: "Je jure de lutter en toute loyauté, sans traîtrise et sans brutalité, pour mon honneur et celui de mon pays. En témoignage de ma sincérité et pour suivre la coutume de mes ancêtres. Je tends à mon émule et ma main et ma joue" (*Contribution à l'étude du folklore bas-breton [danses, luttes, airs populaires] par Nevezadur,* Rennes, 1942, p. 27).

89. René-Yves Creston, *La lutte bretonne à Scaër,* Rennes, 1957, p. 9.

90. ". . . un peu de l'ambiance de leur pays natal." Ibid., p. 11.

91. Fédération des Amis des Luttes (n. 87), p. 48.

92. See chap. 4 in this volume.

93. An 1853 wood engraving at the Musée des Arts Décoratifs, Coll. Maciet, in Paris, is a good example of a Swiss wrestling match in Courbet's time; repro. in *JKH* 22, 1977, p. 154.

94. See Thoré, *Salon,* vol. 2, p. 95: "Les lutteurs en Basse-Bretagne [by Adolphe Leleux], sur une pelouse entourée d'arbres, nous semblent aussi intéressants qu'Atalante et Hippomène disputant le prix de la course dans le cirque antique." On Leleux's interest in depicting regional subjects, see Nochlin, *Style and Society,* pp. 115–117.

95. For the broad sense in which this term was used then, see Jules Michelet, *Le peuple,* Brussels and Leipzig, 1846; and Clark, *People,* pp. 146–148.

96. In addition, according to Ville (n. 28), p. 33, a stadium was opened on rue Lepelletier in conjunction with the World Fair of 1867. Wrestling matches were also held in auditoriums on rue Cadet and rue des Martyrs (see also Desbonnet [n. 28], pp. 8, 10). Binding rules were not established until 1893. On the ensuing enthusiasm for wrestling, see "La lutte et les lutteurs", *L'illustration* 106, Feb. 18, 1899: "On lutte partout . . . " (includes a recapitulation of previous developments).

97. For Meissonier, see Sloane (n. 6), fig. 40; for Thoma, see Henry Thode, *Thoma: Des Meisters Gemälde,* Stuttgart and Leipzig, 1909, p. 49.

98. Maison (n. 55), vol. 1, no. 116, pl. 11 (Paris, Musée d'Orsay, c. 1858).

99. The two aspects are formally combined in a drawing by Géricault (Paris, BN, Cab. des Estampes, Carton Mat. Kg. I) that very probably influenced Julian (fig. 26). See also Géricault's pencil sketch *Wrestling and Boxing Match* (1818–19), repro. in Lorenz Eitner, *Géricault: An Album of Drawings in the Art Institute of Chicago,* Chicago, 1960, fol. 13r; also Daumier's *Four Sketches of Wrestlers* (black chalk, undated, formerly Coll. Guérin, Paris), repro. in K. E. Maison, *Daumier: Drawings,* New York and London, 1960, p. 81. As to boxing, see also Pointon (n. 32).

100. By Champfleury in 1851; see Clark, *People,* p. 127.

101. George Bellows, *Both Members of This Club* (1909), Washington, D. C., National Gallery of Art (repro. in Charles S. Morgan, *George Bellows: Painter of America,* New York, 1965, p. 323). The picture was first entitled *A Nigger and a White Man.* See also Bellows's *Stag at Sharkey's* (also 1909), Cleveland Museum of Art (repro. ibid., p. 320). Other examples are by Eakins, G. B. Luks, Joeckel, C. Bombois, and others, all the way to Mark Robson's film *The Harder They Fall* (1955). Bombois's painting *L'athlète forain* (c. 1930, Paris, Musée National d'Art Moderne) builds logically on Courbet by "exhibiting" the athletes. Courbet's political intention underwent yet another variation in Jürgen Weber's *Wrestler Fountain* (1974–75) in Braunschweig, Germany, where the theme is treated as a metaphor for the conflict between artist and art critic (see exh. cat., Galerie Kühl, Hannover, 1976). The objections raised to this sculpture—that the wrestlers' calves were too thick, that they looked musclebound or had ugly physiques—were literally the same as those made to Courbet's painting. S. Mileev, on the other hand, called Courbet's *Wrestlers* a paradigmatic image in furtherance of physical education, and illustrated it accordingly (*Kunst und Körperkultur,* Moscow, 1931, pp. 137f.).

102. Plaster of Paris; a version in marble once stood in the Jardin du Luxembourg. Its present whereabouts is unknown, as is that of a bronze cast made from the statue.

103. *RDM* 1853, pp. 1155f.: "M. Ottin . . . ne craint pas de mettre un talent, jusqu'ici mieux inspiré, au service de doctrines que la statuaire répudie plus hautement encore que la peinture. Un groupe qu'il a intitulé délibérément le Coup de Hanche représente deux athlètes aux prises, non pas tels qu'on se figure les lutteurs de la Grèce ou de Rome, mais tels que peuvent être des hommes de notre temps et de notre pays débarrassés de leurs vêtements. Quel intérêt . . . peut exciter un pareil spectacle? . . . Quelques personnes accueilleront peut-être comme un progrès cette nouvelle usurpation du réalisme."

104. *L'illustration*, March 20, 1852, p. 192; see also Nochlin, *Style and Society*, p. 186.

105. Caption in *L'illustration*, March 20, 1850, p. 192.

106. Texier (n. 17), vol. 2, pp. 295f. The regionalistic aspect is also evident here: "Tous les membres du Jockey-Club, tous les beaux jeunes gens qui se résignent à voir combattre des hommes contre des hommes, en attendant que le gouvernement permette le spectacle des hommes luttant contre des animaux, s'étaient réunis dans la salle Montesquieu. Des paris étaient engagés; ceux-ci tenaient pour la Savoie, ceux-là pour la Provence." The fight ended with a sensation—Arpin's defeat.

107. "Revue du deuxième trimestre de 1852," *Le journal pour rire*, July 3, 1852: "Les lutteurs de la salle Montesquieu. Rabasson *tombe* Arpin, Arpin *tombe* Rabasson. Le fait est que ces gaillards-là doivent être terriblement forts pour faire un verbe actif d'un neutre!!!" Repro. in *JHK* 22, 1977, p. 159.

108. *Souvenirs . . . des fêtes du 15 Août: Le Lutteur Arpin. Le journal pour rire*, Aug. 21, 1852; repro. in *JHK* 22, 1977, p. 159.

109. Paris, BN, Cab. des Estampes; repro. in *JHK* 22, 1977, p. 160. Also reproduced is another Parisian lithograph which in its dramatic staging shows great similarities to Courbet's composition.

110. In particular, the alternation of concave and convex forms recalls Daumier's chiffres for movement; see Werner Hofmann, "Zu Daumiers graphischer Gestaltungsweise," *Jahrbuch der kunsthistorischen Sammlungen in Wien* 52, 1956, pp. 147–181.

111. L. Dumont, *Corps-de-Fer and Sans-Pitié Wrestling. Le journal pour rire*, Jan. 15, 1853; repro. in *JHK* 22, 1977, p. 163.

112. "La vraie Madame Saqui," text by Edouard Martin, drawings by Bertall [and Dumont], *Le journal pour rire*, Jan. 15, 1853: "Grâce à Corps-de-Fer, la gymnastique a fait des progrès énormes dans toutes les classes de la société. On ne se bat plus comme autrefois en duel dans un coin de Vincennes ou de Saint-Mandé, *on se tombe*. Corps-de-Fer est l'étoile de la Salle Montesquieu. Son nom est en vedette et se pavane orgueuilleusement sur les affiches multicolores qui s'épanouissent à tous les coins de la capitale. . . . MM. Corps-de-Fer et Sans-Pitié se sont engagés sur l'honneur à ne pas quitter l'arène avant qu'il y ait un vaincu. . . . Corps-de-Fer *tombe*, mais il n'a pas été *tombé*. . . . Corps-de-Fer monta l'échelle qui conduisait à la corde. . . . Mais la corde cassa et Corps-de-Fer tomba. Heureusement sa chute fut amortie par un numéro du *Nouveau Figaro* qui gisait sur le pavé."

113. Compare, for instance, D. 2029 (1850) and D. 2153 (1851).

114. Doré, "L'Hippodrome," *Le journal pour rire*, Aug. 7, 1852, p. 3; June 21, 1856, p. 4 ("Réouverture de l'Hippodrome"); Daumier, *L'Hippodrome*, D. 2449 (1853).

115. See Hippolyte Castille, *Les hommes et les moeurs sous le règne de Louis-Philippe*, Paris, 1853, pp. 326–330 ("industrie intellectuelle; l'idée, devenue valeur industrielle").

116. See Courthion, vol. 1, pp. 40, 101, 137f., 309.

117. "Il eut à *lutter* comme personne contre les institutions infirmes qui régissent la France et qui paralysent le génie." Ibid., vol. 2, p. 29.

118. "J'ai *lutté* contre toutes les formes de gouvernements autoritaires et de droit divin,

voulant que l'homme se gouverne lui-même selon ses besoins." Ibid., vol. 2, p. 47. For another example, see p. 48.

119. "Aujourd'hui, j'appartiens . . . à la classe des hommes qui sont morts . . . dévoués sans intérêts égoistes à la République, à l'égalité; car ce sont ces hommes-là qui *luttèrent* sous Louis-Philippe . . . posant la question sociale . . . qui *luttèrent* contre la guerre intentée aux Prussiens." Ibid., vol. 2, pp. 50–51.

120. *Fédération* (n. 87), p. 40.

121. "Chaque homme à Scaër dira / J'ai bien lutté pendant ma vie / Je serai couronné par Dieu / . . . Et lorsque nous lutterons sans crainte / Nous mettrons sur les deux épaules tous les diables." Creston (n. 89), p. 12. Scaër was a center of wrestling in the Bretagne.

122. Parisot: "Lutter, lutter encore, c'est vivre; cesser la lutte, ce n'est plus qu'exister." Mme de Girardin: "En toute chose, la lutte, c'est la vie: en religion, en politique, en littérature, en amour." Parisot was an Encyclopedist and politician who published between 1826 and 1857. Quoted in Pierre Larousse, *Grand dictionnaire universel du 19e siècle*, vol. 10, Paris, 1873; s.v. "lutte." Mme Emile de Girardin, *Lettres parisiennes* (1844), in *Oeuvres complètes*, 6 vols., Paris, 1860; vol. 5, p. 339.

123. Sand: "Sois eunuque et engraisse, ou sois homme et lutte." Balzac: "Le travail est une lutte incessante que redoutent . . . les . . . organisations qui souvent s'y brisent." Both Sand and Balzac are quoted in Larousse (n. 122).

124. "Ceux qui vivent, ce sont ceux qui luttent, ce sont ceux dont un dessein ferme emplit l'âme et le front." Victor Hugo, *Châtiments*, book IV, poem IX, verses 1–2; also verse 10: "Ceux-là vivent, Seigneur! les autres, je les plains" (1848); see Hugo, *Poésie*, Paris (éd. du Seuil), 1972, vol. 1, p. 538. See also *La légende des siècles*, book IV, poem II, verses 17, 23, 24: "Ils luttent, noirs, muets, furieux, acharnés. . . . Et depuis qu'ils sont là, sombres, ardents, farouches, / Un mot n'est pas encor sorti de ces deux bouches" (c. 1846); ibid., vol. 2, p. 36 ("Le mariage de Roland").

125. The hymn was written by Eugène Pottier in 1871.

126. See V. C. Pfitzner, *Paul and the Agon Motif*, Leiden, 1967, pp. 3–6, 165, 177.

127. See, e.g., Theodor W. Adorno, *Minima Moralia* (1951), new ed. Frankfurt am Main, 1971, pp. 174–176, on the intellectual "wrestling association."

128. See Gustav Adolf Erich Bogeng, *Geschichte des Sports aller Völker und Zeiten*, 2 vols., Leipzig, 1926; vol. 1, p. 384.

129. Engravings in Paris, BN, Cab. des Estampes, Carton Mat. Kg. I. See also n. 32.

130. Quoted in Erwin Redslob, *Die Welt vor 100 Jahren*, Leipzig, 1940; 3d ed., 1943, p. 174.

131. *Le journal pour rire*, July 12, 1856. "Revue du deuxième trimestre de 1856," p. 2: "Grande querelle entre Figaro et la Gazette de Paris."

132. D. 3604. Erroneously described as a personification of Chronos in N. A. Hazard and Loys Delteil, *Catalogue raisonné de l'oeuvre lithographiée de Honoré Daumier*, Orrouy, 1904.

133. *Le charivari*, March 1, 1873; repro. in *JHK* 22, 1977, p. 167. How natural the transition between sports and politics was at this period is indicated by the following sports report of June 14, 1870:

> Et c'était aussi un grand événement, avant-hier, le prix de cent mille francs. La grande lutte internationale, la revanche de Waterloo, etc. Sornette, une jument française, a gagné le prix. Les chevaux anglais n'ont pas même été placés. Trois cent mille bourgeois et ouvriers ont après cela repris la route de Paris, en criant: *Vive Sornette! Nous avons battu les Anglais!* Ces sortes de victoire causent une telle joie qu'on eût crié *Vive l'Empereur!* . . . Je n'aime pas l'Empereur, disait derrière moi un bourgeois après la course, mais on est obligé de reconnaître qu'il se passe de grandes choses sous son règne." (Ludovic Halévy, *Carnets*, ed. Daniel Halévy, 2 vols., Paris, 1935; vol. 2, p. 141)

134. Castagnary; see Courthion, vol. 1, p. 146; also Clark, *People*, p. 113.

135. For this topic in general, see Verspohl (n. 20), pp. 61, 73, 74, 77. Hence the conflict takes place on three levels: between the wrestlers, between them and the audience, and between pictorial reality and the reality of the Salon.

CHAPTER 3. *The Painter's Studio*

1. Hélène Toussaint's decoding of the picture has rendered it "more enigmatic than ever," says Werner Hofmann in "Courbet im Grand Palais. Zur Pariser Ausstellung . . . ," *Kunstchronik* 31, 1978, p. 18.

2. Courthion, vol. 2, p. 225.

3. Of course, it is necessary to "refocus our gaze, away from the figure puzzle and back to the formal scaffolding" of the picture (Hofmann, *Wirklichkeiten*, p. 594), but this cannot be done without first solving the pictorial riddle presented by this *world as a stage*. Its dreamlike, abstract quality fairly demands a precise analytical approach. Ironically, Hofmann himself has provided the most profound and detailed analysis of the structural problems of *The Painter's Studio* (Hofmann, *Nineteenth Century*, passim).

4. The fundamental investigation is René Huyghe, Germain Bazin, and Hélène J. Adhémar, *Courbet: L'atelier*, Paris, 1944; also Matthias Winner, "Gemalte Kunsttheorie. Zu Gustave Courbets 'Allégorie réelle' und der Tradition," *Jahrbuch der Berliner Museen* 4, 1962, pp. 150–185; Alan Bowness, *Courbet's "L'atelier du peintre,"* Newcastle upon Tyne, 1972; Benedict Nicolson, *Courbet: The Studio of the Painter*, London, 1973; Hélène Toussaint, in *Cat. Paris*, 1977–78, pp. 241–277; Alex Seltzer, "Gustave Courbet, All the World's a Studio," *Artforum*, Sept. 1977, pp. 44–50. See also n. 3.

5. For Champfleury, see *Cat. Paris*, 1977–78, pp. 246f.; for Bruyas, see Borel, pp. 58–63.

6. Winner (n. 4), p. 162.

7. See Toussaint, in *Cat. Paris*, 1977–78, p. 266, and Seltzer (n. 4), pp. 45, 46.

8. Seltzer (n. 4), p. 46.

9. Ibid.

10. *Cat. Paris*, 1977–78, pp. 251–258.

11. These incoherencies were emphasized particularly by Louis Hourticq (1921), Paul Jamot (1925), Louis Réau (1926), and Henri Focillon (1928), all of whom are quoted in Huyghe (see n. 4).

12. The following characterizations are from Courbet's letter to Champfleury (fall 1854), quoted in *Cat. Paris*, 1977–78, pp. 246ff.

13. The size and massiveness of this figure give reason to doubt the correctness of its traditional identification as a lay figure. Symbolically speaking, it represents a vision of the suffering artist and a counterpart to the female nude—both are *academic* models on whom Courbet has turned his back to devote himself to nature. Also (according to Hélène Toussaint), the male model seems to bear the features of the artist's father, and the female model those of his mother.

14. Peter-Klaus Schuster still finds the earlier identification correct, according to which not Apollonie Sabatier but the singer Mrs. Sabatier-Ungher is represented here (*Cat. Hamburg*, 1978–79, p. 218). However, Seltzer has pointed out that Apollonie Sabatier was perhaps *the* most frequent visitor to Courbet's studio, and that her connections were by no means limited to the political right. Then, too, a singer can hardly be expected to have smoked such big cigars as, according to Quillenbois's caricature, Apollonie did (fig. 71).

15. A similar approach is found in *Departure of the Fire-Brigade* of 1850 (see Toussaint, esp. in the catalogue to the Courbet exhibition, London, 1978, pp. 214–218) and in *The Wrestlers* of 1853 (see chap. 2 in this volume).

16. For instance, by Théophile Silvestre in 1856 ("le modèle vivant ou la Vérité"), or by

Louis Hourticq in 1921 ("sans doute la Vérité, sa muse"); both quoted in Huyghe (n. 4), pp. 26, 29.

17. See Champfleury, "Masques et travestissements," introduction to *Souvenirs et portraits de jeunesse*, Paris, 1972, reprint Geneva, 1970, pp. 1ff.; Champfleury, "Carnavale," *Les excentriques*, 2d ed., Paris, n.d., reprint Geneva, 1967, pp. 164–175.

18. See Shroder, pp. 151–180 (Flaubert), pp. 181–216 (Baudelaire). See also Clark, *Bourgeois*, pp. 162, 163 (Baudelaire), and Hofmann, *Wirklichkeiten*, pp. 590ff. (Flaubert).

19. In this case, the phrase alludes to the liberality associated with the name of this minister. Writing to Castagnary, Courbet expressed the wish that the exhibition be financed with government funds, then went on to say, "Les choses ainsi faites jetteraient déjà *une branche d'olivier dans les arts*." But this was expecting too much; only the overthrow of the government would help: "Tout cela n'arrivera pas parce que les artistes n'aiment pas l'indépendance, et que les autres aiment trop le gouvernement. Dans la casserole de la France, il cuit un fricot, dans lequel il est tombé par hasard un étron [a clod or turd, i.e., Napoleon III]: vous aurez bon rapsoder, relever le goût, avec une pincée de poivre, un clou de girofle, auroit-il cinq feuilles, *une feuille de laurier, voire même d'olivier*—tout cela n'y fera rien, le seul moven c'est de foutre notre fricot à l'eau. . . . Il faut une révolution de 89 sur des bases nouvelles, une constitution faite par des gens libres" (letter to Castagnary dated Feb. 5, 1870; Paris, BN, Papiers Courbet, box 2; my italics).

20. See *Cat. Paris*, 1977–78, p. 260.

21. A comprehensive discussion is found in Jennifer Montagu, "The Painted Enigma and French Seventeenth Century Art," *Journal of the Warburg and Courtauld Institutes* 31, 1968, pp. 307–355. See also Eva Maria Schenk, "Das Bilderrätsel," diss., Univ. of Cologne, 1967, pp. 30–36.

22. Unlike allegories, the hidden meaning of these picture puzzles could be separated from the primary level of meaning; see Montagu (n. 21), pp. 309, 327.

23. Ibid., pp. 310, 316.

24. See Grandville, *Das gesamte Werk*, 2 vols., Munich, 1969; vol. 1, p. 194 (without caption).

25. Montagu (n. 21), p. 310.

26. Courbet's brush pointing to the ruin in the landscape would seem to corroborate this. That ruins could refer to the future as well as the past is well known (see chap. 4, n. 71 below). In 1850 Thoré wrote, "Révolution est à la fois ruine du passé et institution de l'avenir" (*Liberté*, Brussels, 1850, p. 10), and two years later he demanded, "Mais . . . demeurons . . . impavides sous les ruines de la République. Car nous savons bien que la Liberté est immortelle" (*La restauration de l'autorité*, Brussels, 1852, p. 5). Thus an allusion to decay and hope rising from the ruins would seem to be another key aspect of the content of *The Painter's Studio*.

27. See *Cat. Paris*, 1977–78, p. 258.

28. See my *Realismus als Widerspruch*, p. 274, n. 39.

29. Charles Perrier, letter to the editor, *L'artiste*, Oct. 14, 1855.

30. Quoted in Huyghe (see n. 4), p. 26.

31. Philippe Burty, in *Catalogue de trente-trois tableaux et études par G. Courbet et dépendant de sa succession*, Paris, n.d., Hôtel Drouot, introduction. The sale took place in two parts, on Dec. 9, 1881, and on June 28, 1882.

32. We tend to forget how discredited the name of Napoleon III was after the progressive republican forces regrouped. The former emperor was held personally responsible for France's defeat, the loss of Alsace-Lorraine, and the misery of the lower classes.

33. In his diary, Champfleury noted on April 29, 1882: "Big success of the aristocrats. . . . The jury refused Courbet's portrait of Chaudey, the Communard."

34. The statement might conceivably refer to *Departure of the Fire-Brigade* of 1850 (see n. 15), but since this canvas was not exhibited until 1861 and was stored in rolled form, Thoré had

probably not seen it at the time. Nor, since it was pro-Napoleon and executed at an early date, would it have been relevant to his argument.

35. See *Cat. Paris*, 1977–78, nos. 15 (Baudelaire), 34 (Champfleury), and 37 (Courbet).

36. As a rule, Courbet portrayed only persons he had known for a long period of time; his critics even accused him of being "l'esclave du modèle" (see Courthion, vol. 1, pp. 55, 97; vol. 2, p. 298).

37. See, e.g., Eduard Fuchs, *Die Karikatur der europäischen Völker*, Berlin, 1903, vol. 2, p. 127; and the same author, in Arsène Alexandre, *L'art du rire et la caricature*, Paris, n.d., p. 225. A superb example is also found in *L'éclipse*, Dec. 26, 1869. See also chap. 2, n. 76 above (*La lune*, Nov. 3, 1867); and, for a general treatment of the subject, Toussaint, *Cat. Paris*, 1977–78, p. 258.

38. Toussaint, *Cat. Paris*, 1977–78, p. 258.

39. Ibid. See also the proclamations for the presidential election of 1848, in which Napoleon III (Louis-Napoleon) is declared to be a friend of the workers. One of the posters reads in part: "En nommant NAPOLEON-LOUIS BONAPARTE, les ouvriers témoigneront de leur reconnaissance d'avoir pensé à eux alors qu'il était dans les cachots de HAM, s'occupant de l'amélioration du sort de la classe ouvrière, en faisant publier son ouvrage sur le PAUPERISME, ouvrage saisi par la police de Louis-Philippe." Concerning the likeness, see the lithograph published by Dopter in 1849, *Louis Napoléon Bonaparte, Président de la République, passant la revue de la Garde Nationale . . . apperçut . . . le Général Petit . . . .*

40. The French word *braconnier* means "dog-breeder" (a connotation still current as late as 1949), "high-liver" (the sense in which Courbet used it in his letter to Champfleury of fall 1854, where he spoke of a "café de braconniers et des gens du Gai Savoir"), and, finally, "poacher." Yet this term was not necessarily negative for Courbet and his friends, the artist himself having done a bit of poaching (see Borel, p. 26). At any rate, all three terms can be applied to Napoleon III, the last in a figurative sense.

41. At the time, his name was just as proverbial as Tartuffe or Ratapoil, as Pierre Georgel kindly informs me.

42. For a wider discussion of these and the following identifications, see my *Realismus als Widerspruch*, pp. 266–269.

43. According to information provided by the Institut Polonais, Paris, to Hélène Toussaint (1977).

44. As, for example, in *L'artiste*, Dec. 31, 1854: "Tous les regards sont maintenant fixés sur la Turquie"; in *RDM*, April 1, 1855: ". . . effort suprême de conciliation" (in the Orient question and the expansion of Russia as a justification of the Crimean War); or in *L'artiste*, April 8, 1855: "L'Exposition universelle, sous peu de jours, tiendra nécessairement le haut du pavé dans toutes les feuilles publiques, concurremment avec la question d'Orient."

45. It is also noteworthy that the most securely identified portraits (those of Fould, Veuillot, Carnot, Garibaldi, and Napoleon III) are similar in terms of their degree of finish, appear, as it were, individually framed, and stand out from the figures in the background.

46. This theme was already current in the studio-picture tradition of the sixteenth century, for instance in Vasari, who contrasted *ingenium* with *ars* (the workings of inspiration and the actual handling of the medium). See also Winner (n. 4), fig. 5; and conclusions regarding Courbet, ibid., p. 160.

47. See Hofmann, *Wirklichkeiten*, p. 497; idem, *Nineteenth Century*, p. 162f; idem, "Über die 'Schlafende Spinnerin'," in my *Realismus als Widerspruch*, p. 220. The first author to mention the "salle d'attente" was Paul Jamot, in 1925 (quoted in Huyghe [n. 4], p. 29). Linda Nochlin sees the paralyzing influence of the Second Empire in "the melancholy and the remote mood of this painting" (*Style and Society*, p. 222).

48. An example is given in Winner (n. 4), fig. 22 and p. 182. I should like to put up for

discussion a question raised in conversation by Martin Warnke, namely, whether this tradition was taken up, and reversed, in *The Painter's Studio*—Napoleon III as Alexander (as whom French rulers from the time of Louis XIV had themselves portrayed), and the "model" as Campaspe, who evades him and who is in turn disdained by the artist, in favor of "pure" nature.

49. *Le moniteur universel,* April 15, 1853.

50. Although works of art were also exhibited in London, they formed part of each nation's display instead of being united in a separate art exhibition.

51. See Minda de Gunzburg, "La Peinture française et la critique à l'exposition universelle de 1855" (maîtrise), Paris, 1970, pp. 7–39. I am indebted to Mme de Gunzburg for her permission to consult the typescript.

52. *Visites et Études de S.A.I. le Prince Napoléon au Palais des Beaux-Arts . . . suivies des visites du prince aux produits collectifs des nations qui ont pris part à l'exposition de 1855,* Paris, 1856, p. 167. And in another place we read, "Cette grande pensée de la France, qui tend à rapprocher toutes les nations du monde . . . , tous les gouvernements l'ont comprise et accueillie avec enthousiasme" (p. 5).

53. "Discours de l'Empereur distribuant des récompenses, à la suite de l'exposition universelle" [Nov. 16, 1855], in Napoleon III, *La politique impériale exposée par les discours et proclamations de l'empereur Napoléon III depuis le 10 décembre 1848 jusqu'en juillet 1865,* p. 223. See also Hofmann, *Nineteenth Century,* pp. 166–168.

54. See Courbet's letter of Nov. 19, 1851, to the *Journal des faits* (published in the issue for Nov. 21), republished in *Bull. de la Société des Amis de Gustave Courbet* 52, 1974, p. 12.

55. Most authors have neglected to consult this paper and have contented themselves with Théophile Silvestre's general statement that this combination of motifs was "la réponse de l'artiste aux attaques de cette feuille ou la traduction de cette phrase de Proudhon: 'Les journaux sont les cimetières des idées . . . ' " (quoted in Huyghe [n. 4], p. 26).

56. *Le journal des débats,* May 22, 1853 (Delécluze, "Exposition de 1853").

57. Paul Chenavard (1807–95) was a pupil of Ingres and Delacroix and, as a follower of Saint-Simon and Fourier, a convinced republican. Louis Français (1814–97), a pupil of Corot, was in friendly contact with him and the Barbizon painters.

58. The date is controversial. Courthion (vol. 2, p. 84) gives a date of December 1854, which is certainly too late. Nicolson (n. 4), pp. 75f., dates the letter to October 1853, believing it must have been written *prior* to the Ministerial Council meeting of Dec. 29, 1853. But Courbet was not prepared to go so far in 1853. It is more likely that the meeting prompted Nieuwerkerke's invitation to Courbet.

59. Compare the relatively moderate attitude of the National Socialist government which, in view of the Berlin Olympic Games of 1936, was anxious to convey an impression of a civilized Germany to the world.

60. Letter to Castagnary dated Oct. 17, 1868 (Courthion, vol. 2, pp. 111–112).

61. In his *Salons de peinture* (Montpellier, 1852, p. 12), Bruyas listed Napoleon III among those who contributed to a revival of French art, writing that "Delacroix, Rousseau, Troyon . . . tendent tous les jours davantage avec nos célébrités modernes (EN TETE LE CHEF DE L'ETAT), à résoudre le grand problème si difficile." He even called his *Salons* for 1853 a "document venant à l'appui de la vérité du 2 décembre 1851, époque à laquelle la France devait avoir recours plutôt à l'art qu'à l'histoire" (art as playground and alibi?) and went on to quote the emperor: "La puissance et la force viennent des grands maîtres" (Alfred Bruyas, *Salons de peinture,* Montpellier, 1853, p. 5).

62. Pierre-Joseph Proudhon, *Oeuvres complètes,* vol. 9, Paris, 1936, pp. 299–346; see also Georges Cogniot, *Proudhon et la démagogie bonapartiste,* Paris, 1958, p. 34. Proudhon's contacts with the prince were likely based on the fact that they were both Freemasons.

63. Borel, p. 68.

64. His actual words were "qu'ils étaient deux imbéciles." But the context justifies the passive formulation.

65. See n. 15 (*Departure of the Fire-Brigade*); Clark, *Bourgeois*, p. 163 (Wallon); also the pamphlets by Jean Journet, especially *Le socialisme démasqué*, Paris, 1950, and *L'empire c'est la paix*, Paris, 1851.

66. See *L'artiste*, July 15, 1854, p. 183; Sept. 1, 1854, pp. 41–44; Jan. 14, 1855, pp. 36–37; March 25, 1855, p. 182.

67. *L'artiste*, March 1, 1854, p. 16 (Ingres), and April 15, 1854, pp. 81–82 (Delacroix).

68. See Huyghe (n. 4), p. 6; Peter-Klaus Schuster, in *Cat. Hamburg*, 1978–79, p. 494ff.; Shroder, p. 54.

69. On this subject, besides the publications cited in n. 4, see Bert Schug, *Das Atelier* (Reclams Werkmonographien 73), Stuttgart, 1962; Max Kotzloff, "Courbet's L'atelier': An Interpretation," *Art and Literature* 3, 1964, pp. 162–183; Pierre Georgel, "Les transformations de la peinture vers 1848, 1855, 1863," *Revue de l'art* 27, 1975, pp. 62–77, esp. pp. 69–72; Jeannine Baticle and Pierre Georgel, eds., *Les techniques de la peinture: L'Atelier*, exh. cat., Musée du Louvre, Paris, 1976; Gabriele Sprigath, "Courbet: Die Parteilichkeit des freien Menschen," *Tendenzen* 122, 1978, pp. 34–38. Although Hofmann, Kotzloff, and Schug mention the World Fair, they do not discuss in detail its links with the conception of *The Painter's Studio*.

70. See esp. Winner (n. 4); also (without direct reference to Courbet) Rudolf Wittkower, *The Divine Michelangelo*, London, 1964; and Georg Friedrich Koch, *Die Kunstausstellung*, Berlin, 1967.

71. In the Casa Buonarotti; see Wittkower, *The Divine Michelangelo*, figs. 24–27.

72. See also Koch (n. 70), fig. 45, which illustrates a precarious equilibrium between painter and ruler, each serving to enhance the status of the other.

73. On the present state of the discussion, see R. Warning, B. Fabian, and J. Ritter, "Genie," *Historisches Wörterbuch der Philosophie*, vol. 3, Basel, 1974, cols. 279–309.

74. See Francis Haskell, "The Old Masters in Nineteenth-Century French Painting," *The Art Quarterly* 34, 1971, pp. 55–85; Berthold Hinz, *Dürers Gloria. Kunst-Kult-Konsum*, exh. cat., Berlin, 1971, esp. figs. 40–43 and poem by Pocci (fig. 42).

75. By F.-G. Ménageot; see Haskell (n. 74), fig. 1.

76. By P.-N. Bergeret; ibid., fig. 3.

77. Engraving by J.-H. Marlet; ibid., fig. 5.

78. Drawing by O. Schäffer; see Hinz (n. 74), fig. 43.

79. Haskell (n. 74), p. 69.

80. Shroder, p. 75; and for a general discussion, ibid. p. 42.

81. Ibid., p. 73.

82. "Je suis le premier homme de France." Courthion, vol. 2, p. 125; in 1865 Courbet already dreamed of being "un homme sans pareil" (ibid., p. 105).

83. "C'est le monde qui vient se faire peindre chez moi." See Courbet's letter to Champfleury, fall 1854, *Cat. Paris*, 1977–78, pp. 264ff. The term *le monde* is certainly used here in its general sense; see also ibid., p. 251.

84. "Devrais-je parcourir le monde entier, je suis sûr de trouver des hommes qui me comprendront." Borel, p. 21.

85. *Les vignettes romantiques*, Paris, 1883, p. 193: "L'homme, las des révolutions, crut à Napoléon III, sauveur de la société." While acting as a neutral reporter here, in 1853 Champfleury expressed himself in definitely pro-Napoleon terms (*Diary*, p. 3). "La société est sauvée," Napoleon III proclaimed after the *coup d'etat*; see *La politique impériale* (n. 53), p. 125.

86. Charles Baudelaire, "Puisque réalisme il y a" (1855), in *Oeuvres complètes*, ed. Claude Pichois, Paris, 1976, vol. 2, p. 59.

87. See n. 37. Courbet may well have had similar intentions in introducing the allegory of poverty into his *Departure of the Fire-Brigade* of 1850.

88. Based on his landscape painting, Théophile Thoré called Courbet a "doctor" for society (*Salon*, vol. 1, p. 93). On the subject of the artist as redeemer, see also Benno von Wiese, "Das Problem der ästhetischen Versöhnung bei Schiller und Hegel," *Jahrbuch der deutschen Schillergesellschaft* 9, 1965, p. 185.

89. See Huyghe (n. 4), p. 28; Hofmann, *Nineteenth Century*, pp. 12, 17, 19.

90. Hofmann, *Nineteenth Century*, pp. 132, 162, 384. For an extensive discussion, see Max von Boehn, *Vom Kaiserreich zur Republik. Eine französische Kulturgeschichte des 19. Jahrhunderts*, Berlin, 1917, pp. 294–298.

91. "Chez Monsieur Courbet, l'art s'est fait peuple." See Clark, *People*, p. 186, n. 39.

92. Victor Hugo, *Châtiments* [1851–1853], Paris, éd. du Seuil, 1972; *Poésie*, vol. 1, pp. 507f. (the poem is dated Nov. 6, 1851). Pierre Goergel was the first to point out the connection between Hugo's poem and *The Painter's Studio*.

93. Stanley Meltzoff, in "The Revival of the Le Nains" (*Art Bulletin*, 24, 1942, pp. 259–286), has provided the most precise discussion of the metaphor of unsullied nature and the revival of this visual idiom, which is revolutionary in the most profound sense of the word. Based on his insights, I have attempted to show (in "Equality and Authority in Courbet's Landscape Painting") that Courbet and Buchon searched out and represented wild and primordial stretches of countryside out of opposition to the Second Empire and its modernism. For a general discussion of the topics of primordial nature and a rejuvenation of civilization, see Hofmann, *Nineteenth Century*, p. 20f.; and *Wirklichkeiten*, p. 599. However, this author's interpretation that Courbet was not concerned "with a particular event but with a concentrated, enchanted moment . . . in the cyclic process" seems to me doubtful, since it abstracts from Courbet's concrete interest in the depiction.

94. On the pictorial tradition of the poet's and painter's muse, see Joachim Gaus, "Ingenium und Ars. Das Ehepaarbildnis Lavoisier von David und die Ikonographie der Museninspiration," *Wallraf-Richartz-Jahrbuch* 36, 1974, pp. 199–228. In view of this tradition, Courbet's "mundane muse" represents a trivialization (for which the way was paved by David and Hogarth [ibid., figs. 1 and 21]).

95. Hofmann, *Nineteenth Century*, p. 19.

96. Léon Aubineau, "Salon de 1853," *L'univers*, July 3, 1853: "But if painting is meant not only to address the senses, if it has other things to do than provide such impossible pictures as those which Courbet and others . . . have signed this year, if it has the capacity and the mission to converse with and exalt the human soul . . . , then we must return to tradition . . . [for] it is *here* that truth and life are to be found. Look at Overbeck and the entire glorious German school gathered around him—aren't their paintings and names much more beloved of the populace?"

97. Champfleury used this simile as early as his Salon report of 1849 (see Lacambre, p. 155). For an interpretation, see chapter 4 of this volume.

98. See Alain Plessis, *Nouvelle histoire de la France contemporaine*, vol. 9: *De la fête impériale au mur des fédérés, 1852–1871*, Paris, éd. du Seuil, 1973, p. 186. An equal mistrust of this show of industrial might was expressed by the Barbizon artists, and by Delacroix, who after a visit to the World Fair noted in 1855: "The sight of all these machines profoundly depresses me" (Aug. 3, 1855; see André Joubin, ed., *Eugène Delacroix: Journal 1822–1863*, Paris, 1981, p. 529). While the exhibition was intended to celebrate the "victory . . . of world-changing human activity over nature" (Joubin, *Delacroix*, p. 86), Courbet propounded just the opposite: the victory of nature over Bonapartist enterprises.

99. Nature was his sole teacher, Courbet used to emphasize at every opportunity, especially in 1853, when he was mistakenly called a pupil of Hesse. See also my *Realismus als Wider-*

spruch, p. 269, n. 31. On the key role of the new landscape painting, see Castagnary, Vol. 1, pp. 71–72.

100. The two halves of the painting are further characterized as day and night by the fully illuminated female "model" and the male "lay figure" plunged in shadow.

101. See Shroder, esp. pp. 51ff.

102. See Castagnary, *Les libres propos*, Paris, 1864, p. 201.

103. As early as 1845, Laverdant, a Fourierist, wrote: "Ainsi, le TRAVAIL ATTRAYANT, tel est le problème duquel dépend nécéssairement l'avenir de l'art" (Désiré Laverdant, *De la mission de l'art et du rôle des artistes, Salon de 1845*, Paris, 1845, p. 16). This established the mental association that proved decisive for Courbet. For Proudhon's statement, see Pierre-Joseph Proudhon, *Philosophie du progrès* (1853), in *Oeuvres complètes*, vol. 12, Paris, 1946, reprint Geneva, 1982, pp. 88–96.

104. An insight into the German theory of reconciliation that inspired French thinkers is given by von Wiese (see n. 88); by Günther Rohrmoser, "Zum Problem der ästhetischen Versöhnung," *Euphorion* 53, 1949, pp. 351–366; and by Berthold Hinz, "Friede den Fakultäten. Zur Problematik des Verhältnisses von Kunst und Wissenschaft zwischen Aufklärung und Vormärz," in Michael Brix and Monika Steinhauser, eds., *"Geschichte allein ist zeitgemäß." Historismus in Deutschland*, Munich, 1978, pp. 61–65, nn. 38f. Among those who propagated the idea of reconciliation in France were Saint-Simon, Fourier, Comte, Michelet, Proudhon, and Champfleury. Proudhon spoke of a "rêve unitaire du peuple" (P.-J. Proudhon, *Napoleon III: Manuscrits inédits, publiés par Clément Rochel*, Paris, 1900, pp. 16, 19). Laverdant wrote: "Two guiding thoughts have emerged in our era: *Pauperism* occupies the thinkers, worries the statesmen . . . ; the *Theory of universal unity* is born, the law of harmony described . . . Art cannot avoid these tremendous facts. Are the ideas of poverty and harmony foreign to art? Shouldn't the artist inspect himself in their light?" (see n. 96, pp. 21f.). It would almost seem as though Courbet wished to answer these questions, by saying that it was the statesman's concern to worry about overcoming poverty, while it was the artist's to project a vision of harmony (see also Linda Nochlin, "The Invention of the Avant-Garde: France, 1830–80," *Art News Annual* 34, 1968, p. 14).

105. Hofmann, *Nineteenth Century*, p. 230. On the preceding phase, see Hinz, "Friede den Fakultäten" (n. 104), pp. 53–60.

106. See, among others, Berthold Hinz, "Säkularisation als verwerteter 'Bildersturm'," in Martin Warnke, ed., *Bildersturm*, Munich, 1973, p. 118.

107. See Horst Bredekamp's introduction to Ferdinand Piper, *Einleitung in die Monumentale Theologie* (1867); reprint Munich, 1978, p. 11 and n. 49.

108. This touches on a basic problem of nineteenth-century philosophy: "how the socially destroyed, dismembered human being, divided between two imperfect systems, could be restored" (Georg Lukács, *Geschichte und Klassenbewußtsein*, Berlin, 1923; reprint Amsterdam, 1967, p. 153).

109. A hypothesis advanced by Hélène Toussaint, in *Cat. Paris*, 1977–78 pp. 261ff.

110. It might be considered an attempt to create a form of image to which a great variety of social groups could respond—humble people *and* those of higher social strata, bourgeois *and* socialist. This brings up the question—which cannot be answered here—of whether Courbet, in *The Painter's Studio*, might not have anticipated a general aesthetic of reception of the type that is only now being developed. Castagnary seems to have considered this question as well, by demanding an art that could be understood without the aid of intermediaries (quoted in *Realismus als Widerspruch*, p. 171). Courbet's *Studio* fulfilled this demand in a Janus-faced way, by looking back, to history, and ahead, to nature.

111. Eugène Loudun, *Le Salon de 1855*, Paris, 1855, p. 205. Hofmann speaks in similar terms about *The Painter's Studio* itself (*Nineteenth Century*, p. 11).

CHAPTER 4. Equality and Authority in Courbet's Landscape Painting

Translator's note: I thank Peter Chametzky for his kind permission to use his translation of this essay as the basis for my own.

1. Almost all recent publications on Courbet deal with the figure paintings. The last discussion of the landscapes in any detail was that of Riat (1906). Since publication of the present article in 1975, two authors have dealt with Courbet's landscapes: Michael Brötje, "Das Bild als Parabel. Zur Landschaftsmalerei Gustave Courbets," *Jahrbuch der Hamburger Kunstsammlungen* 23, 1978, pp. 75–106 (a structural analysis), and Anne M. Wagner, "Courbet's Landscapes and Their Market," *Art History* 4, 1981, no. 4, pp. 410–431. Wagner's proposals are by no means incompatible with mine; her main concern, Courbet's selling strategy after the Commune, does not affect the political implications of his art nor his advocacy of freedom through depictions of nature from the 1850s on.

2. Clark, *People*, p. 132.

3. See particularly Edmond About, *Voyage à travers l'exposition des beaux-arts*, Paris 1855, p. 205; Théophile Gautier, *Les beaux-arts en Europe, 1855*, Paris, 1856, vol. 2, p. 155; Thoré, *Salon*, passim; Castagnary, passim.

4. On the artist as a "mere eye" (a quip first made by Ingres), see Camille Lemonnier, *G. Courbet et son oeuvre*, Paris, 1878, p. 65; Richard Muther, *Courbet*, Berlin, 1908, p. 31. The concept of the artist as ignoramus was used by Champfleury in the positive sense of "simplicité" (as it was by Castagnary; see Courthion, vol. 1, p. 156), but after the Commune it took on the negative connotation of "stupidité" (see Courthion, vol. 2, p. 305, and Lemonnier, *G. Courbet*, p. 17) and was associated with the still prevailing judgment that Courbet was "un grand peintre bête qui ne faisait pas d'esprit." Among the recent authors to revise this cliché are Charles F. Stuckey, "Courbet's Château d'Ornans," in *Minneapolis Inst. of Arts Bull.* 60, 1971–73; and Jack Lindsay, *Gustave Courbet: His Life and Art*, London, 1973.

5. Courbet was already called an "ouvrier peintre" in 1851, and in 1868 was a member of the First International Association of Labor (see Clark, *People*, p. 146, and Clark, *Buchon*, p. 208). However, his political stance was hardly socialist, as indicated by his skepticism about the "siècle communiste où nous vivons" (Courthion, vol. 2, p. 65). He was an angered republican who remained devoted to the bourgeoisie and its institutions. Ever since Louis Aragon (*Gustave Courbet*, Paris, 1952), most attempts to show the current value of Courbet's political philosophy today have been based on his participation in the Commune; see Maurice Choury, *Bonjour, Monsieur Courbet!* Paris, 1969; and diverse essays published in conjunction with the hundredth anniversary of the Commune. Courbet's relevance cannot of course be explained in terms of any single event which, though certainly connected with his work, was scarcely directly reflected in it. Nor do the antiwar paintings cited by Aragon suffice for an explanation, since they never got beyond the planning stage. Courbet's critical potential is revealed in his oeuvre in general; an exemplary study in this regard is Guido Boulboullé, "Gustave Courbet. Zur Interpretation einer antikapitalistischen Kunst im Frankreich des Second Empire," diss., Univ. of Bochum, 1972.

6. Nochlin, *Style and Society*, p. 2. An early opponent of the conventional separation of socially relevant from socially irrelevant works was Heinz Lüdecke, "Courbet, Ein sozialer Realist," in *Bildende Kunst* 2, 1948, no. 2, pp. 3–6 (includes a discussion of the landscapes); see also Lorenz Dittmann, "Courbet und die Theorie des Realismus," in *Beiträge zur Theorie der Künste im 19. Jahrhundert*, vol. 1, ed. Hans Koopmann and J. Adolf Schmoll (Eisenwerth), Frankfurt am Main, 1971, pp. 215–239.

7. Gabriel Laviron and Bruno Galbacio already saw the new landscape painting as an expression of the current social situation (*Le Salon de 1833 . . .* , Paris, 1833, p. 217). The recent growth of interest in landscape painting has provided a methodological verification of this link; see *Landschaft—Gegenpol oder Fluchtraum?* exh. cat., Haus am Waldsee, Berlin, and Städ-

tisches Museum, Leverkusen, 1974–75; *Schweiz im Bild—Bild der Schweiz? Landschaften von 1800 bis heute,* exh. cat., Aarau, Aargauer Kunsthaus, et al., 1974 (reviewed by Hans-Ernst Mittig in *Kritische Berichte* 2, 1974, vols. 3–4, pp. 12–32).

8. The actual relationships between art and society at any period are dehistoricized when realism and naturalism are treated as timeless principles. An important attempt to reinstate the historical context has been made by J. Adolf Schmoll gen. Eisenwerth (in *Kunstchronik* 27, 1974, pp. 49–52), who defines realism as the critical depiction of social reality (by means of selected subject matter), as opposed to naturalism, which he terms the quasineutral replication of nature (by means of a certain type of representation). However, this still leaves many questions open. For one, Courbet's contemporaries understood realism, too, as a new form of representation (e.g., Charles Perrier, "Du realisme," in *L'artiste* 16, Oct. 14, 1855, pp. 85ff.), and saw in naturalism a form of critical appropriation of reality (e.g., Castagnary, vol. 1, pp. 286, 289ff.). See also Brecht's criticism of the definition of realism as "contentism" (in *Über Realismus,* Frankfurt am Main, 1971, p. 65). It also remains open whether "social reality" includes the relationship of the individual to nature, and, as regards naturalism, whether a "quasineutral" replication of nature is even conceivable. Since the first publication of this article, I have tried to answer some of these questions; see my "Mimesis und Innovation. Überlegungen zum Begriff des Realismus in der bildenden Kunst," in *Zeichen und Realität,* Proceedings of the Third Semiotics Colloquium, Hamburg 1981, ed. Klaus Oehler, Tübingen, 1984, pp. 78–108.

9. "Donner une définition *esthétique* du Réalisme serait du temps perdu; une écluse ouverte à des fleuves de discussion sur les mots." Edmond Duranty, "Esquisse de la méthode des travaux," in *Réalisme,* Nov. 15, 1856, p. 2. Duranty suggests investigating the conditions of intellectual production as *an economist* would. Stylistic criteria certainly do not suffice by themselves, for they have proven to be partly fictions, partly vapid formulas. See Bernard Weinberg, *French Realism: The Critical Reaction, 1830–1870,* New York, 1937, pp. 106, 109ff., and Dittmann (n. 6), pp. 217f. In order to facilitate the development of a new, problem-oriented nomenclature, I use the term *realism* in this essay only when citing the contemporaneous sources.

10. The oppositional French critics recognized the significance of this issue independently of Marx. See, for example, Théophile Thoré on "la séparation du capital et du travail," in *Liberté,* Brussels, 1850, p. 18.

11. On the tensions between city and country and their effect on visual art after 1850, see Clark, *Buchon;* Herbert, esp. pp. 64–67; and my essay "Der Städter auf dem Lande. Daumiers Kritik am bürgerlichen Verhältnis zur Natur," in *Honoré Daumier . . . ,* exh. cat., Berlin, Neue Gesellschaft für bildende Kunst, 1974, pp. 101–126.

12. See Rondo Emmett Cameron, *La France et la développement économique de l'Europe,* Paris, 1971.

13. Thoré alludes to solidarity merely in passing, when discussing his hopes for the future effects of art (Thoré, *Avenir,* p. 254).

14. Hippolyte Castille, *Les hommes et les moeurs sous le règne de Louis-Philippe,* Paris, 1853, p. 340. On competition, egoism, and individualism in the writings of Balzac, see Georg Lukács, *Probleme des Realismus* III, Neuwied and Berlin, 1965, pp. 450f.

15. On the decline of the bourgeois ideal of liberty between 1830 and 1848, and its effects on art, see Stanley Meltzoff, "The Revival of the Le Nains," in *The Art Bulletin* 24, 1942, p. 267. During the Second Empire this ideal was further corrupted in that Napoleon III, for propagandistic purposes, attempted to "combine the idea of freedom with that of authority" (Heinrich Euler, *Napoleon III . . . ,* Miesbach, 1972, p. 11). Courbet's patron Bruyas, writing "à l'appui de la vérité du 2 décembre 1851," used the term *liberty* in precisely this sense, to characterize Napoleon's rule (Alfred Bruyas, *Salons de peinture,* Paris, 1853, pp. 5f., 9).

16. See esp. Helmut Hartwig, "Die Republik und andere allegorische Frauengestalten . . . ", in *Daumier* (n. 12), pp. 127–144.

17. A definition based on Comte's view of science and Proudhon's theory of justice, in order to emphasize their influence on Courbet's notion of equality. In spite of Comte's sharp criticism of anarchy, he lastingly influenced Proudhon, Champfleury, and Courbet. See Proudhon's *Du principe de l'art et de sa déstination sociale* (1865; reprint Farnborough, 1971), and my annotated edition, *Von den Grundlagen und der sozialen Bestimmung der Kunst*, Berlin, 1988, esp. p. 205. Baudelaire, in 1859, even equated realism with positivism (see Weinberg [n. 9], p. 101, no. 637); Buchon specified the realists' conception of truth as "vérité positive" (in *Réalisme*, Feb. 15, 1857, p. 49); Louis de Geofroy introduced the criterion of "exactitude" for realism ("Le Salon de 1850," in *RDM*, March 1, 1851, p. 928). Courbet himself called his stag trilogy of 1861 "exacts comme des mathématiques" (Courthion, vol. 2, p. 90), and to Duranty, finally, completeness of representation was part of the scientific quality of realistic art (Duranty [n. 9], p. 2).

18. Most influential in this connection was probably Pierre Leroux, *De l'égalité*, 2d ed., Paris, 1848; also Philippe Buonarroti, *Conspiration pour l'égalité dite de Babeuf*, 2 vols., Brussels, 1828, a book that was widely read after 1848. On Courbet as a follower of Leroux, see Courthion, vol. 2, p. 27. The connection between economic and political equality is lucidly described by Proudhon; see Karl Diehl, *Über Sozialismus, Kommunismus und Anarchismus*, 3d ed., Jena, 1920, p. 107: "As soon as the economic reforms he proposed were carried out . . . all authority would become superfluous because then everyone would be his own ruler and legislator."

19. Cited in Konstantin Frantz, *Louis Napoleon*, Leipzig, 1852; reprint Darmstadt, 1960, p. 21 (author's own emphasis).

20. See Meltzoff (n. 15), p. 265; and Alan Bowness, *Courbet's "L'atelier du peintre,"* Newcastle, 1972, p. 18. The demand for pictorial equality corresponded with expectations on the current art market. "Egalité pour tous au jour de l'exposition" was declared "indispensable au progrès de l'art" by Laviron and Galbacio, p. 143 (see n. 7). The same authors anticipated Courbet's advocacy, in 1861, of an egalitarian teacher-student relationship (p. 29).

21. *Le constitutionnel*, March 1849; quoted in Linda Nochlin, "The Invention of the Avant-Garde: France 1830–60," in *Art News Annual*, 1968, p. 11. Equality was apparently a more common theme of painting after 1848 than is evident today. Compare Hamon's "L'égalité au serail" (1849; expanded version in *L'artiste*, 1850, p. 112). On Thoré's position, see Henri Marguéry, "Un Pionnier de l'histoire de l'art: Thoré-Bürger," *GBA* 1, 1925, pp. 229–245, 295–311, 367–380; and Pontus Grate, *Deux critiques d'art de l'époque romantique, Gustave Planche et Théophile Thoré*, Stockholm, 1959, as well as Frances Suzman Jowell, *Thoré-Bürger and the Art of the Past*, New York, 1977.

22. Théophile Thoré, *La restauration de l'Autorité ou l'opération césarienne, par un Ex-Représentant du Peuple*, Brussels, 1852, p. 9.

23. Du Camp, p. 106. Du Camp saw the tendency of such contemporary artists as Moreau to call on the authority of the Old Masters in this light. On the topos of the artist as leader of society, see Shroder, pp. 42, 73, 75, 77, and 97. In 1864 the Goncourt brothers pessimistically recapitulated the experience of the Second Empire, writing, "Que le peuple . . . est le plus dénué de ce sentiment d'égalité. . . . Dans tout ce qu'il voit . . . il ne voit partout . . . que la continuelle apparence de l'inégalité" (Edmond and Jules de Goncourt, *Journal*, 4 vols., Paris, 1956; vol. 2, pp. 52f.).

24. See Courbet's report of his conversation with Nieuwerkerke: "Je répondis immédiatement . . . que moi aussi j'étais un gouvernement" (Courthion, vol. 2, p. 81). As early as 1850 he had written, "Il faut que je m'affranchisse même des gouvernements" (ibid., p. 78). And as late as 1868 he was still combating "la gouvernementation autoritaire" (ibid., p. 141). Conversely, Courbet recognized authority as a "nécessité sociale" (p. 52). In his 1870 "profession de foi" he self-critically remarked, "Retranché dans mon individualisme, je luttai sans relâche contre le

gouvernement d'alors, non seulement sans le redouter, mais encore en le provoquant" (p. 48); yet he always thought of himself as one of the "hommes . . . dévoués . . . à l'égalité" (p. 50).

25. Even the colophons of the volumes of *Cours de philosophie positive* contained appeals to the "grande révolution."

26. Auguste Comte, *Système de politique positive . . .* , Paris, 1851–54; reprint Brussels, 1969, pp. 75, 159; also 160f., on the support for existing systems of authoritarian government.

27. See Pierre-Joseph Proudhon, *La révolution sociale demontrée par le Coup d'Etat du Deux-Décembre*, Paris, 1852, in which Proudhon resorts to "a historical *apologia*" for the "heroes of the coup d'état" (Marx in the preface to the second edition of his essay "The 18th Brumaire of Louis Bonaparte"). Further material is found in Peter Heintz, *Die Autoritätsproblematik bei Proudhon . . .* , Cologne, 1956.

28. Schapiro, pp. 183, 188, 190. Champfleury accordingly withdrew from the realist circle (Courthion, vol. 1, p. 126). Charles-Maurice Couyba (*L'art et la démocratie*, Paris, 1902, p. 344) still relies on Champfleury's two-class theory of art.

29. Dupont, originally one of Courbet's friends, wrote a "Chant des Paysans" in 1849 that got him a seven-year ban under the Second Empire (cf. Pierre Brochon, *La chanson française: Le pamphlet du pauvre*, Paris, 1957, pp. 76f., and esp. p. 71, on Dupont's self-abasement before the emperor). Meryon, whose "Collège Henri IV" Courbet may have intended to paraphrase with a view of Paris as an ocean, made an indiscreet comment about the emperor in 1856; in a letter to Foley, however, dated February 17, 1858, he loyally called him "haut et puissant souverain, noble coeur" (Paris, BN). Castagnary (vol. 2, p. 12) cites Meissonier's behavior in 1872 as an example of "à quel degré de servitude morale l'empire de Napoléon III avait réduit les artistes."

30. Examples are, in Millet, *The Gleaners* (intellectually in the Ruth-Boaz opposition, visually in the monumentalization of humble figures); and in Daumier, the caricatures of official authorities (judges) and stereotyped idealizations of the people (intellectually *and* visually most obvious in the lithograph *Je t'ai déjà défendu de m'appeler maître*, D.1303). On Millet's conception of equality, see Eugène Delacroix, *Journal*, ed. André Joubin, 3 vols., Paris, 1932; vol. 2, p. 20.

31. The standard opinion that Courbet's work did not develop was first contradicted by Julius Meier-Graefe, *Courbet*, Munich, 1921, pp. 17, 45 (and 40, 42 on the significance of the landscapes in this regard). The first attempt to clearly distinguish periods was made by John P. Sedgwick, "The Artist's Artist," in *Art News* 58, 1960, pp. 40–44, 65f. While distinguishing an "early type" of painting (1849–53) from a "late type" (1866–71), Sedgwick neglects the middle period, in which the most important changes occurred. Moreover, his analysis is strictly formal, relying heavily on the neo-abstract painting of the 1950s, and should be expanded by reference to the aspect of (primarily ethical) content in Courbet's work.

32. See Nochlin, *Style and Society*, pp. 94ff., 99ff.; Clark, *People*, p. 191, n. 108; Schapiro, p. 171; Meltzoff (n. 15), p. 281 (farmers as "natural poets"). While this hope in regeneration long remained strong in the provinces, in Paris it disappeared for good after the 1857 election.

33. François Sabatier-Ungher saw "la démocratie dans l'art" in *A Burial at Ornans* (*Salon de 1851*, Paris, 1851, p. 62f.); Louis de Geofroy reproached Courbet's equalizing tendencies ("Le Salon de 1850," *RDM*, March 1, 1851, p. 929); Chennevières mocked him in 1851 as "le messie de l'art démocratique" (cited in Riat, p. 86); that same year, *The Stonebreakers* was caricatured as an expression of "démocratisation de l'art" (fig. 71). Still, this does not amount to proof that Courbet's art was addressed to the masses exclusively. Although he wrote to Wey in 1850, "Le peuple jouit de mes sympathies; il faut que je m'adresse à lui directement, que j'en tire ma science, et qu'il me fasse vivre" (Courthion, vol. 2, p. 78), this ambition, inspired by Champfleury, broke down along with his republican hopes. Courbet's statements of 1855 and 1861, seen in light of his view that as an artist he stood above the classes (Courthion, vol. 2, p. 43),

referred to an audience comprising several classes. As Castagnary said, "Ces toiles, faites pour la foule, n'ont jamais eu de prise sur elle" (vol. 1, p. 29).

34. BN, Cab. des Estampes, Papiers Castagnary.

35. Courthion, vol. 2, p. 82.

36. See Linda Nochlin, "Innovation and Tradition in Courbet's Burial at Ornans," in *Essays in Honor of W. Friedlaender,* New York, 1965, pp. 119–126; and *Realism,* Harmondsworth, 1971, p. 60; Clark, *Buchon,* passim.

37. *Précurseur d'Anvers,* Aug. 22, 1861; see Paul Mantz, "Gustave Courbet," *GBA* 1878, no. 2, p. 26.

38. "Lui seul se rengorge, lui seul commande." Clark, *People,* p. 164.

39. See Clark, *Buchon,* p. 288.

40. Nochlin, *Style and Society,* p. 134; see also pp. 136f. and n. 37, p. 121.

41. Clark (*Buchon,* pp. 287f.) shows that between 1847 and 1851 another peasant rising was feared in Paris, but like Champfleury at the time, he cautions that *A Burial* does not depict peasants but well-to-do rural gentry, and that a burial of this kind would have seemed a privilege to 80 percent of the Parisian population. Hence the picture is addressed to two groups: the poor, who would have been stirred up and emboldened by what they thought was a representation of the bourgeoisie, and the upper class, who would have felt both political and aesthetic anxiety in the face of the new demands of the rural population they saw represented there.

42. In the same letter (see n. 34), Courbet expressed the hope that "la commission a renoncé à me faire relever la colonne," and continued, "Laissons marcher, la situation est magnifique. . . . Il y a de quoi rire." He received exhibition offers from London and Berlin, and wrote on March 19, 1873, to the Vienna Exhibition that it would be "la chose la plus heureuse de ma vie" (BN, Cab. des Estampes, Papiers Castagnary).

43. Clark, *People,* fig. 31.

44. While Thoré wrote, "Le sujet est absolument indifférent dans les arts" ("Salon de 1847," *Le constitutionnel,* April 17, 1847, p. 447), Clément de Ris declared, "Nous ne sommes cependant pas de ceux pour lesquels tous les sujets sont également indifférents" ("Salon de 1851," *L'artiste,* March 1, 1851, p. 34). See also Edmond About, "Courbet," *Le journal officiel,* Aug. 28, 1857; cited in Riat, p. 156.

45. Remarked Delacroix in his journal on April 15, 1853 (vol. 2, pp. 18f.; see n. 30).

46. See chap. 2 in this volume. See also Bernard Goldman, "Realist Iconography: Intent and Criticism," *Journal of Aesthetics and Art Criticism* 18, 1959–60, p. 184.

47. Félix Tournachon [Nadar], *Nadar jury au Salon de 1853,* pp. 6ff.; cited at length in Joseph C. Sloane, *French Painting between the Past and the Present,* 2d ed., Princeton, 1973, p. 149.

48. See Léger, *Caricatures,* p. 20.

49. This view characterized both oppositional art criticism, which could thus claim to reflect the *total* historical situation, and the Bonapartist criticism based on idealistic theories. Courbet thought of himself as an evangelist of art (see Borel, pp. 21f., 65, 70, 87, 89) and also as a fighter for democracy through art.

50. See Nochlin, *Meeting,* pp. 209–222.

51. See Bowness (n. 20), p. 13; Choury (n. 5), p. 21, who cites a poem by Vermersch about Courbet titled "Deus, ecce Deus."

52. Reported by Théophile Silvestre, cited in Courthion, vol. 1, p. 44.

53. See Bruyas's statement in his *Salons de peinture* of 1852 quoted above (*Studio,* n. 61). It is also revealing that Bruyas (p. 17) chose as motto for his catalogue of nineteenth-century paintings "Amour, travail, religion, liberté," which makes him sound more like an entrepreneur than a collector. On artistic and political harmony, see Bruyas (n. 15), p. 26. On Bruyas's influence on Courbet, see Bowness (n. 20), p. 20. Courbet seems to have misunderstood his

patron's quest for a social and artistic "solution" as thoroughly as Bruyas misunderstood Courbet's art, in which he saw a necessary liberation from outmoded academic canons, and an analogy to the political "solution" of 1851–52. Courbet, for his part, viewed Bruyas quite unsentimentally as the solution to his financial difficulties.

54. See Riat, p. 3; Clark, *People*, p. 31—hence Courbet's "ambiguity" (Clark, p. 141).

55. Dealt with as a general problem in Shroder, pp. 54, 64ff. (social pretension as a compensation for the isolation of the artist). On Courbet's isolation, see his letter to Bruyas (1854) about "la crainte de se trouver dans une solitude absolue" (Courthion, vol. 2, p. 85); on the later cooling of the relationship with Bruyas, see Clark, *People*, pp. 157, 192, n. 9.

56. "Ses ailes de géant l'empêchent de marcher." See Shroder, p. 37.

57. Ibid., pp. 56–66 (Hugo), 151ff. (Flaubert); on the topos of the Titan, p. 147.

58. *Journal* (n. 30), vol. 2, p. 364 (Aug. 3, 1855).

59. See Leger, *Caricatures*, pp. 29, 38, 51, 68.

60. See Benedict Nicolson, *Courbet: The Studio of the Painter*, London, 1973, p. 65. It has been taken too much for granted that without coming into conflict with the censorship, Courbet depicted opponents of the regime such as Buchon (banned in 1852) and Proudhon (who was excluded from the general amnesty as late as 1859) and showed their portraits at the World Fair.

61. "Aujourd'hui il n'y a en France que des individus isolés et un pouvoir tout-puissant." Thoré (n. 10), p. 127; Thoré (n. 22), p. 10: "L'autorité a pris une forme absolue"; see also Roger Price, *The French Second Republic: A Social History*, London, 1972, p. 32.

62. Courbet's description of the people in the left half of the picture (letter to Bruyas, Dec. 1854); see Borel, p. 50. On the naming of the model "Truth", see Courthion, vol. 1, p. 47.

63. The standard investigations are cited in chap. 3, n. 4 of this volume.

64. He completed a landscape of this type in 1854; see Nicolson (n. 60), p. 20.

65. In fact, Courbet is not painting at all. Cf. Nicolson (n. 60), p. 25.

66. The awareness of living in a "decadent" epoch was widespread, particularly in the fields of literature and art. See, among others, Shroder, pp. 218f. (on Baudelaire) and Thoré *Avenir*, p. 248 (on the "décadence progressive" in art). Concerning the relationship of the big city and the post-romantic turn to nature, see Herbert, p. 38 ("modern life meant rural life"), pp. 64ff.; and Klaus Bergmann, *Agrarromantik und Grosstadtfeindschaft*, Meisenheim, 1970. On the significance of nature, see George Boas, ed., *Courbet and the Naturalistic Movement*, New York, 1967, intro.; and n. 104 below.

67. In the 1830s the escapist experience predominated, and the Franche-Comté region played as much a part in it as Brittany, Normandy, and Auvergne; see Xavier Marmier, "Le Jura," *Le landscape français*, Paris, 1834, p. 23: "S'en aller d'un trait aux montagnes de l'Auvergne . . . , aux sites agrestes de la Franche-Comté, voilà ce qui s'appelle réellement sortir de Paris." From the 1850s the countryside was experienced in conscious opposition to industry, and the primitiveness and authenticity of the rural areas and their inhabitants were accordingly emphasized. On Franche-Comté, see the poetry collection by Max Buchon, *En Province: Scènes franc-comtoises*, Paris, 1858, and the later *Poésies franc-comtoises: Tableaux domestiques et champêtres*, Salins and Besançon, 1862; see also Charles Toubin, "Le paysan d'Alaise: Récit jurassien," *RDM*, Nov. 1, 1861, pp. 371–404. The freedom felt in the country as opposed to Paris resulted, for Buchon, from the fact that primal nature was common and inalienable property: "A nous tous ces vallons . . . où le vent libre et frais souffle à grandes bouffées. . . ." (*Poésies franc-comtoises*, no. 30).

68. Buchon, *Poésies franc-comtoises*, p. 3: "Va, bondis, ô ma Loue! à travers leurs entraves / Et n'imite jamais ces rivières esclaves / Que les hommes, flairant partout un lucre vil / Alignent au cordeau de leur code civil / . . . Ne souffre, surtout, jamais que l'on t'endigue / Car Dieu te créa libre, et, sans la liberté / Que deviendrait ta pure et sauvage beauté."

69. Ibid., p. 5: "Ces grands noms dont l'histoire avide se jalonne / De Vercingétorix et de

Vergassilaune / Ne résonnent-ils pas assez lugubrement . . . / C'est ici que coula, par immense rigoles / Le sang de ces derniers libres enfants des Gaules." See also Toubin (n. 67), p. 371.

70. See Stuckey (n. 4), pp. 28, 31. Ruins (and natural rock formations) are discussed as metaphors current since the Enlightenment for decline *and* unspoiled primitiveness by Robert Rosenblum, *Transformations in Late Eighteenth-Century Art*, 3d ed., Princeton, 1970, pp. 116–120; and by Hubert Burda, *Die Ruine in den Bildern Hubert Roberts*, Munich, 1967, p. 68. On artists' recourse to the Enlightenment, see also nn. 112f. below.

71. See Louvre, Sketchbook RF 9105, fols. 8r, 9r, 10r, 11r, 34v (castle ruins in Germany and Switzerland, 1850s); RF 29234, fols. 27v, 29r (Château sur Salins, which, unlike Aragon [n. 6], I think must probably date from around 1856). See also *Gustave Courbet*, exh. cat., New York, Wildenstein Gallery, 1948–49, nos. 10, 12; *La joie de peindre*, exh. cat., Paris, Galerie Daber, 1974, pl. 3 (*Miroir de Scey-en-Varais sous le château de Saint-Denis*).

72. Rather, he assumes the role of mediator (which is also the quintessence of the generally accepted connection between this picture and Rembrandt's *Hundred Guilder* Print). Here, nature, not Courbet, is the redeemer, and he is subordinated to her. See Nicolson (n. 60), p. 70, and chap. 2 in this volume.

73. See Proudhon (n.17). A general interpretation (*mundus socialibilis* as a continuation of the *mundus naturalis*) is found in Max Raphael, *Proudhon, Marx, Picasso: Trois études sur la sociologie de l'art*, Paris, 1933, p. 35.

74. See, among others, Theodore Zeldin, *The Political System of Napoleon III*, London, 1958, p. 103; and Euler (n. 15), p. 35.

75. Zeldin (n. 74), p. 66; also pp. 69, 120; and Euler (n. 15), p. 40.

76. Eduard Arnd, *Geschichte der Jahre 1860 bis 1867*, vol. 1, Leipzig, 1868, p. 79.

77. Zeldin (n. 74; pp. 91ff., 101–104) refers to the contradictory nature of the government's policy after 1857, which, on the one hand, tried to bring about appeasement through parliamentary reform, and on the other developed serious plans to reduce the metropolis, which had become radical, to an agrarian condition ("Paris . . . must . . . be reduced in size and deprived of its character of an industrial town" [p. 76]).

78. Arnd (n. 76), pp. 68f., 78; Euler (n. 15), pp. 34–38.

79. Emperor Napoleon III himself contributed to the notion that he had created true equality by calling himself a parvenu, thus implying that upward mobility was open to all (Zeldin [n. 74], pp. 49, 121f.).

80. Zeldin (n. 74), p. 120: "There is a myth that the liberal Empire represented the abdication of Napoleon III. . . . It was not the victory of the opposition, but a new party composed of both opponents and supporters of the old régime."

81. See Pierre-Max Angrand, "L'état mécène: Période autoritaire du Second Empire (1851–1860)," in *GBA* 71, 1968, p. 304. I agree with M. Angrand that the period *after* 1860 cannot be considered anti-authoritarian or liberal. As regards the literary upheaval, there was an entire "School of 1857" (Weinberg [n. 9], pp. 159–191).

82. Du Camp, p. 57.

83. See Albert Boime, "An Unpublished Petition Exemplifying the Oneness of the Community of Nineteenth-Century French Artists," *Journal of the Warburg and Courtauld Inst.* 33, 1970, pp. 345–353. Lethargy and opposition both grew after 1857 with the removal of artists from the jury (see Riat, pp. 148f.).

84. Jules-François-Félix Husson [Champfleury], *Le réalisme*, Paris, 1857; and a selection of writings under the same title, ed. Geneviève and Jean Lacambre, Paris, 1973. On Champfleury's political retreat, see n. 28; in 1870 he again glossed over his earlier position when he reminded Courbet that the attribute "democratic" belonged to art in general (Lacambre, *Le réalisme*, pp. 189f.). On the situation in 1857, see Buchon's letter about the "confusions intellectuelles du moment" (*Réalisme*, Feb. 15, 1857, p. 49).

85. Flaubert, and later Zola, eclipsed his reputation; see Schapiro, p. 175.

86. "La poussière et le scandale qu'il avait soulevés . . . sont aujourd'hui bien tombés. Depuis que le courant des idées . . . tend à se réformer . . . on ne s'occupe guère du Réalisme." Castagnary, vol. 1, pp. 27, 29.

87. "[Courbet] a pu croire autrefois que la peinture devait avoir une destination sociale; mais à l'heure qu'il est, il n'en croit plus un mot." Ibid., pp. 29f. See also Thoré, *Salon*, vol. 1, p. 36 (1861), on Courbet's accommodation: "Jugeant que l'époque était difficile . . . il s'est abstenu de risquer sa ménagerie de personnages hors la loi. . . . Il s'est donc rejeté sur les cerfs et les renards, contre lesquels on ne saurait professer d'antipathie." The value of this statement, exaggerated by Sloane (n. 47; p. 72), is qualified by statements to the contrary; Thoré is apparently projecting his own ambivalence onto Courbet. After returning from exile he said about his friend that "l'homme politique est bien mort en effet" (Paul Cottin, ed., *Thoré-Bürger peint par lui-même*, Paris, 1900, pp. 197, 199).

88. See Emile Bouvier, *La bataille réaliste (1844–1857)*, Paris, 1914; reprint Geneva, 1973. Also Sloane (n. 47), p. 158. Nochlin's study (contrary to the title) ends with the year 1855; on *The Painter's Studio* as the end of realism, see pp. 221f.; also Bowness (n. 20), pp. 3, 10, 28; and Nicolson (n. 60), p. 65.

89. All three terms were used to express key demands of the 1856–57 journal *Réalisme* (facsimile reprint Paris, 1970). On *égalité*, see Castagnary, vol. 1, p. 140 ("l'égalité des individus, et . . . l'équation des conditions"). On *indépendance*, see Théophile Silvestre, *Histoire des artistes vivants français et étrangers . . .*, Paris, 1856. On *vérité*, see Edmond Duranty, "Notes sur l'art," *Réalisme*, June 10, 1856, p. 1, especially in connection with landscape painting. See also Meltzoff (n. 15), pp. 273f.

90. Thoré (*Salon*, vol. 1, pp. xiiif.) indeed places the "death of romanticism" in 1857 (see also Grate [n. 21], p. 248; and similarly, Du Camp, p. 104). A clearer marker of the establishment of programmatic realism would be Amand Gautier's *Triomphe du réalisme*, exhibited in the Salon of 1865. Weinberg's (n. 9) division, placing the key period of confrontation between 1843 and 1866, is closer to the facts than Bouvier's (see also Goldman [n. 46], p. 183).

91. See Meyer Schapiro ("Nature of Abstract Art," *Marxist Quarterly* 1, 1937, no. 1, p. 82), dealing with the fact that criticism of impressionism was also fully developed before the works in this style had themselves reached their full potential.

92. See, among others, Jules Assézat, "Profils et grimaces . . . ," *Réalisme*, July 10, 1856, p. 3: "Il nous faut une révolution"; also, Edmond Duranty, "Réalisme," *Réalisme*, Oct. 15, 1856, p. 2.

93. Castagnary, vol. 1, p. 148.

94. Repro. in *Cat. Brooklyn*, 1988–89, p. 127. On the title *Toilette de la morte* (*Dressing the Dead Girl*) see Hélène Toussaint, in *Cat. Paris*, 1977–78, no. 25.

95. Repro. in *Cat. Brooklyn*, 1988–89, pl. 4 (after p. 86).

96. The interpretation of this figure as a self-portrait of Courbet with friends (as in Albert Schug, *Gustave Courbet, Die Jagd in der Kunst* series, Hamburg and Berlin, 1967, p. 24) has since been abandoned (according to Marie-Thérèse de Forges, personal communication). On the question of the figure as huntmaster or landlord, see Schug, pp. 11, 28.

97. For a comparison with Manet and Cézanne, see Christian Zervos, "Les problèmes de la jeune peinture I," *Cahiers d'art* 6, 1931, pp. 117ff.

98. As, for instance, by Schug (n. 96), p. 25, and Dittmann (n. 6), p. 239.

99. Destroyed. See Sloane (n. 47), fig. 58.

100. One of the first examples of a Courbet landscape with small figures that are hardly visible in reproduction is the *Château d'Ornans* (see Stuckey [n. 4], fig. 1); one of the last is *Cliff at Etretat* in the Musée d'Orsay, which has eleven figures of laundrywomen (see chap. 7 in this volume).

101. Schapiro, p. 182. But this did not preclude his remaining their model as an anarchistic painter (see n. 257 below), or his being attacked by Bonapartist-inclined artists: the notion of

anarchy covered both the dissolution of academic hierarchies and republican engagement. Both, his contemporaries felt, could best be approached indirectly, as Arsène Houssaye already advocated: "La meilleure *politique en peinture*, c'est une belle vache dans un paysage flamand. . . . On trouverait plus à rêver aux destinées humaines en face de cette bonne bête qu'au milieud'un phalanstère bien organisé" (*L'artiste*, 1844, p. 164).

102. Letter of Dec. 21, 1865, to Delhasse; see Cottin (n. 87), p. 222. Although in 1847 Thoré still associated rugged cliffs with the proletariat (see Nochlin, *Style and Society*, p. 123), his timidity now even disappointed Millet and Rousseau (Cottin, p. 199). They themselves were not immune to the mood of resignation: "Melancholy and despair swell the pulse of their art because they were urban dwellers, who brought city attitudes with them" (Herbert, p. 65).

103. In 1860 Courbet wrote, "C'est un terrain neutre où chacun s'entend et qui abonde dans la ferveur qu'on a pour le paysage et les animaux" (Léger, *Caricatures*, p. 119). Courbet thus consciously exploited an acute general need, as will be explained more fully below (see n. 194).

104. See Reinhart Maurer, "Natur als Problem der Geschichte," in Kurt Hübner and Albert Menne, eds., *Natur und Geschichte. X. Deutscher Kongress für Philosophie . . .*, Hamburg, 1973, p. 125. On the same problem, see Alfred Schmidt, *Der Begriff der Natur in der Lehre von Marx*, 2d ed., Frankfurt, 1971, pp. 98, 117ff.; and Herbert Marcuse, *Konterrevolution und Revolte*, Frankfurt, 1973, pp. 72ff (on the rediscovery of exterior nature as a part of history).

105. More fully explicated in Shroder, p. 87.

106. Reproduced in *GBA* 2, 1961, p. 158.

107. See Hugo's dedication in *Les travailleurs de la mer* (1866): "Je dédie ce livre au rocher d'hospitalité et de liberté" (in Victor Hugo, *Romans*, vol. 3, Paris, éd. du Seuil, 1963, p. 7). Courbet and the authors of the journal *Réalisme* differed from Hugo not so much in their aims (see correspondence between Courbet and Hugo, in Courthion, vol. 2, pp. 98–101) as in the manner in which they should be treated in art. On the theme itself, see Courbet's *Isolated Rock* (New York, Brooklyn Museum; repro in *Cat. Brooklyn*, 1988–89, p. 62), a picture done in the early 1860s that was possibly influenced by Hugo. Concerning archaic objects as symbols of the future, see Meltzoff (n. 15), pp. 276, 279. Even Champfleury acknowledged that "en étudiant les images du passé, j'ai été naturellement poussé vers celles de l'avenir" (*Histoire de l'imagerie populaire*, Paris, 1859, p. xlvi).

108. Jules Clavé, "Etudes d'économie forestière," *RDM*, Jan. 15, 1860, pp. 454–480; June 1, 1860, pp. 714–736; Oct. 1, 1860, pp. 126–150; June 1, 1861, pp. 446–480. Here, p. 446: "Nous avons . . . fait connaître en quoi consiste la culture des forêts, étudié les moyens d'en accroître la production, recherché à quel système d'exploitation il faut les soumettre pour en tirer les plus grands profits." Emphasized as new, for instance, was "la facilité . . . des transports," which after 1860 permitted the export of all varieties of wood for the first time. Indicatively, this article is followed by a poem by A. Theubiet, celebrating the virgin forest as a giver of comfort and a compensation for social ills (pp. 481f.).

109. "Une fabrique immense de vivres, un laboratoire de subsistences plus productif que la terre même." As by Eugène Noël, cited in Jules Michelet, "Conquête de la mer," *RDM*, Jan. 15, 1861, p. 113.

110. See Champfleury, *Les amis de la nature*, Paris, 1859, esp. pp. 6, 11, 12 ("la violente antithèse"); p. 14: "Il porta dès lors la forêt dans son *cerveau* et dans son *coeur*"; and p. 127: "Il fut question d'établir des trains de plaisir pour Grateloup" (an ironic stab at the commercial exploitation of an aesthetic inclination for nature). Concerning the club itself, see Riat, p. 134.

111. See Nochlin (n. 50), p. 216; Jacques Lethève, *La vie quotidienne des artistes français au 19e siècle*, Paris, 1968, p. 99ff.; Helmut Kreuzer, *Die Bohème*, Stuttgart, 1971, pp. 222–224. The reasoning that a bad political situation caused the flight to nature hardly explains the prevailing attitude toward nature in the Second Empire. Nor did Courbet simply recur to an encoded natural metaphor like that of the German Vormärz. The goals and content of the new

turn to nature in the French boom period of the 1860s were a direct result of the necessity of increased regeneration. For Courbet, who still called himself a "Bohémien" in 1850 (Courthion, vol. 2, p. 78), clear motivations for departure and return took the place of aimless wanderings. Insofar as traditional attitudes were involved, these were preromantic, Enlightenment ones (see nn. 112–115). ". . . *retour sincère,* naïf, un peu sauvage même . . . *à la nature* plus ou moins inculte."

112. Thoré, *Salon,* vol. 1, p. 287; Thoré, *Avenir,* p. 256. On the recourse to Rousseau, see also Du Camp, p. 73.

113. See George D. H. Cole, *Socialist Thought: The Forerunners, 1789–1850,* New York, 1965, p. 216. Rousseau was also the source of Proudhon's attempt to find lost equality in nature.

114. Buchon (n. 67), 1862, preface (unpaginated).

115. ". . . en vue de protester contre le maniérisme et les dérèglements civilisés." Thoré, *Salon,* vol. 1, p. 287.

116. See Burghard Degner, "Wege zum 'Realismus' in der aufklärerischen Darstellung des Landlebens," *Wirkendes Wort* 18, 1968, pp. 303–319; Kathrin Steffen, "Ursprünge schweizerischer Landschaftsdarstellungen . . . ," *Schweiz* (see n. 7), pp. 23–35; and Marianne Matta, "Die schweizerische Landschaftsmalerei im 19. Jh.," *Schweiz,* pp. 36–53, with further literature.

117. Duranty (n. 92), p. 1, traced even the word *réalisme* back to Schiller; Buchon saw in southern German literature both a love of freedom and primal simplicity (see Hugo Frey, "Buchon," diss., Univ. of Besançon, 1940; Nochlin *Style and Society,* pp. 46, 100–105; and Nicolson [n. 60], pp. 39, 44f.). On this subject in general, see Clark, *People,* p. 29.

118. See the color plate in André Fermigier, *Courbet,* Geneva, 1971, p. 68.

119. Thoré connected both aspects when discussing paintings by Théodore Rousseau and Huet: "Ah! qu'il fait bon là en plein air, et comme on oublie les vains tourments des villes. . . . Le Paul Huet donne une impression presque inverse: . . . le ciel est sombre et opaque comme l'eau trouble. On se sent porté à la lutte contre la nature" (Thoré, *Salon,* vol. 1, p. 293). Champfleury's M. Gorenflot detects the same thing: "l'influence sereine de la forêt," and sees *at the same time* "des arbres de nature funèbre qui . . . remplissent l'esprit de réflexions tristes" (Champfleury [n. 110], pp. 6, 12). With this Champfleury placed himself in an old tradition: see Joachim Ritter, "Landschaft," 1963; reprinted in his *Subjektivität,* Frankfurt, 1974, pp. 141–164. Both aspects are perceptible in Courbet's beach and surf paintings (see figs. 41, 42).

120. That I speak of "man" here and not of a specific class or caste corresponds to Courbet's intention, which was to help *overcome* social divisions through art. In the same spirit, Castagnary wrote: "Le seul, le vrai paysagiste, c'est l'humanité" (*Salons,* vol. 1, p. 80).

121. Herbert, pp. 64f. (the attempt to ignore industry, based on the morality of J. J. Rousseau); p. 41 (influence of Th. Rousseau on the Lille painting; see for instance that artist's *Source of the Lison,* repro. in *Théodore Rousseau,* exh. cat., Paris, Louvre, 1967–68, no. 83).

122. See Herbert, p. 64. Industrial views were characteristically considered affirmative (that is, Bonapartist). On the issue itself, see Marx (n. 27).

123. See, e.g., his *Winter Landscape with the Dents du Midi* (Hamburg, Kunsthalle; repro. in *Cat. Hamburg,* 1978–79, p. 302), and the discussion by A. Tzeutschler-Lurie, "G. Courbet, Grand Panorama of the Alps with the Dents du Midi," *Bull. of the Cleveland Museum of Art,* 1966, p. 79, fig. 4.

124. The rail network had doubled in size by 1858. Further information is found in Gerhard Haupt and Dorothee May, "Zur Entwicklung des französischen Kapitalismus im 19. Jahrhundert," in *Daumier* (n. 11), pp. 17f.

125. "Il se mit à peindre au hasard des voyages," remarked Jules-Antoine Castagnary ("Fragments d'un livre sur Courbet," *GBA* 1, 1912, p. 20). *The Sluice at Optevoz* (see Dittmann [n. 6], fig. 4) and the *Cliffs at Bayard* (Riat, p. 267) were favorite retreats; André Chagny (*Un pays aimé des peintres: Sites et monuments de la région de Crémieu,* Lyon, 1929, p. 296) counts

ten artists, besides Courbet and Daubigny, who met in the "Barbizon lyonnais," Optevoz. The government, on the other hand, commissioned artists to depict the sites of successful *expeditions,* whose aim was the conquest and exploitation of nature (e.g., in the stairwell of the Ecole des Mines in Paris; see Angrand [n. 81], p. 332).

126. See completed projects of this type in Paris (Gare Saint-Lazare), Basel, and elsewhere; and for a discussion, Christine Kyburz, "Zum malerischen Schmuck der Bahnhöfe," in *Schweiz* (n. 7), pp. 74–82. Simultaneously with Courbet's plans appeared an *Album du Chemin de Fer de Lyon à la Méditerranée: Recueils de dessins et sites, monuments, costumes etc . . . exécutés sur pierre par J. B. Laurens 1857–1862,* BN.

127. According to Paul Mantz; cited in Riat, p. 181.

128. Sainte-Beuve explained and defended Courbet's idea in a letter to Charles Duveyrier, April 27, 1862 (quoted in full in Courthion, vol. 1, pp. 163f.); Francis Wey took credit for the idea himself (BN, Papiers Castagnary, MS. 22). On Hittorf, see n. 131 below.

129. According to Riat, p. 181. Champfleury, who like Wey took credit for the idea, was more restrained: "Vos pinceaux devaient tracer . . . la nature caractéristique du peuple qui a fourni à la France ces hommes, à l'industrie ces produits" (Lacambre [n. 84], p. 191). Concerning the implications of this "rapprochement de l'art et de l'industrie," see Harold Alfred Needham, *Le développement de l'esthétique sociologique en France et en Angleterre au XIXe siècle,* Paris, 1926, p. 167.

130. See Thoré, *Salon,* vol. 2, p. 264.

131. Paris, 1868, pp. 279–283. Baudry was a republican writer and a friend from Courbet's youth who supported him after the Commune (see Roger Bonniot, "Interventions de ses amis saintais en faveur de Gustave Courbet en exil" [1875], *GBA* 70, 1967, pp. 227–244; also, Bonniot, *Gustave Courbet en Saintonge,* Paris, 1973, pp. 37–43). The key passage related to this theme, in which Courbet is introduced as a member of a fictitious artists' society, is reprinted in part in Lindsay, p. 225. Courbet is cited as wishing to replace the museums "par les gares des chemins de fer . . . qui sont déjà les églises du Progrès, et qui deviendront les temples de l'Art. . . . Car, là où la foule se porte, là est la vie." He then states that his plan has been accepted by the financiers, and goes on: "Bientôt, disais-je à feu Hittorf, vos chemins de fer sillonneront la France; donnez pour mission à l'artiste de faire l'histoire de nos départements. . . . A l'un de peindre les forêts, à l'autre les plaines, à d'autres les fleuves et les rivages de la mer . . . quel puissant moyen vous est offert, de moraliser, en l'instruisant, ce peuple qui jadis inondait les musées . . . songez-y . . . pour enseigner au peuple l'histoire vraie, en lui montrant de la vraie peinture."

132. ". . . d'inaugurer une peinture monumentale qui soit en accord avec la société nouvelle." Sainte-Beuve, cited in Courthion, vol. 1, p. 164.

133. In this sense Courbet's approach resembled Proudhon's. Proudhon envisaged a painting of decidedly socialist tendency which would concentrate on depicting human confrontation with nature through work and on the theme of the proletariat.

134. "Tu as deshabillé ta peinture." Jean Clarétie, *Peintres et sculpteurs contemporains,* Paris, 1882; cited in *Equivoques,* exh. cat., Paris, 1973 (entry on Courbet). On Kleist's statement, see Helmut Börsch-Supan and Karl Wilhelm Jähnig, *Caspar David Friedrich,* Munich, 1973, p. 76 ("as though one's eyelids had been cut off").

135. "Voilà ce que je voulais vous montrer, me dit Baudelaire, voilà le point de vue. Etait-il assez bourgeois, hein! Qu'est-ce que c'est des points de vue? Est-ce qu'il existe des points de vue?" Courthion, vol. 1, pp. 159f.

136. "Où que je me mette . . . ça m'est égal; c'est toujours bon, pourvu qu'on ait la nature sous les yeux." Riat, p. 72.

137. Du Camp, p. 289.

138. On Belgium as a country of political and artistic freedom, see Gerstle Mack, *Gustave Courbet,* New York, 1951; reprint 1970, p. 236; also, Thoré (n. 10), p. 60.

139. The first picture of this type may be *Rocky Landscape near Ornans* (Paris, Musée d'Orsay) of c. 1854; repro. in *Cat. Paris, 1977–78*, p. 140. The later pictures are more determined by a means-ends correlation; examples are *The Gour de Conche*, 1864 (Besançon, Musée des Beaux-Arts; repro. in *Cat. Brooklyn, 1988–89*, p. 153); *The Stream of the Black Well*, 1865 (Toulouse, Musée des Augustins; repro. in Robert Fernier, *La vie et l'oeuvre de Gustave Courbet: Catalogue raisonné*, 2 vols., Paris 1977–78, vol. 1, no. 465); *Snowy Landscape with Boar*, c. 1866 (Copenhagen, Ny Carlsberg Glyptotek (*Cat. Brooklyn, 1988–89*, p. 182); *La Dent de Jaman*, 1877 (Paris, Galerie Schmit; repro. in *Les Impressionistes et leurs précurseurs*, exh. cat., Galerie Schmit, 1972, p. 26); *Snowy Landscape on the Loue*, c. 1867 (Ornans, Musée Courbet; repro. in *Courbet dans les collections privées françaises*, Paris, Galerie Aubry, 1966, no. 20); *Landscape in the Franche-Comté*, 1869 (Paris, Bauchet Coll., Galerie Aubry, fig. 24), and so on.

140. For example, *Roebucks in Winter*, 1866 (Lyon, Musée des Beaux-Arts; Fernier [n. 139], vol. 2, no. 560); *Winter Forest with Deer*, c. 1865 (Cincinnati Art Museum; see Fernier, vol. 1, no. 266); *Hunter in the Mountain Valley*, 1873 (French private coll.; see Courthion, vol. 2, facing p. 225, with set-pieces from *Cliffs by the Sea*, fig. 10).

141. Buchon, 1862 (n. 67), p. 5. Courbet's landscape paintings are often referred to in these terms there. Champfleury even wrote: "Les paysages [de Courbet] représentent presque tous . . . des montagnes et des roches qui ressemblent à des forteresses" (cited in Lacambre, p. 155).

142. Some examples are given in Stuckey (n. 4), p. 33. On the association of cliffs with castles, see Courbet's *View of a Castle*, c. 1855 (Wildenstein [n. 71], no. 4).

143. See Castagnary (n. 126), *GBA* 2, 1911, p. 497. On *vulgarité*, see Goldman (n. 46), p. 191; on *santé*, see Degner (n. 116), p. 313: milk drinking as a sign of moral superiority. The perversion of Enlightenment principles, all the way down to the Nazis' celebration of "blood and soil," deserves a separate investigation. It was facilitated by object-oriented mass production and by the exclusive claims of nonobjective painting. It is indicative that Du Camp, in 1861, already urged Courbet to depict "des choses saines . . . et non point réalistes," in other words, to concentrate on the "healthy" aspects of realism and avoid the "offensive" ones (see Riat, p. 189). Courbet opposed this distinction, particularly in his wave paintings.

144. See Courbet's statements, cited in Stuckey (n. 4), p. 31. Stuckey sees the humble houses on the former grounds of the château as a symbol of the defeat of feudalism, but the castle as an expression of the relative self-sufficiency of the feudal system. In my opinion, the houses and the castle cliffs should be seen as a unity, and both as symbols of a desire to recreate an ancient "independence." Courbet's expressive precision resides not so much in an exact sociohistorical differentiation as in the adequacy of his means of representation (obtrusive and shocking accentuation of renaturalized ciphers for history) and its ends (instrumentalization of the past for the purpose of personal and regional self-assertion).

145. See the two paintings in the Wildenstein exhibition, cited in n. 71 above.

146. See Daber catalogue (n. 71). It remains to be investigated whether the unusually bright colors of the houses were meant to accentuate them in terms of content, and the dirty gray of the *Castle on the Neuenburger See* (repro. in István Genthon, *Die grosse Zeit der neuen französischen Malerei*, Budapest, 1972, no. 17) was intended to reduce its visual importance.

147. See Heinrich Schwarz, "A Landscape by Gustave Courbet," "Museum Notes," *Rhode Island School of Design Bull.* 4, 1946, nos. 5, 2f. Schwarz interprets the mill as a workplace; yet there is nothing in the picture that suggests work. Its latent aggressiveness resides in the very "lack of anecdotal significance" (Goldman [n. 46], p. 189) that has so bothered critics, and in the eerie silence and matter-of-factness with which this plain house fills the picture.

148. A contradiction which is the theme of Cézanne's *Railroad Cutting* (c. 1870; Munich, Bayerische Staatsgemäldesammlungen) and which largely invalidates Courbet's instrumentalization of primitiveness to save society.

149. It was a notion current since the Enlightenment that a view over a landscape repre-

sented dominion; see Jakob and Wilhelm Grimm, *Deutsches Wörterbuch*, vol. 6, Leipzig, 1885, s.v. "Landschaft" (example from Goethe).

150. From Courbet's early period, see for example *Rocks at Mouthier*, c. 1850 (repro. *Cat. Brooklyn*, 1988–89, p. 124). On the difference between Courbet's early and late landscapes, see also Sedgwick (n. 23), p. 65. Courbet's *Stream of the Black Well* (see n. 139 and *Cat. Paris*, 1977–78, p. 181) suggests a comparison with Cézanne's *Forest with Boulders* (Zurich, Kunsthaus; repro. in Lorenz Dittmann, "Zur Kunst Cézannes," *Festschrift Kurt Badt zum 70. Geburtstag*, Berlin, 1961, facing p. 209). See also n. 220 below.

151. "L'homme, le grand modèle, disparaît presque complètement, . . . il semble être devenu je ne sais quel accessoire ennuyeux; la peinture de paysage envahit la peinture de genre, qui elle-même envahit la peinture d'histoire." Du Camp, p. 104.

152. "La révolution dans le paysage . . . a bien restitué la vraie nature, mais la nature pour elle-même; un franc théâtre, mais presque sans auteurs . . . dans cette brillante école de paysagistes la figure humaine n'est qu'un accessoire." Thoré, *Salon*, vol. 2, p. 186.

153. Jules Michelet, *L'étudiant* [posthumously published, 1877], Paris, 1970, p. 115: "Pour enfanter ainsi (comme Géricault), il faut une double condition, être à la fois solitaire, sociable; solitaire, pour concentrer la sève, couver les germes; sociable, pour les rendre féconds" (Jan. 13, 1848). Similarly Hugo, who said his life could be summed up in the words "solitaire, solidaire" (Shroder, p. 79).

154. Herbert, p. 65.

155. Thoré, *Salon*, vol. 1, p. 93.

156. See Schapiro, p. 183, on Champfleury's trips to the Jura. Wrote Castagnary, "On ne peut contempler . . . tous ces paysages frais et éclatants . . . sans recevoir comme une bouffée d'air pur en plein visage" (see n. 125; *GBA* 1, 1912, p. 21).

157. "Qu'il profite donc de la solitude où il se trouve, et quand il sera face à face avec la nature, peut-être que ses bons instincts lui reviendront." See Alexandre Estignard, *Jean Gigoux: Sa vie, ses oeuvres, ses collections*, Besançon and Paris, 1895, p. 45.

158. "Ces médecins . . . des forêts et de montagnes." Thoré, *Salon*, vol. 1, p. 93.

159. For a general discussion, see Rosenblum (n. 70), pp. 180ff. The aesthetic tracts published at the turn of the nineteenth century represented the second phase of Rousseauianism; William Gilpin, for example, recommends that landscape painters choose "objets rudes" and depict nature "dans sa simplicité" (*Trois études sur le Beau pittoresque* . . . , Breslau, 1799, pp. 20, 45). The topos was disengaged from its original moral implications in the 1820s, and after the 1848 revolution was linked with programmatic realism by Champfleury. As a result the term *sincérité*, as opposed to the *hypocrisie* of the Second Empire, gained new moral weight (see Meltzoff, p. 281; Schapiro, p. 188).

160. " . . . de reproduire la nature en l'amenant à son *maximum de puissante et d'intensité*." Castagnary in *Le nord*, May 14, 1863; cited in Marie-Antoinette Tippetts, *Les marines des peintres vues par les littérateurs de Diderot aux Goncourt*, Paris, 1966, p. 84.

161. See Buchon (n. 67), 1862, pp. 7f. (*Les sapins*). Thunder is compared to cannon fire, blasted trees to fallen soldiers, etc.

162. On the legal and political implications of the tree of liberty, see Suzanne Anderegg, "Der Freiheitsbaum. Ein Rechtssymbol im Zeitalter des Rationalismus," diss., Univ. of Zurich, 1968, pp. 27ff., 54, 87 (plays titled "Le chêne patriotique"), 103 (reinstatement of legal symbolism between 1830 and 1848). The link between personal memory and political motivations was established by choosing an object capable of standing for home (*Heimat*) both emotionally and rationally. Depictions of the homeland were common at the time as a protest against academic paintings of the Campagna, and also as a sign of resistance to authoritarian centralism. Hence Buchon (n. 68) could justify love of homeland as patriotism in an oppositional sense in an 1862 afterword.

163. "Je désire que tous les titres et mots appartenant à la Révolution de 89 et 93 ne soient

appliqués qu'à cette époque. Aujourd'hui ils n'ont plus la même signification et ne peuvent être employés avec la même justesse et dans les mêmes acceptions" (Choury [n. 5], p. 101). All the anecdotes about Courbet's political ignorance pale beside this insight into the historicity even of revolutionary concepts.

164. Courbet also used a woodcut of the "Chêne gigantesque de Montravail" (Nochlin [n. 50], fig. 19), a remarkable "model" that served to increase the effect of primeval nature.

165. See Herbert, p. 65.

166. It probably also served agitation within the region, because Ornans (like Flagey) was one of the conservative places in the politically diverse Franche-Comté (see Clark, *People,* pp. 100, 110).

167. References include Meltzoff (n. 15), pp. 272, 276–279; and Thoré, *Avenir,* p. 258.

168. Meltzoff, p. 280f.; Schapiro, pp. 172f., 176; Clark, *People,* pp. 93f., 113f. Dupont's "Chant des paysans" (see n. 29) was omitted from the 1852 edition with an introduction by Baudelaire.

169. Only a few paintings by decidedly oppositional artists were officially purchased, mostly for very low prices (one picture by Yvon was worth fifteen by Rousseau). An exception was Adolphe Leleux's *Noces bretonnes* (see Angrand [n. 81], p. 330).

170. See Nochlin (n. 50), p. 213, and *Cat. Brooklyn,* 1988–89, no. 44, with repro. p. 151.

171. It remains uncertain whether Courbet wished the painting understood in such a decidedly anti-Bonapartist way before its completion. His title may have been a reaction to the Vercingetorix statue commissioned by the emperor from Aimé Millet and shown in the Salon of 1865; see Thoré, *Salon,* vol. 2, p. 259. He may have been similarly affected by the painting of Vercingetorix by Emile Lévy (mentioned by Du Camp, p. 340).

172. See Schug (n. 96) and Nochlin (n. 50), figs. 16, 17.

173. "Le Combat de Cerfs doit avoir, dans un sens différent, l'importance de l'Enterrement" (letter to Wey, April 19–20, 1861; Courthion, vol. 2, p. 89). In his letter to Castagnary of Feb. 1, 1873 (see n. 34), Courbet recommends that instead of *A Burial* he choose for the Vienna exhibition other large-format pictures such as "le combat des cerfs ou l'allali du cerf à la neige."

174. Landseer's stags "stand there in their Sunday best, in their sleekest coats, with their most splendid antlers" (Richard Muther, *Geschichte der Malerei im 19. Jahrhundert,* vol. 2, Munich, 1893, p. 76; see also *Der röhrende Hirsch—Symbol der Männlichkeit,* exh. cat., Kiel, Kunsthalle, 1973–74, pp. 4–14).

175. See for example Grandville's *Revanche ou Grande chasse au tir, an 1830* (BN, photo. 70 C 44178), or Cham's *Pris pour un chamois* (pursuit of Thiers), *Le charivari,* Sept. 13, 1851.

176. "Il fut traqué, comme une bête fauve. . . . En se sauvant, il était tombé dans la gueule du loup." Letter to Castagnary, Dec. 16, 1869 (Courthion, vol. 2, p. 120; also pp. 100f.).

177. Jean Bruno, *Les misères des Gueux,* Paris, 1872, pp. 13, 27, 31.

178. Ibid., pp. 35f.

179. Open letter to the German army, Oct. 29, 1870 (Courthion, vol. 2, p. 131).

180. Edmond Duranty, intro. to Champfleury (see n. 110, p. vii).

181. Courthion, vol. 2, p. 144. Both aspects are discussed in William M. Kane, "Courbet's 'Chasseur' of 1866–1867," *Yale University Art Gallery Bull.* 25, 1960, nos. 3, 37.

182. Courthion, vol. 2, p. 39: "La chasse . . c'est un grand jeu. . . . Le chasseur est un homme d'un caractère indépendant qui a l'esprit libre ou du moins le sentiment de la liberté"; see also pp. 187ff. on the hunts held near Darmstadt and Bad Homburg.

183. Kane (n. 187), p. 37.

184. Letter to Bruyas, Jan. 1854 (Borel, p. 26); see also Riat, p. 154.

185. Nicolson (n. 60), n. 21. Courbet's three paintings of *The Poacher* are reproduced in Fernier (n. 139), vol. 1, no. 381 (Besançon), vol. 2, no. 613 (Rome); and in *Cat. Brooklyn,* 1988–89, p. 184 (Ornans). Adolphe Leleux's painting *Aragonese Smugglers* (repro. in *Art de France* 2, 1962, p. 192) reflects a comparable anti-authoritarian protest. Hélène Toussaint (*Cat. Paris,*

1977–78, p. 193) doubts whether the term *braconnier* was used to refer to a poacher in Courbet's times. See also chap. 3, n. 40 above.

186. See Hans-Wolf Jäger, *Politische Metaphorik im Jakobinismus und im Vormärz*, Stuttgart, 1971, pp. 12–28.

187. On Courbet's stay in Frankfurt in 1858, see Etienne Carjat, in *Echo littéraire illustré*, May 1, 1892; excerpted in Courthion, vol. 1, pp. 133f.

188. See Schug (n. 96), figs. 6–8.

189. "Par ce temps . . . incertain des idées et des sentiments, de la philosophie et de la morale, de la littérature et des arts, de la signification de l'histoire, comme des tendances de la vie présente—la nature et le paysage ont beaucoup d'attrait." Thoré, *Salon*, vol. 1, p. 144.

190. "Je préfère les cerfs de Courbet au chien d'Alcibiade." Thoré, *Avenir*, p. 258.

191. "La nature et la société sont également troublées. En France surtout, inquiétudes permanentes." Thoré (n. 87), p. 208 (letter of Oct. 30, 1866).

192. See *Eugène Delacroix, 1798–1863*, exh. cat., Paris, 1963, p. 29. Herbert was the first to call attention to Courbet's reliance on this painting; see Kane (n. 181), p. 34.

193. See Clark, *Buchon*, p. 208. On the belated liberalization that came with the appointment of Ollivier in early 1870, see Euler (n. 15), p. 46. Castagnary (vol. 1, p. 288) felt a "pressentiment de l'avenir" in the face of Courbet's 1868 *Beggar of Ornans*.

194. Mittig (n. 7) distinguishes between alienation (uncompensated withdrawal from nature) and detachment (aesthetically partly compensated loss of access to rural production); the latter applies in the present context. As Daumier shows (n. 11), aesthetic appropriation also failed, or was unsatisfactory, because it continually attested anew to the opposition between city and country.

195. Courbet's own position remained inconsistent in this regard. Though in 1861 he said that figure painting was more important to him than landscape, he actually devoted all his attention to the latter. See Courthion, vol. 2, p. 94; Meltzoff (n. 15), p. 273f.

196. H. Delaborde, "Le Salon de 1861," *RDM*, June 1, 1861, p. 891.

197. "M. Courbet aime trop la vérité, il ne faut pas aimer la vérité." Castagnary, vol. 2, p. 44. Similarly, Arsène Houssaye said of Potter's landscapes: "toujours vrai, quelquefois trop vrai" (*Histoire de la peinture flamande et hollandaise*, Paris, 1846, p. 203).

198. See letter to Chaudey, March 2, 1867 (BN, Papiers Castagnary; excerpts in Mack [n. 138], p. 216); letter to Bruyas, Sept. 10, 1868 (Borel, p. 132).

199. Du Camp confirms, "La figure, j'entends la figure épique, celle qui doit prendre place dans de grandes compositions, est la pierre d'achoppement de beaucoup de peintres" (p. 74); see also n. 151. With this the principle of individualism, still considered fundamental to realistic art in 1855, was outmoded. This must be seen in connection with the decisive change in all forms of communication in the 1860s, as the masses and mass organizations took on increasing significance in all areas of life (the First International Workers' Association was founded in 1864). See also David I. Kulstein, "Napoleon III and the Working Class . . . ," diss., California State College, 1969, pp. 188f.

200. Klaus Berger, "Courbet in His Century," *GBA* 24, 1943, p. 27; Nochlin, *Style and Society*, p. 144.

201. Ibid., p. 32: " . . . personnages . . . isolés . . . tons brusques et entiers, qui s'opposent les uns aux autres au lieu de s'unir."

202. On scientific influence on painting in general, see Du Camp, p. 74, and Thoré, *Salon*, vol. 1, p. 278. On Courbet's desire for scientific precision, see n. 17. Concerning his study of transitions and changes in nature, see Courthion, vol. 1, pp. 106f. (cloud formations); vol. 2, p. 61 (colored shadows in the snow).

203. Du Camp, p. 73; on "proletarian landscape," see n. 102.

204. See Castagnary, as cited in n. 120. See also Théophile Thoré, *Salons de Th. Thoré, 1844, 1845, 1846, 1847, 1848*, Paris, 1868, pp. xviif.: "Comment rester enfermé maintenant

dans de petits systèmes philosophiques, religieux, politiques, littéraires, artistiques . . . quand toutes ses pensées et toutes les formes . . . ravivent ce qu'elles ont de cosmopolite et de général. . . . Il n'y a plus qu'une race et qu'un peuple, il n'y a plus qu'une religion et qu'un symbole—l'Humanité!" On the internationalism expressed here, see Grate (n. 21), p. 250. This *moral* quality of *humanité*, Thoré says in another place (see n. 10, pp. 18, 20), will not be restored until the partitions that divide the human race are removed; only then could one say that "tout homme est prêtre, guerrier, artiste, savant, propriétaire, travailleur." There is an obvious similarity here to Marx's prediction that a future society would no longer have painters but only men who among other things paint (*German Ideology*). Thoré's bourgeois-revolutionary expectations were picked up by Castagnary (vol. 1, p. 255), who in 1868 declared that the 1848 revolution had been fulfilled in art: "Aujourd'hui la vie a recommencé et la révolution est faite"; he also described painting as a "partie de la conscience sociale" which would give "l'aspect pictural de l'humanité" (cited in Courthion, vol. 2, p. 221). Thoré himself (*Salon*, vol. 2, p. 282) wished in 1866 to "interpréter l'histoire avec un sentiment progressif, et en quelque sorte par une intromission de l'humanité persistante dans ses épisodes variables et temporaires." This was indeed a decided conception of history on the part of the progressive bourgeoisie, which by taking internationalism into account, broadened the "earnest humanitarianism" that existed under Louis-Philippe (see J. M. S. Allison, "The Political and Social Background of Naturalism," in Boas [n. 66] p. 1).

205. See Meltzoff (n. 15), p. 267, on the effects of "free-market competition" on art. On the development of the art market in the Second Empire, see Lethève (n. 121), pp. 141–172.

206. The use of the ground as an effective factor is especially clear in *Snowy Landscape with Boar*, c. 1866 (see n. 140) and in *Seascape*, 1872 (Caen, Musée des Beaux-Arts, repro. in Fernier [n. 139], vol. 2, no. 817).

207. See the excellent discussion in Schug (n. 96), pp. 33f.

208. Berger (n. 200; p. 28) reaches this conclusion solely on the basis of the constitutive individuation of objects that marks the first period.

209. See Thoré (n. 87), p. 223: "Il me semble impossible de parler de Rembrandt, par exemple, sans abîmer l'hypocrisie et le despotisme, sans glorifier *la lumière, qui est la liberté,* et toutes les qualités humaines qui touchent à la politique et à la Révolution" (letter of Dec. 21, 1864). Thoré divides Courbet's painting into periods based on treatment of light (Thoré, *Salon,* vol. 1, p. 100).

210. C. 1875; Paris, private coll.; repro. in Aubry cat. (n. 139), no. 34.

211. According to Thoré (*Salon*, vol. 2, p. 281), Courbet himself used the Aristotelian-scholastic expression *nature naturante;* he may have owed it to Proudhon. The "creative" power radiating from nature is particularly emphasized through the painterly means of the late work; see Sedgwick (n. 31), pp. 65f.

212. See n. 87. Sloane (n. 47; p. 164, and n. 72) rehearses the accepted view that "all hints of humanitarian content had disappeared."

213. Letter to Cuénot, April 6, 1866; Riat, pp. 236f.

214. In 1864 the right of coalition was granted, and in 1868 the right of assembly; but at the same time surveillance was increased. Courbet once alluded to the many secret political groups that existed; when he was assured that "personne ne verrait là une manifestation humanitaire," he replied, "A moins qu'*Ils* n'y voient . . . une société secrète de chevreuils qui s'assemblent dans les bois pour proclamer la République" (Henri d'Ideville, *Gustave Courbet . . . ,* Paris, 1878, p. 37). The ironic comment is meaningful, because it leaves unanswered whether or not a metaphorical encoding had become impossible since the period of Louis-Philippe (see n. 175). The picture's programmatic character is increased by its having been painted over an explicitly social-critical image, *The Source of Hippocrene* (damaged during execution). This was apparently a conscious act of transformation like that of thirteen years before, when Courbet painted *The Wrestlers* over a *Walpurgis Night*.

215. Pierre-Joseph Proudhon, *Solution du problème social,* Paris, 1848, pp. 96 and 95. Proudhon, as much as Courbet, was influenced by Fourieristic ideas of harmony, which Napoleon also exploited. Bruyas was both a Bonapartist and a Fourierist; he even published the "Notes d'harmonie" by Fourier; see Nochlin (n. 21), p. 14, and Needham (n. 129), p. 87. Thoré, by contrast, distinguished between the Bonapartist notion of reconciliation, which he rejected as bad leveling (see n. 22; p. 9), and the Fourierist idea of harmonization of human relations, which he affirmed as utopia (see n. 10; pp. 67, 109).

216. See Shroder, p. 61; Michelet (n. 153), pp. 58ff., 65ff.

217. See Shroder, p. 77 (on Hugo); Courthion, vol. 2, pp. 50, 135 (on Courbet). Thoré, too (see n. 10), envisaged a United States of Europe with a regionally self-sufficient France (pp. 60, 63, 73, 80).

218. Embodied in Corot (Du Camp, pp. 79f.) and Breton (Thoré, vol. 2, pp. 169, 190); and as a reconciliation between idealism and realism. On Champfleury's reconciliation theory, see Schapiro, p. 286.

219. See n. 59, and the caricatures of *The Wrestlers* and of landscape paintings in Léger, *Caricatures,* pp. 52, 72, 115.

220. Max Imdahl, "Die Rolle der Farbe in neueren französischen Malerei . . . ," in W. Iser, ed., *Poetik und Hermeneutik,* vol. 2, *Immanente Ästhetik . . . ,* Munich, 1966, p. 212.

221. Roger Marx characterized this intermediate stage formally as "recherches luministes encore timides, indécises et confuses de Courbet" (quoted in Riat, p. 147).

222. See Imdahl's remarks on Cézanne's "simplifying disburdening" of objects in connection with the conflict between intuitive and rational perception (see n. 220; p. 210).

223. Color repro. in *Jahrbuch preussischer Kulturbesitz* 7, 1969, facing p. 289.

224. "Cette largeur d'exécution et cette beauté de coloris . . . viennent en partie de là" (Castagnary, vol. 2, pp. 272f.).

225. Champfleury, *Souvenirs et portraits de jeunesse,* Paris, 1872, p. 191.

226. Nevertheless, the paint application remains dense, and partially opaque; here as in *The Wave* (D. Coll., Paris) it rises up to three millimeters above the median paint layers, which, as in Van Gogh, intercommunicate—if insularly—regardless of objective designation.

227. Musée d'Orsay: See *Cat. Paris,* 1977–78, p. 71 (color plate); Berlin: *Cat. Hamburg,* 1978–79, color plates 14, 15; Bremen: *Cat. Brooklyn,* 1988–89, p. 189; Frankfurt: *Städelsches Kunstinstitut, Verzeichnis der Gemälde,* 1971, fig. 73.

228. In the case of seascapes, the legitimating function of the Salon in the Second Empire becomes particularly clear. At the same time that Baudry and Cabanel showed their mythologizing seascapes (1863), Napoleon III was working out his colonial plans, and commissioned French engineers to build the Suez Canal. See also n. 251.

229. Unlike the Barbizon school (see Herbert, p. 64). Dittmann (n. 6), who while noting the anarchist aspect of Courbet's painting has remained too general in associating it with "the character of the epic style" (p. 238), sees a limit in Courbet's art, in that "he was unable to see relationships among individuals except in terms of control, which he anarchically opposed" (p. 239). This is to reduce Courbet to the individualistic, anti-authoritarian position of the Barbizon painters.

230. This is the deeper meaning of the statement "J'arrive en plein à l'émancipation de l'individu, et finalement, à la démocratie" (*Précurseur d'Anvers,* Aug. 22, 1861; Courthion, vol. 1, p. 161)—not in positing the individual as an absolute, but in establishing the individual's relation to others.

231. See Tippetts (n. 160), pp. 180, 183.

232. Also noteworthy in this regard is Courbet's materialist perception that "la conception est relative aux moyens d'exécution" (Courthion, vol. 2, p. 32). Silvestre (see Riat, pp. 146f.) recognized the egalitarian structure of the late work by a close observation of Courbet's technique.

233. This metaphor was common in French art and literature of the period; see, among others, Alexis de Tocqueville, "Souvenirs," *Oeuvres complètes,* vol. 12, Paris, 1964, p. 199; Michelet (n. 153), p. 62.

234. See Needham (n. 129), pp. 216f.; Boas (n. 66), p. vi.

235. Champfleury, *Grandes figures d'hier et d'aujourd'hui,* 1861 (reprint Geneva, 1968, p. 262).

236. See Börsch-Supan and Jähnig (n. 134), p. 136 (statement on the occasion of Cornelius's visit of April 19, 1820).

237. See Jäger (n. 186), pp. 91–93, 109.

238. Champfleury (n. 110), pp. 117, 126; perhaps stimulated by Heine, who derived his demand for political freedom from pantheism; see Jäger (n. 186), p. 98.

239. See Riat, p. 121. See also the concept of pandemonium in Baudelaire, which describes artistic behavior as well as artistic form (Shroder, p. 201).

240. "Tout a de l'intérêt dans la nature; tout, présenté par un peintre de talent, peut plaire. . . . Renversons la tradition, disent les réalistes; . . . Exaltons les humbles et les petits: ouvrons une voie large aux nouvelles couches sociales des forêts: . . . C'est une nouvelle forme de la démocratie qui va nous étouffer." Jean-Clément-Léonce Dubosc de Pesquidoux, "Le paysage réaliste," *L'artiste,* 1873, pp. 161f.

241. "Voilà *l'oeuvre de subversion à laquelle tous les paysagistes réalistes ont concouru,* complices inconscients ou non de nos plus dangereux songe-creux, séides trop dociles du fameux déboulonneur de la colonne, le peintre Courbet, *qui n'a fait que transporter en politique ses idées de nivellement* et de table rase artistique." Ibid., p. 162.

242. Perrier (n. 8), p. 88: "Ce n'est point . . . parce qu'il a peint des bourgeois et des paysans que M. Courbet est traité de factieux, mais parce qu'il les a présentés sous un aspect auquel la nature humaine répugne."

243. See Weinberg (n. 9), p. 159.

244. Du Camp, p. 53.

245. Ibid., p. 54. See also Delaborde (n. 196), p. 890: "L'étude" replaces the painting; a "habileté purement matérielle" suffices. Thoré, by contrast, criticizes the "exagération du fini" (Thoré, *Salon,* vol. 1, p. 49).

246. Du Camp, p. 286 (*taches*). J. Massin approves of Hugo: "Et si la tache composait le paysage?" (quoted in Victor Hugo, *Poésie,* vol. 3, Paris, éd. du Seuil, 1972, p. 473). Théophile Gautier complains about Monet that he is satisfied "à poser des taches" (quoted in Imdahl [n. 220], p. 197). Delaborde (n. 196; p. 901) complains that this year painters paid attention only "aux hardiesses, sinon aux impertinences de la touche"; Thoré, by contrast, praises Courbet's "touche franche" (Thoré, *Salon,* vol. 2, p. 278). In *Le charivari,* May 22, 1873, Corot is credited with predicting to Boudin: "Vous finirez par faire vos tableaux avec une seule touche." For a general discussion, see Albert Boime, *The Academy and French Painting in the Nineteenth Century,* London, 1971, pp. 166–184.

247. Du Camp, p. 105: ". . . les éléments de dissolution."

248. Ibid., p. 72.

249. Ibid., p. 72f.: ". . . les ferments de dissolution qu'elle portait en elle."

250. "Nous voulons nous échapper à tout prix, conquérir . . . la liberté de notre individualité . . . et nous allons interroger la nature . . . et réclamer d'elle une paix que nous ne trouvons ni en nous ni autour de nous." Ibid., p. 73.

251. L'espèce de panthéisme vague et consolant que *les écoles socialistes modernes ont promulgué,* n'a-t-il pas appris aux artistes que Dieu est partout, dans l'arbre comme dans l'homme, dans l'animal comme dans la plante? . . . La facilité, la rapidité des communications ont encouragé les peintres. . . . Voyant . . . qu'ils n'arriveront jamais à exécuter . . . l'homme, ils se rabattent sur le paysage, toujours plus facile à traiter, plus obscur, moins défini; en un mot, se sentant impuissants à rendre l'expression, ils se contentent de traduire l'impression." Ibid., p.

74. Thoré had by 1850 grasped that "communication facile" had contributed to the political movement: "Ne voyez-vous pas l'immense mouvement qui s'est opéré en France depuis quelques années, grâce aux chemins de fer, au développement du commerce et de la sociabilité, aux secousses des révolutions?" (see n. 10; p. 78). Now, in 1864, he took up these ideas again on a world scale, in order to explain the realistic renewal of art, and above all of landscape painting, which he, unlike Du Camp, saw in positive terms: "La découverte de l'Amérique . . . était peu de chose comparativement à la découverte du globe entier, dont la possession nous est assurée désormais par la puissance et la rapidité de nos moyens locomotifs" (Thoré, *Salon*, vol. 2, p. 90). Another very clear reference is found in Thoré, *Avenir*, p. 252.

252. Du Camp (p. 136) also quotes, among others, Ingres' statement "Le dessin, c'est la probité".

253. "L'art français est en pleine licence." Ibid., pp. 105f.

254. "Prendre au hasard ce qu'on apperçoit, c'est se réduire à l'état de pantographe. . . . C'est réduire à néant l'observation, la comparaison, l'élection." Ibid., p. 219, where we also read: "La vérité inventée est supérieure à la vérité observée; la première peut être absolue, la seconde n'est jamais que relative." Pantograph stands here for mechanistic, indiscriminate depiction of "everything in sight."

255. "L'avenir seul pourra dire si ce changement a été heureux; notre seule mission est de le constater en gémissant, *car nous croyons qu'il est funeste*." Ibid., p. 289.

256. " . . . une révolution . . . et une révolution par le fond et par la forme." Castagnary, vol. 2, p. 255 (1868).

257. See Clark, *People*, p. 160 (on Picasso); Dittmann (n. 150), pp. 190–193 (on Cézanne and the attacks on his "anarchistic" art made by Gérôme, Constant, and Rochefort); also, Schapiro (n. 91; p. 83) on the "unregulated vision" that in early impressionism implied a criticism of society.

258. *Le charivari*, May 30, 1873.

CHAPTER 5. Proudhon's *Carnets intimes* and Courbet's *Portrait of Proudhon*

1. "Succès. Quatre amis, Chaudey, Madier-Montjau, Courbet, Hagelmann, déjouent l'intrigue pour la propriété littéraire. Les mêmes, moins Hagelmann, font une profession de foi à mon nom, anti-mystique." Pierre-Joseph Proudhon, *Carnets*, 9 vols. (1843–64), Paris, BN, Département des Manuscrits, NAF 14267–14275; vol. 9, p. 594. On p. 602 (following entries for May 4, 1864) Proudhon mentions Courbet for the last time, giving the address "Hôtel du grand lion blanc, rue Ste. Anne, près la rue de la Montagne." On the persons named (except for Hagelmann, about whom I found no information): Gustave Chaudey (1817–71) was a republican and a follower of Proudhon who was exiled after the coup d'état. In the Commune Chaudey was executed by firing squad because he allegedly opened fire on the Federals during the storming of the Bastille. Courbet's role in this affair is still controversial. N.-F. Alfred Madier de Montjau aîné was a jurist and political writer who published between 1845 and 1888, fought for a "République démocratique et sociale," and defended Proudhon. Cf. *Procès des citoyens Proudhon et Duchêne . . . Plaidoirie . . . du citoyen Madier de Montjau aîné et discours du citoyen Proudhon devant le jury. Audience de la cour d'assises de la Seine du 28 mars 1849*, Paris, 1849. Proudhon's entry treats only half of the proceedings. Madier de Montjau cooperated with Courbet in Antwerp, but he also opposed him and his theory of realistic art. Perhaps he felt himself in agreement with Proudhon when he argued that the purpose of art was "d'élever, d'embellir, de poétiser la vie, la nature et la réalité humaines" (see Riat, p. 192).

The BN also contains a typewritten copy of the *Carnets*, entitled *Carnets intimes de Proudhon* (Mscr. Impr. 4° 890/11, vols. I–IV). Only half of the diaries have been published: Pierre Haubtmann, ed., *Carnets de Pierre-Joseph Proudhon*, 4 vols. (1843–51), Paris, 1960–74.

Other manuscripts by and about Proudhon are found in various collections (BN, NAF 14823–25, 14890) and in the Archives Hetzel (BN, NAF 16985).

2. The only men he called friends, apart from the four named, were the Germans Karl Grün and August Wilhelm Eisermann ("ouvrier ébéniste, l'un des philosophes pratiques les plus grands") and the Belgians Delhasse and Haek. On Proudhon's mentality, see Daniel Halévy, *Le mariage de Proudhon,* Paris, 1955, p. 30: "Proudhon l'intraverti, silencieusement actif, écoutait les voix de sa vie intérieure."

3. See Alan Bowness, "Courbet's Proudhon," *BM* 70, no. 900, 1978, p. 125.

4. Of Courbet's many comments on Proudhon, the most significant are those made on the occasion of his death and during the Commune. In a letter of Jan. 20, 1865 to Castagnary, he wrote, "Je veux malgré tout faire un portrait historique de mon ami très intime, l'homme du XIXᵉ siècle. . . . Exaltons l'homme de génie!" To Vallès he wrote in 1871, "Je me suis constamment occupé de la question sociale et des philosophies qui s'y rattachent, marchant dans ma voie parallèlement à mon camarade Proudhon" (see Courthion, vol. 2, pp. 47, 102–104).

5. On Courbet's visits to the prison, see George Woodstock, *Pierre-Joseph Proudhon,* London, 1956, p. 173. That Proudhon felt his wife would merely disturb him at his work is reported in Alexandre Estignard, *Portraits franc-comtois,* 2 vols., Paris, 1885–87; vol. 2, p. 153. After his release on June 6, 1852 the first thing Proudhon did was take a twelve-hour walk with Courbet and others; see Daniel Halévy, *Le mariage de Proudhon* (see n. 2), p. 311.

6. See Emile Zola, "Proudhon et Courbet" (1865), in Gaëtan Picon and Jean-Paul Bouillon, eds., *Emile Zola: Le bon combat. De Courbet aux Impressionistes,* Paris, 1974, pp. 35–56.

7. More on that matter in my introduction to the German edition of Proudhon's *Du principe de l'art,* entitled *Von den Grundlagen und der sozialen Bestimmung der Kunst,* Berlin, 1988, pp. 13–64, 273–310.

8. "*Style.* Chercher les expressions, figures, et tours, propres à chaque spécialité industrielle, et qui se prêtent au langage commun, et à l'art nouveau." *Carnet* I, July 1843, p. 4.

9. See Charles Baudelaire, *Salon de 1846* (XVIII): "De l'héroïsme de la vie moderne"; and "Le peintre de la vie moderne" (1863), in *Oeuvres complètes,* ed. Claude Pichois, 2 vols., Paris, 1976; vol. 2, pp. 493–496, 683–724.

10. See Gottfried Semper, *Wissenschaft, Industrie und Kunst . . . ,* Braunschweig, 1852; also Heinz Quitzsch, "Sempers Kunsttheorie," *Gottfried Semper zum 100. Todestag,* exh. cat., Dresden, 1979, pp. xxv–xxix. Similar thoughts were expressed, before Proudhon, by Saint-Simon.

11. "Il y aussi de nouveaux romantiques. . . . Ils ont inventé la littérature industrielle, la poésie Crampton. Ils soutiennent que le meilleur moyen de régénérer les lettres est de chanter les bienfaits du gaz, de la machine à coudre, etc. De sorte que les inventeurs et notables commerçants n'auraient plus besoin de réclames." Fernand Desnoyers, "Du réalisme," *L'artiste* 16, Dec. 9, 1855, p. 199. Thomas Russell Crampton (1816–88), a British engineer, invented a type of locomotive.

12. See Linda Nochlin, "The Invention of the Avant-Garde: France, 1830–80," *Art News Annual* 34, 1968, pp. 11–18.

13. Karl Marx, *Grundrisse der Kritik der politischen Ökonomie* (rough draft, 1857–58), Berlin, 1974, p. 30.

14. May 7, 1857; *Carnet* IX, p. 322. Doré's *Battle of Inkerman* is now in the Museum of Versailles.

15. "L'Empire a hérité des corruptions du règne de Louis-Philippe, de la littérature romantique, et de l'industrialisme." *Carnet* IX, p. 457.

16. "La littérature suit l'exemple de l'industrie." Ibid., p. 476.

17. For his criticism of Dumas, see the entry for July 20, 1858; see also n. 16. On Ingres as a "sophiste," see *Carnet* I, p. 17, where both Ingres and Gigoux are called "faiseurs" as well. In the

entry for July 15, 1858, Gigoux is again called a "méchant peintre"; see *Carnet* IX, p. 470. Proudhon's polemic against George Sand is especially vehement; in the entry for November 1–5, 1856 he calls her "une bête vénimeuse, une vipère," adding, "Style, composition, morale, me choquent également" (*Carnet* IX, p. 286); similarly on March 29, 1857 (ibid., p. 336).

18. In his *Grandes figures d'hier et d'aujourd'hui* (Paris, 1861, pp. 245–263), Champ-fleury advocates a popular painting that would deal with such subjects as railroads; quoted in Lacambre, p. 185.

19. "Un musée n'est pas la destination des oeuvres d'art; c'est tout simplement *un lieu d'étude,* et de passage, une collection d'antiques, de choses qui par certaines circonstances, ne se peuvent placer nulle part." *Carnet* III, p. 11 (between entries for March 13 and 25, 1846).

20. "Nous avons visité ce matin le musée de Francfort, où il y a de belles choses, mais qui m'intéressent peu." Pierre-Joseph Proudhon, *Lettres à sa femme,* 2 vols., Paris, 1950; vol. 1, p. 241.

21. On July 17, 1858; see *Carnet* IX, p. 472: "Départ de Tournay . . . après avoir visité la cathédrale . . . très beau vaisseau, qui mérite d'être vu."

22. *Carnet* IX, p. 112 (May 4, 1855).

23. Ibid.

24. On Sept. 16, 1858, Proudhon noted, "La lecture des descriptions des musées de Hollande, par Thoré, 1858, vient confirmer tout ce que j'ai dit sur l'art dans mon livre De la Justice" (*Carnet* IX, p. 520). On Dec. 31, 1858, he recorded that he had finished his review "pour la revue trimestrielle" (ibid., p. 552).

25. "Le vrai mouvement de la peinture est dans les écoles des Pays-Bas. On s'étonne que cette nation froide, flegmatique, positive, ait si bien réussi dans l'art. C'est tout simple. Ces gens positifs se sont peints eux-mêmes: et cette peinture vaut mieux que celle des peuples qui font des allégories." *Carnet* IX, p. 520.

26. In the entry for January 10, 1856, we read, "Mardi, 8, funérailles du peintre David (d'Angers). Tout le parti républicain y assiste. . . . Arrestation d'une douzaine de jeunes gens, pour cris de *Vive la liberté!*" (*Carnet* IX, p. 209).

27. June 17, 1856; ibid., p. 250. For Proudhon's opinion on the exhibitions of 1855 and 1857, see Bowness, (n. 3). On the 1846 exhibition, Proudhon noted, "Il semble qu'il y ait progrès chez les artistes, du côté de la composition, de l'expression, et de l'exécution. . . . La composi-tion est pour les artistes chose d'inspiration, chose trouvée, non méditée: voilà ce qui m'a paru. On voit que quelquefois ils tombent juste; mais en général ils ne raisonnent pas"; he goes on to mention paintings by Henri Lehmann (1814–82) and Edouard Baille (1814–88), sculptures by Jean-Claude Petit (1819–1903), and other works. Proudhon also discusses painting technique and differences between various genres, already in cognizance of Thoré's opinion (*Carnet* III, p. 8; between March 13 and 25, 1846).

28. "Ce M. a beaucoup de talent, mais pas de jugement; est engagé dans une voie fausse, la voie du fantastique, du mystique, de l'énorme, de l'horrible. Quelques choses gracieuses, vive-ment contrastées, pour lesquelles on voit qu'il est bien doué par la nature, mais qu'il dédaigne." Sept. 16, 1858; *Carnet* IX, p. 520. On Belgian painting of this period, see *Arbeit und Alltag. Soziale Wirklichkeit in der belgischen Kunst 1830–1914,* exh. cat., Berlin (Neue Gesellschaft für bildende Kunst), 1979. On Courbet's influence in Belgium (from 1852 onwards), the best source is still Riat, p. 191.

29. On July 21, 1858, Proudhon reported on an unexpected meeting with Victor Considé-rant: "Quelle recontre! Les deux socialistes tant caricaturés, se rejoignant sur la terre d'exil" (*Carnet* IX, p. 480).

30. See *Carnet* I, p. 106 (Oct. 1, 1844); on Lessing, see *Carnet* III, p. 61 (June 19, 1846); on Hegel, ibid. and *Carnet* II, p. 53 (Sept. 29, 1845). Whether Proudhon actually read Hegel or only discussed him with Max Grün remains a matter of conjecture.

31. *Carnet* I, p. 106 clearly refers to Hegel's *Aesthetics,* while the notions taken from Hegel's *Phenomenology* occur several times without explicit reference.

32. "Vérité = réalité, ou apparence de l'esprit?" August 31, 1845; ibid., p. 51.

33. See *Carnet* I, p. 103; *Carnet* II, pp. 7–9, 45, for a discussion of Feuerbach.

34. Although Proudhon noted Grün's Paris address in June 1845 (*Carnet* I, p. 109), he did not list him (and Bakunin) among his "connaissances nouvelles" until Oct. 10, 1846 (*Carnet* III, p. 146). According to the entry for Oct. 14, 1858, he remained friends with Grün even in exile (*Carnet* IX, p. 527).

35. "Soleva dire Rafaello che il pittore ha obligo di fare le cose non come le fa la natura, ma come ella le dovrebbe fare. Tout ce qui est contraire à la forme pure de chaque objet, cela est le mal. Le mal est au plus bas degré imperfection, puis laideur, désordre, chaos, monstre, maladie, souffrance, crime et destruction." *Carnet* I, p. 32 (following the entry for Aug. 25, 1843); on Raphael as an ideal, see also *Carnet* III, p. 10 (between March 13 and 25, 1846).

36. On April 11, 1851, Proudhon commented on Courbet's paintings at the Salon (*The Stonebreakers, A Burial, The Return of the Peasants*): "C'est le laid au naturel, mais avec une grande vigueur. Ce n'est point là l'issue de l'art." (*Carnet* IX, p. 69; quoted at length in Bowness [n. 3], p. 124).

37. "J'ai lu Lucrèce: une belle tragédie manquée. . . . Il faut qu'ici comme en peinture, selon le précepte de Raphael, la représentation soit idéalisée, non réelle. Conséquemment le style, le langage, ne peuvent être le langage vulgaire: ils doivent s'élever au contraire, un peu au dessus de l'humain. . . . Il ne faut pas que la couleur locale, les anecdotes locales, le style local, les allusions locales, les moeurs . . . locales, étouffent le côté essentiel de la tragédie, qui est l'Humanité." *Carnet* I, p. 20.

38. On this aspect, see my entry on Gautier in *Realismus als Widerspruch,* pp. 78–85.

39. In the diaries, Proudhon's statements along these lines are devoted particularly to poetry, as on Dec. 6, 1857: "Un poète, en général, est un instrument de perfectibilisation. Ce n'est nullement un initiateur. Il y en a peu de la force d'Homère, Virgile, les prophètes, les psaumes, Boileau, Molière et Lafontaine" (*Carnet* IX, p. 394). Basically this represents a reversal of the academic discussion on genius and talent; to remain true to his doctrines, Proudhon had to insist on the furtherance of talent as the rule. Similar thoughts with regard to visual art are found in *La philosophie du progrès.*

40. *Du principe de l'art et de sa destination sociale,* Paris, 1865; reprint Farnborough, 1971, p. 198.

41. It is surprising how frequently Proudhon's notes on the decline of literature and art are accompanied by reports on immoral behavior, both of which, in his eyes, were results of Bonapartist rule. In particular, tormented by nightmares revealing a *potestas/potentia* syndrome, he detected a link between tyranny and sodomy (by which he meant a form of homosexuality characterized by oppression). Proudhon's seclusion and the necessity of refraining from political activity caused him to suffer from strong feelings of impotence, which he in turn projected on certain aspects of the outside world. This is why he could consider his theory of marriage (an ideology of pure denial) to be a foundation of political theory, writing, "Hors de là, point de famille, point de cité, point de république" (June 15, 1858; *Carnet* IX, p. 427). Indicatively, a man of letters, Sainte-Beuve, remarked on the very same day, "Vous rencontrerez une vive opposition parmi nos *gens de lettres et artistes;* vous êtes trop moral" (ibid.).

The next day Proudhon recorded a dream, to which he gave the heading "L'horreur de la tyrannie et de la sodomie." One passage reads: "Perte de la justice = sodomie . . . le plus grand outrage à l'humanité est l'idéal de l'exploitation, ou de la jouissance de l'homme par l'homme. . . . Le nombre de ces monstres est de plusieurs milliers. . . . *Abaissement rapide et visible de l'art et des lettres. . . .* Un plan général de corruption . . . est en train de se former en France. . . . Il faut poursuivre cette abomination par le fer et le feu, former une association générale contre la tyrannie et la pédérastie: désormais ces ceux mots doivent être unis, soulever l'indignation générale, faire de la pureté une vertu civique et arriver à une déclaration de guerre sociale jusqu'à ce que le monde soit purgé" (ibid., pp. 429–431; my italics). This example also indicates that Proudhon's art theory can be understood only by reference to the political and social aspects of his mental condition.

42. "La véritable école, c'est l'atelier." *Carnet* I, p. 92 (following entry for April 8, 1845).

43. "Maximum de puissance, l'individu. Minimum de puissance, l'Etat ou la puissance de la nation." *Carnet* IX, p. 426 (June 13, 1858). See also *Carnet* III, p. 27 (April 28, 1846), where he writes, "De nouveau, l'Humanité entière rentre dans la loi de l'individu."

44. The phrase is Halévy's; *Le mariage de Proudhon* (n. 2), introduction.

45. For a discussion of the "ouvriers-poètes" in the circle around Victor Hugo and Béranger, see Shroder, p. 74.

46. "Quel élan! Un million de commandes d'objets d'art, du premier coup, pour tous les lieux publics." *Carnet* III, p. 13 (between March 13 and 25, 1846).

47. "Allemands entrepreneurs de métaphysique, comme Anglais d'industrie = misère, misère. Ce n'est ni avec la métaphysique, ni avec le capital, qu'on guérira." Ibid., p. 18 (April 1, 1846).

48. *Carnet* IX, p. 430 (June 16, 1858).

49. On the concept of equality, see especially *Carnet* II, pp. 97–98 (Oct. 15, 1845): "L'égalité étant le résultat du progrès, cette loi doit exister pour l'homme comme pour la Société." Also *Carnet* IX, p. 425 (June 13, 1858): "Notion de l'égalité. Préface. J'appelle égalitaires tous ceux qui reconnaissent que les conditions et fortunes tendent, par l'application de la Justice, à se niveler indéfiniment." About a note on equality of Aug. 31, 1845, Haubtmann remarks: "Nous retrouvons là un des thèmes majeurs de la pensée proudhonienne. Il est persuadé que toutes les sciences, économiques, sociales, morales, prouvent la nécessité de l'Egalité" (*Carnet* I, p. 56). The reconciliatory character of this conception of equality is also made evident in Charles-Augustin Sainte-Beuve, *Pierre-Joseph Proudhon: Sa vie et sa correspondance, 1838–1848* (1872), reprint Paris, 1947, p. 286: "Trouver le moyen, dans les réformes économiques, de satisfaire aux justes exigences du prolétariat, sans blesser les droits acquis de la classe bourgeoise" (from a letter to Prince Napoleon of Jan. 12, 1853). On the contribution of art to a reconciliation of the classes in a projected egalitarian society, see also *Carnet* I, p. 87.

50. "Discipliner cette race d'artistes, chose difficile: il n'y a pour cela que l'égalité." *Carnet* III, p. 11 (between entries for March 13 and 25, 1846).

51. See Picon/Bouillon (n. 6).

52. "Le peuple a besoin d'historiens, de savants, de littérateurs, d'artistes: mais . . . il faut songer que tout ce qu'on leur accorde, est pris sur le bien-être individuel, et que cette prétendue catégorie de travailleurs doit être réduite progressivement, *tout le monde devant être artiste;* tout le monde devant faire de l'art pour soi; tout le monde devant par conséquent contribuer gratuitement aux divertissements publics." *Carnet* I, pp. 91–92 (following entry for April 8, 1845); my italics.

53. Karl Marx and Friedrich Engels, "Deutsche Ideologie" (1845–46), in Marx and Engels, *Werke,* vol. 3, Berlin, 1969, pp. 378–379.

54. "Un troisième agent révolutionnaire est indispensable: C'est l'idéal. L'infini dans la pensée. . . . Cet idéal . . . nous le créons en nous-mêmes, et de nos mains. L'art est la représentation de cet idéal." *Carnet* VIII, p. 317 (Feb. 7, 1851). Here art is considered to be an integral part of a scheme of education that would be the same for everyone; see also *Carnet* I, pp. 94–95.

55. "Les arts, sciences et métiers sont dans l'homme, les formules spéciales de l'absolu." *Carnet* I, p. 18 (before entry for July 26, 1843).

56. "Le fond du réalisme, c'est la négation de l'idéal." *Précurseur d'Anvers*, Aug. 22, 1861; cited extensively in Riat, p. 91.

57. *Carnet* III, p. 29 (April 28, 1846).

58. The year 1853 may be called an ideal date in this respect. Bowness's remark that the age of the daughters would indicate a date of 1856 merely corroborates the supposition that the dating was purposely ideal. I can see no reason to accept a redating of the genesis of the canvas to 1856, as Bowness suggests (p. 126), especially since the photograph on which Proudhon's portrait was based originated after 1862 (and was taken not by Reutlinger, as Courbet said, but by A. Lumière, probably in 1864 during Proudhon's last journey to the Franche-Comté). Rather, Courbet summed up several phases of Proudhon's life in the painting, only *one* of which was the year 1856 and Madame Proudhon's pregnancy with, according to Bowness, the couple's fourth daughter, Charlotte, who was born that year.

59. The emphasis on Proudhon's high forehead in the second state is one of the principal alterations with respect to the first, as it exalts the everyday and mitigates the anecdotal quality of the depiction (see X ray photographs of both states in Martine Ecalle, "A propos du portrait de 'Proudhon et ses enfants' par Gustave Courbet," *Bull. du Laboratoire du Musée du Louvre* 4, 1959, pp. 31–33). For an interpretation of the "front de génie" as a kind of Republican manifesto, see Shroder, *Icarus*, p. 62, where the example given is Hugo caricatured by Daumier (*Le charivari*, Sept. 6, 1849; Delteil no. 1940).

60. In a lecture of 1974 I mentioned Michelangelo's *Jeremiah* as a possible model; in the meantime, Werner Hofmann has suggested Raphael's *Heraclitus* and Klaus-Peter Schuster Dürer's *Melancholy* (*Cat. Hamburg*, 1978–79, no. 262).

61. Reported by André Rousseaux, in BN, NAF 14823, pp. 118–124 (undated newspaper clipping).

62. This view was emphasized at a Frankfurt Courbet symposium in 1979, particularly by T. J. Clark and especially with respect to Proudhon's bourgeois method of raising children.

63. According to Hélène Toussaint at the above Frankfurt Courbet symposium. As this term was presumably widely accepted in 1865, the visual references to graves in the painting would have been immediately understandable to a contemporary viewer.

64. According to Courbet himself; see n. 4 (letter to Castagnary of Jan. 20, 1865).

65. See n. 59.

66. Courbet himself placed emphasis on this aspect; while at work on the portrait, he wrote to Castagnary, "Proudhon tout entier y sera: l'homme et le père, le moraliste et le penseur!" (BN, Cab. des Estampes, Papiers Castagnary, box 5).

67. Overcoming the opposition between manual and mental work was one of Proudhon's prime aims. On this aspect of his philosophy, see Martin Deppner, "Denken und Machen im 'Bildnis des Pierre-Joseph Proudhon im Jahre 1853'," *Kunst und Unterricht*, special issue, 1979, pp. 4–8.

68. "La pensée du siècle, c'est l'individualisme. . . . L'individualisme, né de la grande révolution française, et été reçu dans la famille démocratique comme un enfant difforme." Hippolyte Castille, *Les hommes et les moeurs en France sous le règne de Louis-Philippe*, 2d ed., Paris, 1853, p. 378. Castille's definition of "individualisme" also includes private enterprise; with him the term is usually synonymous with capitalism.

69. " . . . morcellement de la société française." Ibid., p. 340.

70. Ibid., pp. 15, 378. Castille's perceptiveness is not diminished by the fact that he opposed Proudhon at one time (*Carnet* IX, pp. 443, 457).

71. Used derogatorily in *Carnet* IX, p. 227 (March 8, 1856) and p. 292 (Nov. 26, 1856).

72. As for example in *Carnet* III, p. 8.

73. *Carnet* IX, pp. 25–28 (Jan. 1, 1855); my italics:

Un des mes amis me demandait l'autre jour si je regrettais d'être marié. J'essayais de lui faire comprendre que la question était mal posée; qu'elle ne pouvait avoir de sens qu'autant qu'elle était personnalisée, et se rapportait, non au mariage, mais à la femme.

Sous ce dernier rapport, un mari ne confie jamais ses sentiments secrets; mais il peut m'être permis de les confier au papier.

Je regrette donc de m'être marié tard. . . . Je regrette de ne m'être pas marié par amour . . . , chose qui d'ailleurs m'était devenue, depuis plus de vingt ans, impossible: mais chose que je crois cependant bonne en soi, et par conséquent regrettable. Mon unique amour, non communiqué, n'a été qu'un rêve. . . .

Je regrette que ma femme ne soit pas riche: cela n'a nul besoin d'explication. . . .

Je regretterais peut-être de n'avoir pas choisi une femme d'un esprit et d'une éducation plus distinguée: car l'esprit, l'éducation, les talents, les connaissances, sont en soi, comme la richesse, de bonnes choses. Mais, aujourd'hui comme à l'époque où j'ai connu ma femme, je suis et je demeure fermement convaincu de deux choses: la 1ère, que n'éprouvant plus d'amour, et *mon individualité voulant rester impitoyablement elle-même,* une éducation plus soignée des talents, etc., chez ma femme devenaient incompatibles avec le genre de vie que je me proposais de mener et que je mène en effet dans l'état de mariage; la 2e, que ces mêmes qualités, incompatibles avec mon objet, le devenaient encore bien davantage avec les qualités que je requérais en ma femme, savoir une abnégation absolue, un dévouement sans borne, un zèle pour le travail domestique qui ne recule devant aucune fonction répugnante, une abstention complète de toute immixion dans mes affaires, mes travaux, mes idées, mes relations, etc.

Ma femme ne lit rien; n'a jamais lu une page de mes publications, ne s'informe point de mes études, ne furète pas mes manuscrits: dans l'état de mon coeur, nul ne se fera d'idée des avantages précieux que je trouve en cette conduite, et ces relations conjugales.

Avec tout cela, cette femme possède un fond de vertu sévère, une abnégation, une générosité naturelle que je prise très-haut, et que des talents supérieurs et d'autres avantages ne compenseraient pas pour moi.

J'abrège ce chapitre des regrets, plus ou moins longs, pour tous ceux qui se marient, et qui ne prouvent rien absolument contre le mariage en lui-même. . . .

Pour moi, le mariage est une des formes périodiques essentielles de l'existence. . . .

D'abord, il y a la paternité, qui est pour moi comme un doublement de l'existence, une sorte *d'immortalité.* De nos jours, la paternité est redoutée. . . . Cet égoisme est à mes yeux la mort même. Un cercle d'enfants est une couronne pour le père de famille, au point de vue de la société, comme de la nature. . . . Je suis si profondément homme de famille et *patriarche* que pendant plusieurs années, mon premier et unique amour évanoui, j'eus l'idée de devenir père, moyennant indemnité pécuniaire, avec entremise de qq. jeune fille pauvre que j'aurais séduite. . . .

Après la paternité, j'ai le ménage, le domicile, l'une des choses les plus substantielles de la vie civile et naturelle. Un célibataire n'a vraiment pas de chez soi. . . . Le domicile, la paternité, en un mot le mariage, . . . ont produit pour moi d'autres biens inestimables: 1° une plus grande somme de *travail* . . . ,

2° un affranchissement à peu près complet de l'aiguillon de la chair . . . , enfin un ordre de vie, une discipline, une puissance de moi-même, une consistance, telle que je ne me la suis jamais sentie dans le célibat. En un mot, *avec le travail, le mariage a augmenté en moi la liberté.* . . .

De mon côté, le travail et l'âge, du côté de ma femme, les fatigues de la maternité et l'épuisement qui s'ensuit, ont amené une cessation presqu'absolue de relations conjugales:

nous avons même chacun notre lit séparé. J'ai la satisfaction de penser qu'au moins, si je n'ai plus d'enfants, ce n'est pas que je trompe, ni en moi, ni en ma femme, la nature; c'est la nature elle-même qui se montre impuissante, et qui nous dit: assez.

74. Particularly apparent in later works (*Amour et mariage*, posth. ed., 1875; *La pornocratie ou les femmes dans les temps modernes*, 1858), but already anticipated in "Qu'est-ce qu'est la propriété?" (1840). See among other commentaries Juliette Lamber, *Idées antiproudhoniennes sur l'amour, la femme et le mariage*, 2d ed., Paris, 1868, where the author replies to Proudhon's view of marriage, "Heureusement, il existe un rémède contre . . . l'amour, c'est le mariage" (p. 20); and to his definition of woman, "La femme . . . un moyen terme entre l'homme et le singe" (p. 48).

75. The political significance of marriage and family resulted for Proudhon, among other things, from the fact that his wife was of proletarian origin. One might even contend that in marrying Euphrasie Piégard, he had the intention of marrying the proletariat.

76. "Quelle est la fonction de l'autorité? Où est son siège? Je la place dans la famille, vous la placez dans l'Etat, ce qu je nis." *Carnet* IX, p. 95 (April 4, 1855).

77. "Si je trouve 12 tissérands, je suis sûr de conquérir le monde: quelle rage de poursuivre la propriété! *Carnet* III, p. 6 (March 8, 1846).

78. As Victor Hugo said of himself; see Shroder, p. 79.

79. Ibid., pp. 151–180 (on Flaubert); pp. 190, 197, 201 (on Baudelaire); conclusion, p. 231.

CHAPTER 6. Color and Worldview

Translator's note: In preparing this translation I relied on an English-language version of the essay by Peter Chametzky, whose permission to use it I should like to acknowledge here.

1. Courthion, vol. 2, p. 76.

2. There is a useful, if fragmentary study: Max Imdahl, "Die Rolle der Farbe in der neueren französischen Malerei . . . ," in W. Iser, ed., *Poetik und Hermeneutik* II, *Immanente Ästhetik* . . . , Munich, 1966, pp. 195–225. Delacroix and Cézanne are the corner posts of Imdahl's investigation; Courbet isn't even mentioned. That makes investigations in the area even more necessary. An important preliminary to this: Guido Boulboullé, "G. Courbet: Zur Interpretation einer antikapitalistischen Kunst im Frankreich des Second Empire," diss., Univ. of Bochum, 1972.

3. Delacroix often spoke in critical admiration about Courbet; he already called him revolutionary in reference to *After Dinner at Ornans*, repro. in *Cat. Paris*, 1977–78, p. 96.

4. Courthion, vol. 2, p. 125 (1870); also p. 82.

5. Courthion, vol. 1, pp. 35, 208.

6. I am indebted to Christoph Krämer, with whom I examined most of the works cited, for many insights into painting technique and usage.

7. Courbet also discovered the large format at this time (Courthion, vol. 2, pp. 71f.).

8. Repro. in *Cat. Paris*, 1977–78, p. 83.

9. On the grounds of palette, both versions (Oslo and Luxeuil), contrary to *Cat. Paris*, 1977–78, should be dated *after* the still smoothly painted *Portrait of Juliette*, ibid., no. 8.

10. Delacroix, *Journal*, ed. Jouin, Paris, 1932, pp. 18–19 (April 15, 1853).

11. Color repro. in Toussaint, "Mystères et symboles chez Courbet," *Conn. des Arts* 308, Oct. 1977, p. 60.

12. Courbet himself used this image (Courthion, vol. 1, p. 51).

13. The full-length *Portrait of the Singer Louis Gueymard* (*Cat. Paris*, 1977–78, no. 54)

is an exception, an isolated attempt to mimic Delacroix. See also the remarks on *The Sleep* of 1866.

14. In *Le charivari* of Jan. 4, 1847, the caption of a caricature on Ingres' style reads, "Quelques-uns se vouent au blanc, d'autres se vouent au bleu; M. Ingres s'est voué au gris." Also spoken of there is "la belle nuance grise qu'affectionne tant l'auteur du Saint-Symphorien."

15. Color repro. of the painting in *Cat. Brooklyn,* 1988–89, p. 103.

16. Color repro., ibid., pl. IV (after p. 86).

17. See *Cat. Hamburg,* 1978–79, color plate 1.

18. For example, in the face of the sacristan, or the *Portrait of Baudelaire*. A comparison of the two versions of *Château d'Ornans* is also instructive.

19. As in Schapiro, passim.

20. Clark, *Buchon.*

21. Original text in Charles Léger, *Courbet,* Paris, 1929, p. 17.

22. Courthion, vol. 1, p. 199.

23. See Clark, *Buchon,* and idem, *People.*

24. Radio script, 1976. I thank Clark for letting me see the text. For a color repro. of the painting, see *Cat. Brooklyn,* 1988–89, p. 108.

25. Original text in Riat, 1906, p. 98.

26. Clark, *Buchon.*

27. See Hippolyte Castille, in Max Buchon, *Le réalisme,* Neuchâtel, 1856, pp. 26–30; also in "Welcher philosophischen Richtung . . . ", *Realismus als Widerspruch,* pp. 95–97.

28. Hélène Toussaint takes a different position; *Cat. Paris,* 1977–78, p. 140.

29. Redating: *Mouth of the Seine (Cat. Paris,* 1977–78, no. 2) already shows the use of the spatula; this and the fluffy painting of the clouds excludes a dating in the 1840s. *Le Pont de Scey (Paris,* no. 24), a painting of 1850, is much more comparable. See also n. 9. Misattribution: Nos. 56 and 86a of the 1978 London exhibition catalogue, and above all the London National Gallery version of *The Young Ladies on the Banks of the Seine (Summer)*. Here spatula and palette knife are not used, the paint is applied evenly with bristle brush. The surface is homogeneously covered, and the underpaint doesn't show anywhere. The light-dark system of alternating horizontal bands of cool and warm color that characterized the Paris version and authentic studies is not grasped. The unclear contours, Renoir-like, also speak against an attribution to Courbet, as do the puppet-like little heads, the scratched-in index finger of the foremost figure—a procedure never used by Courbet—and the misunderstanding of the complexion (the left arm of the reclining figure is darker, the right lighter than the gloves). The whole picture lacks the "obtrusiveness" of Courbet.

30. See *Cat. Paris,* 1977–78, no. 28.

31. Color repro. in *Cat. Brooklyn,* 1988–89, pl. VI (after p. 86).

32. Color repro., ibid., p. 111.

33. Above all Théophile Gautier, cited in chap. 2 of this volume. Alphonse de Calonne already called Courbet's picture in 1851 "l'orgueilleux charbonnage signé Courbet." See Clark, *Buchon,* p. 135.

34. See, among others, Augustin-Joseph du Pays, in *L'illustration,* June 8, 1853, pp. 392f: "M. Courbet reste définitivement le chef de l'ecole du laid, et ce qui est plus triste, du laid, non dans sa grandeur et dans sa force, mais du laid vulgaire, du laid ignoble" and, about *The Wrestlers,* "On sera dominé invinciblement par la répugnance que cause cet ensemble voué au noir, voué au laid, au grossier, au trivial".

35. Courthion, vol. 2, p. 78.

36. Ibid., vol. 1, p. 160.

37. See chap. 8 of this volume.

38. Color repro. in *Cat. Brooklyn,* 1988–89, pl. V (after p. 86).

39. Thoré, *Salon,* vol. 1, p. 93. This 1861 statement admittedly applies only with reserva-

tions; for *The Young Ladies of the Village,* for example, nature has no recuperative value, though it is not they but city-dwellers whom the painting addresses.

40. Color repro. in *Cat. Brooklyn,* 1988–89, p. 177.

41. Above all in the sense of allowing the landscape to burst the picture, as Delacroix noticed; see *Journal* (n. 10), vol. 2, p. 364 (March 3, 1855).

42. See chap. 4; a further aspect in Imdahl (n. 1), preface and introduction.

43. A topos that remained current into the 1890s; see Lorenz Dittmann, "Zur Kunst Cézannes," *Festschrift Kurt Badt,* Berlin, 1961, esp. pp. 190–193.

44. Color repro. in Nationalgalerie Berlin SMPK, *Verzeichnis der Gemälde und Skulpturen des 19. Jahrhunderts,* Berlin, 1977, color plate 20.

45. Repro. in *Cat. Paris,* 1977–78, p. 140.

46. See, among others, Delacroix's *Bouquet of Flowers* (Paris) and Cézanne's copy of it (Moscow). Color repros. in *De Renoir à Picasso,* Grand-Palais, Paris, 1978, nos. 7 and 8.

47. See n. 13. Delacroix remained Courbet's lifelong secret guide, especially in theory and color. Courbet admired the *Massacre of Chios* (Courthion, vol. 1, p. 36), alluded to Delacroix in his self-portrait *The Wounded Man,* and excluded him and Théodore Rousseau from his general condemnation of romantics (Courthion, vol. 1, p. 160). Although he didn't believe in his concept of the imagination, he was finally called of one mind with Delacroix by Castagnary (Castagnary, vol. 1, p. 397).

48. Courthion, vol. 2, p. 297.

49. See *Cat. Hamburg,* 1978–79, color plate 6. Green is used similarly in *Portrait of Madame de Brayer* (1858) as a background color used planarily, almost nonobjectively (*Cat. Paris,* 1977–78, no. 56), probably the first example in Courbet's work of this.

50. Courbet: *Cat. Hamburg,* 1978–79, color plate 5; Quaglio: *Städelsches Kunstinstitut, Die Gemälde des 19. Jahrhunderts,* Frankfurt, 1972, pl. 3.

51. Color repro. in *Cat. Brooklyn,* 1988–89, pl. VIII (after p. 86).

52. Color repro. ibid., p. 139; better in *Cat. Hamburg,* 1978–79, pl. 10.

53. See chap. 4 of this volume.

54. Original text in Riat, p. 188.

55. See Imdahl (n. 1), p. 197, n. 7; pp. 209–210, n. 54, p. 211.

56. See Riat, pp. 223f. The only praise came from Carjat. Similarly to *The Wrestlers,* the question of political motives for Courbet's aesthetic disqualification arises.

57. See *Cat. Hamburg,* 1978–79, no. 275.

58. For *The Source of the Lison,* see *Jahrbuch preussischer Kulturbesitz* 7, 1969, color plate facing p. 289; as to *Forest Glen,* see Julius Meier-Graefe, *Gustave Courbet,* Munich, 1921, p. 53.

59. Klaus Berger, "Courbet in His Century," *GBA* 24, 1943, p. 27.

60. This structure finds a personal and philosophical equivalent in Courbet's striving for reconciliation; on the rapprochement with Bonapartism, see chaps. 3 and 4 of this volume.

61. Color repro. in *Cat. Brooklyn,* 1988–89, p. 127.

62. See *Cézanne, Die Badenden,* exh. cat., Basel, 1989.

63. *Woman at the Well:* see *Cat. Hamburg,* 1978–79, no. 277; *The Woman in the Waves:* see *Cat. Brooklyn,* 1988–89, p. 179.

64. Color repro. in *Cat. Brooklyn,* 1988–89, p. 181.

65. See Courthion, vol. 1, pp. 133f.

66. Color repro. in *Cat. Hamburg,* 1978–79, cover plate (no. 278).

67. "Un art nouveau apparaît, sérieux et convaincu, ironique et brutal, sincère et plein de poésie" (in *Grandes figures d'hier et d'aujourd'hui,* Paris, 1861, pp. 231ff., cited in Lacambre, p. 166).

68. See Champfleury, *Grandes Figures* . . . (n. 67); Lacambre, p. 262; Castagnary, vol. 1, pp. 396–397.

69. Repro. in *Cat. Hamburg*, 1978–79, p. 292.

70. Courbet expressed himself in these terms particularly to Baudelaire; see Léger (n. 21), p. 191.

71. Castagnary, vol. 1, p. 397.

72. *Cat. Hamburg*, 1978–79, color plate 12.

73. See *Hamburger Kunsthalle. Meisterwerke*, Cologne, 1969, color plate 297.

74. John P. Sedgewick ("The Artist's Artist," *The Art News* 58 1960, pp. 40–44, 65–66) recognized Courbet's importance for abstract expressionism; Julius Meier-Graefe (*Corot und Courbet*, 2d ed., Munich, 1912, pp. 187f.) established a contrast to impressionist painting of light, above all in the negation of atmosphere.

75. See Michael Wilson, *The National Gallery Schools of Painting: French Paintings after 1800*, London, 1983, pl. 21.

76. See, as opposed to this, the mundane beach life at Etretat in contemporary woodcuts— for example, in *L'illustration*, Nov. 1, 1862: repro. in *Cat. Hamburg*, 1978–79, p. 299.

CHAPTER 7. A Note on the Late Work

1. See *Cat. Paris*, 1977–78, no. 131 (St. Gallen) and no. 127 (Paris). *Château de Chillon* (Essen) is on loan from the Krupp family to the Folkwang Museum there (not in catalogue).

2. See Julius Meier-Graefe, "Courbets Niedergang. Zur Ausstellung im Petit Palais in Paris," *Berliner Tageblatt*, June 18, 1929; Champfleury, *Souvenirs et portraits de jeunesse*, Paris, 1872, p. 191. Even before Meier-Graefe, Riat (p. 281) headed his discussion of Courbet's final period "Le déclin."

3. Among others by Martin Warnke, *Peter Paul Rubens* (1977), English ed. New York, 1980, p. x. (". . . the works are counterproposals to his actual life"); and Albert Erich Brinckmann, *Barockskulptur*, Handbuch der Kunstwissenschaft, Potsdam, 1917, pp. 325, 328. It is not my purpose in the following remarks to extensively discuss the various theories of artists' late or mature periods. Most of the more recent attempts to derive general criteria from diverse art forms and epochs rely on Richard Hamann, *Der Impressionismus in Leben und Kunst*, Cologne, 1907, pp. 218ff. See also Joseph Gantner, "Der alte Künstler," *Festschrift für Herbert von Einem*, Berlin, 1965, pp. 35f. and 71ff.

4. Theodor W. Adorno, "Spätstil Beethovens," *Moments musicaux*, Frankfurt, 1964, pp. 13–17. Adorno's sober analysis ends with the verdict "In the history of art, late works are the catastrophes."

5. For a more detailed discussion of Courbet's paint application and palette, see chap. 6 of this volume.

6. Oil on canvas, 21.5 × 40 cm, inscribed lower right: "la brême, 15 nov. 1836, G. C." This small canvas, not mentioned in Robert Fernier (*La vie et l'oeuvre de Gustave Courbet*, catalogue raisonné, 2 vols., Paris and Lausanne, 1977–78), represents the Brême, a right-hand tributary of the Loue, covered with ice in early winter. The wooded gorge through which it flows was to become one of Courbet's favorite painting sites. The sketch-like painting was one of the artist's earliest works; as Riat recounts (see n. 2), Courbet began doing portraits in 1834—that is, at the age of 15—and in 1836–37 began depicting "des paysages d'Ornans et des environs" (Riat, pp. 5, 11, 21f.). Fernier lists three landscapes executed between 1836 and 1838 (nos. 2–4). The painting represents the ice-covered stream in gradations of gray and blue in which the reddish underpainting shimmers through in places. Snow and bushes are rendered with a broad-bristle brush; supplementary colors are red, ocher, and white apparently taken straight from the tube and occasionally mixed with green.

7. 195 × 257 cm; *Cat. Paris*, 1977–78, no. 18.

8. 56 × 46 cm; ibid., no. 28; a good color repro. in *Apollo* 76, 1962, pl. VII, p. 403. For a wider discussion of this portrait, see chap. 6 of this volume.

9. See Lacambre, p. 155.

10. See chap. 4 of this volume.

11. 67 × 52 cm; *Cat. Paris*, 1977–78, no. 65. Related in this regard is *Forest Landscape*, 157 × 115 cm, Fernier (see n. 6), cat. 637. In connection with Courbet's collaboration with Corot, see especially *View of Saintes*, 33 × 46.5 cm, Fernier, cat. 346. This small painting also evinces the rapid brushwork characteristic of the later works.

12. *Cat. Paris*, 1977–78, nos. 72f.; *Cat. Hamburg* 1978–79, color plate XIII; *Cat. Brooklyn*, 1988–89, pp. 154f. (color plates); also, Fernier (see n. 6), nos. 387, 393–394.

13. Color plate in *Cat. Brooklyn*, 1988–89, p. 187.

14. See Thoré, *Salon*, vol. 2, p. 269.

15. Ibid., p. 276.

16. Courbet is known to have addressed issues associated with the Commune only in drawings. The sole exception among the paintings done after the Commune may be a caricature-like portrait of a Swiss clergyman; yet the attribution of this painting, which I have seen, is by no means secure. The key idea Courbet expressed as a minority representative in the Commune nevertheless entered his art, namely, the notion of a decentralized coexistence based on the model of Switzerland and the United States. In other words, there was no need for Courbet to change his art, since the Commune simply corroborated his own regionalistic ideas (sources quoted in my *Realismus als Widerspruch*, pp. 34–39).

17. The Zurich canvas is inscribed: " . . . 71, in vinculis faciebat." Actually done at a later date, it reflects the injuries sustained by the artist as a result of imprisonment and trial. In a second version (65 × 99 cm; Paris, Orsay) the space surrounding the trout is even more oppressive in effect, and its forms evince an even greater disruption. In the latter regard, this version of *The Trout* is related to *Fisherman at Lake Geneva*, a canvas discussed below. For more on the culprit-victim syndrome, see chap. 1 of this volume.

18. On *The Wave* (80 × 100 cm), see Fernier (n. 6), cat. 752; on *The Dents du Midi* (73.5 × 101 cm), see *Cat. Hamburg*, 1978–79, no. 302.

19. On the series of the cliff at Etretat, see Fernier (n. 6) nos. 718–721, 723–725, 745; also *Cat. Hamburg*, 1978–79, nos. 284 and 285, with a detailed discussion of the differences. On the series of the château de Chillon, see Fernier, nos. 931–945, 989–993; and *Courbet et la Suisse*, exh. cat., Château de La Tour-de-Peilz, 1982, pp. 61–65.

20. "Les peintres arrivent dans notre pays. Nous avons déjà Rapin, Jean-Jean Cornu, des Suisses et Pata." See Courthion, vol. 2, p. 146 (Courbet's letter to Castagnary from Ornans, Aug. 14, 1872). Alphonse Rapin (1839–89) exhibited at the Paris Salon in 1870; the Musée des Beaux-Arts in Besançon has seven paintings by his hand. On the other artists listed, see the following note, and also Musée d'Ornans, cat., 1975, nos. 87–102.

21. To briefly characterize these artists: Brigot was a portrait, landscape and genre painter who exhibited portraits and hunting pieces at the Paris Salon between 1863 and 1876. In the *Bulletin des Amis de Gustave Courbet* (cited below as *AGC*) he is mentioned among the "peintres mineurs de la Tour de Peilz" (no. 26, 1960, p. 16, and no. 72, 1984, p. 36). Morel was initially a punchmaker (*poinçonneur*) before becoming Courbet's apprentice on Lake Geneva, "au même titre que Pata" (Riat, quoted in Courthion, vol. 1, p. 294); Courbet used to foregather "avec ses familiers, Pata, Morel et Slomczynski" (Courthion, vol. 1, p. 296). On Nov. 4, 1877, he wrote to Castagnary, "J'arrive de la Chauds-de-Fonds"—this letter was mailed from La Tour de Peilz, where Morel and his wife, refugees of the Commune, had gone so as to be able to take Courbet in and care for him (letter from the physician, Collin; Courthion, vol. 2, p. 262). On Jan. 8, 1878, Morel wrote to Castagnary that he had known Courbet for three and a half years (Courthion, vol. 1, pp. 336–341). Morel's studio was located in an annex to Courbet's house (Courthion, vol. 1, p. 254), but nothing more is known about his painting.

Ordinaire, born near Ornans, was the son of a former representative of the Doubs *département;* he was furthered as a landscape painter by Courbet from childhood (Courthion, vol. 1, p.

300) and accompanied Courbet into exile (Riat, pp. 350f.; Courthion, vol. 1, pp. 290f.). Ordinaire owned the sketch to an antiwar painting by Courbet (Courthion, vol. 1, p. 284); Dr. Collin lists him, with Pata and Slomczynski, as one of "les plus distingués" of Courbet's pupils (Courthion, vol. 2, p. 263).

Slomczynski (alias Slom), a painter and draughtsman of Polish origin, "qui avait été condamné à mort, après la Commune" (Courthion, vol. 1, p. 296), preceded Courbet into Swiss exile and became one of his most outstanding pupils (Courthion, vol. 2, p. 263). After Courbet's death he and Bocion were named expert consultants for the sale of his paintings (Courthion, vol. 1, p. 343); later, in Paris, Slomczynski contributed to numerous periodicals and did book illustrations (see *Exposition de 47 tableaux de Marcel Ordinaire*, exh. cat., Besançon, 1897; and Thieme-Becker, *Allgemeines Künstlerlexikon,* Leipzig, vol. 31, 1937, p. 141).

Pata, a Swiss artist from Tessin, accompanied Courbet as early as the Ornans period (Courthion, vol. 2, pp. 146 and 154) and rejoined him in Switzerland in October 1873 (Courthion, vol. 1, p. 298). According to Gros-Kost, Pata reported on the sale of several of his own landscapes "que l'on avait revêtus de la signature du maître" (Courthion, vol. 1, p. 299). According to Riat, "il lui arriva de ne plus finir ses oeuvres, et de s'en rendre . . . aux soins, inhabiles et inférieurs, de Pata et de Morel, qui empâtaient la fluidité de ses couleurs et les assombrissaient" (Courthion, vol. 1, p. 301). Pata was the only one of Courbet's pupils to treat themes of a social character, such as the sufferings of the unemployed (this and other information in: Thieme-Becker, vol. 26, 1932, p. 290; and *AGC* 14, 1954, pp. 13ff.). See also exh. cat. *Chérubino Pata 1827–1899, le vrai faux-Courbet,* Ornans, Musée Courbet, 1988.

22. Bocion, a Swiss landscape and seascape painter from the canton of Vaud, is mentioned by Riat (p. 358) as a companion of Courbet's Swiss exile, and with Slom (see above) was a consultant after his death (Courthion, vol. 1, p. 343); further information in Thieme-Becker (n. 21), vol. 4, 1910, p. 156, and in Franz Zelger, *Katalog der Stiftung Oskar Reinhart,* Winterthur, vol. 1, *Schweizer Maler des 18. und 19. Jahrhunderts,* Zurich, 1977, pp. 65–75, with numerous illustrations.

Baud-Bovy, a portrait, genre, and landscape painter of Geneva, became an instructor at the art school there in 1869 and first exhibited at the Paris Salon in 1875. According to Riat (pp. 358 and 365), Baud-Bovy was a pupil of Courbet's during his Swiss exile and reported enthusiastically to Castagnary on Courbet's new pictures in 1875; further information in Thieme-Becker (n. 21), vol. 3, 1909, p. 53; and in Zelger, *Katalog,* pp. 57ff., with illustration.

23. Hector Hanoteau (1825–90) is represented, for example, by a painting in the Musée Courbet, Ornans, titled *La mare aux grenouilles;* for further information, see Thieme-Becker (n. 21), vol. 15, 1922, pp. 597f.

24. "Personne n'a, aussi bien qui lui, réussi les faux Courbet." Quoted in *AGC* 26, 1960, p. 16. Further information about Courbet forgeries is found there as well.

25. See *Le temps,* Aug. 26, 1890; reproduced in Fernier (see n. 5), vol. 2, pp. 340f. and *AGC* 54, 1975, pp. 1ff. See also Guy Isnard, *Faux et imitations dans l'art,* vol. 2, Paris, 1960, pp. 191ff. (also in *Jardin des arts* 72, 1960, pp. 46–53). To the forgery story must be added the cases of mistaken identification. Paintings by Gustave Colin, whose flourish "G. C." was extremely similar to Courbet's, and even works by the Hungarian artist Gyula Benzcur, have been confused with authentic Courbets (see *AGC* 26, 1960, p. 17 [sample signatures] and *Frankfurter Allgemeine Zeitung,* May 3, 1957 [acquisition of a Benzcur painting as a Courbet by the Öffentliche Kunstsammlungen, Basel]).

26. On *Covert of Roe-Deer,* see *Cat. Paris,* 1977–78, no. 97 (174 × 209 cm.). On the marketing of Courbet's works, especially the landscapes, see Anne M. Wagner, "Courbet's Landscapes and Their Market," *Art History* 4, no. 4, 1981, pp. 410–431.

27. I have identified a number of forgeries in my review of Robert Fernier's catalogue, in *Pantheon* 39, 1981, pp. 282–286. Subsequently, about thirty forgeries not listed in Fernier have been presented to me.

28. See *AGC* 73, 1985, p. 20, with illustration. The dating suggested there, 1874, seems to me too late; in view of Pata's other, more original works, this one is characterized by a relatively tame derivativeness that points to a considerably earlier date of execution.

29. 91 × 162 cm; Ornans, Musée Courbet; ill. in the first publication of the present article, *Pantheon* 44, 1986, p. 78, fig. 7.

30. 48.5 × 64.5 cm; Ornans, Musée Courbet; ill. ibid., p. 78, fig. 8.

31. 64.5 × 81 cm; see *Millet, Courbet et le réalisme français*, exh. cat., Tokyo, 1978, no. 68.

32. The first-named type includes, for example, *The Wave* (45.0 × 59.5 cm), Sotheby's, London, auction cat., April 25, 1968, p. 102; or *The Source in the Rocks* (33.3 × 41.0 cm), Fernier (n. 6), vol. 2, p. 249 (collaborations, no. 27). The latter category includes *The Cliff at Etretat* (46 × 55 cm), Fernier vol. 2, p. 256 (suppl. 13), identical with Hauswedell, Hamburg, auction cat. no. 227, June 1, 1978, no. 260; or *Mill at the Loue* (98 × 148 cm), Basel, Öffentliche Kunstsammlungen (despite signature "G. Courbet" already identified in the museum as "Pata[?]"); see Fernier, vol. 2, p. 241 (collaborations, no. 6). Pata may also be the author of the following paintings listed in Fernier as works by Courbet: nos. 192, 259, 714, 717, 915, 494, and 951; collaborations, no. 3(?), 12, 16, 17, 21, and 28; also *Cat. Hamburg*, 1978–79, no. 268.

33. 52 × 76 cm; Ornans, Musée Courbet; repro. in *Pantheon* 44, 1986, p. 79, fig. 11.

34. On *Scey-en-Varais* (35 × 81 cm), see *Cat. Hamburg*, 1978–79, no. 295 (the attribution goes back to Hélène Toussaint); on *The Pool* (72.5 × 58.5 cm), see Fernier (n. 6), vol. 2, p. 249 (collaborations, no. 30); on *Swiss Landscape* (81 × 65 cm), Fernier, vol. 2, p. 251 (collaborations, no. 37).

35. 46.5 × 56 cm; Fernier, cat. 922.

36. 92 × 72.5 cm; Fernier, cat. 760.

37. "Nous gagnons 20,000 francs par mois." See n. 24 above.

38. See my essay in *Pantheon* 42, 1984, p. 369.

39. Color repro. in *Cat. Brooklyn*, 1988–89, p. 205.

40. On the issue of "modernity versus modernism," see Timothy J. Clark, *Paris in the Art of Manet and His Followers,* New York, 1985; also, *Modernism and Modernity,* the Vancouver Conference Papers, ed. Benjamin H. D. Buchloh et al., Halifax, 1983.

41. More information is found in chap. 4 of this volume, especially in connection with fig. 32.

42. " . . . il s'arrêta de peindre, découragé, brisé." Quoted in *Cat. Paris*, 1977–78, no. 132.

43. The signature in red lead, a color Courbet often used and that peels easily, was repaired at a later date. The picture was superbly restored in 1984 at the Schweizerisches Institut für Kunstwissenschaft, Zurich. It was doubled, cracks and other damage repaired, and the back fitted with a protective sheet. For a good color reproduction, see the first publication of this article, *Pantheon* 44, 1986, p. 81.

44. See Hélène Toussaint, in *Cat. Paris*, 1977–78, facing no. 69.

45. For examples and further interpretation, see chap. 4 of this volume.

46. See *Cat. Hamburg*, 1978–79, no. 234.

47. A particularly good example is *The Source of the Lison*, Staatliche Museen Preussischer Kulturbesitz, Nationalgalerie, West Berlin (color plate in *Jahrbuch preussischer Kulturbesitz* 7, 1969, facing p. 289). For an interpretation, see esp. chap. 4 of this volume and the review cited in n. 27, esp. pp. 486ff.

48. Repro. in *Cat. Brooklyn*, 1988–89, p. 135.

49. For paintings related in terms of motif and facture, see Fernier (n. 6), cats. 179, 254, 305, 547, 549, and 581.

50. Color repro. in *Cat. Brooklyn*, 1988–89, 139; better in *Cat. Hamburg*, 1978–79, pl. X.

51. As regards the boulder in the stream, the closest parallel is found in the drawing *The Ravine,* published by the present author in *Pantheon* 42, 1984, p. 369.

52. For his contemporaries, however, both connotations were closely related; for references, see chap. 4 of this volume, n. 257.

53. See n. 43 above. The interruption in the lower third of the C resulted from a flaw in the paint surface. Otherwise, the unwieldy signature with its extremely upright letters, including the date, corresponds very well with that of *Grand Panorama of the Alps;* see also the signature sample in Fernier (n. 6), vol. 2, p. 337, no. 74. The only feature missing is the dot after the *t.* The painting was also restored in 1985 at the Schweizerisches Institut für Kunstwissenschaft. For a good color reproduction, see the first publication of this article, *Pantheon* 44, 1986, p. 84.

54. 32.6 × 40.3 cm; see Fernier (n. 6), cat. 1047. This sketch, which is known to me only in reproduction, appears to be more summarily painted than the canvas published here. In several of its details there is an affinity to Fernier, cat. 1044 and 1049.

55. The old stamp is still visible on the reverse: "Paul Pia / Tableaux / Et articles pour peinture / 28 Place de l'Entrepôt / Genève." The same stamp is found on the painting *Barque at Lake Geneva* (46 × 38 cm), reproduced in *Courbet et la Suisse* (see n. 19), p. 61, fig. 109.

56. I have discussed this point in more detail in *Pantheon* 39, 1981, p. 285.

57. On *Bon Port* (27 × 35 cm), see Fernier (n. 6), cat. 957; on *The Dents du Midi* (24 × 33 cm), ibid., cat. 946.

58. On *Château de Chillon,* see the versions reproduced in Fernier, cats. 941 and 944; on *View of Lake Geneva* (38 × 55), ibid., cat. 950; also, *Cat. Brooklyn,* 1988–89, p. 204.

59. Warsaw (55 × 65 cm): Fernier (n. 6), cat. 351 (color reproduction in Dario Durbé, *Courbet und der französische Realismus,* Munich, 1974, pl. 43). Caen (38 × 46 cm): Fernier (n. 6), cat. 817 (color reproduction in Bruno Foucart, *Courbet,* Paris, 1977, p. 71). London (38 × 55 cm): Fernier (n. 6), cat. 950.

60. *Cat. Paris,* 1977–78, no. 38.

61. The statement about *A Burial* is quoted from a letter from Courbet to Jules-Antoine Castagnary, dated Feb. 9, 1873 (Paris, BN, Papiers Castagnary). On the quality of abstraction inherent in realistic art, see my essay "Mimesis and Innovation" (1984), quoted above (chap. 4 of this volume, n. 8).

CHAPTER 8. Courbet's Modernity as Reflected in Caricature

1. Contemporary caricatures of works of art frequently use them as a mere pretext to criticize conditions that have little or nothing to do with art, e.g., Ivan Steiger's drawing of the Nefertiti bust in West Berlin, captioned "Now Property of the People" (alluding to East German claims to ownership), in *Frankfurter Allgemeine Zeitung,* June 14, 1978; or Plantu's caricature of Velazquez's *Infanta Margarete* reading the newspaper and discomfited by the headline "82% des touristes sont sur les plages," in *Le monde,* June 17, 1978. An excellent overview of twentieth-century art caricature is found in *"A Child of Six Could Do It!" Cartoons about Modern Art,* exh. cat., Tate Gallery, London, 1973. Apart from the general literature in which this genre is mentioned only in passing (Arsène, Fuchs, Gombrich, Hofmann, Kris, Melot), two sources contributed substantially to my line of argument: Charles Baudelaire, "De l'essence du rire . . . ", *Oeuvres complètes,* ed. Claude Pichois, Paris, 1976, vol. 2, pp. 211–232; and Champfleury, "La caricature," reprinted in Lacambre, 1973, pp. 201–212.

2. See the remarks by Théodore Duret quoted in Léger, *Caricatures,* pp. 1–7.

3. Not on his own initiative but in reaction to a petition submitted by the painter Jacques-Th. Véron in 1861 (information kindly supplied by Geneviève Lacambre).

4. *Le Salon de 1843 . . . Appendice au livret. Avec 37 copies par Bertall. Extrait du Martyrologe Parisien pour l'année 1843,* pp. 90–104.

5. See Marie-Claude Chadefaux, "Le Salon caricatural de 1846 et les autres salons

caricaturaux," *GBA* 71, 1968, pp. 161–176. The attached bibliography is extremely spotty; no sources are given for forty Courbet caricatures alone.

6. See Clark, *Buchon*, p. 209.

7. Bertall, *The Pictures and Statues Commented Upon by the Artists Themselves* . . . , *La vie parisienne*, June 5, 1869; repro. in *Cat. Hamburg*, 1978–79, p. 503. For Courbet's *The Beggar's Alms*, see *Realismus als Widerspruch*, color plate 10.

8. See Courthion, vol. 2, p. 225; see also pp. 299–305. As Louis Peisse wrote at the time, "M. Courbet continue . . . ses cruelles expériences sur le goût public" ("Le Salon de 1853," *Le constitutionnel*, May 20, 1853). Théophile Gautier uttered, "Il nous donne la caricature et non le portrait de la vérité" (see chap. 2 of this volume). Writing in 1853, Eugène Loudun stated that "tant qu'il ne prouvera pas qu'il est capable d'avoir une pensée et de l'exprimer, nous le regarderons comme un caricaturiste, non comme un peintre" ("Salon de 1853," *L'union*, June 5, 1853). Edmond About expressed himself similarly in *Voyage à travers l'exposition des beaux-arts,* Paris, 1855, p. 202.

9. Julius Meier-Graefe (*Der Fall Böcklin*, Stuttgart, 1905), a fiery advocate of modernism, declared that Böcklin entirely lacked artistic instinct. In Courbet's case, it was just the opposite—the same verdict on him was passed by conservative critics.

10. The caricature relates to the first version of 1850, now lost, whose composition differed from the surviving version of 1855 (see *Realismus als Widerspruch,* color plate 4). The differences, however, are immaterial for my argument.

11. See Nadar's caricature of Puvis de Chavannes's *The Return from the Hunt, Le journal amusant,* July 16, 1859; repro. in the first publication of this article, *Cat. Hamburg,* 1978–79, p. 503. Nadar's caption, however, relates to color, reading, "I regret very much that this second issue on the Salon is not colored like the previous one; it would have permitted me to lend *The Return from the Hunt* some color, which Puvis entirely avoided."

12. See Clark, *Buchon,* passim.

13. "The enthusiasm with which Courbet's pictures are received by the public is without compare. This is the *real truth,* without artifice or polish. One detects none of the Academy clichés, nor is any account taken of the absurd traditions of classical art. Everything is naive, and joyous. Courbet was eighteen months old when he painted this picture" (French caption in Léger, *Caricatures,* p. 13).

14. For sources on this topic, see my essay "Meryons 'Eaux-fortes sur Paris'—Probleme der Verständigung im Second Empire," *Kritische Berichte,* n.s. vol. 4, 1976, nos. 2–3, p. 59, n. 53.

15. "Being a sharp observer, Courbet wanted to prove that the village girls are not worth two cents. So he represented them as carnival dolls, and because in this strange world the animals are smaller than human beings, he retained the proportions of . . . the carnival. They say this picture was sold to monsieur de Morny for 5,000 francs—congratulations!" Nadar's caricatures also point out errors in perspective and proportion (*Album du Salon. Nadar, Jury,* Paris, 1952), as do Cham's (*Cham au Salon de 1852*). A good reproduction of Courbet's picture is now available in *Cat. Brooklyn,* 1988–89, p. 108.

16. See his polemic against German painting: "Ils sont tous dans les *qualités négatives* de l'art. Une des principales qualités, c'est la perspective. On parle de cela toute la journée" (letter to Castagnary, Nov. 20, 1869; quoted in Courthion, vol. 2, p. 114).

17. The caricaturist is alluding here to *White Bull and Blond Heifer* (ill. in *Cat. Brooklyn,* 1988–89, p. 105), and to *Rocks at Mouthier* (ill. ibid., p. 124).

18. Clark, *Buchon,* passim. A color repro. of *A Burial* is in *Cat. Brooklyn,* 1988–89, facing p. 14.

19. Borel, p. 23.

20. Historically speaking, this effect was first realized in realistic *painting,* since it could hardly be achieved with the photograph of the time. The most striking example was provided by

Courbet himself, in *Deer Hunting in the Franche-Comté: The Ruse* (repro. in *Cat. Brooklyn*, 1988–89, p. 181).

21. *The Young Ladies* is reproduced in *Cat. Brooklyn*, 1988–89, p. 135; *The Rest*, ibid., p. 187. One more example of *The Rest* caricatured is reproduced in *Cat. Hamburg*, 1978–79, p. 507 (Bertall, *Le journal amusant*, May 29, 1869).

22. *Rocky Landscape near Ornans* (formerly *La roche de Dix Heures*) is reproduced in *Cat. Paris*, 1977–78, p. 140. For Bertall's caricature of the picture, see *Cat. Hamburg*, 1978–79, p. 508.

23. Repro. in *Cat. Paris*, 1977–78, p. 71.

24. Repro. in Léger, *Caricatures*, p. 72.

25. Repro. in *Cat. Hamburg*, 1978–79, p. 296.

26. As, for example, the painting *Vue de la Hougue—Effet de nuit* by Jean-Louis Petit (no. 938 in the 1843 Salon), caricatured by Bertall in *Le Salon de 1843* (n. 4), p. 95; or Alphonse-Hippolyte Leveau's *Macbeth et les sorcières* (1852 Salon), likewise caricatured by Bertall in the *Journal pour rire*, May 8, 1852, p. 2. Similarly, framed white surfaces functioned as spoofs (that were actually exhibited in the Salon, such as Alphonse Allais's *Première communion de jeunes filles chlorotiques par un temps de neige* of 1883; see *Equivoques*, exh. cat., Paris, Musée des Arts Décoratifs, 1973) or, as caricatures, such as André Gill's on *Effet de neige* by Ludovic Piette (no. 1999 in the 1868 Salon), in "Gill-Revue," *Le salon pour rire*, 1868, p. 6.

27. See Léger, *Caricatures*, p. 56; also Hans Graber, *Edouard Manet*, Basel, 1941, p. 8.

28. See Castagnary, vol. 1, pp. 288f.; also Léger, *Caricatures*, p. 81.

29. For *The Stonebreakers*, see *Realismus als Widerspruch*, color plate 2; Cham's caricature is reproduced in *Cat. Hamburg*, 1978–88, p. 565.

30. See chap. 2 of this volume.

31. Repro. in *Cat. Hamburg*, 1978–79, p. 510. The former *Fox Hunt* (now labeled *Horse in Forest*, since the fox has been deleted) is reproduced in *Cat. Hamburg*, 1978–88, p. 249.

32. Caricature by Bertall (*Le charivari*, 1864), repro. ibid., p. 510.

33. There is a similar caricature, done by Nadar, of Daubigny's *Seine Landscape* (no. 707 in the 1859 Salon), published in the *Journal amusant*, July 16, 1859 (repro. in *Cat. Hamburg*, 1978–88, p. 512) which relates to Daubigny's naturalism in general. Its caption reads, "Effet produit sur un visiteur du salon par l'eau des merveilleux tableaux de M. Daubigny" (a spectator has undressed and is about to jump into the painted river).

34. References in Erwin Panofsky, *Idea*, 3d ed., Berlin, 1975, p. 7.

35. Wilhelm Busch, the German satirist, addressed the subject by caricaturing the distorted proportions in close-up photography; see his illustrations to "Ehre dem Fotografen, denn er kann nichts dafür!" *Fliegende Blätter* 2, 1871, p. 145 (repro. in *Sämtliche Werke*, vol. 1, Munich, 1943, pp. 430–438). Another related caricature, by Rudolf Wilke, and an exhaustive discussion of the problem of close-ups are found in Hans Jantzen, "Die Raumdarstellung bei kleiner Augendistanz," *Über den gotischen Kirchenraum und andere Aufsätze*, Berlin, 1951, pp. 41–48.

36. See my review "Gustave Courbet (1819–1877)—Zum Forschungsstand (1. Teil)," *Kunstchronik* 30, 1977, p. 456.

37. "M. Courbet s'est posé en peintre du Danube, à la bonne heure, mais il ne faut pas qu'il s'y trompe: la grossièreté n'est pas la force, non plus que la brutalité n'est la franchise, ni le scandale la réputation" (Nadar, *Jury au Salon de 1853*, Paris, 1853, unpaginated).

38. Schapiro, pp. 170–171.

39. References in chap. 4 of this volume.

40. French original in Courthion, vol. 1, p. 102.

41. Critics of the period like Elisabeth de Mirbel (cited in Clark, *Buchon*, p. 209) apparently projected Courbet's imagery onto his audience, calling them "populaires avinés" (drunken bums, winos). The dangerousness of the figures, underlined by their huge hammers, was turned

back against the artist himself, for one of the stonebreakers is shown smashing the reversed letters of his name. In other words, Courbet himself was considered highly dangerous.

42. See Clark, *Buchon,* passim.

43. References in chap. 2 of this volume.

44. Eugène Delacroix, *Journal,* ed. André Joubin, vol. 2, Paris, 1932, pp. 18f.

45. The other caricature of *The Bathers* is Cham's, in *Le charivari,* May 29, 1853; repro. in *Cat. Hamburg,* 1978–79, p. 515.

46. Wood engraving after the painting in Julius Meyer, *Geschichte der modernen französischen Malerei,* Leipzig, 1867, facing p. 642.

47. Ibid., p. 617 (discussions of the "most recent realism").

48. As Clark noted, "To be in Paris, but not of it: that was what Courbet wanted" (*People,* p. 31).

49. Popular figure during the French Revolution—Little John, sympathetic dupe, and man of the people.

50. On shoes as an attribute of realistic painting, see Nadar, "Un peintre réaliste," *Le journal pour rire,* Jan. 17, 1857 (reprinted in *Als guter Realist . . . Internationaler Realismus heute,* exh. cat., Hamburger Kunstverein, Hamburg, 1978, p. 16).

51. Also, Courbet compared Manet's pictures to playing cards, while Manet spoke of Courbet's figures as billiard balls; see Léger, *Caricatures,* p. 56.

52. "Oui, M. Peisse, il faut encanailler l'art!" (letter to Wey, Nov. 26, 1849; Courthion, vol. 2, p. 76).

53. A striking example is Auguste Bouquet's caricature *The Last Supper of Republican Liberty,* the personification of which is being betrayed, after the July revolution, by Louis-Philippe in the figure of Judas (*La caricature,* May 17, 1832); repro. in *La caricature,* exh. cat., Münster, Westfälisches Landesmuseum, 1980–81, no. 39, p. 124.

54. This reading is corroborated by the fact that there are two veterans of the French Revolution in the picture. See *Cat. Paris,* 1977–78, p. 102; also my review of Clark, *Kritische Berichte,* n.s., vol. 6, 1978, no. 3, pp. 45, 48.

55. Repro. in *Cat. Hamburg,* 1978–79, p. 273; Courbet's picture, ibid., pp. 271f.

56. Proudhon's words were " . . . l'effet de cette consécration constitutionelle des principes de 89, doit être évidemment de subordonner l'Eglise à la Révolution" (Pierre-Joseph Proudhon, "La justice poursuivie par l'Eglise", *Oeuvres complètes,* vol. 12, Paris, 1946, p. 329).

57. Gill, *Courbet's Deer . . . , La lune,* May 13, 1866; repro. in *Cat. Hamburg,* 1978–79, p. 519. The caricature might be an allusion to *Remise de cerfs au crépuscule,* Paris, Musée d'Orsay (ill. in *Hommage à Gustave Courbet,* exh. cat., Ornans, Musée Courbet, 1977, plate 14).

References

Borel — Borel, Pierre. *Lettres de Gustave Courbet à Alfred Bruyas*. Geneva, 1951.

Castagnary — Castagnary, Jules-Antoine. *Salons 1857–1879*. 2 vols. Paris, 1892.

Cat. Brooklyn, 1988–89 — *Courbet Reconsidered*, exh. cat., Brooklyn Museum and Minneapolis Institute of Arts, 1988–89.

Cat. Hamburg, 1978–79 — *Courbet und Deutschland*, exh. cat., Hamburg, Hamburger Kunsthalle, and Frankfurt, Städelsches Kunstinstitut, 1978–79.

Cat. Paris, 1977–78 — *Gustave Courbet (1819–1877)*, exh. cat., Paris, Grand Palais, and London, Royal Academy of Arts, 1977–78.

Clark, *Bourgeois* — Clark, Timothy J. *The Absolute Bourgeois: Artists and Politics in France, 1848–1851*. London 1973.

Clark, "Buchon" — Clark, Timothy J. "A Bourgeois Dance of Death: Max Buchon on Courbet." In *The Burlington Magazine* 111, 1969, pp. 208–212, 286–290.

Clark, *People* — Clark, Timothy J. *Image of the People: Gustave Courbet and the 1848 Revolution*. London, 1973.

Courthion — Courthion, Pierre, ed. *Courbet raconté par lui-même et par ses amis*. 2 vols. Geneva, 1948–50.

Cousin — Cousin, Victor. *Du vrai, du beau, et du bien*. Paris, 1837.

Du Camp — Maxime Du Camp. *Les Beaux-Arts à l'Exposition Universelle et aux Salons de 1863, 1864, 1865, 1866 et 1867*. Paris, 1867.

Herbert — Herbert, Robert L. *Barbizon Revisited*. New York, 1962.

Herding, *Realismus als Widerspruch*   Herding, Klaus, ed. *Realismus als Widerspruch. Die Wirklichkeit in Courbets Malerei.* Frankfurt, 1979. 2d rev. ed., 1984.

Hofmann, *Nineteenth Century*   Hofmann, Werner. *Art in the Nineteenth Century* (1960). English ed. London, 1961.

Hofmann, "Wirklichkeiten"   Hofmann, Werner. "Courbets Wirklichkeiten." In *Courbet und Deutschland*, 1978–79, pp. 590–613.

Lacambre   Lacambre, Geneviève and Jean, eds. *Champfleury: Le Réalisme.* Paris, 1973.

Léger, *Caricatures*   Charles Léger. *Courbet selon les caricatures et les images.* Paris, 1920.

Nochlin, *Style and Society*   Nochlin, Linda. "The Development and Nature of Realism in the Work of Gustave Courbet: A Study of the Style and Its Social and Artistic Background." Ph.D. thesis, New York University, 1963. Published under the title *Gustave Courbet: A Study in Style and Society.* New York, 1976.

Nochlin, *Meeting*   Nochlin, Linda. "Gustave Courbet's *Meeting.* A Portrait of the Artist as a Wandering Jew." *The Art Bulletin* 49, 1967, pp. 209–222.

Riat   Riat, Georges. *Gustave Courbet.* Paris, 1906.

Schapiro   Schapiro, Meyer. "Courbet and Popular Imagery: An Essay on Realism and Naiveté." *Journal of the Warburg and Courtauld Institutes* 4, 1941, pp. 164–191.

Shroder   Shroder, Maurice Z. *Icarus: The Image of the Artist in French Romanticism.* Cambridge, Mass., 1961.

Thoré, "Avenir"   Thoré, Théophile. "De l'avenir de l'art." *Revue germanique française et étrangère* 15, no. 2, 1861, pp. 248–259.

Thoré, *Salon*   Thoré, Théophile. *Salon de W. Bürger, 1861 à 1868.* 2 vols. Paris, 1870.

Articles on Courbet
by the Author

Articles collected in this volume were first published as follows:

CHAPTER 1
"Erlöser und Scharlatan, Zerstörer und Märtyrer. Zur Rolle Courbets." In Herding, ed., *Realismus als Widerspruch,* pp. 12–20.

CHAPTER 2
"'Les lutteurs détestables'—Stil- und Gesellschaftskritik in Courbets Ringerbild." *Jahrbuch der Hamburger Kunstsammlungen* 22, 1977, pp. 137–174.

CHAPTER 3
"Das 'Atelier des Malers'—Treffpunkt der Welt und Ort der Versöhnung." In Herding, ed., *Realismus als Widerspruch,* pp. 223–247.

CHAPTER 4
"Egalität und Autorität in Courbets Landschaftsmalerei." *Städel-Jahrbuch,* n.s. 5, 1975, pp. 159–199.

CHAPTER 5
"Proudhons 'Carnets intimes' und Courbets 'Bildnis Proudhons im Familienkreis'." In *Malerei und Theorie. Das Courbet-Colloquium 1979,* ed. Klaus Gallwitz and Klaus Herding, Frankfurt, 1980, pp. 153–173.

CHAPTER 6
"Farbe und Weltbild. Thesen zu Courbets Malerei." In *Cat. Hamburg,* 1978–79, pp. 478–492.

CHAPTER 7
"Zu Courbets Spätwerk." *Pantheon* 44, 1986, pp. 75–86.

CHAPTER 8
"Courbets Modernität im Spiegel der Karikatur." In *Cat. Hamburg,* 1978–79, pp. 502–521.

Other articles on Courbet by the author:

"Nur eine Woge." Begleitheft zu Dokumentarfilm über Courbets Berliner Meereslandschaft, Neue Gesellschaft für Bildende Kunst, Berlin, 1977: "Courbets Leben. Sein Verhältnis zur Politik, Kunst und Literatur seiner Zeit," pp. 34–37; "Zur politischen Bedeutung der Landschaftsmalerei im Hinblick auf Courbet," pp. 53–56.

"Gustave Courbet (1819–1877). Zum Forschungsstand." *Kunstchronik* 30, 1977, pp. 438–456, 486–496.

"Von der Kraft des Widerspruchs, Courbets Bedeutung." *Tendenzen* 120, 1978, pp. 41–47.

"Realismus—eine Frage des Ziels." In Uwe M. Schneede, ed., *Als guter Realist muß ich alles erfinden. Internationaler Realismus heute,* exh. cat., Hamburger Kunstverein, Hamburg, 1978–79, pp. 12–23.

Review of Robert Fernier, *Gustave Courbet: Catalogue raisonné, vols. 1 and 2,* Lausanne and Paris, 1977–78. *Pantheon* 39, 1981, pp. 282–286.

Klaus Herding, ed., with Katharina Schmidt. *Les voyages secrets de Monsieur Courbet—Unbekannte Reiseskizzen aus Baden, Spa and Biarritz,* exh. cat., Baden-Baden, Staatliche Kunsthalle, and Zürich, Kunsthaus. Stuttgart, 1984: "Die Lust, aus Gegensätzen eine Welt zu bauen. Courbet als Zeichner," pp. 11–56; "Kritischer Katalog," pp. 159–325.

"Nachträge zur Ausstellung 'Les voyages secrets de Monsieur Courbet' in Baden-Baden und Zürich." *Pantheon* 42, 1984, pp. 369–371.

"Mimesis und Innovation. Überlegungen zum Begriff des Realismus in der bildenden Kunst." In Klaus Oehler, ed., *Zeichen und Realität, Akten des 3. Semiotischen Colloquiums der deutschen Gesellschaft für Semiotik e.V., Hamburg, 1981,* Tübingen, 1984, vol. 1, pp. 83–113.

"Fortschritt und Niedergang in der bildenden Kunst: Nachträge zu Barrault, Baudelaire und Proudhon." In Wolfgang Drost, ed., *Fortschrittsglaube und Dekadenzbewußtsein im Europa des 19. Jahrhunderts. Literatur—Kunst—Kulturgeschichte,* Heidelberg, 1986, pp. 239–258.

"Lautmalereien. Zu einigen unbekannten Gedichten und Briefen Courbets." In Christian Beutler et al., eds., *Kunst um 1800 und die Folgen. Werner Hofmann zu Ehren,* Munich, 1988, pp. 233–243.

"Courbet Reconsidered, Brooklyn and Minneapolis" (review). *The Burlington Magazine* 131, 1989, pp. 244–246.

Index